The Silence in Progress of Dante, Mallarmé, and Joyce

Currents in Comparative Romance Languages and Literatures

Tamara Alvarez-Detrell and Michael G. Paulson
General Editors

Vol. 82

PETER LANG
New York • Washington, D.C./Baltimore • Boston
Bern • Frankfurt am Main • Berlin • Vienna • Paris

Sam Slote

THE SILENCE IN PROGRESS OF DANTE, MALLARMÉ, AND JOYCE

PETER LANG
New York • Washington, D.C./Baltimore • Boston
Bern • Frankfurt am Main • Berlin • Vienna • Paris

Library of Congress Cataloging-in-Publication Data
Slote, Sam.
The silence in progress of Dante, Mallarmé, and Joyce / Sam Slote.
p. cm. — (Currents in comparative Romance languages and literatures; vol. 82)
Includes bibliographical references and index.
1. Style, Literary. 2. Dante Alighieri, 1265–1321—Style. 3. Mallarmé,
Stéphane, 1842–1898—Style. 4. Joyce, James, 1882–1941—Style. 5. Silence
in literature. 6. Narration (Rhetoric). I. Title. II. Series.
PN203.S56   809—dc21   98-26872
ISBN 0-8204-4179-1
ISSN 0893-5963

Die Deutsche Bibliothek-CIP-Einheitsaufnahme
Slote, Sam:
The silence in progress of Dante, Mallarmé, and Joyce / Sam Slote.
–New York; Washington, D.C./Baltimore; Boston; Bern;
Frankfurt am Main; Berlin; Vienna; Paris: Lang.
(Currents in comparative Romance languages and literatures; Vol. 82)
ISBN 0-8204-4179-1

The paper in this book meets the guidelines for permanence and durability
of the Committee on Production Guidelines for Book Longevity
of the Council of Library Resources.

© 1999 Peter Lang Publishing, Inc., New York

All rights reserved.
Reprint or reproduction, even partially, in all forms such as microfilm,
xerography, microfiche, microcard, and offset strictly prohibited.

Printed in the United States of America

Acknowledgments

This book began its life as a dissertation and no doubt retains traces of this origin. As with its previous incarnation, I am indebted to numerous individuals who have helped shape my thinking. These acknowledgments can in no way recompense the few stout individuals herein named for their pains, but can only note my gratitude and appreciation for their kind efforts and travails. Despite this welcome aid, there will no doubt remain in this dissertation errors, omissions, misjudgments, blunders, mistakes, inaccuracies, misinterpretations, unfortunate phrasings, and many, many *faux pas*, the responsibility for which must—as ever—belong to me and me alone.

First, I would like to thank David Hayman for his patience, advice, encouragement, criticism and especially for his keen and perspicacious understanding of some of the more imperspicacious texts ever hoisted upon a community of exegetes. I also wish to thank Próspero Saíz for the numerous suggestions and criticisms which he has offered over the years. I am very grateful to Jane Tylus for her painstaking, thorough and helpful criticisms, her knowledge and her good humor. I would also like to thank some of my other professors at the University of Wisconsin–Madison for their help and advice: Elaine Marks, Matthew Gumpert, Phillip Herring, and Kristiaan Aercke.

I also thank our friends and colleagues in Madison for providing inspiration, distraction and some warmth in the improbably cold Wisconsin winter: Najat Rahman, Scott Bonneville, Jed Deppman, David J. Califf, Roger Cooper, Christopher Bjork, and Dana Bultman.

I am especially grateful to Geert Lernout for his encouragement during the initial phase of writing. I have greatly enjoyed and benefited from his company, his wit, his knowledge and his dedication to Joyce. I would also like to thank my friends and colleagues at the awkwardly named "Centrum voor de wetenschappelijke studie van het werk van

James Joyce" and at the appropriately named University of Antwerp for helping me have a most enjoyable and productive two years in the fair city of "Gnantwerp," a *remémoration d'amis belges*: Dirk Van Hulle, Ingeborg Landuyt, Vivian Liska, Luc Herman, Nico Cuyvers, Ilja Grauls, and Barbara de Bakker.

I would also like to thank the Ministerie van de Vlaamse Gemeenschap for the Flanders Community Scholarship which allowed me to work in Antwerp for the academic year 1995–1996, and the Belgian American Educational Foundation for allowing me to remain in Antwerp for 1996–1997 to complete this project.

I also thank some friends and colleagues in realms Joycean: Lucia Boldrini, Jean-Michel Rabaté, Laurent Milesi, Valérie Bénéjam, Daniel Ferrer, Pascal Bataillard, Luca Crispi, Wim Van Mierlo, Fritz Senn, and Lesley McDowell. I am also very grateful to Jeremy Tambling for his suggestions on the Dante section of this dissertation.

Lest anyone be omitted from this blitzkrieg of obsequiousness, I would like to thank some friends who also, in their own way, contributed to this project: John Wyeth, Elizabeth Festa, Alex Neidell, Steve Beckner, Kelsey Goss, Daryl Edelman, Garry K. Schumacher, Pierre de Gentil, and most especially James DiGiovanna, *primo de li miei amici*.

I am grateful to the *James Joyce Quarterly* for permission to reprint material originally published in that journal. I thank the Estate of James Joyce for allowing me to quote from Joyce's works.

I would also like to acknowledge the fine work of my editors at Peter Lang: Heidi Burns and Lisa Dillon.

Although it goes without saying, I will say it nonetheless: I thank my parents and my sister. In ways too many to be counted they have made my work possible.

Contents

Editions and Abbreviations	ix
1 Worse Words for Worser Still: An Introduction	1
2 Language and Loss in the *Divina Commedia*	21
3 The Lot of Mallarmé	73
4 The Syntaxes of *Un coup de dés*	127
5 The Desistance of Narrative in Joyce's Work	185
6 Some Inconclusive Unscientific Comments with Constant Reference to *Finnegans Wake*	235
Bibliography	297
Index	319

Editions and Abbreviations

The following editions and citation conventions will be used throughout:

Dante Alighieri. *Rime.* Ed. Gianfranco Contini. Turin: Einaudi, 1939, 1995 (R + page.line).
———. *La divina commedia.* Ed. Fredi Chiappelli. Milan: Mursia, 1965 (Canticle + canto.line).
———. *Convivio.* Ed. Piero Cudini. Milan: Garzanti, 1980 (C + book.chapter.line).
———. *La vita nuova.* Ed. Marcello Ciccuto. Milan: Rizzoli, 1984 (VN + chapter.line).
———. *Monarchia.* Ed. and trans. Frederico Sanguineti. Milan: Garzanti, 1985 (M + book.chapter.line).
———. *De vulgari eloquentia.* Ed. Vittorio Coletti. Milan: Garzanti, 1991 (DVG + book.chapter.line).
———. *Epistolam ad Canem Grandem della Scalla. Opere Minori, volume III, tomo II.* Eds. Arsenio Frugoni, Giorgio Brugnoli, Enzo Cecchini, and Francesco Mazzoni. Milan: Riccardo Riccardi, 1996. 599–643 (CG + section).

U. Boscolo, ed. *Enciclopedia Dantesca.* Rome: Instituto dell'Enciclopedia Italiana, 1970–78 (ED + volume.page).

James Joyce. *Finnegans Wake.* New York: Viking, 1939 (FW + page.line).
———. *Letters, Volume I.* Ed. Stuart Gilbert. New York: Viking Press, 1957 (LI + page).
———. *Stephen Hero.* Eds. Theodore Spencer, John J. Slocum, and Herbert Cahoon. New York: New Directions, 1963 (SH + page).
———. *Letters, Volume II* and *III.* Ed. Richard Ellmann. New York: Viking Press, 1966 (LII, LIII + page).
———. *A Portrait of the Artist as a Young Man.* Ed. Chester G. Anderson. New York: Viking, 1968 (AP + page).

———. *Selected Letters*. Ed. Richard Ellmann. London: Faber and Faber, 1975 (SL + page).

———. *The James Joyce Archive*. Eds. Michael Groden, Hans Walter Gabler, David Hayman, A. Walton Litz, and Danis Rose. New York: Garland Publishing, 1978 (JJA + volume.page).

———. *Ulysses*. Eds. Hans Walter Gabler *et al*. New York: Vintage, 1986 (U + chapter.line).

Stéphane Mallarmé. *Œuvres complètes*. Eds. Henri Mondor and G. Jean-Aubry. Paris: Gallimard, 1945 (OC + page).

———. *Correspondances*, Volume I. Eds. Henri Mondor and Jean-Pierre Richard. Paris: Gallimard, 1956 (CI + page).

———. *Correspondances*, Volumes II–XI. Eds. Henri Mondor and Lloyd James Austin. Paris: Gallimard, 1965–84 (CII–CXI + page).

———. *Un coup de dés jamais n'abolira le hasard*. Eds. Mitsou Ronat *et al*. Paris: Change/d'Atelier, 1980 (UC + page; each double page will be referred to by a single number from 1 [the cover page] to 12, and divided into verso/recto pairs by adding a or b, respectively; references to this poem will be keyed in to both the Ronat and the Mondor editions, but all matters of layout will derive from the Ronat edition).

———. *Œuvres complètes. I. Poésies*. Eds. Carl Paul Barbier and Charles Gordon Millan. Paris: Flammarion, 1983 (OCP + page; references to Mallarmé's poems will be keyed in to both the Barbier and the Mondor editions).

Worse Words for Worser Still: An Introduction

In his study of *Un coup de dés*, Robert Greer Cohn offers the following assessment of the poetic work of Stéphane Mallarmé: "Sa carrière tout entière, littéralement son existence tout entière, était orientée vers un Œuvre dépassant par son ambitieuse conception les rêves les plus extravagants d'un Dante ou même d'un Joyce."[1] The problem with such a grandiose claim is, quite simply, that Mallarmé did not exactly leave behind a work of such magnitude that it could be easily compared with either Dante's *Commedia* or Joyce's *Finnegans Wake*. Despite many promises, Mallarmé never managed to write the Grand Œuvre whereof he so often spoke. To be sure, he did orient his writings *towards* the Œuvre in that everything he wrote could be construed as a component of the still as yet unrealized Book. At the beginning of *Le livre, instrument spirituel,* one of many essays offered in place of the Œuvre, Mallarmé wrote that "tout, au monde, existe pour aboutir à un livre" (OC: 378). That is then the Book or what impacts into a book: everything, in the world. All the fragments that he left behind (including essays such as *Le livre, instrument spirituel*) end up in a book. Yet with Mallarmé there is no Book there. With Mallarmé, the very possibility of the Book becomes coordinate with the absence of the Book.

It is not so much that Mallarmé's ambition to write the Book unites him with Dante and Joyce, since this ambition is hardly unique. There have been many writers who have variously been engaged with the project of writing the Book, the Book as some kind of *summum*: Ovid, Aquinas, Cervantes, Sade, Blake, Hugo, Baudelaire, Balzac, and Queneau. Rather, Dante, Mallarmé, and Joyce can be united in that each of them did write the Book, but only by silencing it. They are united by the attempt to silence their works. This silencing is obviously paradoxical since as difficult as it may be to write a Book of all earthly experience, it is redoubtably more difficult to write silence—to achieve silence upon the printed page. To be more precise, in different ways, the works of Dante, Mallarmé and Joyce *approach* silence.

It is neither our intention nor our desire to write an influence study, nor shall we undertake a study of common themes or tropes. Such work has already been done, and done well.[2] In brief, our essay is to read the works of Dante, Mallarmé and Joyce under certain of the propositions of Maurice Blanchot concerning silence and accomplishment. We aim to show how the possibility of writing the Book, of writing the complete Book (such as, for example, Dante's *Paradiso*, Mallarmé's Grand Œuvre and Joyce's *Finnegans Wake*), is marked by an inachievement which can be termed *silence*. The book silences itself, *terminates* in silence by its writing. To take seriously Blanchot's notion of silence here means that there will be some aspect of the text—Dantean, Mallarméan, Joycean—that does not submit to a judicious reckoning, some aspect that is fundamentally *apart* from coherence and sense. One could merely call this aspect "obscurity," purse one's lips and gloss away. Instead we will be asking how these texts can be said to be "difficult," and how they might stand apart from normal and normative discourse. Ultimately we will be claiming that Dante, Mallarmé and Joyce discover in language an ability to say nothing and thus for them, literature, the literary *work* becomes an interval of nul iteration.

> Le don d'écrire est précisément ce que refuse l'écriture. Celui qui ne sait plus écrire, qui renonce au don qu'il a reçu, dont le langage ne se laisse pas reconnaître, est plus proche de l'inexpérience inéprouvée, l'absence du « propre » qui, même sans être, donne lieu à l'avènement. Qui loue le style, l'originalité du style exalte seulement le moi de l'écrivain qui a refusé de tout abandonner et d'être abandonné de tout. Bientôt, il sera notable; la notoriété le livre au pouvoir: lui manqueraient l'effacement, la disparition.
> Ni lire, ni écrire, ni parler, ce n'est pas le mutisme, c'est peut-être le murmure inouï: grondement et silence.[3]

The only authority possible is to the work's unworking. The gift of writing is predicated as a silence, the burning whiteness of the page that admits no speaking and no authority (and no mark of an *auctor*, such as stylistics). Writing is thus not exactly productive. Even within the work of culture there might be an inachieved or neutral term: a *crisis* in which silence resounds, an enunciation that dissimulates silence through an operation of *unworking*.

We will, in this introductory chapter, begin our study by investigating the implications of the critical presupposition that these three writers are difficult and obscure, since it is this assumption that underlies much of the work on these authors, either individually or in combination. Indeed the early critics of both Joyce and Mallarmé are united in their leveling of charges of pointless, sterile and excessive obfuscation.[4] There is something there—some muddle—that is unclear and therefore *scandalous* (σκανδάλη, that which causes to stumble or give offense) to the refined tradition of commentary.[5] The *riposte* would be that that muddle can be accounted for by critical methodologies; that there is a tradition of difficulty and that tradition can and should now welcome a new, happy member upon the bookshelf.[6] Such criticism, at its most facile, finds "l'amor che move il sole e l'altre stelle" (Par: XXXIII.145) hidden within "una selva oscura" (Inf: I.2). Even Sade has been numerated by the Dewey-Decimal *Aufhebung*. Maurice Blanchot—himself no stranger to obscurity—characterizes this work of restitution as follows:

> La culture travaille pour le tout. C'est là sa tâche et c'est une bonne tâche. ... Pour elle, la signification d'une œuvre, c'est son contenu, et ce qui est posé et déposé dans les œuvres, leur côté positif, c'est la représentation ou la reproduction d'une réalité extérieure ou intérieure. ... L'idéal de la culture, c'est de réussir des tableaux d'ensemble, des reconstitutions panoramiques qui permettent de situer dans une même vue Schœnberg, Einstein, Piacsso, Joyce—et, si possible, Marx par-dessus le marché et, mieux encore, Marx et Heidegger: alors, l'homme de culture est heureux, il n'a rien perdu, il a ramassé toutes les miettes du festin.[7]

Restitution is inevitable. One is always already spoken for in the first-person plural of culture and exegesis. However there may be some *interval* temporarily unassimilable to this happy work of restitution, that which Blanchot, following from Bataille's notion of *la dépense*, calls "l'exigence fragmentaire de l'œuvre" (507). Instead of being a work obscure, perhaps the work—the work of, say, Joyce, Dante and Mallarmé—stands apart from the very possibility of sense and nonsense.

Calling a work obscure assumes that there is already a sense and meaning there in the work that has been obscured.

Blanchot directly addresses this issue in his review of Charles Mauron's *Mallarmé l'Obscur,* "La poèsie de Mallarmé est-elle obscure?" Surprisingly, Blanchot's answer to this question is a counterintuitive *non*: Mallarmé's poetry is not obscure, or more precisely, obscurity is not the issue here. Blanchot rigidly distinguishes between poetic and normal signification: "Le premier caractère de la signification poètique, c'est qu'elle est liée, sans changement possible, au langage qui la manifeste."[8] Unlike normal language, poetic language is inseparable from its words. "Ce que le poème signifie coïncide exactement avec ce qu'il est" (Blanchot 1943, 128). The poem reveals itself as a *singularity* void of communicative imperative. Blanchot characterizes rational language as a language of transparency in which individual words bear no tangible effect upon communication, and that explication—by *translating* obscurity into discourse—obviates the poetic utterance (130). In contradistinction, in poetry language is not communicative, it ceases to be a tool. "Et l'on comprend un poème, non par lorsqu'on en saisit les pensées ni même lorsqu'on s'en représente les relations complexes, mais lorsqu'on est amené par lui au mode d'existence qu'il signifie, provoqué à une certaine tension, exaltation ou *destruction de soi-même*" (129; emphasis added). The overtly Heideggerian phraseology of the first portion of this statement yields a decidedly non-Heideggerian punchline: *destruction de soi-même*. That which appears obscure threatens intelligibility, to the extent of even threatening its own intelligibility, if not its ontological status.

Then, this shall be our thesis: in language—in the languages of Joyce, Dante and Mallarmé—there is an enunciation that aims towards some achievement, and in so doing it aims towards the very destruction of itself-as-enunciation. Each writer set out to write a book of all earthly experience, *the Book,* and indeed each, in their own manner, wrote that book, each acheived their promise. *Yet* each achievement, each handsome volume, can only be said to have been achieved because of some formidable negation. There is, *there,* in achievement, the utterance's silencing. These are thus three different works that work upon a neutrality. This is obviously a precarious affinity to describe because it is suceptible of becoming a trait around which one can organize three highly disparate works. One can easily make silence speak as a *genre* of difficulty. Derrida, in an uncharacteristically strong Blanchotian register calls this *force*:

> la voix de M. Blanchot nous rappelle avec l'*insistance* de la profondeur qu'il est la possibilité même de l'écriture et d'une *inspiration* littéraire en général. Seule l'*absence pure*—non pas l'absence de ceci ou de cela—mais l'absence de tout où s'annonce toute présence—peut *inspirer,* autrement dit *travailler,* puis faire travailler. Le livre pur est naturellement tourné vers l'orient de cette absence qui est, par-delà ou en deçà de la génialité de toute richesse, son contenu propre et premier. Le livre pur, le livre lui-même, doit être, par ce qui est en lui le plus irremplaçable, ce « livre sur rien » dont rêvait Flaubert.[9] Rêve en négatif, en gris, origine du Livre total qui hanta d'autres imaginations. Cette vacance comme situation de la littérature, c'est ce que la critique doit reconnaître comme la spécificité de son objet, *autour de laquelle* on parle toujours.[10]

The works of Dante, Mallarmé and Joyce are—by simple virtue of being works—subject to force: they can be called *obscure*. Yet, even as much as this is the case (and we make no pretense otherwise), and indeed, *precisely because this is the case,* these works effect a negative interval upon discourse. This is what we call their *silence*.

> Je ne donnerai qu'un example de *mot* glissant. Je dis *mot:* ce peut être aussi bien la phrase où l'on insère le mot, mais je me borne au mot *silence*. Du mot il est déjà, je l'ai dit, l'abolition du bruit qui est le mot; entre tous les mots c'est le plus pervers, ou le plus poétique: il est lui-même gage de sa mort.[11]

In an essay admirably contra-thetic (actually two distinct essays yoked together under a similar thesis), Jean-Luc Nancy, following very closely from Bataille and Blanchot, names this negativity "exscription" and describes the paradoxical problem of fragmentary irruption, which always risks becoming a force, becoming a book, just another book:

> In order—but the gesture of writing is never satisfied with a teleology—to dissolve—but in a dissolution itself dissociated from the values of solution

always conferred on it by metaphysics—not only the ideal identity inscribed in the blinding whiteness of the Book (for in the depth of eternal light, everything scattered throughout the universe is reunited, as if bound by love, into a single book; Dante) but to dissolve even the privation, which also forms the privation, the privitization, of the Book. The Book is there—in each book occurs the virgin refolding of the book (Mallarmé)—and we must *write on it*, make it a palimpsest, overload it, muddy its pages with added lines to the point of the utter confusion of signs and of writings [here we muddy the waters of Nancy's merrily unconvoluted prose and add the name Joyce]: we must, in short, fulfill its original unreadability, crumpling it into the shapeless exhaustion of cramp.[12]

Nancy's proposed imperative of fulfilling an originary unreadability is impressive, and under other circumstances perhaps we would listen to it. But it would seem, following from Blanchot's argument above, that this *original unreadability* is not an origin after all. Unreadability is the preposition of reading that cannot be pinned down. The double-motion that we will be traversing in our three writings then is this paradox that in the happy reuniting of the book there is the intervallic dissolution, *and* this intervallic dissolution, rather than sunder unity, is also the mark of the possibility of the book. Dante, too, dissolves the privation. *Meaning-* (an absolute achievement of auto-coincidental being), as such, is not even possible for Dante. Indeed it is our aim in the next chapter to disprove Nancy's brief characterization of the lovesick Florentine.

The subject, then, of our book is this interval of exscription, an interval which—as Paul Celan noted—"shows a strong tendency towards silence."[13] As Nancy implies, this tendency is the tendency of the book, the book as conceived by Mallarmé, and also by Dante and Joyce, a project "à ne donner force et existence poétique qu'à ce qui *est* hors de tout (et hors du livre qui est ce tout), mais, par là, à découvrir le centre même du Livre" (Blanchot 1959, 304). Our thesis then is that *the book* for Dante, Mallarmé and Joyce is this interval apart, the interval of silence, a *pas au-delà* that betrays silence for it can do nothing else.

We will attempt to refrain from employing a consistently theorized principle to our readings of Dante, Mallarmé and Joyce, preferring instead to develop a logic and terminology through their works rather than from the works of others. The above discussion of silence and the fragment in Blanchot is proffered only as a means of setting a stage for our investigations. The overall logic of our argument may be at times circuitous, and for this we make no apology.

Henri Mondor, in his biography of Mallarmé, makes a slightly florid claim: "Sa fidélité aux engagements de sa jeunesse lui a fait commencer, remplir et finir par l'amour une vie que la recherche de la Beauté et la vocation de Poésie ont seules fascinée."[14] Stripped of a certain nostalgia, this claim could be easily applied to Dante and Joyce as well. All three writers—whilst engaged in writing the works that are now called, for better or worse, their "masterpieces"—followed from certain tenets and implications of their early work. The results of these delineations—in as much as they could be claimed to have *faithfully fulfilled* the original notions and plans of their projects—involved a silencing or an annulation of the very idea subtending their work. *To follow the logic of the originary idea entails its silencing or desistance.* They all fulfilled their promises faithlessly, by, in a certain way, exscribing the originary idea. They each wrote their book by proffering the withdrawal of its possibility.

∴

We begin then with Dante. There is much to be careful with the *Divina Commedia*, as Philippe Sollers astutely warns: "Peu d'œuvres sont aussi séparées de nous que la *Divina Commedia*: plus proche dans l'histoire que l'*Énéide*, où elle prend sa source, elle nous paraît cependant plus lointaine; commentée et répétée avec une érudition maniaque, elle garde à nos yeux son secret."[15] The reason for this, perhaps, is that there is no secret *there*—in the *Commedia*—to be revealed, at least not one that could be called, after the fact, a secret. In a text so apparently concerned with approaching a definite and definitive *revelation* (and a divine one at that), there may be very little that can be revealed. To be sure there will always be myriad matters to gloss and annotate, but such commodious comprehensiveness alone will not recover the *Commedia*'s trajectory for us.

As Curtius notes, Dante reconfigures the trope of the book into a *summum* of human knowledge, a *summum* that leads to God (Curtius, 326). The trope of the book appears early in Dante's work, from the poem *E' m'incresce di me sí duramente*: "Lo giorno che costei nel mondo venne, / secondo che si trova / nel libro de la mente che vien meno" (R: 65, ll. 57–59). From such wishful beginnings, Dante opens up the problem of the book: the book as the pentecostal path of access to divinity and he figures his own work as the inscription of this *codex* that leads him to God. The *Vita Nuova* opens by announcing that it is a transcription of the opening of this path:

> In quella parte del libro de la mia memoria dinanzi a la quale poco si potrebbe leggere, si trova una rubrica la quale dice: *Incipit vita nova*. Sotto la quale rubrica io trovo scritte le parole le quali è mio intendimento d'assemplare in questo libello e se non tutte, almeno la loro sentenzia. (VN: I)

The life of Dante is inscribed as this transcription of "the book of the opening of the mind to light" (FW: 258.31–32), an opening figured throughout the book by Dante's evolving appreciation of the beatific quality of Beatrice.[16] Domenico de Robertis has called the *Vita Nuova* the first book in Italian literature because it gathers and articulates a set of poems into a narratologically coherent unity or sequence.[17] Its *novelty* is its unity, the subsumption of a life into *a life under God*.[18] The act of transcribing the book of memory *makes* a unity out of disparity. However the transcription of the divine *inscripting* is left incomplete, at the end of the *Vita Nuova* the scribe breaks off and announces that he has yet to undertake his work:

> Appresso questo sonetto apparve a me una mirabile visione, ne la quale io vidi cose che mi fecero proporre di non dire più di questa benedetta infino a tanto che io potesse più degnamente trattare di lei. E di venire a ciò io studio quanto posso, sì com'ella sae veracemente. Sì che, se piacere sarà di colui a cui tutte le cose vivono, che la mia vita duri per alquanti anni, io spero di dicer di lei quello che mai non fue detto d'alcuna. E poi piaccia a colui che è sire de la cortesia, che la mia anima se ne possa gire a vedere la gloria de la sua donna, cioè di quella benedetta Beatrice, la quale gloriosamente mira ne la faccia di colui *qui est per omnia secula benedictus*. (VN: XLII.1–2)

In concluding the book of his memory, the poet announces that he has not yet accomplished his task of properly praising Beatrice. Literally this passage states that an interval of silence is to be required in order to represent Beatrice. It is as if at the moment he is unable to undertake the final step of his spiritual pilgrimage.[19] The *Vita Nuova* then could be called a book in its very emphasis upon its lack of an autotelic conclusion. In place of a conclusion it proffers silence, tentatively. The slowly progressing figuration of Beatrice throughout the narrative remained *inadequate* to Beatrice. However, perhaps out of tact, the mirabile visione named in the final chapter does not even lie within this rarefied economy of *adequate signification*, it stands apart.

The *Vita Nuova* began by resuscitating the images of memory and ends with a visionary venture into the future. The future is a project of writing which cannot be subsumed by the present. In the open-endedness of this conclusion the poet gives us the thought of another, futural poet who awaits inspiration to *speak of Beatrice in an absolutely new way*. Once inspired, all that the poet can affirm is that there is nothing to affirm and nothing that he can write about. In this sense Dante's inspiration by Beatrice is not without analogy to Mallarmé's *crise*. The poet is *he who cannot write*, the figure of a writer surrendered to a *crise de vers*, a crisis of inspiration. To be a pilgrim then is to be a poet, to venture forth into darkness and submit (submit by transgression) to the economy of the interval. This could then be the project of the *Commedia*. *The* book begins with disjunction, it begins as a figuration of this disjunction.

Our concern with Dante in the following chapter is to show that the *Paradiso* does not redress this disjunction, rather it written in the wake of the impossibility of a book of pentecostal resolution.[20] The *Paradiso* ends just as apart from divinity as the *Vita Nuova*. Through the manipulation of languages, through the marks of the separation of human tongues from a divine plenitude, the path to God remains impassable even as this transversal is transcribed. *Indeed, the transcription both denies and is the mark (inscription) of this denial of transversal*. The experience of the book is post-babelian and this leads to a rupture or *generative discontinuity*, the book is already inscribed by the plurality and plurability of languages.

Through an unparalleled access to God (an access without possible analogue) at the close of the *Paradiso*, Dante writes the désœuvrement of the book.

This experience of désœuvrement then comes to be the major problem for Mallarmé: the necessary inability to write the book. Chapters 3 and 4 will detail the poetic manifestations of this inability. As noted at the start of this chapter, all the fragments that Mallarmé has left behind end up in a book. The book then is the planning and reckoning that he had formulated *vers le livre*. As he wrote to his friend Henri Cazalis in July 1868: "Mon œuvre est si bien préparé et hiérarchisé, représentant comme il le peut, l'Univers, que je n'aurais su, sans endommager quelqu'une de mes impressions étagées, rien en enlever" (CII: 99). This hierarchy had been well planned, as testified to by the notes Mallarmé had left behind and that have been collected and edited by Jacques Scherer.[21] Scherer claims that the book would have been autotelic: "Le Livre est réel dans toute la mesure où il est superposable à lui-même. Sinon, il n'est que fantasie gratuite, jeu de ce hasard que la fonction première de la littérature est, très exactement, d'abolir" (Scherer, 94; cf. 84–94). These notes are thus framed as an imperfect record of a thinking *of and towards* the book, Scherer has then defined them by some *missing* book which *would have been* their fulfillment. But Mallarmé never wrote this book, never was able to write this book. In its never-present place is another book, the *crise de vers, vers le livre*.

Blanchot criticized Scherer's volume in the essay "Le livre à venir." He only directly addresses Scherer's project in two lengthy footnotes but the entire essay could be construed as a rebuttal against Scherer's project. In the first of these footnotes Blanchot notes the editorial difficulty of subsuming the heterogeneous fragments under the title of a single project. Further he notes the Apollinairian dictum to publish all (also an Apollonian dictum, as well as one suggested by Sade's Juliette). Blanchot articulates this injunction concerning communication as *the exigency that communicates:* "L'écrivain n'a aucun droit sur elles et il n'est rien en face d'elles, toujours déjà mort et toujours supprimé.... Quelle est cette puissance?... [Mallarmé] l'a appelée le Livre" (Blanchot 1959, 314 n.1;

cf. 312–14 n.1). In the second footnote on Scherer, Blanchot points out that Scherer's claims that the published work points to a singular ontogenetic Livre-as-idea is untenable because the performative aspect to the Livre (which are most extensively detailed in the notes) guarantees that the Livre will always be iterated variably, with no original. The Livre is always process and "est toujours autre... il n'est jamais là, sans cesse à se défaire tandis qu'il se fait" (330 n.1). The book remains conjugated in the conditional, and this *conditionality* is what has impacted into a book, which is still, always, a livre à venir. The book thus *oscillates* between manifestation and disappearance, a hypothetical disappearance of what never had been.

Like Dante, Mallarmé planned a book, the evidence of which is fundamentally discontinuous with the conception. Indeed, it is this very discontinuity which informs the book that has been left behind to read. In chapter 3 we will pursue this notion of oscillation in Mallarmé's critical work and in some of his poems (*Salut, Brise marine, Le vierge, le vivace et le bel aujourd'hui,* and *À la nue accablante tu*). The poems *Salut* and *À la nue accablante tu*—which both concern tempestuous sea-voyages—were planned by Mallarmé to serve as the beginning and end for the edition of his collected poems published in Brussels in 1899 by Edmond Deman (OC: 1406, 1341; OCP: 749–57). The poems fall as book-ends to a book Mallarmé did write. We will argue that these poems constitute an interval (a legible trace) of the illegibility of the book: how, through lexical manipulations, these poems retract the possibility that they might be read and understood as *complete* iterations. These sea-faring poems entail some of the possibilities of traversal that haunted Dante (specifically the disastrous and "folle volo" [Inf: XXVI.125] of Ulysses), but instead of iterating a progression-towards-disaster (or, for that matter, salvation), instead of iterating a teleologically bounded and defined passage, the poems iterate a neither/nor experience of the interval, an interval unsubsumed by an economy of completion. The interval is neither calamitous nor knowable.

> L'écriture fragmentaire serait la risque même. Elle ne renvoie pas à une théorie, elle ne donne pas lieu à une pratique qui serait définie par

> *l'interruption*. Interrompue, elle se poursuit. S'interrogeant, elle ne s'arroge pas la question, mais la suspend (sans la maintenir) en non-réponse. ... L'exigence fragmentaire, liée au désastre. Qu'il n'y ait cependant presque rien de désastreux dans ce désastre, il faudra bien que nous apprenions à le penser sans peut-être le savoir jamais. (Blanchot 1980, 98–99)

In chapter 4 we will discuss how *Un coup de dés* extends this fragmentary intervallic illegibility to include the notion of the Livre itself. Explicitly playing words against the whiteness of the page, the possibility of the book is suggested only to undergo perdition. By being a contested fragment of the Livre, *Un coup de dés* puts into play the generative discontinuity of the Livre.[22] As with Dante, the book is discontinuous with its legible form, and this discontinuity is precisely what there is left to read.

And then, in the wake of Dante and Mallarmé, Joyce. Despite Dante and Mallarmé's obvious influence on Joyce (as documented in some of the works listed in note 2),[23] the Joycean œuvre seems, at first glance, to be entirely different, overloaded as it is with all manner of detail and stylistic eccentricity. *Finnegans Wake* is neither a clear albeit convoluted pilgrimage to divinity like the *Divina Commedia*, nor is it a brazen lexical tempest like *Un coup de dés*. Yet there are some affinities between this triad of works in their exploration and exploitation of the post-babelian possibilities and implications of language. The *Wake* begins from the possibility of a discontinuity between language and the plenitude that is named by the Book. Like the *Paradiso* and *Un coup de dés*, the book is the interval of this discontinuity. All of these works are derived from their ceaseless deferral of a linguistic pentecost.

Our Joycean investigation will begin with a consideration of the narrativity of *Ulysses* and *Finnegans Wake*. We will argue that *Ulysses*, in that it remains within a *genre* of narrative, still follows the ("Ulyssean") path of a progression, that it remains circumscribed within some teleology, albeit a teleology under the absence of a telos, "the apathy of the stars" (U: 17.2226). In *Finnegans Wake* this becomes "the irony of the stars" (FW: 160.22). It is *here* then—with *a withdrawn and ironic absentation* of a telos—that there is obscurity and difficulty, the dissolution or *suspension* of the possibility of meaning achieved in the interval of a tenebrific play of writing, "every splurge on the vellum" (179.30–31). The irony is there unrelieved, a bottomless rupture *dès astre*:

> *Si la rupture avec l'astre pouvait s'accomplir à la façon d'un événement, si nous pouvions, fût-ce par la violence de notre espace meurtri, sortir de l'ordre cosmique (le monde) où, quel que soit le désordre visible, l'arrangement l'emporte toujours, la pensée du désastre, dans son imminence ajournée, s'offrirait encore à la découverte d'une expérience par laquelle nous n'aurions plus qu'à nous laisser ressaisir, au lieu d'être exposés à ce qui se dérobe dans une fuite immobile, à l'écart du vivant et du mourant; hors expérience, hors phénomène.* (Blanchot 1980, 92)

Our final chapter will argue how *Finnegans Wake* stands apart from an economy of completion by *redegenerating* writing one splurge at a time. We will argue that through the dense concatenations of diverse meanings, the *Wake* lacks both whither and whence, that it remains apart from a defining and delimiting meaning precisely because it engorges so many meanings and possibilities of meanings into its pages. *Finnegans Wake* assimilates so many disparate meanings that it effects a disparition of meaning. *Finnegans Wake* stands as the work of writing an indefinite cyclical prolongation of the recounting of a cryptic loss: the memorial (or crypt) indistinguishable from the ostensibly memorialized (or *en-crypted*). "Only for that these will not breathe upon Norronsen or Irenean the secrest of their soorcelossness" (023.18–19). The deepest, most arcane and cryptic secret is *soorcelossness:* a preterite loss of origin which remains most secret. The crypt does not merely conceal but also *hides* the event of its concealing as a *secrest*. The crypt, as such, is effaced by *cryptic marks*. It is a palimpsest of dissimulated marks inscribed over a still illegible writing. The crypt is at once intelligible and illegible. Each word—whether one would be so crude as to call it Joycean, Mallarméan or Dantean—utters a suggestiveness (an expansion of evocative referentiality) encrypted. The world is proffered and yet nothing is there on the page except words.

From *L'action restrainte*: "L'encrier, cristal comme une conscience, avec sa goutte, au fond, de ténèbres relative à ce que quelque chose soit: puis, écarte la lampe. Tu remarquas, on n'écrit pas, lumineusement, sur champ obscur, l'alphabet des astres, seul ainsi s'indique, ébauché ou interrompu; l'homme poursuit noir sur blanc" (OC: 370). The inkpot purveys the possibility of darkness which disturbs the clarity of the blank page into a wake or écume of suggestions. However this inkpot—l'encrier—is also that which submits *crise;* to write is to surrender to the *interval* that is subsisted by the totality of inscription—the purlieu of the alpha to omega of the alphabet *des astres*. The Books then are these "obscure" and "secrest" stellar crypts, the writing that takes place *after* the Book is no longer possible. These books—*Paradiso, Un coup de dés* and *Finnegans Wake*—are books *that take the place of the possibility of the Book*. Yet, despite their pervasive difficulties, there is still enough of a book there to read. These books remain subject to *force*; despite their silences they are made to speak, as if they had secrets to be unconcealed and lessons to teach. Even, or perhaps especially, exscription comes to be reinscribed into an archive. But by being written and bound into folio, these books perturb and pervert the insouciant stellar silence whence they ironically and perpetually speak. These books prematurely give themselves over to silence with only the preterite traces of perjured perdition left in their perilously periphrastic wakes. These books perplex their readers precisely because they perpetuate this discontinuity in perishable words inflicted upon the arrogance of a blank page.

Notes

[1] R.G. Cohn, *L'œuvre de Mallarmé*, Paris: Les Lettres, 1951, 15.

[2] Much comparative work has been done between Joyce and Dante and between Joyce and Mallarmé, but little work—aside from fleeting references—has been made on a connection between Mallarmé and Dante. Comparisons of Joyce and his august Florentine counterpart date back to Samuel Beckett's "Dante... Bruno. Vico.. Joyce" which appeared while *Finnegans Wake* was still a Work in Progress (Samuel Beckett, et al, *Our Exagmination Round His Factification For Incamination Of Work In Progress*, New York: New Directions, 1939. 1–22). Later, Louis Gillet proposed a Dantean foufolded allegorical hermeneutic for *Finnegans Wake* (*Claybook for James Joyce,* trans. George Markow-Totevy, London: Abelard-Schuman, 1958. 58). The most thorough exposition of Joycean modulations of Dante is Mary T. Reynolds's *Joyce and Dante* (Princeton: Princeton UP, 1981). Numerous articles have appeared since, adding further to our knowledge of Dantean glosses in Joyce's work. Recent work has shifted the focus away from a description of influence towards an analysis of certain theoretical implications of said influence.

Joyce's affinities with Mallarmé have been better documented as both breathe within the heady atmosphere of modernism, Mallarmé as precursor and Joyce as full-fledged participant. Marshall McLuhan briefly examined both Joyce and Mallarmé's attitudes towards the popular media of communication in "Joyce, Mallarmé and the Press" (*Sewanee Review* 62 [1954]: 38–55). David Hayman undertook a systematic study of Mallarmé's influence on Joyce in the two volumes of *Joyce et Mallarmé* (Paris: Lettres Modernes, 1956). Recently, there have been further studies of these two writers: William Carpenter's thematic *Death and Marriage: Structural Metaphors for the Work of Art in Joyce and Mallarmé* (New York: Garland, 1988); Jean-Michel Rabaté's typographic study "'Alphybettyformed verbage': the shape of sounds and letters in *Finnegans Wake*" (*Word and Image* 2.3 [July–September 1986]: 237–43); Simone Verdin's brief "Mallarmé et Joyce, somptuosités vitales et magnifique veille de la pensée" (*Courrier de Centre International d'Études Poétiques* 84 [1971]: 17–28); and Adam Piette's stylistic analysis of prosody in Mallarmé, Proust, Joyce and Beckett, *Remembering and the Sound of Words* (Oxford: Oxford UP, 1996).

Joyce and Mallarmé have provided much fodder for the post-structuralists. Philippe Sollers has written (separate) essays on Joyce, Mallarmé and Dante, and he has suggested connections, some quite intriguing, between the three; see his *Logiques* (Paris: Seuil, 1968) for the Dante ("Dante et la traversée de l'écriture" [44–77]) and Mallarmé ("Littérature et totalité" [97–117]) essays. His main critical essay on Joyce is "Joyce et c^{ie}" (*Tel Quel* 64 [Winter 1975]: 15–24). Jacques Derrida has written extensively on both Joyce and Mallarmé, both of whom appear to occupy a privileged position in his continuing *response* to the dysfunctional vagaries of writing; for his work on Joyce see *L'origine de la Géometrie de Husserl. Introduction et traduction* (Paris: PUF, 1962. cf. 104–7), *La carte postale* (Paris: Flammarion, 1980. 255–58) and the two essays in *Ulysse gramophone* (Paris: Galilée, 1987) as well as sundry other references peppered throughout his work; for his readings of Mallarmé see "La double séance" (*La dissémination,* Paris: Seuil, 1972. 199–317). The history of Joyce's reception by the French post structuralists has been extensively covered by Geert Lernout in *The French Joyce* (Ann Arbor: U of Michigan P, 1990).

[3] Maurice Blanchot, *L'écriture du désastre,* Paris: Gallimard, 1980. 154–55. This follows from something that Heidegger had said in *Being and Time*: "the primary substance of literature is not the unnamable, but on the contrary the named…. The writer does not 'wrest' speech from silence, as we are told in pious literary hagiographies, but inversely, and how much more arduously, more cruelly and less gloriously, detaches a secondary language from the slime of primary languages afforded him by the world, history, his existence, in short by an intelligibility which preexists him… the whole task of art is to *unexpress the expressible*" (Martin Heidegger, *Being and Time*, trans. John Macquarrie and Edward Robinson, New York: Harper and Row, 1962. 211).

[4] Max Nordau called Mallarmé a "lamentable eunuch" with a "weak mind" who only exhibited "moments of versification" (quoted in D. Hampton Morris, *Stéphane Mallarmé, 20th Century Criticism 1901-71,* Valencia: Romance Monographs, 1977. 14). Joyce suffered many accusations of insanity during the serial publication of *Finnegans Wake*, especially from Wyndam Lewis and Ezra Pound, many of these were worked into the text in a manner that paradoxically refutes this charge whilst agreeing with it. One example: in a letter to Joyce, Pound wrote "Nothing short of divine vision or a new cure for the clapp [*sic*] can possibly be worth all the circumambient peripherization" (LIII: 145). Joyce then worked this comment into his text as "*A New Cure for an Old Clap*" (FW: 104.23–24).

[5] Dante is here the *exceptional figure* in the tradition of commentary, since until the *Divina Commedia* mere texts were considered unworthy of comment and painstaking gloss as such activity was reserved for the Bible (the word of God!) and secular works in the Classical languages of unquestioned authority (the word of Aristotle!). The commentary tradition then *deifies* and colors the *Divina Commedia*

by placing it within this highly esteemed tradition. Such enframing has implications for the question of deciding between the allegory of the poets of the allegory of the theologians (see our argument in chapter 2), since, by suggesting a value to the text even roughly analogous to the Bible, one has already decided upon the allegory of the theologians.

Rapidly canonized through commentary, Dante suffered critical resistance after an early enthusiastic welcome. "The process by which the Florentine Dante's poem came to be canonized as an 'Italian' classic roughly parallels the process by which the Florentine vernacular came to be adopted as the literary language throughout the peninsula, thus reducing the regional languages of Italy to dialect status. Finally however, the history of the critical reception of Dante's poem during the Renaissance is also a story about the poem's decline in popularity. The prophetic claims and religious fervor of the *Divine Comedy*, no less than the poem's unorthodox language and style, were incompatible with the neo-classicism of Renaissance literary culture, which preferred the lyric poetry of Petrarch" (Theodore J. Cachey, Jr, *Introduction. Renaissance Dante in Print (1472–1629),* Online, Internet. January 3, 1996). Ernst Robert Curtius notes that unreserved appreciation for Dante returned only in the latter half of the eighteenth century and cites a less-than-flattering assessment from Goethe as exemplary of Dante's wilderness years: "I had never been able to understand how anyone could spend time over these poems; that, as for me, I found the *Inferno* monstrous, the *Purgatorio* ambiguous, and the *Paradiso* boring" (quoted in Ernst Robert Curtius, *European Literature and the Latin Middle Ages,* trans. Willard R. Trask, Princeton: Princeton UP, 1953. 348; cf. 348–50).

[6] In the first full-length study of Mallarmé—*La poésie de Stéphane Mallarmé* (1912)—Albert Thibaudet attempted to show that the standard critical methods of explication could be applied to Mallarmé as efficiently as with any classical author (Albert Thibaudet, *La poésie de Stéphane Mallarmé,* 9th edition, Paris: Gallimard, 1926. cf. esp. 10). This exemplifies the typical critical response to accusations of obscurity: demonstrate that the work can be rendered legible by paring away difficulty through parsing, thereby establishing the work within a genealogy of commentary.

[7] Maurice Blanchot, *L'entretien infini,* Paris: Gallimard, 1969. 587–88.

[8] Maurice Blanchot, *Faux pas,* Paris: Gallimard, 1943. 127. Blanchot's rapport with Mallarmé could be characterized as an elaboration of the implications of this claim; see our discussion of this in chapter 3.

[9] Blanchot proposes an affinity between Bouvard and Pécuchet's failures and Flaubert's attempts at prose: the question for Flaubert is "comment la nullité fait œuvre et comment peuvent coïncider, au niveau de la littérature, la totalité du savoir encyclopédique (donc, le maximum de substance) et le rien sans lequel Flaubert soupçonne qu'il n'y a pas d'affirmation littéraire" (Blanchot 1969, 490). Flaubert's project thus runs the same risk as that of Bouvard and Pécuchet, of literalizing Mallarmé's claim that "tout, au monde, existe pour aboutir à un livre" (OC: 378). But then, in the *Dictionnaire des idées reçus*, they gloss a livre with "Quel qu'il soit, toujours trop long" (Gustave Flaubert, *Bouvard et Pécuchet*, Paris: Flammarion, 1966. 366).

[10] Jacques Derrida, "Force et signification," *L'écriture et la différence*, Paris: Seuil, 1967. 9–49. 17.

[11] Georges Bataille, *L'expérience intérieure*, Paris: Gallimard, 1954. 28.

[12] Jean-Luc Nancy, "Exscription," trans. Katherine Lydon, *The Birth to Presence*, Stanford: Stanford UP, 1993. 319–40. 322. We regret citing a translation, but the full version of both parts of this essay exists only in English.

[13] Paul Celan, "The Meridian," *Collected Prose*, trans. Rosmarie Waldrop, New York: Sheep Meadow Press, 1986. 37–55. 48.

[14] Henri Mondor, *Vie de Mallarmé*, Paris: Gallimard, 1941. 7–8.

[15] Philippe Sollers, "Dante et la traversée de l'écriture," *Logiques*, Paris: Seuil, 1968. 44–77. 44.

[16] In his inordinately influential essay, Charles S. Singleton considers Beatrice in terms of her Christological allegorical relevance to the Dantean project. The poet's retrospection of the events of Beatrice's life and death signify a revelation of Christian *caritas* (Charles S. Singleton, *An Essay on the "Vita Nuova,"* Baltimore: Johns Hopkins UP, 1949. 75; 111–13). With differences in modulation, virtually all critical responses after Singleton posit Beatrice as the ineluctable point of alterity (*beatitude*) to which Dante's writing tends. Some recent work has tended to diminish the overtly theological comportment granted to Beatrice by Singleton's essay, but the insistence on Beatrice as the figure for Dante's epiphanic experience of writing nevertheless remains (cf. Guiseppe Mazzotta, "The Language of Poetry in the *Vita Nuova*," *Rivista di studi italiani*, 1.1 [June 1983]: 3–15. 11; Robert Pogue Harrison, *The Body of Beatrice*, Baltimore: Johns Hopkins UP, 1988. 44).

[17] Domenico De Robertis, *Il libro della "Vita Nuova,"* second edition, Florence: Sansoni, 1970. 18.

[18] Such theological autobiography is of course not so novel. In many ways it repeats the gestures of Augustine's *Confessions* in which a "life" is made in its accounting and recollection before God. Augustine's is a life that is explicitly predicated as a life that has deviated and separated from God and its unity exists only in that it can be *narrated* in the face of God. The (Augustinian) self exists in its narratologic expenditure before God.

[19] This conclusion is foreshadowed by the poem *Tanto gentile e tanto onesta pare*, where Beatrice is figured as a gentle spirit of love and the only response that the poet is capable of to this is a sigh: "par che de la sua labbia si mova / un spirito soave pien d'amore, / che va dicendo a l'anima: Sospira" (VN: XXVI.7, ll. 12–14). The poet is reduced to describing the inability to write of her and instead writes of his inability to write which is figured as a *ex-spiration* in the encounter with *in-spiration*.

[20] In his historical account of the modern privileging of silence as the asymptotic point to which poetic discourse tends, George Steiner writes: "The election of silence by the most articulate is, I think, historically recent. The strategic myth of the philosopher who chooses silence because of the ineffable purity of his vision or because of the unreadiness of his audience has antique precedent. ... But the poet's choice of silence, the writer relinquishing his articulate enactment of identity in mid-course, is something new" (George Steiner, *Language and Silence*, Harmondsworth: Penguin, 1969. 68). Steiner relegates Dante to the former category—where silence is just a trope of *ingegno* (60–2)—whereas he allows Mallarmé and Joyce, among others, the discovery of silence as the subversive mark of an insufficiency of language (48–53). In the next chapter, we will argue that Dante's tendency towards silence does not necessarily operate with reference to an autotelic presence that authorizes a purity of vision.

[21] Upon his death, Mallarmé wished all remaining incomplete manuscripts to be burned. A loose-leaf notebook survived which is what Scherer has edited and published as *Le "Livre" de Mallarmé* (Jacques Scherer, *Le "livre" de Mallarmé*, nouvelle édition, Paris: Gallimard, 1957, 1977. cf. esp. 145–52 for a discussion of the manuscript); Scherer also includes a lengthy essay on the possibility of the form

Mallarmé's book would have taken based on the evidence that had not been destroyed.

[22] There is a polarity of critical opinion concerning the status of *Un coup de dés* and the Grand Œuvre. On the one hand, critics such as Thibaudet, R.G. Cohn and Suzanne Bernard claim that the poem is at least an initial attempt in earnest to write the Work, if not the Work *itself,* after so many previous abortions and miscarriages (Thibaudet, 417–21; Cohn, 23–24; Suzanne Bernard, *Mallarmé et la musique,* Paris: Nizet, 1959. 133). On the other hand, critics like Paul Valéry, Jean-Pierre Richard and Gardner Davies claim that *Un coup de dés* announced the abandonment of the grand project of writing (Paul Valéry, *Écrits divers sur Stéphane Mallarmé,* Paris: Gallimard, 1951. 18; Jean-Pierre Richard, *L'univers imaginaire de Mallarmé,* Paris: Seuil, 1961. 563–64; Gardner Davies, *Vers une explication rationnelle du « coup de dés »,* nouvelle edition, Paris: José Corti, 1992. 157). As we will argue in the appropriate chapter, the possibility of this contestation between the equivalence or non-equivalence of *Un coup de dés* and the Livre is precisely the issue of the poem.

[23] David Hayman has written that shortly after completing his dissertation on Mallarmé's influence on Joyce, he asked Beckett to offer his opinion on the matter. Beckett disagreed with Hayman's premise and stated "I think [Joyce] took a lot from Dante" (David Hayman, "Beckett," unpublished).

Language and Loss in the "Divina Commedia"

The *Vita Nuova* ended with a "mirabile visione" (VN: XLII.1), an impasse and a promise to write of Beatrice thereof what had not been written before. Such a heroic task could well be taken to mark the inception of the *Divina Commedia*, and one would perhaps not find oneself horribly astray if one were to claim that the *Divina Commedia* is the fulfillment of the project announced by the *Vita Nuova*. Much impressive work has been done to elaborate this claim, and indeed the first two *cantiche* of the *Divina Commedia* almost seem to be fulfilling this promise.[1] We take as example, almost at random, *Inferno* X when just after being warned by Farinata of his forthcoming exile, the pilgrim is told by Virgil "La mente tua conservi quel che udito / hai contra te... quando sarai dinanzi al dolce raggio / di quella il cui bell'occhio tutto vede, / da lei saprai di tua vita il viaggio" (Inf: X.127-32). Beatrice is to provide the benediction for the pilgrim's cursèd life, she will consecrate his memories and through her blessedness he will know his life. And indeed this fulfillment appears to be taking place in the earthly paradise at the close of the *Purgatorio* when the pilgrim sees Beatrice for the first time since her untimely earthly demise: "E lo spirito mio, che già cotanto / tempo era stato che a la sua presenza / non era di stupor, tremando, affranto, / sanza de li occhi aver più conoscenza, / per occulta virtù che da lei mosse, / d'antico amor sentì la gran potenza" (Purg: XXX.34–39). The pilgrim is restored to a proximity with a scopically apprehensible intoxicating beatitude. It is this vision, at the culmination of the pilgrim's travels that will restore him to the promise shown in his, as Beatrice says, "vita nova" (XXX.115). By ensuring his return to her, she guarantees the fulfillment of this *past* vita nova. The *Divina Commedia* would thus be the *achievement* of a *recherche d'un vita nova perdu*, a vita nova that itself had not been achieved, but one that had been deferred in and by the transcription of the book of memory, the *Vita Nuova*.

All is, however, not sweetness and light, not even in Eden. The pilgrim has to undergo one more tangible journey, the passage through the "beata riva" (XXXI.97) Lethe. The passage beyond can only be accomplished by a passage through forgetting. Indeed the argument of this *cantica* has been intimately involved with *exscription* as the seven *peccato* Ps are gradually wiped off the pilgrim's brow during his passage: "Sette P ne la fronte mi descrisse / col punton de la spada, e « Fa che lavi, / quando se' dentro, queste piaghe » disse" (IX.112–14). The progress of the journey through purgatory is *marked* by the erasure of the marks of the sins of earthly life.[2] Past Lethe the pilgrim is enjoined by Beatrice to write what he will see there: "quel che vedi, / ritornato di là, fa che tu scrive" (XXXII.104–5). From this point on the pilgrim is beholden to a certain *responsibility to write*.[3] Giuseppe Mazzotta notes that the lethic experience emphasizes the role of forgetting for the pilgrimage: "Memory and forgetfulness are coextensive in his moral progress; they implicate and complement each other."[4] The leap to paradiso, then, is based upon writing and upon oblivion. In some sense, forgetting and the figurations thereof will have constituted the paradisic experience. The *Purgatorio* closes with a statement that interlaces both the forgetfulness of Lethe and the injunction to write:

> S'io avessi, lettor, più lungo spazio
>   da scrivere, i' pur cantere' in parte
>   lo dolce ber che mai non m'avria sazio;
> ma perché piene son tutte le carte
>   ordite a questa cantica seconda,
>   non mi lascia più ir lo fren de l'arte.
> Io ritornai da la santissima onda
>   rifatto sì come piante novelle
>   rinovellate di novella fronda,
> puro e disposto a salire a le stelle. (XXXIII.136–45)

The *cantica* ends because it has to, it is beholden to the mathematical form of its project of writing which demands thirty-three cantos. The parchments upon which the poet writes are pre-ordained, and the apportioned length granted to recount the passage through purgatory have been filled. In this sense the leap to the account of paradiso is figured as dependent upon the exigencies of transcription. "The poet ends his second *cantica* with an address to the reader, claiming a certain limit of art, as though only so many pages and no more could be allotted to this *cantica*" (Singleton 1973, 824).[5] A notion of limited and delimited art perdures throughout the *Paradiso*. The conventions of the poem thus excise the account of the Lethic experience, and so because of poetic τέχνη, Lethe is withdrawn. "That's the lethemuse but it washes off" (FW: 272.F3). The project of writing thus enframes, because of its very enframing, the erasure of the project of writing. Almost quite literally the poem *exscribes* its exscription because of the very exigencies imposed by its project of inscription. This notion of exscription at the end of the *Purgatorio* is purely a conceit of the poet's *ingegno*[6] (and of how such *ingegno* is figured as being ordained), but it does announce a predicament of writing that will be not without consequence for the *Paradiso*. The end of the *Purgatorio* announces a writing based upon both erasure and inscription, a double writing.

This double motion at the end of the *Purgatorio* of a retreat of memory and a responsibility of writing anticipates a crucial aspect of the *Paradiso*. For there are two modes of language in the *Paradiso*. On the one hand, there is the *iterable language*, the language that proceeds *as if* the paradisic experience could be, and perhaps even should be, sayable. This is the language of poetic *ingegno*, and is thus affiliated with the exigency to write. On the other hand, there is the initerable language, the language that proceeds *as if* the paradisic experience were not accessible to, and thus apart from, language. This is the language of *ingegno* confounded. Of course these two modalities had been present in Dante's earlier work (such as at the close of the *Vita Nuova*), but the tension is nowhere more extreme than in the *Paradiso*. The rapport between these two languages in the *Paradiso* constitutes an exigency of writing in whose interval or wake the paradisic experience is constituted.

The problematic interlacing of a language of iterability and a language of initerability has been phrased by *dantiste* through the dueling typologies of the allegory of the poets and the allegory of the theologians. The split between these two typologies derives from the apparently incompatible emphases concerning allegory in the *Convivio* and the *Epistle to Can Grande*, the former favoring the poets' allegory whereas the latter prefers the allegory of the theologians by advocating that the *Commedia* is to be read according to the fourfold exegesis normally reserved for scripture.[7] Mazzotta has very precisely articulated the differences of these typologies:

> The proponents of the allegory of poets see the *Divina Commedia* essentially as a *fabula*, a poetic construct in which theology, figuralism and Dante's prophetic vocation, which manifestly are the props of the poem, are part and parcel of the fictional strategy, the literal sense of which is a pure fiction. For those critics, such as Singleton, who argue in favor of the allegory of theologians, the poem is written in imitation of God's way of writing and, like Scripture, it exceeds metaphor and comes forth with the 'irreducibility of reality itself.' (Mazzotta, 230–31)[8]

Part of the blame for this state of apparently contradictory typologies is inherent within allegory itself, since allegory (ἀλληγορια) denotes a *speaking otherwise*: a hidden or secret speaking which—as Qunitillian was perhaps the first to have noted—inverts the literal level of discourse whilst remaining obliquely related to that literal level.[9] The problem allegory opens is *how* the *rapport* between what is iterated and what is not iterated (initerated but implied, somehow, through iterative and iterable inversion). The problem of allegory is thus the differentiation of iteration through iteration.[10] Allegory works as a departure from iteration but also as a reassertion of a possibility of iteration (some thing is being iterated without being within the proffered iteration): it restitutes iterative deficiency,[11] but the price for this restitution is the implication or indication that the language within which iteration speaks is less than ontogenetically pure (this is a point with which Mallarmé will not be disinterested). We will return to the possibility of this implication and its consequences after a brief elaboration of the typologies of poetic and theological allegory. In a sense the controversy of these typologies, which becomes a hermeneutic undecidability, bespeaks an insufficiency of discourse that invites *allegorizations* of reading. Furthermore the disjunction of allegorical typologies reflects a disjunction within the *Commedia* itself: the disjunction between a language of iterability and a language of initerability.

Following from Mazzotta's characterization of the two typologies, the poet, inasmuch as he produces allegory, writes "una veritade ascosa sotto bella menzogna" (C: II.i.3), an *allegoria in verbe,* whereas the theologian uncovers *the* truth (ideally God's truth) within the obscurities of the world, an *allegoria in factis*. The former produces and hides allegory in *verbe* and the latter elucidates the truth from *res*. Such distinction obviously assumes a stable differentiability between *res* and *verba*. The operative distinction between these two modes of allegory is thus the attribution of authority: the allegory of the poets grants the power of *allegoresis* to the poet's rapport with language (his *ingegno*) and, unsurprisingly, the allegory of the theologians grants it to the poet's rapport with God, and so the poet's task is merely one of *translating* God's power of signification onto the page. Whitman finesses this typological tension into his scheme of compositional and interpretive allegories. Whitman's rephrasing of the problem enables him to briefly propose that the writing of the *Divina Commedia* enstages a convergence of these two allegories, that the act of the poet creating his allegory (his book) is itself an *interpretation* (and not only an imitation as Singleton claims) of divine *allegoresis*: "It is the *Divina Commedia* that preeminently displays this reciprocal motion in allegory, demonstrating that from one perspective creatural activity has its own force, while from another perspective it simply reveals obliquely the force of the Creator" (Whitman, 199).

The author of the *Epistle to Can Grande* grants more veracity and authority to the literal level than does the author of the *Convivio* and so the levels of polysemy *include* the literal level, it is no mere ornament. Even though the *Epistle* favors a theological allegory, it admits a freedom of referentiality even as it posits a filiation of hermeneutic strategy between the *Commedia* and holy scripture: "Ad evidentiam itaque dicendorum sciendum est quod istius operis non est simplex sensus, ymo dici potest polisemos, hoc est plurium sensum; nam primus sensus est qui habetur per litteram, alius est qui habetur per significata per litteram" (CG: VII). As Lucia Boldrini states: "in the 'Epistle' [the author] comments on the *Divina Commedia*, whose literal surface he has to present as a historically true pilgrimage in the other world."[12] In other words—and allegory is always speaking other words—the literal level is itself already constituted as polysemous; and the uncertainty of the authorship and authority of the Epistle exacerbates rather than alleviates this polysemy of the literal *intendamente*.[13] Neither the literal nor the figurative levels abolishes each other since both remain within a polysemic rapport. Erich Auerbach writes: "Both entities in the figurative or typological relationship are equally real and equally concrete; the figurative sense does not destroy the literal, nor does the literal deprive the figured fact of its status as a real historical event" (quoted in Scott, 588). The rapport then between the literal and the allegorical is not so much one of authorization (whether poetic or divine), but more importantly one of the maintenance of a differentiation through polysemy. This would make the *Epistle* a less reliable guarantor of the theologians' allegory than Hollander maintains.[14] The mere possibility of allegorical meanings (the possibility of *other* meanings) suggests a failure or insufficiency of language. Jeremy Tambling formulates this problem quite precisely through Auerbach's notion of *figura*: the polysemy of the figura can work *both* ways and therefore one no longer has a stable level of adjudication between a poetic or a theological allegory.[15] Furthermore, the constant *reconfigurations* of these *figuræ* (which Tambling characterizes as palinodes) denies the stability of a referent: "It seems more profitable to urge that Dante's image of the book, and his ability to write and re-write with perfect freedom in the 'copying out' from that book, turns him into a *believer* in the centrality of writing, and accepting all writing as *essentially* fictional, so that allegorical meanings may be mounted onto poems that may or may not have had a precise original referent, without any sense of deception... and earlier positions may be retracted formally without their loss being felt as more than the switch from one mode of writing to another" (Tambling 1988,

134; cf. 130–35).[16] The question then is not *where* the authority for *allegoresis* lies (with the poet or with God) but rather *if* any position of authority or mastery over language can be achieved. The *Divina Commedia* is perhaps not reducible to a specific type of allegory.

If language is subtended by this possibility of polysemy then communication can not proceed on a straightforward path to some divine plenitude (a point Dante considers in the *De vulgari eloquentia*, and one which we will examine shortly), what then could the rapport be between iteration and the divine in the *Commedia*? Mediæval notions of fourfold allegory (as noted by Dante in the *Convivio,* II.i.2–7) imply some level of *correspondence* or transference between an order of truth and the letter: theological allegory insists that *there is* a code that can mediate and translate between language and Being. In other words, the allegorical phrasing of a double language necessarily articulates the initerable (the "poetic") as an *iterability* insofar as the poetic resorts to the codes of *allegoresis*. Through de Manian notions of allegory, Mazzotta has rephrased the polemic between poetic and theological allegory explicitly onto the hermeneutic scene. Reading itself becomes a spiritual pilgrimage and is thereby inscribed within the overall allegory, as Mazzotta notes in the following subtle point: "the question of whether Dante's allegory belongs to a theological or fictional mode cannot be simply solved, as critics would have it, by some *a priori* decision about the fictiveness or reality of the literal sense. Dante's reader is constantly reminded, in effect, that the practice of reading deals precisely with how that decision can be made, that reading is an imaginary operation in which truth and fiction, far from being mutually exclusive categories, are simultaneously engendered by the ambiguous structure of metaphoric language" (Mazzotta, 233). Allegoresis is itself a trope (but then such a conclusion was already implied by the *Epistle to Can Grande*).

In his ambitious and recent study *Dante's Interpretive Journey*, William Franke appears to be following the typology of a theological allegory by reading the *Commedia* through Heideggerian notions of poiesis, hermeneusis and truth. "The human work gives itself out to be merely a means for facilitating a more direct encounter with the divine Word. In effect, Dante employs poetry as a way of gaining a hearing for the Logos."[17] According to Franke, this Logos is heard through the discursive event of the poem: truth is *unveiled* or *unconcealed* (thereby securing for itself its being truth-as-$ἀλήθεια$[18]) by the poem's "being an event for the reader" (Franke, 40; cf. 39–47). It is through the reader's exegesis, through a pilgrimage of building, dwelling and thinking which responds to the figured passage of the pilgrim, that the divine Logos is to be vouchsafed: "the reader qua reader gains self-awareness of her own reality only insofar as this is disclosed in, and in responding to, the text" (43). Franke thus arrives at a conclusion similar to Mazzotta: allegory in the *Divina Commedia* is itself allegorical of the hermeneutic act (cf. Mazzotta, 233). For both Franke and Mazzotta, the reader embarks upon a pilgrimage, but for Franke this is through an ontologically authentic truth and not through the vicissitudes of figural language as Mazzotta claims. Franke's reading seems to use Heideggerian vocabulary in order to assert a theological allegory as extreme as Josipovici's (see note 7), but Franke proffers a not unimportant qualification, one which recognizes the negativizing potential of language hinted at by the poets' allegory: "The divine truth revealed through the poem *is not identical* with what Dante himself however skillfully and earnestly, says in his work" (Franke, 96; emphasis added). Franke emphasizes the reader's requisite hermeneutic efforts in this *entretien* of unconcealing divine truth, yet this formulation bespeaks another difficulty of the poem, the difficulty of an iteration's rapport with the initerable: how iteration is never self-identical, not even in—but perhaps *especially in*—divine plenitude. Dante himself theorized this inability of iteration and of language (specifically in his discourse concerning Babel in the *De vulgari eloquentia*, which we will discuss shortly). *Between* the possibilities of a theological and a poetic allegory there is a *difference*, a difference of authority, and it is this difference which constitutes the book known as the *Divina Commedia*. Our argument will proceed by first elaborating the interplay of iterability and initerability in the *Paradiso* (and how that follows from but radicalizes the lethic experience that closes the *Purgatorio*). We will then enumerate some of the consequences of this interplay for the possibility of a rapport with divinity constructed through language, memory and loss.

⋯

The *Paradiso* begins with an almost insufferable modesty in the face of having witnessed divinity:

> La gloria di colui che tutto move
> >   per l'universo penetra, e risplende
> >   in una parte più e meno altrove.
> Nel ciel che più de la sua luce prende
> >   fu' io, e vidi cose che ridire
> >   né sa né può chi di là su discende;
> perché appressando sé al suo disire,
> >   nostro intelletto si profonda tanto,
> >   che dietro la memoria non può ire.
> Veramente quant'io del regno santo
> >   ne la mia mente potei far tesoro,
> >   sarà ora matera del mio canto. (Para: I.1–12)

Memory will be unable to perform a restitutive task and therefore an order of writing different from those of the preceding *cantiche* is required for the poet of this *cantica*.[19] The poet is thus to limit himself to the constraints imposed by his faculties and circumstances. *And yet* mere lines after this *propositio* concerning the limitations of poetic iteration, the *invocatio* requests an amplification of both the powers of the poet and of language, it is as if the poet expresses his inability only that he might be granted poetic puissance:

> O divina virtù, se mi ti presti
> >   tanto che l'ombra del beato regno
> >   segnata nel mio capo io manifesti,
> venir vedra'mi al tuo diletto legno,
> >   e coronarmi allor di quelle foglie
> >   che la materia e tu mi farai degno (I.22–27).

There are numerous ways in which this apparent contradiction between the *propositio* and the *invocatio* can be construed. There is, on the one hand, a sense of modesty concerning the poet's abilities in the face of the experience to which he is beholden. What is of course notable here in the *invocatio* is the absence of Beatrice as a figure of inspirational force. Although she inspires the pilgrim, she does not inspire the poet; or more precisely she inspires the poet only in that (the poet can remember how) she had inspired the pilgrim: "Così Beatrice a me com'io scrivo" (V.85). The implication is that there is a disjunction of authority between the pilgrim and the poet that cannot be reconciled, a disjunction that concerns both the responsibility and the authority for the poet to write.

The apparent contradiction between the *propositio* and the *invocatio* is a point supported by the *Epistle to Can Grande* in a gloss for lines 5–6: "nescit quia oblitus, nequit quia, si recordatur et contentum tenet, sermo tamen deficit. Multa namque per intellectum videmus quibus signa vocalia desunt" (CG: XXIX). Language itself lacks the resources to accommodate the divine, and therefore a craftsman of language is doubly deficient. But then, on the other hand, in the *invocatio* there is the pledge made to overcome these deficiencies with divine aid. Indeed, elsewhere in the Epistle these statements concerning inability and promise are labeled rhetorical tricks enacted in order to excite the readers, thereby rendering them disposed to learn from the poem (XIX). Such a claim would tend to reassert *ingegno*. In a sense then the poet is asking—even forcing—poetry to do something that it normally cannot do while still remaining within the register of the poetic. This is how Mazzotta characterizes the *Divina Commedia* "the metaphoric movement of the poem denounces the illusoriness of the project and draws the theological structure of sense into the possibility of error, that Dante writes in the mode of theological allegory and also recoils from it" (Mazzotta, 237). John Freccero has neatly summarized this predicament of *poiesis* in the *Paradiso* as an "attempt to create a non-representational poetic world" and so the boldly daring task of the poet of the *Paradiso* is "to represent non-representation without falling into unintelligibility or into silence."[20] The *Paradiso* is thus articulated within both inability and progress.

Perhaps the most compact instance of a simultaneity of these two modalities in language can be found in the following tercets:

Nel suo aspetto tal dentro mi fei,

> qual si fe' Glauco nel gustar de l'erba
> che 'l fe' consorte in mar de li altri Dei.
> Trasumanar significar per verba
> non si poria; però l'essemplo basti
> a cui esperienza grazia serba. (Para: I.67–72)

The word *trasumanar* is a neologism of the poet, the poet's *ingegno* makes a new word to signify the motion towards transcendence[21] only to have that possibility retracted *per verba*. Initerability is claimed as a withdrawal (the *non si poria* clause) of the announcement of *trasumanar significar per verba*. Such a syntactically enacted and deferred retraction, an enjambment past the cæsura of the line-break, operates in a manner not unlike the title *Un coup de dés jamais n'abolira le hasard*. *Significare* is thus asserted as being within the poet's domain only to be adamantly denied. This phrasing recalls Dante's gloss on ineffability in the *Convivio*: "cioè che la lingua non è di quello che lo 'ntelletto vede compiutamente seguace" (C: III.iii.15). There, in the service of an explanation, the possibility of language is denied in a straightforward manner. However this articulation in the *Convivio* is not isomorphic with the above passage from the *Paradiso* because in the latter the statement of ineffability itself wavers between iterability and initerability: it is *as if* the poet can speak, if only to be silenced.[22]

After the palinode of this line, the poet writes: "però *l'essemplo* basti a cui esperienza grazia serba." After the retraction one is left with an *essemplo*, presumably the simile of the fisherman Glaucus transformed, itself an example of a *trasumanazione* (cf. ED: II.728; Singleton 1975, 18). Ovid's story of Glaucus offers an example which must supplement the inability to iterate the *trasumanazione*. But syntactically *essemplo* could also refer to the *very action of designating the process of exemplarity*. The *essemplo* that remains is not just the allusion to Glaucus but is also that breaking off (or aposiopesis) of the iteration of the experience of *trasumanazione*. The poet thus communicates the *brisure* that proscribes his communication (setting forth the experience *per* verba). Once *ingegno* is withdrawn and denied all that is left is the analogy. The essemplo then is the interval of iteration itself: an interval in which similes and other figures are used and abused. This would then be the point that Sollers

makes of the *Paradiso*: "C'est le lieu de l'écriture s'écrivant elle-même. ... Passer au-delà de l'homme (trasumanar), dit Dante, ne pourrait pas être signifié par des mots (per verba), et nous devons sans doute comprendre: pusique ce passage s'effectue au sein du langage, il ne saurait être dit *par lui*."[23] Mazzotta makes a similar point: "[Dante] implies that, as readers, we lodge in a world of language and that to interpret we must *travel the distance* that separates signs and meanings" (Mazzotta, 11, emphasis added). The passage through humanity—the *tra* of *trasumanar* ("posizione localmente intermedia" [ED: V.675])—is effected *as* an *interval* of the poem's iteration. Indeed, after the paradisic experience Dante will have remained a poet, nothing but a poet: "Se mai continga che 'l poema sacro / al quale ha posto mano e cielo e terro /... ritornerò poeta; ed in sul fonte / del mio battesmo prenderò 'l cappello" (Para: XXV.1–9). After the encounter with divine plenitude there is the language of poetry (and the tokens of its earthly rewards), a poetry which by its very perdurance renders the divine experience belated.[24]

Of course the question of the possibility of an analogue or *essemplo* is by no means a simple one in the *Divina Commedia*. The very possibility of analogicity is located at the intersection of the poet's *ingegno* and the resources available to him through and with language. In a certain sense the possibility of an analogue underlies each of the two modalities of paradisic language. The statements in the *Paradiso* are not necessarily motivated by a logic of *mimesis* so much as by a logic of tropic substitution putatively governed by *analogos*.[25] This is a conclusion Freccero draws from the following statement by Beatrice to the pilgrim: "Così parlar conviensi al vostro ingegno, / però che solo da sensato apprende / ciò che fa poscia d'intelletto degno" (Para: IV.40–42). "The extraordinary implication of Beatrice's remark is that the whole of the *Paradiso*, at least until the crossing of the river of light toward the poem's ending, has no existence, even fictional, beyond the metaphoric" (Freccero, 211; cf. 222). Following from the logic of Freccero's point, the language of the *Paradiso* is not unlike a simile without an apodosis or tenor. The *ingegno* of the pilgrim and of the poet can only deal with tropic displacements divested from *that* whereof they cannot understand nor speak.

The possibility of the iterability of analogy has implications beyond a mere enstaging of the *cantica* as a purely hermetic text, for in the *Paradiso* referentiality impacts upon and against the possibility of an elocutory interval of the Book. It is this intersection that more precisely marks the interlacing of the two modalities of paradisic language.

> Imagini, chi bene intender cupe
>   quel ch'i' or vidi e ritegna l'image,
>   mentre ch'io dico, come ferma rupe,
> quindici stelle che 'n diverse plage
>   lo cielo avvivan di tanto sereno,
>   che soperchia de l'aere ogne compage;
> imagini quel carro a cu' il seno
>   basta del nostro cielo e notte e giorno,
>   sì ch'al volger del temo non vien meno;
> imagini la bocca di quel corno
>   che si comincia in punta de lo stelo
>   a cui la prima rota va dintorno,
> aver fatto di sé due segni in cielo,
>   qual fece la figliuola di Minoi
>   allora che sentì di morte il gelo;
> e l'un ne l'altro aver li raggi suoi,
>   e amendue girarsi per maniera,
>   che l'uno andasse al primo e l'altro al poi;
> e avrà quasi l'ombra de la vera
>   costellazione e de la doppia danza
>   che circulava il punto dov'io era:
> poi ch'è tanto di là da nostra usanza,
>   quanto di là dal mover de la Chiana
>   si move il ciel che tutti li altri avanza. (Para: XIII.1–24)

Following from Peter Hawkins's reading of this passage, there are here three separate injunctions to *imagini*, each followed by a simile, or rather an *image*: "an emphatic command not only to etch in mind 'come ferma rupe' the image inscribed on the page, but also to heighten our awareness of the poet's activity: the making of the metaphor 'metre ch'io dico'" (Hawkins, 15). But then the complex cathexis of images is discredited and thus retracted: "The effect of the lines [19–24] is radically to undermine the preceding *imago*. And yet, if the poet rejects his analogy as only a shadow of the truth, it is still a shadow" (*ibid*). The passage thus begins within the first modality of paradisic language: the attempt to proffer multiple analogues to the experience in the sun's sphere, and yet this attempt, once boldly made, is retracted. Therefore analogues may not be possible within the sphere of this work in progress, yet they are all that remain of the experience. They remain divested of correspondence. By proffering similes to account for an unaccountable experience, the poet highlights a certain inability or insufficiency of his ingenuous use of language, and this inability is figured as a trope of allegoresis. The inability itself becomes a cathexis of differential figurations. The difference between the two modes of paradisic language is thus tropic. This can be illustrated by the following passage in which the cross is beheld, also in the fourteenth canto:

> Qui vince la memoria mia lo 'ngegno;
> > ché 'n quella croce lampeggiava Cristo
> > sì, ch'io non so trovare essempro degno:
> ma chi prende sua croce e segue Cristo,
> > ancor mi scuserà di quel ch'io lasso,
> > vedendo in quell'albor balenar Cristo. (Para: XIV.103–8)

There is no possibility of *essempli* for the Christic experience by the poet's *ingegno* ("non so trovare essemplo degno"), and consequently the poet proffers Cristo as a rhyme with itself. Cristo is so unique—a "venerabil segno" (XIV.101)—that only he can be made analogous to himself.[26] However this rhyming auto-affective non-differentiation is achieved through a repetition of his name: his uniqueness is designated in its multiple iteration. The impossibility of an analogue for Christ is registered through the specific form of the poet's craft: the rhyme structure of *terza rima*. In this way the formal constraints of the poem allow the poet to ingeniously deploy an instance of his *ingegno* confounded by the pure presence of the divine since he characterizes himself-as-poet as being fundamentally incapable of wrapping Cristo into a rhyme. Therefore, in this sequence, the difference between the two modes of paradisic language—the difference between the iterable and the initerable—is iterated through one identical rhyme sequence which serves as a metaphor for an impossible allegorization. The metaphor of being confounded is itself a metonymic displacement of an impossible allegory.

There is one word other than Cristo, and only one other word, which also rhymes with itself in the *Divina Commedia*:

> Poi come gente stata sotto larve
>   che pare altro che prima se si sveste
>   la sembianza non sua in che disparve,
> così mi si cambiaro in maggior feste
>   li fiori e le faville, sì ch'io vidi
>   ambo le corti del ciel manifeste.
> O isplendor di Dio, per cu' io vidi
>   l'alto triunfo del regno verace,
>   dammi virtù a dir com'io il vidi! (XXX.91–99)

In a canto of the account of the "novella vista" (XXX.58), vision is enunciated as a singularity, as a statement without analogue—perhaps not unlike Cristo after all. Indeed vision is intertwined with the possibility of the analogue. Richard Lansing notes that the strong visual impact of Dantean simile registers the Mediæval concern that things manifest, the *visibilia*, register the existence of the *invisibilia*. In this sense, following very closely from Augustine, the order of the world, *res*, proffers signs for the numinous world and so every thing signifies beyond itself towards God. "The only access to an understanding of the *invisibilia* is through the *visibilia*.... In St. Thomas's words, *nihil est in intellectu nisi prius fuerit in sensu.* ... What Eliot like Macaulay and others failed to grasp was that Dante's visually oriented similes were not intended to make the reader see the scene more clearly as an end in itself, but to call attention to the process of visualization as the means of cognition" (Lansing, 45–46). What is interesting about Lansing's claim is the idea that similes enframe not just a specific analogy, but that they would also register the very process of analogicity (of tropic substitution) *as* the means of access to divinity. Similes thus remark the passage the pilgrim takes and makes towards God (this is similar to the claim Mazzotta made, quoted on page 27). Analogicity is itself analogous to a pilgrimage towards God.

The simile in the above passage—which enstates the pilgrim's new vision, a vision that thrice rings forward—registers a profound confusion of analogics since the relation between protasis and apodosis is sylleptic. The denuded face of the protasis ("Poi come gente stata *sotto larve* che pare altro che prima, se *si sveste*") could be analogous to either the pilgrim who can now see clearly, *or* to the *vista* he beholds ("così mi si cambiaro in maggior feste li fiori e le faville"). The confusion follows because in the logic of the protasis the "enmasked" seem different, with *parere* assuming the ambiguity of semblance as both semblance of perception and semblance of appearance. Therefore in this statement of perspicacity renewed, there is a fundamental undecidability as to whether the unmasked is the pilgrim or the pilgrim's perception of heaven (and consequently there is the ambiguity of who or what had been concealed). In that the simile proffers a polyvalent rapport between terms of the protasis and apodosis. The simile obscures as much as it enlightens. The effect of this simile's black light in this specific context of divine vision without analogue is to destabilize the possibility of any apprehension of the divine *invisibilia* ("Lume è là che visibile face / lo creatore a a quella creatura" [Para: XXX.100-1]). As Marguerite Chiarenza says in reference to similes of vision which enstate an inability of seeing, "visibility is described only through... near invisibility: reflections not in a mirror but in glass or shallow water so clear as to offer virtually no reflection at all.... Dante tells the reader what he saw in terms of visual experience in which the eye fails."[27] One could thus read this simile in Canto XXX as the enstatement of the attaining of a vision (*vidi, vidi, vidi*) that does *not* see the analogue. If *essempli* already serve as supplements to an absent experience—an experience that remains *other* to the genres of presence and representation—then the *essemplo* here is itself an example of absence: an example of a lack supplementing an absence. If analogicity is analogous to a pilgrimage, it is a pilgrimage without an organizing *telos*. The poet's *ingegno* thus ultimately appears to proffer a tropic circumlocutory supplement to apophasis.

•••

The odd thing about *apophasis* is that the word already registers the problem of the *Paradiso*'s two modalities of language because apophasis is already *two words*. The word ἀπόφασις, derived from ἀποφαίνω (to come to light, to prove) means a statement or proof; and the word ἀπόφασις, derived from ἀπόφημι (to deny) means a negation or retraction. The *difference* between apophasis-as-statement and apophasis-as-retraction is nowhere inscribed in the one word ἀπόφασις. The one word can thus mean both a statement and a statement denied; the statement of this one word can retract its own meaning. In the essay "Comment ne pas parler: dénégations," Jacques Derrida considers Negative Theology through the intersection of the word *apophasis* as an economy of discourse circulating around that which remains other to being: "comment ces deux modes se rapportent-ils l'un à l'autre? Quelle est la loi de leur traduction réciproque ou de leur hiérarchie?"[28] Therefore the issue here concerns the *possibility* of some code that transfers between these two modalities of ἀπόφασις, and across the non-difference of inscription that names them. The problem of Negative Theology that Derrida addresses is that the nominative gesture subscribes to a metaphysics of immanence and so always categorically inscribes the alterity to which it is beholden into a discourse of the same.

Hawkins's article on ineffability performs many of the tropes of a Negative Theology that Derrida discusses (although in a perhaps negative move, Hawkins never names Negative Theology in his essay). Hawkins articulates the two modalities of the language of the *Paradiso* as "a dialectic of ineffability, which moves from the claims of language, through a recognition of its limits, to the intimation of a transcendent, unrepresentable reality—a move that Dante describes in *Paradiso* XXIII.61-3 as a 'jump' into silence ["e così, figurando il paradiso, / convien saltar lo sacrato poema, / come chi trova suo cammin riciso"]" (Hawkins, 9). Therefore one mode of the language of Negative Theology, the thetic, *crosses* into a language of silence in order to access that which is inaccessible to language; to approach God one must deny the existence of the path (cf. Derrida 1987a, 536). In this way the poets' allegory—in its emphasis on the bella menzogna—could attain divinity by ingeniously negating the props and conceits of *ingegno*. And so Negative Theology betrays a certain attitude towards language in which "le nom de Dieu serait alors *l'effet hyperbolique* de cette négativité ou de toute négativité conséquente en son discours" (538, emphasis added). "God" is thus the name given to an unnamable experience registered through language.[29] The residual problem here—the problem of the remainder—is that by naming God as that which cannot be named, the nominative gesture still remains. Language is not transcended in words (*trasparlar* significar per verba non si poria).

> Mais la réappropriation onto-théologique en est toujours possible et sans doute *inévitable* tant qu'on parle, précisément, dans l'élément de la logique et de la grammaire onto-théologiques. On peut toujours dire: l'hyperessentialité, c'est justement cela, un étant suprême qui reste incommensurable à l'être de tout ce qui est, qui n'*est* rien, ni présent ni absent, etc. (542)

In the negation the statement or thesis endures as the hyper-effect of language. This is precisely the point to which Hawkins tends in positing a dialectic of ineffability. Essentially Hawkins's argument is exemplary for Negative Theology: the *via negativis* becomes a moment of *translatio*. Hawkins's reading, while insightful in places, remains an allegory of the poets in the *hyper*-form of a Negative Theology. "La négativité sert le mouvement en *hyper* qui la produit, l'attire ou la conduit" (564). A Negative Theology *translates* the merely earthly and ontic into an ontotheology, into the *hyperousios*, the "Dieu *sans* l'être" that authorizes being (540). By characterizing this hyper movement as one of conversion, of μεταφόρειν, Hawkins's argument becomes eminently theological, in a negative way: "the language of the *Paradiso* is busy with its own elimination, *with the conversion of speech into silence*" (Hawkins, 13; emphasis added). Hawkins's dialectic thus decides ἀπόφασις as a moment of ἀποφαίνω and thus as a moment of being. For Hawkins's dialectic to operate, the dual valences of ἀπόφασις must be determinably inter-translatable, discourse must be able to *pass into silence*.

The problem with Negative Theology is thus that it remains oriented· as a *via*, or as a *tra* that remains between-two, an *entretien* between mortals and the divine. The communication is thus "vers ce contact ou cette vision, cette intuition pure de l'ineffable, cette union silencieuse avec ce qui reste inaccessible à la parole" (Derrida 1987a, 543). In this way Negative Theology chiasmically constitutes ἀπόφασις as a negation of statement which arrives at a statement of negation, a silent communion. However the two words named in ἀπόφασις might not be that easily reconciled. Derrida—following from Plato's *Timæus*— names a third possibility of *apophasis* with the name *khôra* (χώρα, place, position, land, provenance, dwelling, situation, euphemism for the genitalia): a third genre between sensibility and intelligibility and thus the site of difference (566). Following from Derrida's reading of Plato, *khôra* names a fundamental ontological ground that cannot be subsumed under and by any nominative or figurative discourse; it remains the *necessarily indifferent* aporia that calls forth an impassable answer. In Derrida's reading of the *Timæus*, *khôra* names the alternative language in Plato's discourse to a thetic language and to a nihilistic language. *Khôra* thus names the *responsibility* with which one is beholden to the unspeakability of the differentiation, discontinuity and immensity which serves as the principle of an economy of finite beings. "L'espacement de *khôra* introduit une dissociation ou une différence dans le sens propre qu'elle rend possible, contraignant ainsi à des détours tropiques qui ne sont plus des figures de rhétorique" (568). The possibility of linguistic sense is already disjunctive and dissociative and it is within this differential nexus that the *Commedia* is written. This leads to Sollers's main thought concerning Dante, already noted above, that the *transversal* of being is effected through an interval of writing: "*La Divine Comédie*... va donc être pour nous un texte en train de s'écrire" (Sollers, 45). The difference marked in the word ἀπόφασις is thus subordinate to the dissociative difference that Derrida terms *khôra*. The difference between iteration and initeration is likewise disjoined and disjunctive: the statements Dante ingeniously makes concerning *ingegno* confounded do not necessarily resolve either comportment of ἀπόφασις, his palinodic writing thus becomes a *neither/nor* of iteration and initeration. In this way, Dante *re-marks* the difference between iteration and initeration; this re-mark is the redoubling trace of a mark, "une marque marque à la fois le marqué et la marque, le lieu re-marqué de la marque."[30] The re-mark is not an essence, not a definitive and deciding trait (which would enable taxonomies of generic qualification and comprehension), but rather a *place* (not unlike the *khôra*), a place in which designations are delegated.

⋯

According to Sollers, the central organizing myth for Dante is Babel—the event of the transversal of language*s*—because it registers both the impossibility and discord of communication (as opposed to paradisic immediacy). The consideration of Babel in the *De Vulgari Eloquentia* anticipates the more radical theory of writing of the *Commedia*. There is within the *De Vulgari* a tension between the Augustinian problem of attributing a singular event of *trapassare* and the possibility of writing in the wake of Babel. Unlike Augustine in the *De civitate dei*, Dante explicitly names Babel as *the* (uninterrupted singular) *event* of the *dispersion* of languages: "cum celitus tanta confusione percussi sunt, ut qui omnes una eademque loquela deserviebant ad opus, ad opere, multis diversificati loquelis, desinerent, et nunquam ad idem commertium convenirent" (DVG: I.vii.6). For Dante, Nimrod is but *one* victim of babelian folly.[31] Dante's most radical claim in the *De Vulgari* concerns the status of dispersal: the event of Babel is remembered as the *gift* of the multiplicity of languages. The destruction of Babel is His "correctione... memorabili" (I.vii.5). The retribution—the imposition of linguistic exile—is remembered in the existence of *lingue*. The existence of plurality of languages, the discontinuity between languages, is the *memorable* trace of the event of the divine advent at Babel. Language is thus infected not with Him, but His correction which *is* His confusion, His correction and His *gift* (delle lingue). "Cette confusion, il est remarquable qu'elle se marque pour Dante par un *oubli* de la langue première, et que cet oubli soit à la source de... la parole elle même" (Sollers, 51). The event of Babel vitiates the possibility of a singularity of the event (and thus of a *single* language) and remains a ruin commemorated by its very dispersion and forgetfulness. The memorable correction enstates confusion as the punishment of the single pre-babelian language. Language comes to commemorate the *effect* (or *trace*) of Babel, linguistic diaspora, and not the *event* of a divine cæsura.

There is still an insistence in the *De Vulgari* upon a singularity for the event of Babel and thus also for man's transgression. The *De Vulgari* seems to intend towards a linguistic pentecost. Dante's hope (*esperanto*) is to found the *singular* vernacular in the wake of having forgotten Latin. In this light it is not unsurprising that Dante would claim that the Adamic *Ur-sprache* had survived Babel, and he explicitly identifies it as Hebrew (DVG: I.vi.7). Following from Augustine, Dante also claims that man's first venture into speech is his first woe, the first proffered word is also the first transgression: "Quid autem prius vox primi loquentis sonaverit, viro sane mentis in promptu esse non titubo ipsum fuisse quod Deus est, scilicet 'El'... post prevaricationem humani generis quilibet exordium sue locutionos incipit ab 'heu'" (I.iv.4). Dante maintains that the originary utterance of the name of God, *El*, was said in joy: a blissful statement of man's state with God. God does not participate in human speech—His discourse is *other* to speech (I.iv.6). Man's first statement of joy remarks the enstatement of rupture between divinity and mortality. In this way *speech* is a *memorable crisis:* a recollection of the expulsion from Eden and the decisive point of Dante's eschatology. In the *De Vulgari* Dante is trying to state a privileged moment for the originary profferal of God's name—a privilege of the originary event of language as *singular* trespass into sin.

This issue of linguistic fallenness is taken up by Adam in the *Paradiso* with specific reference to *trapassare*. In the *Paradiso* Adam refutes a number of the specific claims that had been made in the *De Vulgari*. Perhaps his most radical modulation comes when he states that the first sin, the reason for God's wrath, was "il trapassar del segno" (Para: XXVI.117).[32] On a literal reading this sin would be pride, a trespassing of limits, or of the borders established by God.[33] However this limit (segno) also names a sign and mark. The downfall is a trespassing of the sign, or rather a trespassing by (use of) the sign coeval with transgression. The very statement that names a singular ætiology for the linguistic fall is enstated through an ineluctable linguistic plurality; the statement of singularity is *already plural*. Because of this double valence the very phrase "trapassar del segno" is itself a *trapassare del segno*: a statement of the confusion that makes the very enstatement possible. Adam's statement re-marks itself as a *trapassare del segno*. The polyvalence of *segno* confuses the event of trapassare in the attempt to enstate it. The implication of polyvalence then is a radical destabilization, differentiation and undecidability between *res* and *verbe* which can never be named except through (*tra*) linguistic differences. Babel is thus the name given to this effect.[34] That Adam can say *trapassare del segno* in ascribing an ætiology of fallen language shows that language had never been a locus of immanence. The language in which the poet writes is *other* to and separate from an immanence of God.[35] Babel is just a trope for a non-originary origin to the plurality of languages: its iteration as a singular cause is transgressed by the *segno* of which it is also taken to be the *Ur-trapassare*. The condition of humanity is peregrinism: exile across borders both material and linguistic. The human condition is thus a confused (or babelized) *trapassare del segno*.

At the beginning of canto XXVI, the temporarily blinded pilgrim is commanded by the enflamed St. John to supplement consumed sight ("vista che hai in me consunta" [XXVI.5]) with discursive reasoning, "ragionando" (XXVI.6). This command establishes an odd equilibrium between discourse and sight: "fa ragion che sia / la vista in te smarrita e non defunta" (XXVI.8–9). He is commanded to reason that his sight is merely confused and not destroyed. One could say that the pilgrim's blindness is a babelization or confusion of his sight. Intellect advances where the vision is denied in order to purify vision. This movement towards love is not simple, and the pilgrim's first answer is not quite satisfactory. He responds that "Lo ben che fa contenta questa corte, / Alfa ed O è di quanta scrittura / mi legge amore o lievemente o forte" (XXVI.16–18). Here the pilgrim claims that the good is expressed through its technical manifestation in scripture: the alphabet as $\tau\acute{\epsilon}\chi\nu\eta$ of lingua. The pilgrim is then told that he must think harder, to the source of this reasoning (XXVI.23–24). He then responds that this love "in me s'imprenti" (XXVI.27): love is felt in its inscribed impression and thusly after the singular event of its being-there. Love is perceived by the intellect only after it had been there. The cause of love—Him—is apprehended only afterwards in the *after-words* imprinted· within the pilgrim. Furthermore, the effect can only be represented figurally, as if the event had been there, the inscription upon the pilgrim is known only through the supplementary reinscribing of the poet. The figure of the mental imprint is thus an imperfect metonymy of divine light; or more precisely, the divine light is constituted by the figure of its tracing in the after-words of the poet.[36] This event is thus figured as a trace: "con· quanti denti questo amor ti morde" (XXVI.51). Love is thus figured not as presence motivating its trace, but instead as *excessive* effect of inscription. Love is the hypereffect (see page 38) of inscription upon memory.

The pilgrim is able to employ his reason to progress beyond the "mar dell'amor torto" (XXVI.62) by advocating a *figure* of divine timeless language:

> Le fronde onde s'infronda tutto l'orto
>   de l'ortolano etterno, am'io cotanto
>   quanto da lui a lor di bene è porto. (XXVI.64–66)

This metaphor has resonances throughout the *cantica*. The leaves are beloved to the extent that they are a product of God, however this divine attribution remains ambiguous in that the "ortolano etterno" could also be Adam. The trace of God is ambiguously attributed. The trace—indicated by the figure of the leaves—insofar as it suggests Him, can also suggest someone else. This ambiguity exfoliates onto the larger problem raised in this canto: the ontological status of language, or the attribution of a technicity (human or divine) to language.

The burning questions on the pilgrim's mind, perceived by Adam, concern sin and language. Adam corrects the assertion in the *De Vulgari Eloquentia* that Hebrew is the singular Adamic language, since his language had already faded by the time of Nimrod's act of hubris. Hebrew remains one of many vulgar and postlapsarian languages:

> chè nullo effetto mai razionabile,
>> per lo piacere uman che rinnovella
>> seguendo il cielo, sempre fu durabile.
> Opera naturale è ch'uom favella;
>> ma così o così, natura lascia
>> poi fare a voi, secondo che v'abbella.
> Pria ch'io scendessi a l'infernale ambascia,
>> *I* s'appellava in terra il sommo bene
>> onde vien la letizia che mi fascia;
> e *EL* si chiamò poi: e ciò convene,
>> chè l'uso de'mortali è come fronda
>> in ramo, che sen va e altra vene. (XXVI.127–38).

These last two lines echo the following passage from Horace's *Ars Poetica*: "Vt siluæ foliis pronos mutantur in annos, / prima cadunt ita uerborum uetus interit ætas, / ... Debemur morti nos nostraque."[37] Language—figured as a leaf—is a vehicle re-marked by loss and death. The being of language—its ontological ground—is natural (inhuman), and yet the existential specificity of languages is human and technical. Individual languages suffer the vicissitudes of time (like Horacian leaves), while language is timeless. Man merely embellishes, establishes earthly and mortal adornments and divagations for, language. As existential, language is technical, and remains destined for human use. Along this axis, Adamic language would be no more privileged than any of its successors since his is only the first: "l'idioma ch'usai e ch'io fei" (XXVI.114), and as such it was but the first idiom to undergo "lextinction" (FW: 083.25). In confusion the originary language has been forgotten, but it was no more ontologically privileged than its successors. The previous example of the leaves of the *ortolano etterno* forms just one example of such embellishment.

Adam remarks that אל is now just one name of God and not the originary *trapassare* as indicated in the *De Vulgari*, however Adam does still insist upon an originary name for God, *I*. In denying one originary name he has imposed another. However this insistence upon His name remains an instance of "l'uso de' mortali"; an instance of appellation and (still) not an event of His being. In this manner the multiple names of God are not without analogy to the "ortolano etterno": both evidence the trace of the divine as subject to the vicissitudes of human mortality and obsolescence. *He* is already an *ortolano*, His being already amidst the fall, decay and dispersion of the leaves. The *I* whereof Adam speaks would be a reference to the unspeakable name of God: *Yahweh*. Instead of supplying a name that would name Him, he proffers the mark of the deferral of the name. The name names no thing outside an onomastic chain. The usage of mortals is here the supplement to His name; a supplement of that which cannot be said and which obligates silence. The language Adam speaks is already loss, and that loss has itself been lost amidst the falling leaves. Language is not just a product or a register (or document) of loss; it *is* loss, and this loss and dispersion are all that remain. Languages themselves are the correctione memorabili. Hawkins's emphasis on the negativity of Dante's discourse thus obviates or *loses* this notion of language and loss by supplementing it with the possibility of a present statement of silence. However such ingeniously apophatic statements remain within the absentation of language. A trope of *ingegno* confounded, rather than being merely a conceit of *ingegno*, remarks its constitutive absentation without recourse to a presentation (a making present). Following from Adam's statements, Language is the mark of loss that remarks loss.

∴

A belated etymological leaf (an old usage of mortals) to which Dante would not have had access is the derivation for the word *planet*: πλανήτης, from πλανάω, to wander, lead astray, deceive. In his pilgrimage through the heavens, the pilgrim is but one more planet, and just as the planets obey the influence of the Sun, so too does the pilgrim subscribe to the powers of God. As he mentions in the sphere of Jupiter: "'l mio girar dintorno / col cielo insieme avea cresciuto l'arco" (Para: XVIII.61–62). And yet, the only force that guides the pilgrim—steering him apart from the nastier aspects of his *planetary motion*—is the force of God. God's influence ostensibly guides the pilgrim's planetary peregrinations to meaning and to unity.

The problems associated with such a situation of central guiding authority are elaborated in Canto XVIII with the delineation of the eagle of justice.

> Io vidi in quella giovial facella
> lo sfavillar de l'amor che lì era,
> segnare a li occhi miei nostra favella.
> E come augelli surti di rivera
> quasi congratulando a lor pasture,
> fanno di sé or tonda or altra schiera,
> sì dentro ai lumi sante creature
> volitando cantavano, e faciensi
> or *D,* or *I,* or *L* in sue figure. (XVIII.70–78)

A seemingly random wandering of heavenly sparks (likened to a flock of birds) *traces out* a pattern organized by a higher authority which then begins to give itself to intelligibility and therefore slowly becomes legible to the pilgrim. The path of the spirits becomes a *favella*. But the pilgrim's reading of this favella has been lost as the poet invokes a generic muse[38] to help him recall his interpretation: "O diva Pegasea che li 'ngegni / fai gloriosi e rendili longevi, / ed essi teco le cittadi e' regni, / illustrami di te, sì ch'io rilevi / le lor figure com'io l'ho concette" (XVIII.82–6). The pilgrim's scopically gathered apprehension of the shapes (io l'ho *concette;* from the Latin *conceptae* [Singleton 1975, 309]) is now deficient and needs to be supplemented by an infusion of fresh poetic $\tau\acute{\epsilon}\chi\nu\eta$, not unlike the withered and belated Horacian leaf.

The flying sparks are, of course, an instance of writing,[39] markings yield to a lisibility that is subtended by a higher authority or *auctor.* Indeed the initial description of the markings proceeds through the simile of the birds *as if* the inscribed phrase of justice in the heavens were already within an economy of writing. It is of course also no coincidence that the initial description involves a simile of birds as the final *M* of the inscribed phrase "QUI IUDICATIS TERRAM" (XVIII.93) itself becomes a bird, an eagle:

> E vidi scendere altre luci dove
> era il colmo de l'emme, e lì quetarsi

> cantando, credo, il ben ch'a sé le move.
> Poi, come nel percuoter de' ciocchi arsi
>   surgono innumerabili faville,
>   onde li stolti sogliono augurarsi;
> resurger parver quindi più di mille
>   luci, e salir, qual assai e qual poco,
>   sì come il sol che l'accende sortille;
> e quietata ciascuna in suo loco,
>   la testa e 'l collo d'un'aguglia vidi
>   rappresentare a quel distinto foco.
> Quei che dipinge lì, non ha chi 'l guidi;
>   ma esso guida, e da lui si rammenta
>   quella virtù ch'è forma per li nidi.
> L'altra beatitudo che contenta
>   pareva prima d'ingigliarsi a l'emme,
>   con poco moto seguitò la 'mprenta. (XVIII.97–113)

The terminal *M* gathers the other lights onto itself and then disperses them to form a new pattern, that of an eagle represented in the flame of the dispersed sparks or embers ("rappresentare a quel distinto foco"). The delineated Latin *favella* has now become the *faville* forming a new and different locus of signification. The eagle is a sign emerging from a pilgrimage of signifiers. There is thus a very close correlation—almost an indifference—between the protases and the apodoses here; this section abounds with pseudosimiles (the sparks of the souls flying off the burning *M* likened to sparks off a burning log).[40] One could almost call the eagle a figure for polysemous figurality. That the poet in recounting this occurrence, in recounting his interpretation-perception of this event compares the sparks to sparks off a log from which "li stolti sogliono augurarsi" is of some implication and import. Within this structure of interpreting variable inscription—inscriptions which always already rely upon differentiations in order to be apperceived—interpretation itself becomes highly suspect. The traces whereof the poet speaks are no longer present and in speaking of them he speaks of them through figures, through *other* traces. There is no present trace here. That which is interpreted—the *favella*-yielding trace—is already within an economy of loss, an economy of the *faville* (as we will soon show, this is the situation of the final canto). The writing of the poem is already a hyperactive shifting scrim of absentations divested from any possibility of original authority.

This comes quite close to Mazzotta's point concerning Dante's exilic writing: the poet finds himself writing in the place where "univocal meaning is elusive and itself exiled" (Mazzotta, 274). The language in which the poet writes is already an errance, a planetary pilgrimage that cannot have any rapport with a belated and defunct truth (cf. 271). And so reading itself is exilic, *hermeneusis* takes place in the desert. But then such a reading casts the *Divina Commedia* into a register of melancholic nostalgia: as if there had been some plenitude which now remains inaccessible, as if there had been a path for the pilgrim. Like Tambling (see note 16), Mazzotta reads a melancholic condition into the processes of signification, but perhaps Adam's comments should have put this melancholy to rest. Perhaps melancholy is not the tenor of the *Divina Commedia,* but perhaps there still would be a path, but that path is all that there is. Perhaps there is only the interval for the pilgrim and perhaps any notion of *telos* is but the hypereffect of the path's incinerated quirks.

• • •

The problem of iteration that the poet continually faces in the *Paradiso* is deceptively simple: he speaks (makes, ποιεῖν) whereof he cannot. Within the *Paradiso* he is to proffer a simile for the divine, the absolutely unsimilar. The entire *Paradiso*, thus construed, is an extended apodosis without *any* possible protasis (statable or inferable by human means). One solution to reading Dante would be to consign this conundrum as being effected or even resolved through ingenious tropic legerdemain. These readings would thus enframe the *Paradiso* into one of the various registers of *apophasis,* as discussed above: either the poet nihilates language through an impressive mastery (the poet silences language; he imposes, through a redoubtable force of will, silence upon language) thereby preserving the divine as inaccessible to a peregrine language condemned to a fallen hermeticism; or the poet holds out faith as a possibility out of human wretchedness (of course the first possibility is already a moment of the second). The conflict between the allegory of the poets and the allegory of the theologians is but one modulation of this problem. Other modulations include Hawkins's notion of *translatio* (discourse *into* silence), and Mazzotta's notion of exilic writing: "[The *Divina Commedia*] tells the story of the persistent ambiguity of metaphoric language in which everything is perpetually fragmented and irreducible to any unification. Alongside the presence of a representation adequate to its spiritual reality [i.e., the first modality of paradisic language], the poem repeatedly dramatizes a world of dissemblance, empty forms and illusory appearances which the poet repeatedly demystifies but to which the poem is irrevocably bound [i.e. the second modality]. In this sense, the poem always places us in the land of unlikeness of *Inferno* I" (Mazzotta, 269–70). In other words Dante—the *master* poet, the one who deserves his laurels—cunningly uses his *ingegno* against itself in order to surrender it and himself to the divine mastery and authority of "la voce del verace autore" (Para: XXVI.40).

There is however a very different possibility to the notion of this admirable and laudable progression. The lesson of Babel is that meaning, as such, is never present and moreover never could have been present, and that language speaks this absence and loss. Language is the medium in which a truth that had never been present dissipates, and this dissipation bears the force of a trace, a trace of the difference between the iterable and the initerable which motivates the poet to write. Therefore the question concerning the *Paradiso* is not merely a question concerning mastery or *ingegno* over language since it is not *a priori* certain that the *uso de' mortali* can assume mastery. Language thus might lack the very resources needed for the poet to engage within an economy of apophasis. The gift the poet makes in and by language remains always forthcoming. And so the *Divina Commedia* might not so much be the presentation of the promise made at the end of the *Vita Nuova*, but rather a *prolongation of that aposiopesis hardened into the pages of a book*. The language consumes itself within this interval, within this interval language is *imparadised*.[41]

> chè la mia vista, venendo sincera,

> e più e più intrava per lo raggio
> de l'alta luce che da sé è vera.
> Da quinci innanzi il mio veder fu maggio
> che 'l parlar nostro, ch'a tal vista cede,
> e cede la memoria a tanto oltraggio.
> Qual è colui che somniando vede,
> che dopo il sogno la passione impressa
> rimane, e l'altro a la mente non riede,
> cotal son io, chè quasi tutta cessa
> mia visione, ed ancor mi distilla
> nel core il dolce che nacque da essa.
> Così la neve al sol si disigilla;
> così al vento ne le foglie levi
> si perdea la sentenza di Sibilla. (XXXIII.52–66)

The pilgrim surrenders the overpowered faculties of speech and memory since his vision has come to exceed his discourse: "nel qual son si dee creder che s'invii / per creatura l'occhio tanto chiaro" (XXXIII.44–5). That the pilgrim's sight could have beheld God is inconceivable and exceeds the powers of the intellect. The vision has become purer than the speech. The memory of beholding God is too excessive to submit to inscription and this excess cannot be registered by discourse and so it remains a trace or track under erasure. The remembrance of the experience is ineluctably forgotten (not unlike Adamic language). The experience of the divine is invariably canceled: all that remains is the erased trace (the melted track in the snow).[42] The cause of this erasure can be remarked only after the putative event as effect of the erasure: the simile of the sun that has melted (*disigilla*, to lose form [Singleton 1975, 573; we will discuss this word in more detail shortly]) the imprint. The memory of beholding God is effaced by having beheld God: beholding God is an inscription which de-inscribes itself upon memory.[43] The cause remains *re-marked*. God—the Λογός—is completely irrecuperable to the figure and He cannot be gathered by the ἀναλογός. The simile of His being re-marks an erasure of the impression of His experience. In the final canto what Dante *gives*[44] is the trace of an originary inscription under erasure. Loss is withdrawn in its being given or written: he gives the absentation of loss.

The problem remarked in this passage is that the originary remembrance of things past is absolutely absent, and is only to be supplemented by a trope (a trope from Virgil's *Æneid*, no less, and after the "poeta che mi guidi" [Inf: II.10] had ostensibly been jettisoned from the pilgrim's progression). The Sibylline leaves could be construed as a figure of vatic poetry, a figure authorized by the poet. It is thus the vatic "vista nova" (Para: XXXIII.131) that is effaced in the poetic iteration.[45] The experience of the divine can thus only be remarked as the re-mark of the poetic *sign*. "Are those their *fata* which we read in sibylline between the *fas* and its *nefas*?" (FW: 031.35–36). All that the poet can do to register said transphenomenality is to deploy similes of aporia. An example of which would be the second simile from the above passage. If the progression of earthly languages had earlier been likened to leaves ("fronda in ramo" [Para: XXVI.137–38]), then, now, the translinguistic is likened to the Sibylline leaves. In canto XXVI, the pilgrim was able to employ his reason to progress beyond the Ulyssean "mar dell'amor torto" by advocating a figure of divine timeless language. Supposedly when the pilgrim is beyond the temporal figure, the polysemic sign, and has attained the eternal singularity, Dante retains a figural language only to the extent that it is always already an annulled trace. The numinal experience remains, nominally registered, as disseminated leaves. Dante's complete book of all earthly experience thus remains like Mallarmé's, a *livre à venir*, awaiting its final moment of overpowering which is at once a moment that is forever gone and the moment that inspires the task of writing.

It is precisely *here* at the most formidable aporia (ἀπορία: the privation of passage, πόρος, or even of *pilgrimage*) that the poet phrases one final injunction to write, an *invocatio* addressed to God:

O somma luce che tanto ti levi
    da' concetti mortali, a la mia mente
    ripresta un poco di quel che parevi,
e fa la lingua mia tanto possente,
    ch'una *favilla* sol de la tua gloria
    possa lasciare a la futura gente;
ché, per tornare alquanto a mia memoria

> e per sonare un poco in questi versi,
> più si conceperà di tua vittoria. (XXXIII.67–75; emphasis added)

The poet asks that his *lingua* (his tongue and perhaps also his very language, the language he makes with his tongue) will retain some *favilla* of the divine experience so that the experience returns *alquanto* to memory. He asks that the experience be *rewritten*, if only barely, in his mind. He asks to *supplement* the defunct experience with a *cinder* or trace. For as he said much earlier in the *cantica*: "Poco favilla gran fiamma seconda" (I.34). The poet is here, apparently, putting the *faville* to work: making the cinder speak by unerasing the wasting temporal effacement of forgetting. All that remains—if it remains, for God may never have answered the poet's call—is the *favilla*: a testimony that a fire *had taken place* and to nothing else. The experience had taken place, but is no more, and perhaps there will be no more *gran fiamma seconda*. With the eagle in canto XVIII the path or trace had become a *favella*, here the trace is just a *favilla* and nothing more. The place of the trace, its *avoir lieu*, is belated: an *irreducible dov'è*. Indeed the poet's account remains troubled, as is indicated in the use of the subjunctive in "La forma universal di questo nodo / credo *ch'i'vidi*" (XXXIII.91–92; emphasis added). Even the defunct *favilla* will exceed discourse: "Omai sarà più corta mia favella, / pur a quel ch'io ricordo, che d'un fante / che bagni ancor la lingua a la mammella" (XXXIII.106–8). The *favella* of the *Commedia* is the supplement for the supplementary *favilla*. In this sense, the *favella* erases the *favilla* just as the *favilla* had erased the original flame, which is not unlike the *disigillare* of the snow tracks. And so the two modalities of paradisic language—the inscription of the *favilla-favella* and the exscription of *disigillare*—are coterminous, but only within the possibility of the poetic iteration, within the *tra* of the *trapassar del segno*. Once the segno has been transgressed, all that is left is further transgression: further tropes which multiply in supplementarity only to withdraw within their proliferation.

At the end the poet writes of the loss of poetic puissance. "All'alta fantasia qui mancò possa" (XXXIII.143). The poetic phantasy consumes the poetic craft or τέχνη. Within the register of the divine, the trace consumes itself through the possibility of multiple figurations. The figure (*favilla, favella*) no longer affirms. If peregrinism—the babelian scene—invites a re-mark of *lingue* then the experience of God remains within a register of the affirmation's re-mark: the *segno* doubles back and re-marks not *trapassare* but withdrawal. The complete book is supplement to nothing—nothing that can be proffered by an ingenious *lingua*.

> A l'alta fantasia qui mancò possa;
>   ma già volgeva il mio disio e il velle,
>   sì come rota ch'igualmente è mossa,
> l'amor che move il sole e l'altre stelle. (XXXIII.142–45)

This is how Sollers reads the close of the *Paradiso*, the close of the *Divina Commedia*, as a *ricorso* back to the obscured forest: "Au moment où il devient ce qu'il voit, et où, peut-être, il se rend compte qu'il était depuis le début ce qu'il voyait (ce qu'il écrivait), il cesse d'être pour faire place au texte: *l'Amour qui meut le soleil et les autres étoiles renvoie à la constellation du sens et des mots dont l'entrée se trouve au milieu du chemin de notre vie*" (Sollers, 75). At *the* moment of fulfillment *Dante* (as both pilgrim and poet) withdraws in order that the text *takes place*, in order that the text *takes its place within and as a selva oscura*.[46] The love that elevates at the close of the *Divina Commedia* is a love that cannot be accessed in a human manner; whereas this love provides no possibility of *transference*, no translation (tropic or otherwise) to the divine. It is an event that can only be announced in the erased trace of God (*favilla*) that subsists within the interval of the poetic iteration (*favella*).

The initial problem faced by the poet at the close of the paradisic experience is of writing a totality apperceived and lost. The truth—God's Truth—had been granted, had taken place, but not within the "sacrato poema" (XXIII.62). Mazzotta emphasizes this by noting that like the *Vita Nuova*, the *Commedia* is also a book of memory with its initial invocation to the Muses: "O musa, o alto ingegno, or m'aiutate; / o mente che scrivesti ciò ch'io vidi, / qui si parrà la tua nobilitate" (Inf: II.7–9). Tropes of forgetfulness abound throughout the *Paradiso* until the final farrago of oblivion in the final canto: "this oblivion is as important as the act of remembrance. For by forgetting the final vision Dante *gives what is forgotten a unique and unrepeatable presence and preserves it intact and inviolate*" (Mazzotta, 263, emphasis added). Mazzotta seeks to preserve and vouchsafe an imminence for the poet's forgetfulness, to grant forgetfulness a present mimetic status, this then implies a tenor of semiotic melancholy. However, the sacred vision stands absolutely apart from its iteration in the *Paradiso*. Indeed, Marguerite Chiarenza claims that this apartness is *dictated (spoken)* by the poet's figurations of the numinous experience as a *book*: "Nel suo profondo vidi che s'interna, / legato con amore in un volume, / ciò che per l'universo si squaderna" (Para: XXXIII.85–87). "When the universe is transcended, what was separate becomes unified just as all the pages when bound become the book. ... Vision of unity and totality are not a part of the poem but a result of it. ... The pilgrim does not see the last page of the book in God's face, he sees the book bound together, for when the poem is complete it is no longer a sequence but a unity" (Chiarenza, 80). Within the paradisic iteration, totality is *achieved* as a book, as an analogue to the *volume*, and indeed the last page turns to the first—as if from a hermetic bindery—with the Love that moves the stars, but what Chiarenza has forgotten is that the achievement of totality is an achievement of forgetting. The divine experience remains other*:* different from and inaccessible to the belated writing that purportedly it had inaugurated. The gathering of the experience into a book disperses an experience that never had been. Therefore the volume here is not quite the *libro della mia memoria*. Or rather it *is* the *libro della mia memoria*—it is the fulfillment of this book—only inasmuch as that book, announced in the Vita Nuova, had already been a book of forgetting. It is here, at the erased track in the snow, the whiteness of the page, the lexical chaos of *silva* that one can speak of a Mallarméan moment in Dante, as does Sollers who calls the *Commedia* "un text en train de s'écrire, et plus encore le premier grand livre pensé et agi intégralement comme *livre* par son auteur" (Sollers, 45).

The paradisic experience, *the* beatific vision is iterated only to be *disigillato*. Mazzotta precisely locates a rupture of memory here in this word, and a rupture that counters Chiarenza's reading. *Disigillare* is the privation of *sigillare* (inscripting, imprinting, more commonly *suggellare* [cf. ED: V. 472–73]): "The *sigillum* marks the act of creation, the process of imposing a form and sealing it with authority: 'disigilla,' thus, traces the distance between the book as a gathering Logos and the dispersion and openness of the poet's book of memory; it stresses Dante's technique of giving up the myth of the poet as *Autore*" (Mazzotta, 265).[47] *Disigilla* is thus a re-mark of an *exscription*. The book of memory *inscribes* (and, as Mazzotta notes, for Mediæval theorists, the act of inscription is analogous to the operation of memory), and the book of the *Divina Commedia* retracts that very possibility in that the only possible trace of the beatific paradisic experience is an effaced trace. Indeed in the first canto the motion of the heavens is described through *suggellare* (the unprivated *disigillare*): "con migliore stella / esce congiunta, e la mondana cera / più a suo modo tempera e suggella" (Para: I.40–42).[48] More importantly the word *sigilla* is used in a description of poetic optimism in the face of the paradisic experience, as a clear expression of the first modality of paradisic language. It is always *favelle* that are *sigillano*: "Ciò che da lei sanza mezzo distilla / non ha poi fine, perchè non si move / la sua imprenta quand'ella sigilla" (VII.67–69).[49] And—as noted earlier (see page 46)—in canto XVIII a *favella* was imprinted upon the pilgrim's eyes (XVIII.72). The love that moves the stars ("move il sole e l'altre stelle") submits to *disigillare* and only the account that is firmly imprinted "non si move"—only an impossible act is inviolate and unerasable. The divine remains *sous rature,* indeed the divine is coterminous with auto-annulling *raturage*. In this way, Dante's *disigillare* anticipates Derrida's critique of Freud in that *disigillare* marks the only possible scene of a writing of the divine, a writing of a recollected pure plenitude that cannot be distinguished from a writing-as-absence.

Derrida identifies the problem of representing forgetfulness in Freud's model of memory as a *wunderblock* (mystic-writing pad); and *modeled* as such, it bears affinity to Mediæval analogies of memory. In figuring the operation of memory as an inscription upon a mystic pad, the inscription is itself an erasable trace inscribed upon two surfaces with the inscripted trace removed from a singular event of inscription. The inscription is divorced from a single referent. In this way, Freud did not describe the psychic apparatus but rather a model or prop for that apparatus. The model supplements the psychic apparatus as if it had existed prior to Freud's speculations. In order for the *psyche* to be represented, to be made present, it must be replaced—a technical model (a machine for inscription) takes its place. By citing Freud's use of the term *darstellung* (with its pictorial quality) to depict the psychic operation of memory, Derrida claims that memory always already exists (is figured) as a representation. Memory is thus always different and never present: memory is not the *frayage* but rather the *différence* between the *frayages*: "La trace comme mémoire n'est pas un frayage pur qu'on pourrait toujours récupérer comme présence simple, c'est la différence insaisissable et invisible entre les frayages."[50] This thus implies that a system of translation (or even access) between the levels of the trace is impossible. For Derrida, Freud is constantly gesturing to a possibility (perhaps even a *theology*) of translation (Derrida 1967b, 311), that there can be some code that will act as a guarantor (thereby lending its *imprimatur*) of metaphoric writing, that *translatio* will be the *auctor*. This would ignore the materiality of significations, a materiality whose reinstatement makes poetry (312). In *La dissémination,* Derrida will argue that Mallarmé provides an alternative to such a (Platonic) notion of textuality, but this possibility is already *there* in Dante's *faville*.

> Il n'y a pas de texte écrit et présent ailleurs, qui donnerait lieu, sans en être modifié, à un travail et à une temporalisation… qui lui seraient extérieurs et flotteraient à sa surface. Il n'y a pas de texte présent en général et il n'y a pas même de texte présent-passé, de texte passé comme ayant été-présent. Le texte n'est pas pensable dans la forme, originaire ou modifiée, de la présence. La texte inconcient est déjà tissé de traces pures, de différences où s'unissent le sens et la force, texte nulle part présent, constitué d'archives qui sont *toujours déjà* des transcriptions. (314–15)

This is a scene of writing (the Freudian *model*) which depends upon and performs a metaphor, a *form* of writing. But there is not necessarily a model of writing in the *Commedia*: *disigilla* is a sigil of lexical annulment and the point to which the pilgrimage beatifically tended: an operation of and by the word. *Disigillare* is thus the *trapassare del segno*: the word's remarking itself as being exscribed. It is here, with and in this one word that there is, also, Mallarmé (who did after all claim that "La Destruction fut ma Béatrice" [CI: 246]): "Telle est l'expérience qu'exige de nous le livre—'expansion totale de la lettre,' comme le dira Mallarmé" (Sollers, 47). But this expansion *totale* is not an encyclopædic totalization since the work for Mallarmé (as for Dante) is a detraction; the book is an event of disaster to the totality that is the world. The word is the (unit of) interval and suspension (*entre dire*) of enunciation and the profound absence of meaning (and of the production of meaning) in the work is an annulment more profound than the longest book. In the word *disigilla* language undertakes its pilgrimage towards silence. Language herewith speaks silence without silence being present.

The volume of the *vista nova* is established, perhaps even achieved (in some other modulation of that accursèd word) only to yield a melted trace (but this is already too much). The experience with the limit-experience of what is to be called God (what has been called, and such is the operation of apophasis, such is the apophatic operation) provides a case or instance of a certain set of conditions that Mallarmé had called the "jeu insensé d'écrire… la goutte d'encre apparentée à la nuit sublime" (OC: 481). The pilgrim beheld God (and one can only have beheld God in a past imperfect) and the poet is left with a book: a trace of the divine experience that takes the place of an originary place of being that had never been there. And as with Freud's writing machine: "L'écriture supplée la perception avant même que celle-ci ne s'apparaisse à elle-même" (Derrida 1967b, 332). The experience that impacts into (*aboutit à*) Dante's book is an experience that has slipped away through the difference between the iterable and the initerable. The *Commedia* is not just the complex figuration of a totality lost, as advocated by Mazzotta, but rather the very difference between loss and a belated pure presence of God. Dante has given a book, *neither* iterable *nor* initerable, just a book which traverses the distance and difference between the two. The experience slips through what gathers and binds it: "l'amor che move il sole e l'altre stelle."

> come procede innanzi dall'ardore
> per lo papiro suso un color bruno
> che non è nero ancora e 'l bianco more. (Inf: XXV.64–6)

The poetic iteration—iterated *through* a language that has been submitted to loss—is an iteration *vers: le silence*. This is Mallarmé's discovery and it is also a moment for the poet of the *Divina Commedia*. The poem speaks of a double perdurance, a loss that expands and expends itself excessively within the space of its iteration. The cold gradations of the lunar surface, the marks of God, of God's authority, lose themselves. By ending with the melted snow, the *Paradiso* does not close with the order of lunar differentiation which grounds manifestation, instead it closes with the writing of the place where that would have taken place. Paradisic language is a subjunctive effacement. This is what happens in a book and this is the poet's discovery: the double loss of the beatific vision that is recounted in the *Commedia*. The poet is not responsible to what he cannot communicate (which can be called with some naïveté "God") but rather if he is responsible to anything, it is to the inability to communicate. And so both modes of paradisic language impact into the book. This then becomes the scene of his writing, the *volume*. For Dante the possibility of the book is that it communicates a non-totalizable experience which cannot *subscribe* to a logic of presence and representation. The *Vita Nuova* ended with silence and the *Divina Commedia* is the iteration of that silence, an iteration of failure.

Notes

[1] In one of his early notebooks for *Finnegans Wake*, Joyce wrote: "div. Commedia just what you would expect Dante to write" (JJA: 28.196). As an example of a more vigorous interpretation of the *Commedia* as the sequel to and fulfillment of the *Vita Nuova*, Charles S. Singleton reads the journey to Beatrice as a justification (or coming to divine justice) of the pilgrim's human existence: "Beatrice is the end toward which the journey with Virgil always moves. Beatrice is also a beginning as well as an end, for she too must guide as Virgil does, and she leads to the celestial paradise. ... But the goal is a justice which in the poem is acknowledged to include all Beatrice and her seven handmaids represent, a justice which Christian doctrine knows to be attainable only through the grace and charity of Christ" (Charles S. Singleton, Journey to Beatrice, Baltimore: Johns Hopkins UP, 1958. 266–67). Beatrice is thus construed as the path to the goal of justice, which exists as a telos that incorporates its approach.

[2] In his commentary Singleton notes that none of the other souls in purgatory, who are already dead, receive these peccato marks. Only the living pilgrim is duly inscribed, exscriptive penance is a resource reserved only for the living (Charles S. Singleton, *"Purgatorio": Commentary,* Princeton: Princeton UP, 1973. 189–90).

[3] This responsibility differs substantially from the orders of the invectives to write and to remember that the pilgrim had encountered in his journeys through hell and purgatory. In hell he becomes a curator of the narratives of the sinners so that they can be represented to the living, but the sinners nevertheless remain without any possibility of succor below: "sappiendo chi voi siete e la sua pecca, / nel mondo suso ancora io te ne cangi, / se quella con ch'io parlo non si secca" (Inf: XXXII.137–39). In purgatory this task takes on a greater urgency since by reminding the living of the repentant, their purgation might be accelerated with acts of contrition on their behalf from the living. In both cases the requested remembrances are authorized by the tangible reality of past sins.

[4] Giuseppe Mazzotta, *Dante, Poet of the Desert,* Princeton: Princeton UP, 1979. 266.

[5] Singleton notes that the three *cantiche* are "remarkably close to being equal in length" (Singleton 1973, 824). Curtius also notes the delimitation figured through the trope of the mechanics of transcription (Ernst Robert Curtius, *European Literature and the Latin Middle Ages,* trans. Willard R. Trask, Princeton: Princeton UP, 1953. 328–29).

[6] "Più volte il termine indica specificamente l'ingegno poetico, l'ispirazione, la capacità inventiva dell'artista. Per la tradizione oratoria, retorica e letteraria latina l'*ingenium* costituisce la dote naturale dell'oratore e del poeta, il talento spontaneo che predispone all'ispirazione musica e che va congiunto con la padronanza degli strumenti tecnico-retorici (*ars*) per una compiuta opera d'arte" (ED: III.442).

[7] The problematic rapport between theology and poetry in the *Commedia* (rendered all-the-more intractable by Dante's other writings) has been a concern of *dantiste* almost ever since the poem first appeared. In 1373, Benvenuto de Rambaldis noted the isomorphism of the two: "sicut in isto libro est omnis purs philosophiae, ot dictum est, ita est omnis pars poetriae" (Benvenuti de Rambaldis, *Comentum super Dantis Aldigherij Comoediam*, 5 volumes, ed. J.P. Lacaita, Florence: Barbera, 1887. I.19). Recent trends have been to loosen such tight inter-relation in order to favor one mode of allegory over the other. Singleton emphasizes that the *Commedia* is an imitation of God's writing, therefore the possibility of signifying otherwise (or allegorically) rests within this *imitatio* that is grounded in and by divine plenitude. Dante's account is vouchsafed by the approach towards divinity, the account of the pilgrimage is essentially true (even if it is in-and-of itself only a bella menzogna) because it also, and more fundamentally rests within God's truth: "the fiction of the *Divine Comedy* is that it is not fiction" (Charles S. Singleton, "The Irreducible Dove," *Comparative Literature* 9.2 [Spring 1957]: 129–35. 129; cf. *"Commedia": Elements of Structure*, Cambridge: Harvard UP, 1954. 1–42; 84–98). Bruno Nardi emphasizes that the vatic comportment of the *Commedia* completely obviates any and all of the dissimulative interference occasioned by poetic *ingegno*: "Poesia, e poesia altissima, è certamente il poema dantesco, come permeati di poesia sono i liber profetici della Bibbia; ma il motivo centrale che anima siffratta poesia è un motivo morale e religioso" (Bruno Nardi, *Dante e la cultura medievale*, new edition, ed. Paolo Mazzantini, Bari: Laterza, 1983. 308; cf. 307–26). Hollander's reading is slightly different, he emphasizes the historical comportment of the pilgrimage through which one individual (the pilgrim, or indeed any eligible Christian) can attain God: the account may be fictive in part but fiction and history are consecrated by divinity (Robert Hollander, *Allegory in Dante's "Commedia,"* Princeton: Princeton UP, 1969. 15–56; "Dante *Theologus-Poeta*," *Studies in Dante*, Ravenna: Longo, 1980. 39–89. cf. esp. 79–89). Gabriel Josipovici has staked out an extreme position by claiming that all authority is ceded to God: "Dante's allegory signifies what it does, not because *Dante* meant it to, but because *God* does" (Gabriel Josipovici, *The World and the Book*,

London: Stanford UP, 1971. 37). In this sense the poet's task of writing is coterminous with interpreting God's will in the things of the world. It is notable that the massive commentary tradition surrounding the *Commedia* reinforces the theological allegory by enframing the text with the same reverence as holy scripture.

Proponents of the allegory of the poets emphasize the irreducible fictivity of the "bella menzogna," that ultimately the *Commedia* is a *fabula*. Therefore the *Commedia* is to be read as scrip rather than as scripture. An early statement of this was made by Robert Green in a challenge of Singleton's position: "But [Dante's] illusion of historical reality is his fiction" (Richard Hamilton Green, "Dante's 'Allegory of the Poets' and Medieval Theory of Poetic Fiction," *Comparative Literature* 9.2 [Spring 1957]: 118–28. 128). In his review of Hollander's book *Allegory in Dante's "Commedia,"* John A. Scott notes the persistence of fictive figuration throughout the *Commedia*. He points out that in the *De vulgari eloquentia* Dante explicitly defined poetry on the basis of fictivity and invention: "Si poesim recte consideremus: que nichil aliud est quam fictio rethorica musicaque poita" (DVG: II.iv.2; quoted in John A. Scott, "Dante's Allegory," *Romance Philology* 26.3 [February 1973]: 558–91. 579; cf. 571–91). Recently, Teodolinda Barolini has advocated that any theology of the poem must be analyzed through the formal and technical figurations that would necessarily constitute a "divine truth" (Teodolinda Barolini, *The Undivine Comedy: Detheologizing Dante,* Princeton: Princeton UP, 1993. chapter 1). For an excellent and relatively unbiased summary of this numbing typological polemic see Jean Pépin, *La tradition de l'allégorie: de Philon d'Alexandrie à Dante* (Paris: Études Augustiniennes, 1987) 251–85, as well as his entry in the *Enciclopedia dantesca* (ED: I.151–65).

[8] The provenance of Mazzotta's citation is Singleton 1954, 12–13.

[9] Quintillian, *Institutio Oratoria,* ed. and trans. H.E. Butler, Cambridge: Harvard UP, 1921. VIII.vi.44. For an excellent etymology of the word allegory see Jon Whitman, *Allegory,* Oxford: Oxford UP, 1987. 263–68. In the *Epistle to Can Grande,* allegory is defined through its etymological derivation from the Greek ἄλλη (*otherwise*) and the Latin *alienum* (CG: VII).

[10] This is precisely why Paul de Man claims that allegory and irony "are two faces of the same fundamental experience of time"; they both indicate the unreliability of signification: "They are... linked in their common demystification of an organic world postulated in a symbolic mode of analogical correspondences or in a mimetic mode of representation in which fiction and reality could coincide" (Paul de Man,

"The Rhetoric of Temporality," *Blindness and Insight,* revised edition, Minneapolis: U of Minnesota P, 1983. 183–228. 225 & 222).

[11] The classic paradigm for this, and one which is not without influence for Dante, is Augustine's description of allegory (and of figural language in general) as the hermeneutic strategy to restitute *caritas* (God's truth) out of and from a deficient literal meaning: "Whatever appears in the divine Word that does not literally pertain to virtuous behavior or to the truth of faith you must take to be figurative. … But Scripture teaches nothing but charity" (St. Augustine, *On Christian Doctrine,* trans. D.W. Robertson, jr., New York: Macmillan, 1958. III.10). The literal level has meaning only in that it *points to* the allegorical, and so Augustine issues an important qualification and delimitation for allegorical hermeneutics: "it is a carnal slavery to adhere to a usefully instituted sign instead of to the thing it was designed to signify" (III.7). The differentiability of the sign implies that the potency of the sign is always beholden to its divine signified. Allegorical meaning begins when the literal level is construed as breaking off or erring away from *caritas.*

[12] Lucia Boldrini, "Let Dante Be Silent… Wakean Transformations of Dante's Theory of Polysemy," unpublished paper, fn. 3.

[13] Obviously the proponents of the allegory of the theologians favor reading Dante as the author of the Epistle (cf. Hollander 1969, 40–47), Hollander does provide an escape-clause by noting that even if spurious, the Epistle reveals a great deal about the poem and about Mediæval notions of allegory (41–42). (See ED: II.706–7 and Robert Hollander, *Dante's Epistle to Cangrande,* Ann Arbor: U of Michigan P, 1993. for a history of this authorial debate.) It is ironic that a key text for the question concerning allegorical authority is itself authorially contested: the often-bitter debate about the Epistle's authenticity shows that designations of authority are potentially susceptible to the vicissitudes of the bella menzogna.

[14] Hollander redresses the lamentable lacuna of a discussion of the theologians' allegory in the *Convivio* in such a way as to highlight the issue of *transference* and of the hermeneutic *decoding* demanded by allegory: "Under this scheme the poetry of the *Convivio* is to be understood as being literally and allegorically fictive, but occasionally, in the moral and analogical senses, theological" (Hollander 1969, 39).

[15] Jeremy Tambling, *Dante and Difference,* Cambridge: Cambridge UP, 1988. 53.

[16] In a subsequent essay, Tambling argues that a consequence of this bottomless negativity of the fictionalizing figurations of allegoresis is a melancholic "nostalgia for the lost body, for a lost moment of fullness" (Jeremy Tambling, "Dante and Benjamin: Melancholy and Allegory," *Exemplaria* 4.2 [Fall 1992]: 341–63. 343). Following from de Man, this melancholy-without-remission is the condition for allegory in language: "Allegory may appear to defend the clarity of meaning and truth, but the very necessity to speak differently itself deconstructs the meaningful universe of which it speaks: if such meaning is indeed immanent, why resort to allegory?" (354; cf. de Man, 207).

[17] William Franke, *Dante's Interpretive Journey,* Chicago: The U of Chicago P, 1996. 21.

[18] "The fundamental trait of presencing itself is determined by remaining concealed and unconcealed. One need not begin with a seemingly capricious etymology of ἀληθεσία in order to experience how universally the presencing of what is present comes to language only in shining, self-manifesting, lying-before, arising, bring-itself-before, and in assuming an outward appearance" (Martin Heidegger, "Aletheia," *Early Greek Thinking*, trans. David Farrell Krell and Frank A. Capuzzi, New York: Harper and Row, 1984. 102–23. 106–7).

[19] This stands in marked contrast to the poet of the *Inferno* who betrayed a blissful confidence in the happy power of memory: "O Muse, o alto ingegno, or m'aiutate; / o mente che scrivesti ciò ch'io vidi, / qui si parrà la tua nobilitate" (Inf: II.7–9; cf. III.131–32).

[20] John Freccero, *Dante: The Poetics of Conversion,* ed. Rachel Jacoff, Cambridge: Harvard UP, 1986. 210–11.

[21] Singleton reads *trasumanar* as a passing beyond the human, the pilgrim thus passes beyond the human to a divine state not unlike Glaucus (cf. Singleton 1958, 30–3 and *"Paradiso": Commentary,* Princeton: Princeton UP, 1975. 18).

[22] Such interplay between the two modalities of the language of the *Paradiso* would put us squarely within the register of a Negative Theology, and indeed that is how this passage has been read by Peter Hawkins: "whatever the *Paradiso* offers with one hand, it resolutely withdraws with the other; what it speaks cannot be set forth in

words" (Peter S. Hawkins, "Dante's *Paradiso* and the Dialectic of Ineffability," *Ineffability*, eds. Peter S. Hawkins and Anne Howland Schotter, New York: AMS, 1984. 5–21. 8). Hawkins reads the poet's allegory as an allegory of initerability. Rather than read this passage as an ontological linguistic undecidability, Freccero reads it as "a compromise short of silence" (Freccero, 211)—thereby reasserting the modality of linguistic *ingegno* and decidability.

[23] Philippe Sollers, "Dante et la traversée de l'écriture," *Logiques*, Paris: Seuil, 1968. 44–77. 71–72.

[24] This motion of differentiating the poetic account from the divine pilgrimage is itself figured as a part of the pilgrimage. Throughout the *Paradiso*, Dante frequently deploys similes involving a figure of the pilgrim. For example, the pilgrim's reaction to beholding the celestial rose is described as "E quasi peregrin che si ricrea / nel tempolo del suo voto riguardando, / e spera già ridir com'ello stea, / su per la viva luce passeggiando, / menava io li occhi per li gradi, / mo su, mo giù, e mo recirculando" (Para: XXXI.43–48). The encounter is already constituted by its being-towards-figural representation.

[25] In the *Purgatorio* an unusual number of similes do *not* involve a drastic tropic displacement, indeed most of the similes there are almost simple restatements or *paraphrases* of the literal level. Antonino Pagliaro counts almost one hundred of these in the *Purgatorio* (*Ulisse: ricerche semantiche sulla Divina Commedia*, 2 volumes, Florence: Messina, 1967. II. 669; see also his entry on simile in the *Enciclopedia Dantesca*, ED: V.259). Richard Lansing terms these *pseudosimiles* which tend to universalize the pilgrim's experience by representing the individual in terms of the generic through detached poetic paraphrasis. He also counters Pagliaro's claim and states that the number of pseudosimiles in the *Purgatorio* is only slightly greater than in the other two *cantiche* (22 as opposed to 20 in the *Inferno* and 16 in the *Paradiso*) (Richard H. Lansing, *From Image to Idea*, Ravenna: Longo, 1977. 30–32).

[26] Other instances of a Cristo rhyming with itself can be found at Para: XII.71–75; XIX.104–8; and XXXII.83–87. In his commentary on XII.71, Isidoro de Lungo notes the conventional wisdom concerning the triple-Cristo rhyme scheme: "il santo nome di Cristo... in fine di verso, no comporta alta rima" (Isidoro de Lungo, Commentary, 1926, *Dartmouth Dante Project*, Online, Internet. October 26, 1995).

[27] Marguerite Mills Chiarenza, "The Imageless Vision and Dante's *Paradiso*," *Dante Studies* XC (1972): 77–91. 84.

[28] Jacques Derrida, "Comment ne pas parler: dénégations," *Psyché*, Paris: Galilée, 1987. 535–95. 557.

[29] This is a problematic statement to elaborate. It *calls for* elaboration and yet the elaborative gesture (by aiming towards completing the statement in a thorough, thetic, and perspicacious manner) remains bound within a certain exigency of communication which it will try, always try, to name. On the other hand, that said, if communication is predicated on the inachievement of totality, then the work of communication would be rife with discontinuity, differentiation, and rupture. These dislocative aspects would not have, would never have, the status of *presence*: dislocation is never here, it is always there, *elsewhere*. In this way communication is haunted by something that is both fundamental to communication and yet remains incommunicable. This aporetic exigency cannot be communicated but it is precisely this exigency *that communicates*. The aporia of this exigency has been allegorized and it has been named; it has been named "God." "« Il n'y a pas de nom pour cela »: lire cette proposition en sa *platitude*. Cet innommable n'est pas un être ineffable, dont aucun nom ne pourrait s'approcher: Dieu, par exemple. Cet innomable est le jeu qui fait qu'il y a des effets nominaux, des structures relativement unitaires ou atomiques qu'on appelle noms, des chaînes de substitutions de noms, et dans lesquelles, par exemple, l'effet nominal « différance » est lui-même *entraîné*, emporté, reinscrit, comme une fausse entrée ou une fausse sortie est encore partie du jeu, fonction du système" (Jacques Derrida, "La différance," *Marges de la philosophie*, Paris: Minuit, 1972. 3–29. 28). In this sense God, too, is Godot, the belated, awaited and undefined end that defines a scene. In the *Divina Commedia* the phrasing of this exigency has become twisted through the double-bind of apophasis.

À propos of divinity and its names, early in the *A Portrait of the Artist as a Young Man* Stephen discovers the disturbing possibility of linguistically unseating the plenitude of God: "God was God's name as his name was Stephen. *Dieu* was the French for God and that was God's name too; and when anyone prayed to God and said *Dieu* then God knew at once that it was a French person that was praying. But though there were different names for God in all the different languages in the world and God understood what all the people who prayed said in their different languages still God remained always the same God and God's real name was God" (AP: 16). Much like Augustine—albeit evincing a lack of technical sophistication appropriate for a small child—Stephen quickly becomes suspicious of onomastic authentication as he notes that the word "God" is hardly a stable ground since it itself rests within a linguistically—even a translinguistically—labile chain of naming. The grounding Stephen provides for himself is hardly stable, and yet after perplexing himself, he resorts to simply reaffirming God's name as being *God*, as if that affirmation would expunge linguistic negativity. Young Stephen is thus a theological allegorist.

[30] Jacques Derrida, *Positions*, Paris: Minuit, 1972. 63.

[31] In the *Inferno* Nimrod stands as a victim of singularity in being damned to a singular language. After uttering "Raphèl maỳ amèch zabì almì" (Inf: XXXI.67), Virgil explains that "chè così è a lui ciascun linguaggio / come 'l suo ad altri, ch'a nullo è noto" (XXXI.80–81). Nimrod has been completely excluded from comprehension within the confusion his hubris had wrought. He is an "anima confusa" (XXXI.74) excluded from any possibility of signification. His tongue has become witness to its own pride: "Elli stesso s'accuso" (XXVI.76), witness to the folly of singularity. Ultimately, Nimrod's punishment is being overpowered by the very *lingua* he had tried, in vain, to use to exert power. The specific event of his *lingua* is lost in his punishment of a confused tongue. Nimrod's power has been overpowered by having been fulfilled in singularity. This is emblematic of the condition Sollers ascribes to the *Inferno*, the place where one is "chassé par soi-même de sa propre parole" (Sollers, 67). In the *Inferno* the damned *become* their sins: "*Le langage se retourne et possède celui qui s'en est cru possesseur alors qu'ils n'en était qu'un des signes*" (68). And as the pilgrim hears from the blasphemers: "Qual io fui vivo, tal son morto" (Inf: XIV.51).

There is a tradition of attributing the construction of the tower of Babel to Nimrod. This tradition is in part based on the claims Augustine makes concerning Nimrod's wickedness in the *De Civitate Dei*, which are based on the Old Latin (*Vetus Latina*) *mistranslation* of Genesis: X.8–10 in the Greek bible (*De Civitate Dei*, seven volumes, ed. and trans. Eva Matthews Sanford and William MacAllen Green, Cambridge: Harvard UP, 1965. XVI.4).

[32] This interpretation is repeated later when Beatrice tells the pilgrim that "Principio del cader fu il maladetto / superbir di colui che tu vedesti / da tutti i pesi del mondo costretto" (Para: XXIX.55–57).

[33] Paolo Costa's gloss of this line is typical of the commentaries: "Intendi il trapassare oltre i termini prescritti dal volere di Dio, cioè la disubbidienza" (Paolo Costa, Commentary, 1819, *Dartmouth Dante Project*, Online, Internet. October 27, 1995; this point has been traced to Aquinas's *Summa Theologica* II.ii.q. 163, a. 1; cf.

ED: V.692). Carlo Steiner notes that the affiliation between *segno* and the Latin *signum* "donnde il senso di trascurare un comando" (Carlo Steiner, Commentary, 1921, *Dartmouth Dante Project,* Online, Internet. October 27, 1995).

[34] This is a point that Derrida makes in the essays "Des tours de Babel" and 'Deux mots pour Joyce." This possibility of babelization—the possibility of peregrinism *as* the event of language—that Adam indicates in *Paradiso* XXVI opens up the possibility of *Wakean* miscegenation. Babel is also a linguistic exigency for Joyce. We will explore this in more detail in the penultimate chapter.

[35] In a very astute reading of this canto in concert with *Inferno* XXVI and *Purgatorio* XXVI, Tambling notes that "no more than in the *Purgatorio* is there [in *Paradiso* XXVI] a full presence, a final knowledge to be gained. Language presupposes absence of full knowledge (angels do not need speech because of their intuitive insight which means that they have full grasp of another's thought: men need language), and language is a *sign* (*De vulgari eloquentia* I.3) presupposing absence of full understanding, absence of presence. If everything has a sign-value for Dante in this canto (just as the *Commedia* itself is setting forth signs), then the reality of the sign is not there" (Tambling 1988, 144).

[36] Earlier Beatrice had warned the pilgrim that his faculties of sight and love might become overpowered by the divine light: "e s'altra cosa vostro amor seduce, / non è se non di quella alcun vestigio, / mal conosciuto, che quivi traluce" (Para: V.10–12). Singleton glosses this with the following from the *Monarchia*: "cum totum universum nichil aliud sit quam vestigium quoddam divine bonitatis" (M: I.viii.2; Singleton 1975, 98). The universe is but a *vestige* of divinity, an imperfect metonymy. And just as any corruption corrupts because it is imperfect and vestigial, so too is the *memory* of the perfect light vestigial. "La trace n'est pas seulement la disparition de l'origine, elle veut dire aussi… que l'origine n'a même pas disparu, qu'elle n'a jamais été constituée qu'en retour par une non-origine, la trace, qui devient ainsi l'origine de l'origine" (Jacques Derrida, *De la grammatologie,* Paris: Minuit, 1967. 90). (This *trace* is thus also the supplement of Heidegger's *trait* of presence, see note 18). Divine love is reduced to the imprint; we will return to this at the close of this chapter. See Jeremy Tambling's "'Nostro peccato fu ermafrodito': Dante and the Moderns" (*Exemplaria* 6.2 [Fall 1994]: 405–27. 408–12) for a discussion of the necessary condition of materiality of poetry-as-*vestigio* in *Purgatorio* XXVI (this article expands upon his argument in Tambling 1988, 138–44).

[37] Horace, *Ars Poetica, Épitres,* ed. François Villeneuve, Paris: Belles Lettres, 1967, 181–227. ll. 60–63. cf. Singleton 1975, 424; Tambling 1988, 145. Dante cites this line from Horace in the *Convivio* (C: II.xiii.10).

[38] "The muses are associated with the winged horse Pegasus. It is not clear whether Dante had in mind any special muse" (Singleton 1975, 308–9).

[39] This is a point that Tambling brings out: "A measured nine letters (significant number) for IUSTITIAM gives way to the other nine letters of IUDICATIS: as though meditation on the one word produces the other: suggestive of the very process of writing" (Tambling 1988, 54).

[40] In the following canto the eagle is again likened to a bird: "Quasi falcone ch'esce del cappello, / move la testa e con l'ali si plaude, / vogila mostrando e faccenndosi bello, / vid'io farsi quel segno" (Para: XIX.34–37) (Lansing discounts this from being a simile as it uses the comparative term *quasi* [Lansing, 28–29]). The eagle here *is itself a sign*, and not some definite and defining signified.

[41] At the start of the twenty-eighth canto, the action of memory's recording of events is itself rendered analogous to the *imparadising* of the pilgrim's mind: "Poscia che 'ncontro a la vita presente / de' miseri mortali aperse 'l vero / quella che 'mparadisa la mia mente, / come in lo specchio fiamma di doppiero / vede colui che se n'alluma retro, / prima che l'abbia in vista o in pensiero, / e sé rivolge per veder se 'l vetro / li dice il vero, e vede ch'el s'accorda / con esso come nota con suo metro; / così la mia memoria si ricorda / ch'io feci riguardando ne' belli occhi / onde a pigliarmi fece Amor la corda" (Para: XXVIII.1–12). But this imparadising is immediately preparatory to Beatrice's withdrawal from the text in canto XXXI. Later in that canto Beatrice departs just as the pilgrim has been refreshed, like a pilgrim who had viewed the veil of Veronica in Florence (XXXI.103–4) — and thus suspiciously also not unlike the pilgrims at the close of the *Vita Nuova*. She departs just as the pilgrimage has been consecrated (as we have never undertaken such a pilgrimage, we can scarcely divine why the pilgrim would have been happy to see the wizened Bernard take the place of blissful Beatrice). Such withdrawal concomitant with plenitude foreshadows the close of the text.

Borges reads the departure of Beatrice in this canto in a manner that could only be called an allegory of separation: "the scene has been imagined by Dante. For us it is very real; for him it was less so. (For Dante, the reality was that first life and the death snatched Beatrice away from him.) Forever separated from Beatrice, alone and perhaps humiliated, he invented the scene in order to imagine that he was with her" (Jorge Luis Borges, "Beatrice's Last Smile," trans. Virginia Múzquiz, *Dispositio* XVIII.45 [1993]: 23–25. 25). Rather than construe the *Commedia* as a "journey to Beatrice" (and by extension, to divinity), Borges proposes to read it as a making or poeticizing of distance and separation: the journey is consecrated in and by its sundering.

[42] Charles Singleton notes that this confession of the poet's failure is the fulfillment of the initial admission of poetic inability in *Paradiso* I.4–9 (Singleton 1975, 571; cited in Hawkins, 16), and would thus be just another trope of modesty, thereby preserving the integrity of the theological allegory. Perhaps more importantly, lines 52–7 in canto XXXIII rephrase the following from the first canto: "Nel ciel che più della sua luce prende / *fu'io*" (I.4–5; emphasis added). The vision, excessive, is belated, it always already *had been*.

There is a parallel between the aporetic image of the melted tracks in the snow and the simile that opens *Inferno* XXIV: "In quella parte del giovenetto anno / che 'l sole i crin sotto l'Aquario tempra / e già le notti al mezzo dì sen vanno, / quando la brina in su la terra assempra / l'imagine di sua sorella bianca, / ma poco dura alla sua penna tempra" (Inf: XXIV.1–6). The frost attempts to copy the image of the snow in an attempt to become indifferent with it, but ultimately it will fail at this task since its white ink will be depleted under the approaching heat. But once it has melted, it will achieve indifferentiation with the snow in that both of them will have melted and evaporated. The pen does achieve indifference, but it is an indifference of a different kind. The trace that is left is undecidable and indifferent again in that after the snow has melted, there might have been neither snow nor frost there to begin with. The trace thus re-marks this residual absence of loss.

[43] Jacopo della Lana's commentary phrases this quite precisely: "Cioè sì come la nove si dissigilla perdendo al sole lo calore e la figura, così le spezie delle memorie che fantasticando reduceno allo intelletto la cosa che ha veduta, sì si dissigillono per quello sole, che è padre d'ogni lume, cioè Dio" (Jacopo della Lana, Commentary, 1324, *Dartmouth Dante Project,* Online, Internet. October 24, 1995).

[44] There is a tradition beginning with Boccaccio of construing the name "Dante" as *dante,* the present participle of *dare,* to give (Giovanni Boccaccio, *Esposizioni sopra la Commedia di Dante,* ed. Giorgio Padoan, *Tutte le opere di Giovanni Boccaccio,* volume 6, ed. V. Branca, Milan: Mondadori, 1965. 8).

[45] Mazzotta notes that the Sibyl's leaves are already ironized in the *Æneid* since "after leading Æneas over every scene of his future, Anchises dismisses the Sibyl and his son through the gate of polished ivory (*Æneid* VI.893–901) [the gateway to delusions and false dreams]. Just as in the *Æneid*, there is no univocal truth in the vision at the end of the *Divina Commedia*" (Mazzotta, 268).

[46] For his reading of the *Inferno,* Tambling cites Cristoforo Landino's assertion that *selva* is related to the Latin *silva*: "'the customary translation of the Greek *hyle*—prime matter—the unformed chaotic stuff out of which corporeal things are made. *Silva* itself is unintelligible; Chalcidius in fact says that our knowledge out of it is *obscurus*'" (quoted in Tambling 1988, 72). Tambling then notes that in the *Inferno*—specifically with Nimrod and Bonangiunta—language is in danger of returning to this primordial unformed and chaotic *silva* (72–4). Unnoted by Tambling here is a cross-reference with the canto in the Moon in the *Paradiso* where Beatrice explains to the pilgrim—correcting his mistaken belief (also espoused in the *Convivio* [C: II.xiii.9])—that the unevenness in the Moon's reflectivity is caused by "i corpi rari e densi" (Para: II.60)—that the material universe is itself a *sign of God* (in a properly Augustinian sense of signification, that the universe cannot give an account of itself without the illumination of God's power): "Da essa vien ciò che da luce a luce / *par differente,* non da denso e raro: / essa e il formal principio che produce, / conforme a sua bontà, lo turbo e 'l chiaro" (II.145–48). In other words manifest differentiation—the opposite of unformed, chaotic *silva*—can only be perceived through God, through God's signification and writing of the universe (cf. VIII.100–12). It is God Who obscures the clarity of whiteness (*silva*) with writing. The word *selva* thus names *silva* (the name of chaotic indifference) through a metonomasic lexical difference. One could even claim that the argument of the *Paradiso* is announced by the following rhyme in the Moon canto: "accender ne dovrìa più il disio / di veder quella essenza in che si *vede* / come nostra natura e Dio s'unìo. / Lì si vedrà ciò che tenem per *fede*" (II.40–43; emphasis added). The pilgrimage is nothing if not the coming-to-union of vision and faith; but the poem remains another story and another pilgrimage.

[47] This etymology was first remarked in the commentary of Niccolò Tommaseo (Niccolò Tommaseo, Commentary, 1837, *Dartmouth Dante Project,* Online, Internet.. October 24, 1995. cf. ED: II.499).

⁴⁸ *Disigillare* is thus related to Beatrice's explanation in the Moon canto as: "Or come ai colpi delli caldi rai / delle neve riman nudo il suggetto / e dal colore e dal freddo primai, / così rimaso te nell' intelletto / voglio informar di luce sì vivace, / che ti tremolerà nel suo aspetto" (Para: II.106–11).

⁴⁹ This word is also deployed elsewhere to denote a divine inscripting: "Surge ai mortali per diverse foci / la lucerna del mondo… e la mondana cera / più a suo modo tempera e suggella" (Para: I.37–42). And in the *Purgatorio*: "e avea in atto impressa esta favella / '*Ecce ancilla Dei*,' propriamente / come figura in cera si suggella" (Purg: X.43–45).

⁵⁰ Jacques Derrida, "Freud et la scène d'écriture," *L'écriture et la différence*, Paris: Seuil, 1967. 293–340. 299.

THE LOT OF MALLARMÉ

If one needed to share in Dante's belief in God in order to read the effaced imprintings of the *Divina Commedia,* then the difficulty in reading Mallarmé is redoubtably more extreme, for there one needs to share his belief in poetry, a belief that in poetry, in *vers,* a certain predicament of language might be said to appear, but that would already be saying, even at the outset, too much. Perhaps instead of *faith*, the issue is of the *fate* of issuance. The lot of Mallarmé is the residual, constitutive issue of a *poiesis sans issue.* The work of the poet, the lot of literature is the allotment of absence, and nothing else. "Oui, que la Littérature existe, et si l'on veut, seule, à l'exception de tout" (OC: 646). At its most emphatic there is a subjunctive affirmation of a hypothesized singularity of literature as apart from all else. The experience of literature announced is that of the interval: words enunciated and gone, enunciated as gone; silence proffered within a duration as a detraction or exscription. Blanchot's earliest phrasing of this experience is very precise: "un arrangement méthodique des mots, par une intelligence toute particulière des mouvements et des rhythmes, part un acte intellectuel pur, capable de tout créer en n'exprimant *presque rien.*"[1] A certain *rhythm* occasions a play of negativity. As we will attempt to elaborate in the first half of this chapter, for Blanchot this rhythm is semantic, it lies within the word whereas for Derrida it is syntactic, it lies in the phrasing. But for both Blanchot and Derrida, the *presque rien* is of course the problem, since ultimately Mallarméan writing lacks the resources of the incredible negativity (the *formidable lack*) to which it invariably tends. This is the predicament suggested by the essays under the name *Divagations,* the wanderings of the poetic voice into prosaic meditations of *poiesis* which are also the wanderings of prose into vers, errant planetary wanderings that re-mark a certain *crise de vers:* "La littérature ici subit un exquise crise, fondamentale" (OC: 360). Here, in *vers,* literature submits an exquisite and foundational crisis (or cry): in the poem literature *gives itself over to crise*, surrenders to a suspension of decidability.[2] Within this suspension, this interval, there is nothing (*rien*) that can be definitively decided or acted upon. As Mallarmé announced to Cazalis in 1867:

> Je viens de passer une année effrayante: ma Pensée s'est pensée, et est arrivée à *une Conception pure*. Tout ce que, par contrecoup, mon être a souffert, pendant cette longue agonie, est inénarrable, mais, heureusement, je suis parfaitement mort, et la région la plus impure où mon Esprit puisse s'aventurer est l'Éternité, mon Esprit, ce solitaire habituel de sa propre Pureté, qui n'obscurcit plus même le reflet du Temps. (CI: 240; emphasis added)

Leo Bersani has very precisely and eloquently phrased the double bind of this poetic task to which Mallarmé has *assigned* himself: "Poetic composition heightens the poet's sense of alienation from poetry."[3] For Mallarmé the implication of writing was to be unable to write, to *inachieve writing*. As Bersani quotes from one of Mallarmé's letters to Cazalis: "le simple acte d'écrire installe l'hysterie dans ma tête… je ne suis pas encore tout à fait quitte de la crise puisque la dictée à mon bon secrétaire et l'impression d'une plume qui marche par ma volonté, même grâce à une autre main, me rend mes palpitations" (Bersani, 2–3; CI: 301). Bersani sustains a study of *Hérodiade* and *Igitur* on the basis of this crisis of writing announced through claims of a visceral inability to write: "The very crisis which threatens the writing of poetry sustains poetic composition" (3). The conclusion would be that Mallarmé is perhaps the poet *par excellence*, precisely because he found himself so often unable to write. The status of his poetry lies in this inability of production or manifestation.[4]

The *crise de vers* has begun, thought has exhausted itself to arrive at a conception pure. Poetry is realized by exhausting the detritus of habit and convention, but this purity cannot be written, it does not write. The poem, even literature *is* because it does not, can not appear; hence *crise*. Mallarmé too is a pilgrim, a pilgrim of the crise. Mallarmé, so captivated by the processes of writing, surrenders himself (je suis parfaitement mort) to the negativity of the poem.[5]

For Blanchot this *crise* is opened by the negativizing possibility of a symbolism: "Le symbole est un récit, la négation de ce récit, le récit de cette négation; et la négation, elle-même, apparaît tantôt comme la condition de toute activité d'art et de fiction et, par conséquent, celle de ce récit, tantôt comme la sentence qui en prononce l'échec et l'impossibilité, car elle n'accepte pas de se réaliser dans un acte particulier d'imagination, dans la forme singulière d'un récit achevé."[6] The symbol proffers itself into iterative sacrifice, negating the very rapports upon which its iteration is founded, perhaps even negation. In adducing meaning beyond the literal, the symbol speaks of an insufficiency of language, a negativity fundamental to *poiesis*. Unlike allegory, such a notion of symbolism would be *a priori* divested from reference, it is not simply that an apodosis is denied, but rather that an apodosis never had existed and so it can be neither denied nor affirmed. Symbolism thus re-marks a virtuality or irony of inscripting, and the very possibility of any sense and signification becomes fictive within an endless downward spiral of negativity with no present chance of sublation.[7] As Blanchot points out, once this negativity is discovered within the operation (œuvre) of language, language itself becomes the *work* of absence: "Quand on a découverte dans le langage un pouvoir exceptionnel d'absence et de contestation, la tentation vient de considérer l'absence même de langage comme envelopée dans son essence et le silence comme la possibilité ultime de la parole" (Blanchot 1949, 41). *Symbolism* thus names an experience of a possibility of negativity within language, a possibility which could also be found in Dante's turn to divine *raturage*.[8] Mallarmé speaks of this negativity as being fundamental to Poe:

> L'armature intellectuelle du poëme se dissimule et tient—a lieu—dans l'espace qui isole les strophes et parmi le blanc du papier: significatif silence qu'il n'est pas moins beau de composer, que le vers. (OC: 872)[9]

The poem does not exist, or rather (since the ontological is not a category that can be unquestioningly and unquestionably ascribed to poetry, at least not since Heidegger) the poem does not *take place (avoir lieu)* in the "Signs on a white field" (U: 3.415). The poem—that which is made or composed—rests within the iterative dimension of the *whiteness* of the page, a dimension which is *apart* (see our reading of *Le vierge, le vivace et le bel aujourd'hui* on page 98 and following). In a letter to Catulle Mendès, Mallarmé explained his project: "Je voudrais un *caractère assez serré*, qui s'adoptât à la condensation des vers, mais de *l'air entre les vers, de l'espace,* afin qu'ils se détachent bien les uns des autres, ce qui est nécessaire encore avec leur condensation" (CI: 212). The space then *articulates* the verse, detaching it (also *dé-tacher,* to ex-scribe) into attenuated iteration. The form of the unrealizable book, the book that cannot be divined by human genius is that of "l'hymne, harmonie et joie, comme pur ensemble groupé dans quelque circonstance fulgurante, des relations entre tout" (OC: 378). The work of negativity in the poem is hymnal, rhythmic.

⁂

According to Suzanne Bernard, musicality is suggested through Mallarmé's poems by rhythmically aligned and agitated silences, just as the words on the page are rendered intelligible by the blanks of whiteness shining through.[10] Music is a play of silence. *And yet,* coordinate with this foundational "Significatif silence" is the fact that here *silence,* as Blanchot points out, "pour s'exprimer, fait appel à quelque chose de matériel, se rend présent d'une manière qui ruine l'orgueilleux édifice élevé sur le vide et lui, l'absence même, n'a, pour s'introduire dans le monde des valeurs signifiées et abstraites, d'autre ressource que de se réaliser comme une chose" (Blanchot 1949, 44). The paradox of silence is its reliance upon the monumental language which it renders possible, "Monument en ce désert, avec le silence loin" (OC: 361). To write, then, is to succumb to the vanity of the manifest: "Les individus, à son avis, ont tort, dans leur dessein avéré propre—parce qu'ils puisent à quelque encrier sans Nuit la vaine couche suffisante d'intelligibilité qui lui s'oblige, aussi, à observer" (OC: 383).

Bernard notes that in the analogy to music, poetry suffers because it still depends upon words, upon economies of signification (Bernard, 43). However, the very economies of manifestation and signification surrender to the whiteness of the page, and consequently music might be crippled by its apparent advantage—its freedom from signification. Lacoue-Labarthe argues that the apparent divestiture from meaning that music enjoys too easily elicits overdetermination (Lacoue-Labarthe, 125–29).[11] "La Poésie, proche l'idée, est Musique, par excellence—ne consent pas d'infériorité" (OC: 381). Poetry, although like music can be invested with meanings, has a language—better, it has language*s*, the wasted detritus of Horacian leaves—to *squander*.

> Appuyer, selon la page, au blanc, qui l'innaugure son ingénuité, à soi, oublieuse même du titre qui parlerait trop haut: et, quand s'aligna, dans une brisure, la moindre, disséminée, le hasard vaincu mot par mot, indéfectiblement le blanc revient, tout à l'heure gratuit, certain maintenant, pour conclure que rien au-delà et authentiquer le silence— (OC: 387)

In the poem both silence and manifestation are betrayed. Silence is the *cendre*, it is never *here, it is apart, it is the interruption*. This apartness marks Blanchot's fascination in Mallarmé since he writes of "l'étrange possibilité que nous avons de créer du vide autour de nous, de mettre une distance entre nous et les choses" (Blanchot 1949, 46).[12] For Mallarmé everything in the world ends up (*aboutit*) within this distance or interval, everything winds up within a "disparition vibratoire" (OC: 368). Pressed upon the page, insouciant to context (to its title), the poem enunciates silence within the *disappearance* of its enunciation. The poem applies to blankness its exscription.

Oscillational absentation is occasioned for Mallarmé, in part, through the concern with evocation: "*Nommer* un objet, c'est supprimer les trois quarts de la jouissance du poëme qui est faite de deviner peu à peu: le *suggérer*, voilà le rêve" (OC: 869).[13] Naming *res* suggests or *makes* (ποιεῖν) *rien*. The word *rien*, as Littré shows, also means *something*, its belated Horacian leaf of positivistic meaning is *res*. *Rien* is an apophatic word: thing and thing negated. To evoke is thus to *make* rien mean the one within the other, to oscillate between the positive and negative modalities enjoined by and re-marked within the σύμβολον of the lexical reserve of *rien*. To evoke is thus to surrender *res* to the operations and initiatives of *verbe*, a surrender which pre-positions the poetic iteration. Yves Bonnefoy precisely identifies this lexical effect as the manifestation of disparition: "words in their own way betray us as much as empirical existence, and they do so for essentially the same reason, which is that they also exist, caught as they are in the contingency of sound when seemingly determined by the necessity of the Idea."[14] Lexical negativity arises from precisely the fact that it depends upon the contingencies of monumental language to arise.

Derrida's reading of this oscillatory interval emphasizes the dissolutional force of syntax within the parameters of Mallarméan evocation. The ῥυθμός (cadence and character of writing) of disparition is articulated through spacings upon the page. The poet does not enunciate a thing (*res*) into being, rather he periphrastically pronounces an effect thereby suggesting some thing *else*, and so *res* is iterated as and through *rien*. The thing is suggested or *it*erated in that *it qua res* is an effect of the poetic circumlocution (or circumnavigation). Derrida provides an uncharacteristically concise formulation for this: "La *chose* est comprise, comme *effet de chose* dans cette longue *citation* de la langue."[15] The word gives itself up to possibilities that can be neither fixed nor arbitrated within an exchange that is not *purely* semantic (an example which Derrida deals with in the 1974 essay is sonority).[16] Derrida argues that the Mallarméan credo—"*Peindre, non la chose, mais l'effet qu'elle produit*" (CI: 137)—is effected *syntactically*.

The implications of this point are developed in *La dissémination* where Derrida proposes that in Mallarmé's *Mimique* "Nous sommes devant une mimique qui n'imite rien, devant, si l'on peut dire, un double qui ne redouble aucun simple, que rien ne prévient, rien qui ne soit en tous cas déjà un double. Aucune référence simple" (Derrida 1972, 234).[17] Recalling Derrida's argument concerning Freud's *wunderblock*, μιμῆσις is already a simulacra within an economy of difference and repetition. Representation then would not deal with a bringing to presence *again* (a metaphysics of repeatable imminence), but rather with the *effect* of repetition (an effect which de Man squarely associates with rhetoric). For Derrida this marks a deviation from a reliance upon the word as such. The word gives itself to syntactic possibilities of evocation that cannot be fixed. "Ce qui compte ici, ce n'est pas la richesse lexicale,

l'infinité sémantique d'un mot ou d'un concept, sa profondeur ou son épaisseur, la sédimentation en lui de deux significations contradictoires (continuité et discontinuité, dedans et dehors, identité et différence, etc.). Ce qui compte ici, c'est la practique formelle ou syntaxique qui compose et le décompose" (Derrida 1972, 249). And more forcefully: "Ce qui suspend la *décision*, ce n'est pas la richesse de sens, la ressource inépuisable d'un mot, c'est un certain jeu de la syntaxe" (Derrida 1974, 371, emphasis added). Syntax debilitates the power of criticism to decide. Syntactically, *la critique aboutit à crise*.[18]

Following Derrida, the concern within Mallarméan poetics is not representation, but the putting into play of the effects of representation syntactically, deferring writing away from a manifest issue (or issuance) and towards a play of rhythmically aligned absentation: "Sur la ligne introuvable de ce pli, l'hymen se ne présente jamais, il n'est jamais—au présent—, il n'a pas de sens propre, il ne relève plus de sens comme tel, c'est-à-dire, en dernière instance, comme sens de l'être. Le pli (se) multiplie mas (n'est) pas (un)" (259). The *pli* is already multi*pli*ed, thereby perpetually deferring a very possibility of meaning, iterative or even otherwise.

For Derrida, the word through syntactic cross-concatenations, is divested from a rapport with *res*; the word stands as an experience of negativity in which there is no appearance and no original reference (Derrida 1972, 219). The word does not put into play a simple binary cathexis of contradiction (a diction-contradiction, as such could be easily subsumed within the cunning machinations of a Hegelian dialectic), but rather marks and re-marks (re-marks as marking) *the very possibility* of a semantic diction-contradiction; syntactically (deferred through syntactic espacement) the word re-marks the possibility of naming *rien* (cf. 251–52).[19] *Designations* of absence (of "blanks") are themselves enunciated *within* supplementary chains, therefore definitive ascription and attribution are impossible operations. One cannot even decide upon undecidability within this proliferation, which Derrida terms *dissemination*; the σημεῖον (boundary, limit, sign of the gods, flag, trace) of meaning withdraws within a play of extrapolated profligacy. "Dès que

le blanc (est) blanc, (se) blanchit, dès qu'il (y) a quelque chose à voir (ou à ne pas voir) avec une *marque* (c'est le même mot que *marge* et que *marche*), soit que le blanc (se) marque (la neige, le cygne, la virginité, le papier etc.,) ou (se) dé-marque (l'entre, le vide, l'espacement etc.), il se re-marque, se marque deux fois. Il se plie autour de cette étrange limite. Le pli ne lui survient pas du dehors, il est à la fois son dehors et son dedans, la complication selon laquelle la marque supplémentaire du blanc (espacement asémique) s'applique à l'ensemble des blancs (pleins sémqiues), plus à soi-même, pli sur soi du voile, tissu ou texte. En raison de cette application que rien n'aura précédée, il n'y aura jamais de Blanc majuscule ou de théologie du Texte" (290). Mallarméan syntax transgresses the σημεῖον. Such a notion of syntax runs away from the more traditional notion of syntax as a disciplined arrangement of subordination and coordination that marches in unison (σύνταξις, *arranging in order*; from σύν, *in company* and τάξις, *military arrangement*). His syntax deploys multiple patterns of arrangement that tend towards canceling out the subsistence of a single subsumptive σύν. For Mallarmé, syntactic operation thus establishes a constellation of (sylleptic) differences that cannot be subsumed under and by any present (238). Instead of meaning, there is an intervallic site of a suspension, a deferral away from (a singular) presence. And yet, one might ask,

> Quel pivot, j'entends, dans ces contrastes, a l'intelligibilité? Il faut une garantie—
>
> La syntaxe— (OC: 385)

Syntax curbs disseminal proliferation of meaning (that is its guaranty, its responsibility, its concern). And yet there has never been *one syntax*, one guaranty of meaning. There have always been *syntaxes*. Added to the formal austerity of a French syntax (perhaps even that is already plural), there is the syntax of the page, of the compressive espacement and tenebrific articulations of ink against white. The effect, then, is a play between different articulations of statement and statability. "Un balbutiement, que semble la phrase, ici refoulé dans l'emploi d'incidentes multiplie, se compose et s'enlève en quelque équilibre supérieur, à

balancement prévu d'inversions" (OC: 386). The Mallarméan iteration is this intervallic équilibre supérieur achieved, briefly, tenuously, by the play between different syntaxes, different modes of articulating inscriptive logic.

> Tout devient suspens, disposition fragmentaire avec alternance et vis-à-vis, concourant au rythme total, lequel serait le poëme tu, aux blancs; seulement traduit, en une manière, par chaque pendentif. (OC: 367)

The Mallarméan *coup de poème* thus falls at an odd remove from circumstance. The poem depends upon its circumstance of enunciation in order for it to be silenced and in order for the circumstance to disappear,[20] much as the pilgrim needed to traverse through the conditions of sin and redemption in order to behold the God that is silenced at the close of the *Paradiso*. Most of Mallarmé's œuvre—the œuvre that can be compiled,[21] the œuvre that has left its marks—could be construed as being circumstantial, even, and perhaps especially *Un coup de dés*.[22] The circumstance of the Mallarméan work is one prone to none. The Mallarméan experience of writing, the experience of *having had* destruction as Beatrice ("La Destruction *fut* ma Béatrice" [CI: 246; emphasis added]) is an experience of writing in the wake of belated disparition, a disparition that can be neither denied nor affirmed. The constitutive white page already annihilates, and so what remains for the work of the poet? This question could be asked of Dante after the final beatific vision which had already *disigillato* in his mind. In a sense the allegory of the theologians could have been partially correct, since after all is said and done, the poet could have been imitating a divine writing by reinscribing a non-originary original excription. Effacement precedes the poet's pen, it is the pre-position. If for Dante the (ineluctably) postlapsarian poet writes in the wake of a "correctione... memorabili" (DVG: I.vii.5), then for Mallarmé the poet writes *in and with* the wake or echo of a *mémorable crise*:

> L'œuvre pure implique la disparition élocutoire du poëte, qui cède l'initiative aux mots, par le heurt de leur inégalité mobilisés; ils s'allument de reflets réciproques comme une virtuelle traînée de feux sur des pierreries, remplaçant

> la respiration perceptible en l'ancien souffle lyrique ou la direction personnelle enthousiaste de la phrase. (OC: 366)

The conception pure is the poet's work of ceding initiative to words, to surrender to the *spirit* (*souffle*) of poetic enunciation. Inspiration is now a lexical surrender. The poetic voice is *exceeded* by the vers. Such surrender is precisely the event of the *crise de vers*, a crisis coordinate with the event of the *book*, that spiritual instrument.

Fundamental to the *circumstance* of the *crise* de vers is the pause or cæsura—an undoing of the traditional forms of French versification (i.e. the Alexandrine): "Au traitement, si intéressant, par la versification subi, de repos et d'interrègne, gît, moins que dans nos circonstances mentales, la crise" (365). The crise de vers is also a crisis for those "fidèles à l'alexandrin" (362) once confronted by the possibility of a "vers libre"; such is the ostensive concern—or occasion—for the lecture *La musique et les lettres* (and also for *Crise de vers*).[23] In an excellent article on Mallarmé's eventual preference for the octosyllabic sonnet, David Scott notes that the alexandrine, by virtue of its wide syllabic span, tends towards containing complete and integral syntactic units, thereby retaining a typically prosaic quality. In contradistinction, the more abbreviated octosyllabic form relies frequently on *disrupting* normal syntactic flow (especially by the frequency of enjambment), thereby suggesting other modes of organization (rhythm, rhyme, vertical rather than horizontal associations, *&c.*): "in Mallarmé's octosyllabic sonnets, each line does not so much move itself forward under the impetus of its own logical or verbal energy as itself becomes catapulted on to the page."[24] This notion of fragmentation, of submitting to other syntaxes, is also at work in Mallarmé's alexandrines and, more problematically, in his prose.

The question concerning the prose poem subtends a vaster question of *poiesis*, for in the crise both versification and literature have *subi*: "On a touché au vers. ... Faut-il s'arrêter là et d'où ai-je le sentiment que je suis venu relativement à un sujet plus vaste peut-être à moi-même inconnu, que telle rénovation de rites et de rimes; pour y atteindre, sinon le traiter" (643–45). Elsewhere Mallarmé writes that "Le vers est partout dans la langue où il y a rythme, partout, excepté dans les affiches et à la

quatrième page des journaux. ... Toutes les fois qu'il y a effort au style, il y a la versification" (867). It is thus not with poetry-as-such or rather a *poesy* that Mallarmé is concerned, rather it is the *possibility of language's being poetic*, a possibility which is not apart from the possibility of *crise*. *Vers* is, quite simply, the *crise*. The *crise*, thus construed, is not just the crisis of metricized verse undergoing new strange rhythms, but is also not without relation to the crise of the Mallarmé's infamous inability to write.[25] The *crise de vers* is thus this triple impasse: the freeing of verse from the Alexandrine, the musical disparition in and of vers, and the disempowerment of the poet. The new rhythm of crise, this *new music* oscillates and plays between in- and ex-scription, between appearance and disparition upon the pages of the book.[26]

> Tandis qu'il y avait, le langage régnant, d'abord à l'accorder selon son origine, pour qu'un sens auguste se produisît: en le Vers, dispensateur, ordonnateur du jeu des pages, maître du livre. Visiblement soit qu'apparaisse son intégralité, parmi les marges et du blanc; ou qu'il se dissimule, nommez-le Prose, néanmoins c'est lui si demeure quelque secrète poursuite de musique, dans la réserve du Discours. (375)

In the crise the poet, the poetic voice, is given to the rhythms of the *vers,* and in this *action restrainte,* there is a poetry as the *virtuality of poetic iteration:* "Au contraire d'une fonction de numéraire facile et représentatif, comme le traite d'abord la foule, le dire, avant tout, rêve et chant, retrouve chez le Poëte, par nécessité constitutive d'un art consacré aux fictions, sa virualité" (368). Language is the field of the surrender of everything to the crisis at sea.[27]

∙∙∙

Rather than locate the poet's surrender to language in a rhythm between syntaxes, Blanchot valorizes the notion of an impossible *lexical* purity of annulation. This reading was developed between the essay "Le mythe de Mallarmé" (1949)[28] and *L'espace littéraire* (1955). Blanchot insists upon a lexical reserve of annulation. Central to this reading are the concluding paragraphs to *Crise de vers:*

> Je dis: une fleur! et, hors de l'oubli où ma voix relègue aucun contour, en tant que quelque chose d'autre que les calices sus, musicalement se lèvre, idée même et suave, l'absente de tous bouquets.
>
> Au contraire d'une fonction de numéraire facile et représentatif, comme le traite d'abord la foule, le dire, avant tout, rêve et chant, retrouve chez le Poëte, par necessité constitutive d'un art consacré aux fictions, sa virtualité.
>
> Le vers qui de plusieurs vocables refait un mot total, neuf, étranger à la langue et comme incantatoire, achève cet isolement de la parole: niant, d'un trait souverain, le hasard demeuré aux termes malgré l'artifice de leur retrempe alternée en le sens et la sonorité, et vous cause cette surprise de n'avoir ouï jamais tel fragment ordinaire d'élocution, en même temps que la réminiscence de l'objet nommé baigne dans une neuve atmosphère. (OC: 368)

The pure word—*stranger to language*—effects a transformation of the possibility of sense. The pure word is a completely isolated nul instance of novelty and reminiscence: the word of the future awaiting a present that never comes. The flower is not said, it retreats in the profferal of letters. The only word available for profferal in this floral example is the calyx: chalice used for sacrifice. The only word not absent is the word for *giving up*. In the immediacy of recollection and anticipation there is the solitude and decomposition of the word. In its very invocation on the page—in black on white—the word (say, *fleur*) is silenced. By being alluded to, it eludes.[29] In *vers* a word becomes something else, or rather *somewhere else, étranger à la langue*. It becomes its own virtuality. Not even its elusiveness can be named since the disappearance is rhythmic and virtual, as if it were not even there. Therefore the pure word must already be translated in order to *appear* on the page (our concern with the issue of translation will be deferred to the following chapter).[30] The word is already *sub-scribed* to an ineluctable modality of the lisible: "C'est que les mots ont besoin d'être visibles, il leur faut un réalité propre qui puisse s'interposer entre ce qui est et ce qu'ils expriment" (Blanchot 1949, 39). *The pure language is given up in the very approach that evokes it*. In a sense literature is a distraction from itself; poetic language is *virtual* language, a disparition virtually re-marked on the page.[31]

Bersani's reading of the conclusion to *crise de vers* harmonizes with Blanchot's notion of the fragment: "A verse creates a new 'total word' from its several individual words, a word 'étranger à la langue et comme incantatoire.' The 'isolement de la parole' in poetry is not only… an isolating of language from nature, but also a separation of language from itself, the creation of new linguistic units on the basis of sound" (Bersani, 43). From this possibility Blanchot formulates his distinction between the parole brut and the parole essentiel, the "double état de la parole, brut ou immédiat ici, là essentiel" (OC: 368; cf. 379–80). The essential word is never here, but always *there*, pure (or *essential*) absentation is always à venir. This distinction between the two modalities of parole is, as Blanchot admits, obviously crude:

> Pur silence, la parole brute…. Silencieuse, donc, parce que nulle, pure absence de mots, pur échange où rien ne s'échange, où il n'y a rien de réel que le mouvement d'échange, qui n'est rien. … La parole brute « a trait à la réalité des choses ». « Narrer, enseigner, même décrire » nous donne les choses dans leur présence, les « représente ». La parole essentielle les éloignes, les *fait* disparaître, elle est toujours allusive, elle suggère, elle évoque. (Blanchot 1955, 38, emphasis added)

The crude word re-marks negativity, it *reports* the absentation effected in and by language. The pure word is not content to report absence, it *makes and proffers* absentation (the divine effaced and lost within a chain of pure supplementarity).[32] Blanchot sees Mallarmé's *langue suprême* as this pure thought which is the almost-disappearance of the essential word. The essential word is a de-enunciation of being (and not quite the renunciation of being that one can find in *Igitur*). The poem aims towards the excellence of destruction. But this excellence is neither in the past (Hölderlin's gesture with the proclamation of destitution, if not nostalgic is at least a gesture to a past), nor is it in the future, instead it is in the *exposure* of death—a passivity towards death; a passivity that never happens in the present. The present lack to be remunerated is *not there*. It is crucial to note that the distinction made between the parole brute and the parole essentiel is not a dialectic since both modes ultimately end with silence. The only difference, and a slight one at that, is that the

parole essentiel delivers language itself to silence as "l'absente de tous bouquets."[33]

> Mais, ayant ce pouvoir de faire se « lever » les choses au sein de leur absence, maîtres de cette absence, les mots ont aussi pouvoir d'y disparître eux-mêmes, de se rendre merveilleusement absents au sein du tout qu'ils réalisent, qu'ils proclament en s'y annulant, qu'ils accomplissent éternellement en s'y détruisant sans fin, acte d'auto-destruction, en tout semblable à l'événement si étrange du suicide. (Blanchot 1955, 45)[34]

This is the point at which the ineluctable vanity of the word reasserts itself. If language has the nonmasterable power of absentation, it is also a power which is not absolute. Language itself lacks the resources needed to effect absentation precisely because in effecting absentation, absentation is betrayed. The pure language does not exist.[35]

> Les langues imparfaites en cela que plusieurs, manque la suprême: penser étant écrire sans accessoires, ni chuchotement mais tacite encore l'immortelle parole, la diversité, sur terre, des idiomes empêche personne de proférer les mots qui, sinon se trouveraient, par une frappe unique, elle-même matériellement la verité. ...
> —*Seulement*, sachons n'existerait pas le vers: lui, philosophiquement rémunère le défaut des langues, complément supérieur. (OC: 363–4)

This passage describes a moment of *translation*.[36] But such an idea of translation should not be read as an ensurance of survival of an *original*. The literary language—the literary idiom—exists because a perfect language is missing. The literary language owes itself, is indebted to, this ineluctable lack, subtended by the babble of multiple languages. Coordinate with this indebtedness is the poem's status as remuneration of the lack; hence the *double-bind* of the poem. Derrida argues in "Des tours de Babel"—following from Walter Benjamin's infamous "Task of the Translator"—that both poet and translator are indebted to an impossible gift of redemptive transposition. "Le traduction est transposition poètique (*umdichtung*)" (Derrida 1987, 222). The gift is impossible because both poetry and translation are ineluctably *within* language and thus inexorably *without* relation to any phenomenal originality.[37] For Mallarmé, the pure language can only be announced as a *translation*; it can be said to have existence only in that it is subtended by a multiplicity of language; but the very *fait* by which *it could be said to exist* already marks its ineluctable withdrawal into a nothingness of dead and autopsy-turvy'd words. This is precisely the point around which Derrida, Blanchot and Sollers's readings of Mallarmé align: the notion that words do not align around meaning. Words *exhaust* meaning.[38] By naming the *parole essentiel*—even as an impossibility—Blanchot runs the risk of having fixed a locus of disparition. But according to Mallarmé, were such a locus possible, there could be no poetry. The Mallarméan poem is the futile remuneration for this *lack* of pure disparition: the exscribed articulation of the absence of disappearance. This would, also, be the situation *named* by Dante's pure word "disigillare" as well as the gallimaufry of tongues in *Finnegans Wake*: babble supplements and remarks the originary and autotelic Babel that had never been (we will return to this point in chapter 5). Derrida's emphasis on syntax avoids this problem precisely by *deferring absentation* to the exhaustive and exhausting play of syntax. Syntactically there is not even the *chance* to designate exscription. Language does not even have the resources for such a poetry and so the pure word remains fictive and its œuvre *à venir*. Because of this prepositioning *lack*, Mallarméan awaiting is fundamentally different from Heideggerian awaiting. As Graham Robb rather wittily points out, "if language had been perfect, Mallarmé would have had nothing to do but write textbooks and edit fashion magazines."[39] Because of language's insufficiency, there can be work for Mallarmé, there can be an œuvre, albeit an œuvre à venir.

The uneasy junction between syntax and the word can be traced in the poem *Ses purs ongles très haut dédiant leur onyx* with the interlacing of the inscrutable nonce-word ptyx, a "mot intact et nul" (OC: 374), into a bizarre rhyme-scheme. For the sake of space we will only examine the second strophe:

> Sur les crédences, au salon vide: nul ptyx,
> Aboli bibelot d'inanité sonore,
> (Car le Maître est allé puiser des pleurs au Styx
> Avec ce seul objet dont le Néant s'honore). (OC: 68; OCP: 356 ll. 5–8)

In a letter to Cazalis, Mallarmé explained this setting of the salon vide as "une nuit faite d'absence et d'interrogation" (OC: 1490; CI: 279). This ascription of figuration becomes especially difficult to decide in that the sonorous elements are interlaced or crossed with the *-yx* rhyme. The difficult rhyme sequence determines the poem, one of its syntaxes is this rhyme. Mallarmé called this rhyme scheme an "étude projetée sur *la Parole*: il est inverse, je veux dire que le sens, s'il en a un… est evoqué par un mirage interne des mots mêmes" (OC: 1489; CI: 278). Sense comes from the *superficiality* of its typography—the vanity of its inscription—and not from a lexical reserve. The rhyme is deployed purely for affect and not for meaning, but then this ostensible lexical insouciance is already a *significant* matter.[40] Amidst rhyme—the -yx rhyme of the quatrains and the -or rhyme of the tercets, the rhymes of the son or that reverberate whence the Néant s'honore—significance is supplemented through lexical affect (cf. Derrida 1972, 295–97 fn. 54 and see also note 16 in this chapter). Rhyme *re-marks* a mirage of signification. "So all rogues lean to rhyme" (FW: 096.03).

The *re-mark* of annullation in this poem revolves around the singular nonce word ptyx—a word Mallarmé claimed, in a letter to Lefébure, to be absolutely *unique* in any language, a word unknown to all men. This word was chosen apparently for the exigency of the *meaningless* rhyme-scheme (OC: 1488; CI: 274).[41] Ptyx is the singular word *made for poetry*. In the poem, ptyx falls as the sigil of an *originality* nullified in an empty room. This ostensibly original and unique word is a perfect transposition of the Ancient Greek word πτύξ: *fold* (as in literally a folding of garments, but with numerous metaphorical resonances; the word "diptych" derives from πτύξ).[42] There is *potentially* a formidable linguistic weight behind this supposedly nonce word; however it would be remiss to call ptyx either a straightforward translation, or even a transcription, of the *jadis* word πτύξ. Ptyx is perhaps the poetic word *par excellence* because it *is* a nothingness imbricated within a rhythmic scene, or it even (if this Greek meaning is to be acknowledged) *names* a folding, it names *the very act of folding itself into a poem*. It either *is* or it *names* an interlacing of vacuity into a sonnet or small sound (*sonnetto*). In this way *ptyx* is the perfect allegorical word since it both *is and is not* allegorical of itself and of its role within the poem. And, of course, in this sonnet there is "nul ptyx." This blank cipher of and for rhyme is not even *there,* the nought of naming is already nulled, the nought of poetic enunciation is enunciated as negation. The word, "neuf, étranger à la langue," is *made* to disappear, as Mallarmé explained: "or, c'est bien clair, le ptyx est insolite, puisqu'il n'y en a pas; il résonne bien, puisqu'il rime; est ce n'en est pas moins un vaisseau d'inanité, puisqu'il n'a jamais existé!" (OCP: 222). This annulling action is in the poem when the Néant *s'honore*: nothing honors itself, and the *reflexive* action of this is interlaced with sonority, the sonority of the poem's rhymes with, for example, the *or* that expires into *décor* (or a decorous mirage). Ptyx (the space of poetic enunciation) takes over, *takes the place* of the *tongue:* the poetic remuneration of the absence of the langue suprême. In this way the nul ptyx is the double negation—or denegation—of the tongue's power to affirm both itself and its being through its enunciation. In this way, in this weighty absence of affirmative meaning, the Maître of this poem comes to be lost within his parenthetical (alongside or paratactic) elaboration of vacuity absented. The word ptyx is *folded* into the rhyme in which is enfolded the disappearance of the fold, nul ptyx. The pure word is folded into the poem only to be retracted, isolated and nullified. Neither the poem's syntax (its rhyme-schemes), nor this one word nullify: their nullification is interlaced. And so Blanchot's emphasis on the pure word and Derrida's emphasis on syntax cross and fold into the nullification of ptyx. Mallarmé's word plays with syntax and his syntax plays with the word, and in this play of the pure word are redoubling disparitions.

The pure word's deployment is coordinate with its effacement and so confront the pure word is thus to confront death—an expenditure of a reserve which can never be made present: to absolutely give what is absolutely not present. To write is to give oneself up. And Mallarmé *gives* what he does not have: the pure word, he poisons it by syntactically tortured and torturous profferal. The Mallarméan word is *désœuvrement*; such is his pyrrhic lyric. This profferal is precisely what is hardened into the interval of a book, the interval set between the *plis* of a volume: "Le livre, expansion totale de la lettre, doit d'elle tirer, directement, une mobilité et spacieux, par correspondances, instituer un jeu, on ne sait, qui confirme la fiction" (OC: 380). This then is the *crise de vers* according to Blanchot, "une pause de la poésie, de l'intervalle qu'elle traverse" (Blanchot 1959, 317). The livre stands as the circumstance of an inachievement of negativity in that this inachievement is achieved only as a fiction, an interregnum of totality. It is the œuvre made manifest and circulable within circumstance, and as such it *is* (not merely reports) the inevitable failure of the work, the failure of the work to become a totality and the failure of the work to escape from economies of totalization. "Le livre est le mode, par excellence, du langage, à la fois parce qu'il n'en retient que le pouvoir d'abstraction, d'isolement, de transposition, parce qu'il éloigne le hasard, reste de la contingence des choses réelles, parce qu'enfin il en écarte l'homme même, celui qui parle et celui qui écoute... Tout proférer, c'est aussi proférer le silence" (Blanchot 1949, 43). The livre is *disigillare* put into play upon a page, a virtual reality of syntactic annihilation: its work is its unworking. "Disparu et supprimé comme auteur, il est, par cette disparition, en rapport avec l'essence apparaissante et disparaissnte du Livre, avec son oscillation incessante qui est sa communication" (Blanchot 1959, 330).[43] In this way, all the *Divagations*, proffer the Livre, as a fleur—absente de tous bouquets. The Livre, in that it is à venir, all hype and no publication, is the Mallarméan word par excellence. "Le Livre, où vit l'esprit satisfait, en cas de malentendu, un obligé par quelque pureté d'ébat à secouer le gros du moment. Impersonifié, le volume, autant qu'on s'en sépare comme auteur, ne réclame approche de lecteur. Tel, sache, entre les accessoires humains, *il a lieu tout seul: fait, étant*. Le sens enseveli se meut et dispose, en chœur, des feuillets" (OC: 372, emphasis added). The livre *is* only in that it is insouciant to being.[44]

For both Dante and Mallarmé writing exhausted the possibility of meaning in a restrained action of excription. For the former excription came before an eternally proximate yet never present divinity, and for the latter excription exhausted even its own resources within the vanity of inked signs on the page.

∙∙∙

At this point we interrupt our consideration of the loftier blur of the "ancien souffle lyrique" in order that we might both defend and illustrate the claims above by navigating a reading through some of Mallarmé's poems. The twin concerns of circumstance and of the Livre are intertwined in the sonnet *Salut,* a poem in which *confluence* is of no small import.[45] The poem (originally entitled *Toast*) is one that could be considered a vers de circonstance since it was written for performance at a banquet of poets organized by the editors of *La plume* on February 13, 1893. Mallarmé subsequently took the poem to serve as *exergue* for the edition of his verse prepared by Edmond Deman (Brussels, 1899), which—with the exception of this poem—was organized more-or-less chronologically (OC: 1406; OCP: 749–53).[46] Because of this key position in the first collection of Mallarmé's verse, Marchal calls *Salut* "Dédicace de l'œuvre entière," and furthermore in dedicating his glass (*verre*), Mallarmé also dedicates and sends off his *vers*.[47] This poem, the *coup de vers* of one circumstance has become frontispiece to an œuvre.

> Rien, cette écume, vierge vers
> À ne désigner que la coupe;
> Telle loin se noie une troupe
> De sirènes mainte à l'envers.
>
> Nous naviguons, ô mes divers
> Amis, moi déjà sur la poupe
> Vous l'avant fastueux qui coupe
> Le flot de foudres et d'hivers;
>
> Une ivresse belle m'engage
> Sans craindre même son tangage
> De porter debout ce salut
>
> Solitude, récif, étoile
> À n'importe ce qui valut
> Le blanc souci de notre voile. (OC: 27; OCP: 402)

Although a salutation, the poem does not begin auspiciously. Indeed the address begins by addressing itself, by addressing its action of salutation (à ne designer que la coupe), and then by addressing this action as *rien*. "Mallarmé is apologizing for the slightness of the offering compared to the lifelong Dream he had not yet offered to the public and, particularly, to his youthful admirers."[48] The proffering of the *coupe* supplements the profferal of the *Œuvre,* which within this designation remains *à venir* and is thus, presently, *rien*. The salut is a *small sound* (*sonnetto*) silencing itself for not having been a *vaster silence*. The poem offers *rien*, a thing that is no thing in the place of a lacuna of work. The coupe thus designates a lack which it fulfills, but *only* in that it designates itself as a mere trifle, as *rien*. In designating itself as rien, the poem designates an absent œuvre. Indeed through a tremendously tightened self-reflexivity the poem conflates *more* into the wake of *rien*. Coordinate with the champagne undulating within the raised glass of the toast is a turbulent maritime scene, a fatal navigation from swerve of shore to bend of bay. That which is designated under the rien, the toast, in that it is being designated within the iteration also designates a hazardous navigation. Bénichou notes—in his commentary for *Le vierge, le vivace et le bel d'aujourd'hui*— that a typical vehicle or formula for Mallarméan verse is "des symboles dont les deux termes fussent si naturellement suggestifs l'un de l'autre, qu'il pût remplacer les deux discours par un seul" (Bénichou, 245).[49] Each isotope suggests the other, and these suggestive matrices are intercalated through a minimal constellation of terms. Said confluence is not without effect for its *renewed* circumstance as exergue: "En plaçant ainsi toute l'œuvre sous le signe du néant, même si le néant affecte ici par ironie l'insignifiance d'un « Rien » de modestie, le poème fait de l'expérience poétique une navigation prommise à un naufrage fatal, et désamorce à l'avance toute lecture dramatique, ou dramatisante, des *Poésies*" (Marchal 1985, 14).

The fourteen lines of the sonnet embark upon a multiple cruise directed through syntactic and metaphoric cathexes which ultimately designate no more than the iterative dimension in which the poetic cruise (or *crise*) takes place—upon this general statement critics such as Cohn, Bénichou, Marchal, Sugano and Kaufmann agree. Here, *rien* is *evoked*. It is of course just a bit bizarre that these witnesses to the poem's circumstantial auto-reflexivity were not present at the banquet of *la Plume*. Their claims are sustained precisely because of their absence at the event. Indeed the account given in *la Plume* of the occasion barely hints at such inter-reflexive fuss: "cet homme délicieux, Stéphane Mallarmé, se lève, prend sa coupe et d'une voix sonore, quoique mal assurée, dit l'exquis poëme qui s'inscrit au fronton de cette revue" (OC: 1407; OCP: 403). This testimony of the original performance suggests that it had already been imperfect, and that this original, imperfect performance had itself been a repetition of a prior, inscribed poem, and consequently the circumstance or *origin* of the poem could not be merely its original performance. The performance was already prepositioned by the poem on the page. Indeed there may be a self-reflexivity suggested by *Salut* (and a self-reflexivity not unlike that proposed by these esteemed critics), *but* this circumstantial self-reflexivity is borne by the *absence* of the iterative voice. The *salut* was already belated.

Despite the insistence upon the self-referentiality of the performative context—the circumstance of the poem's first *salut*—there is also a suggestion of a voyage of *reading* the words across the page—"Nous naviguons, ô mes divers"—*we* also navigate through the *vers*. The poem has adapted to—has saluted—its circumstance upon the page. After *rien* there is cette écume, vierge vers: an unnavigated path through a suggested wake of whiteness (the foam being one of many evocations of the whiteness of a page).[50] The poem splattered upon the virginal vellum of the page ("virginité de la feuille de papier" [OC: 400]) is but a wake of whiteness disturbed by the poet's ink, the *rien* of an *action restreinte*. And in the procession of this *vers*, the singing sirens—*telle loin*[51]—are *en vers*: the song of the sirens is both reversed and (inscribed) *in* verse. As Marchal kindly notes "Pour les amateurs de paragrammes, notons que le *rien* est inscrit au cœur de la *sirène*" (Marchal, 14 fn.4). Rien is sounded again *en vers*. If *vers* is to carry an external reference to the circumstance of the toast—to the raised and proffered *verre* (which is also *rien*)—then *vers* also plays across the rhyme scheme of the poem with *envers, divers* and *hivers*. Vers is itself given up to the rhythm of the words in a melodic "effacement de rien qui ait été beau dans le passé" (OC: 363). That (thing) which the poem *is* (*rien*) is lost within the very voyage that it has occasioned. The voyage, the *envoi,* fails to progress to a destination, to a *work* that could be completed or achieved. The navigation through the *parages* of designating the cup and its écume is ateleological.

The first tercet enumerates a steadfastness to the voyage: "Une ivresse belle m'engage / Sans craindre même son tangage / De porter debout ce salut."[52] Rather than auto-reflexively refer to the circumstance of its toast, this tercet can be read as citing the *effect* of a *salut,* of citing a "voix sonore, quoique mal assuré" in the sound of a *son* tangage. This tercet suggests a prosopopoeia of a drunken toast. There had been no original presentation of salutation, merely repetitions of a *son tangage.* The final tercet reestablishes the virginity of the "blanc souci de notre toile." The page re-engulfs the *vers:* the vers heads towards (*vers*) whiteness, à n'importe ce qui valut. All that is left then is the ivresse belle of solitude, récif, étoile. All that is left is the nautical disaster within the blankness of its preposition of absentation, hardly an auspicious departure.

• • •

In the earlier poem *Brise marine* one finds many of the tropes of *Salut* (such as drunkenness, whiteness, the frothy sea-foam and the inevitable *naufrage*) coupled with a dark revising of Baudelaire's *Parfum exotique*.[53]

> La chair est triste, hélas! et j'ai lu tous les livres.
> Fuir! là-bas fuir! Je sens que des oiseaux sont ivres
> D'être parmi l'écume inconnue et les cieux!
> Rien, ni les vieux jardins reflétés par les yeux
> Ne retiendra ce cœur qui dans la mer se trempe
> Ô nuits! ni la clarté déserte de ma lampe
> Sur le vide papier que la blancheur défend
> Et ni la jeune femme allaitant son enfant.
> Je partirai! Steamer balançant ta mâture,
> Lève l'ancre pour une exotique nature!
>
> Un Ennui, désolé par les cruels espoirs,
> Croit encore à l'adieu suprême des mouchoirs!
> Et, peut-être, les mâts, invitant les orages
> Sont-ils de ceux qu'un vent penche sur les naufrages

Perdus, sans mâts, sans mâts, ni fertiles îlots...
Mais, ô mon cœur, entends le chant des matelots! (OC: 38; OCP: 176)

Cohn's reading of the poem is strongly informed by its circumstance: Mallarmé herewith expresses a desire to flee from the burdensome responsibilities of his new family; an explanation provided from a letter he wrote on February 8, 1866 to Cazalis's cousin, Mme. Le Josne: "ce désir inexpliqué qui vous prend parfois de quitter ceux qui nous sont chers, et de partir" (Cohn 1980, 288; OC: 1433; CI: 200). Thus construed, the poem becomes an elaboration—if not an explanation—of this *désir inexpliqué*. However, within the poem—rendered into Alexandrines—tintinnabulations take over from the forward direction of the rhyme-scheme, thereby distorting any sense of coherent reference. The Alexandrine form is distended through the suggestion of other, less rigid metrics. The poem breaks off or decomposes into internal echo rhymes thereby suspending the possibility of *fuite*, even as *fuir* is itself one of the sounds surrendered to repetition.[54] These echoed soundings could be (partially) tabularized as follows (end-rhymes are excluded):[55]

line 1: *est... hé*las... j'*ai*; l*u*... t*ous*   line 2: *Fuir* [là-bas] *fuir*; & *sens*... *sont*
lines 3–4: c*ieux*... v*ieux*   lines 4–5: *Rien*... jard*ins*... ret*ien*dra
lines 3–6: parm*i*... n*i*... qu*i*... n*uits*... n*i* lines 8–9: allait*ant*... enf*ant*... balanç*ant*
line 14: qu'*un* v*en*t p*en*che   line 15: fert*iles îl*ots (cacemphaton)
line 15–16: s*ans*... s*ans*... *en*t*en*ds... ch*ant*

Even *sens* yields to *sont*, and ultimately to *sans* and *chant* in lines 15–6. Indeed the *sens/sont* rhyme suggests, in both its sound and by its reliance upon repeated soundings, *son;* the name of sonority is evoked here as its effect is played out throughout as one is to *entend* the *chant*. The iterative space of the poem can thus be characterized as a disseminated constellation of rhymes producing interferences with each other (such as the interruption of the repetition of *fuir* by the unit *là-bas*).[56] Occasionally the internal rhyming expands and illustrates the sense of the line, such as the echo of *ant* in "la jeune femme allaitant son enfant": the *ant* is transferred from the *sein* of the woman to her child.

In most cases the internal rhymes fall at unevenly spaced or dissymmetric intervals with the exception of "qu'un vent penche" in line

14 and the "fertiles îlots" in the following line. The direct and forceful concatenation of "qu'un vent penche" contrasts strongly with the titular *Brise marine* (which finds resonances in the invective *fuir*). This compacted rhyming unit is anticipated by the *allaitant / enfant / balançant / invitant* cluster above (*allaitant, balançant* and *invitant* form a cross-rhyme as they occupy the same metrical location within the Alexandrine line) and expands below into the last two lines of the poem with the rhyme scheme *sans / sans / entends / chant* (and the twin *sans* themselves participate within the doubled *sans mâts*). This *vent penchant inclines* the naufrages towards a loss which is stated through repetition: "Perdus, sans mâts, sans mâts, ni fertiles îlots." The masts which had earlier invited the winds ("les mâts, invitant les orages") are now lost amidst an echo of their loss as they have translated the *orages* into a *naufrage* with neither means of propulsion (*mâts*) nor destination (*fertiles îlots*); neither possibility remains within the space of echoes.

The sonorous cross-echoing is itself echoed by the main syntactic organization of the poem, which is concentrated in—but reverberates from—the first strophe. The clauses in lines 4 and 6–8 are actually (negative) subordinate clauses (which themselves also project further subordinate clauses) to the apodosis (consequent clause) in lines 4–5: "Rien… / Ne retiendra ce cœur qui dans la mer se trempe"; said subordination is stated through the *(rien) ni… (ne)… ni… ni* construction. The first protasis—"ni les vieux jardins…"—interrupts the negative apodosis "Rien ne." The interpolated placement of this subordinated clause violates the integrity of the main clause. In effect the subordination is stated through the paratactic juxtaposition of these clauses articulated by ni/ne, and this paratactic subordination is itself porous to the various sonorous juxtapositionings of the entire poem.[57] Indeed this extended clause is echoed in the penultimate line—the line of loss—with "ni fertile îlots."[58] This poem plays multiple *syntaxes* with and against each other within its enunciation.

One subordinate clause is not without relevance here: "Ô nuits! ni la clarté déserte de ma lampe / Sur le vide papier que la blancheur défend." Again a sonorous echo intensifies a sense here as the paper defends (d*é*fend) the clart*é* d*é*serte. The visible clarté is indeed defended by the repetition of the *sound* of the word; clarté is defended in a synæsthesia. This synæsthesia is crucial since it brings together both the echolalic aspects of the poem and the restrained action of writing (or rather of *not* writing, since the page is, after all, blank)—the action from which the poet wishes to flee, but cannot as he is to be hypothetically overtaken by the brise of *un vent penche*.[59] The poet cannot flee that which will hold him back (the clearness of the lamp and the page) as the poetic voice has already surrendered to being written, and what has been written is written through the rhythm of the naufrage. The whiteness of the page and the whiteness of the "adieu suprême des mouchoirs" become the sea's foam, the mother's milk, the ship's steam and the sails on its masts that invite the storm. In order to "lève l'ancre," the poet has had to *lève l'encre*. Writing destroys the escape that had destroyed the writing but could only destroy it by being written. The first strophe thus enstates a neither/nor clause of escape which becomes engulfed within a poetic iteration *as* interval of escape denied, which denies escape. The escape is suggested, suspended and denied all through a *disastrously fleeting interval*. The poem comes into being and *comes to naught*.[60] Even this fleeting interval of the poem's postulate and denial is itself denied with the final call to supplement the poem by hearing "le chant des matelots." The postulated departure and disaster are further relegated away from the poet to a faintly heard proximity. There is the poem's disaster, the disaster *evoked* in the poetic iteration (through all its cunning tricks) and then, there is, *there,* the evocation of *another* disaster. The poem thus has progressed as another, supplementary, sequence of contrary juxtapositionings which develop through concatenated interferences (not unlike the tightly intermixed detractive associations of *Salut*): the written poem supplements the sailors's song which itself supplements the naufrage which was postulated to supplement naughty nautical escape which was postulated to supplement the *ennui* of not being able to write a bloody poem in the first place (the circumstance of family turmoil insisted upon by Cohn as the singular occasion for the poem becomes but one more partial metonym in this chain).[61] *Brise marine* is thus a *crise de* *vers* in all its modalities: interrupted alexandrine, inability to write and désœuvrement. The poem is both a metonym for the *chant des matelots* while also simultaneously being completely apart. There is the *naufrage* of the burning white page, *there*.

∴

What then is the *issue* of this burning white page? What—if *rien*—survives the *don du poëme*? What is proffered there in the lieu of poetic iteration?

> Le vierge, le vivace et le bel aujourd'hui
> Va-t-il nous déchirer avec un coup d'aile ivre
> Ce lac dur oublié que hante sous le givre
> Le transparent glacier des vols qui n'ont pas fui!
>
> Un cygne d'autrefois se souvient que c'est lui
> Magnifique mais qui sans espoir se délivre
> Pour n'avoir pas chanté la région où vivre
> Quand du stérile hiver a resplendi l'ennui.
>
> Tout son col secouera cette blanche agonie
> Par l'espace infligée à l'oiseau que le nie,
> Mais non l'horreur du sol où le plumage est pris.
>
> Fantôme qu'à ce lieu son pur éclat assigne,
> Il s'immobilise au songe froid de mépris
> Que vêt parmi l'exil inutile le Cygne. (OC: 67–68; OCP: 308)

Marchal notes that *too easily* this poem lends itself to a symbolic reading, one could gloss the virginal white swan haplessly trapped upon the "blanche agonie" of a sheet of ice as a figuration for the poet striving and failing to achieve a work of writing upon blank pages, "le poème blanc de l'œuvre avortée" (Marchal 1985, 153).[62] This would produce a reading of the poem as an allegory of signification, an allegory for a *cygne* trying to free itself and become a *signe* or a producer (*assigner*) of signs; "this total defeat [of the trapped swan] through an absurd dilemma springs, via a meta-paradox, obliquely, into an unhoped-for victory, the poem" (Cohn 1980, 129). The poem, *selon* Cohn, is successful because it survives the swan as a monument of language. The facile glossing that Marchal decries would treat the poem as *reportage*: there is an incident there to be reported, restituted and *translated* into clear discourse, no matter how synæsthetically self-reflexive it may be. Furthermore, this translates the poem into a récit, a narrative of *signification* (even Marchal succumbs to this temptation; cf. Marchal 1985, 155–59). In order to read the poem symbolically there needs to be a minimal legibility that can be decoded, there needs to be a minimal *sign* that can be *reassigned*. For example: "The ice in which the bird is trapped is, at one level, these frozen layers of his past history, deep, crystallized dream-memories: *un cygne se souvient*" (Cohn 1980, 124). The poem, such a reading of this poem, is thus a *recherche d'un signe (cygne) perdu*. But perhaps, this perdurance of the sign is irrecoverable, perhaps—as Blanchot has suggested (see page 75)—the symbolic act negates even the accountability (ability to be subsumed as a récit) of itself, a "négation perpetuellement active" (Blanchot 1949, 84). To read the symbol in this way is to read it as the achievement of the *parole pur* precisely in that it achieves nothing.

In this poem each barest assignment of a sign is retracted. The first strophe establishes a subject but only through paratactic adjectival attributes (male, virginal, lively and lovely, all of which are contemporary, *aujourd'hui*) that could also function as separate nouns (*Le vierge, le vivace et le bel*). There is nothing in the first strophe to explicitly designate a cygne, said assigning falls in the second strophe, "Un cygne d'autrefois." However this assignment of a swan fails to exactly gloss the first line since the cygne is a cygne *d'autrefois*, as opposed to le vierge, le vivace et le bel *aujourd'hui*. In definitively assigning a *cygne*, the cygne becomes belated rather than contemporaneous. In this belatedness the "cygne d'autrefois *se souvient que c'est lui*." In belatedness the cygne remembers itself *to itself*, but this recollection does not guarantee it a presence other than this self-reflexivity. The cygne, once named as such, is already redoubled, without referent.[63]

Returning then to the first strophe—where the cygne remains temporarily anonymous in its very contemporaneity—the question there, as in *Brise marine,* concerns the possibility of *fuir*. This strophe poses the question or possibility that the as-yet unspecified subject might escape, "Va-t-il nous déchirer avec un coup d'aile ivre." But that from which he is to tear himself is already *not there*, it is a "lac dur *oublié*." Escape is useless because there is no thing to escape from.[64] Rather, that which is to be escaped from is only that which leaves a ghostly trace upon the frost above ("Ce lac dur oublié *que hante* sur le givre"). Like the cygne, the lake is belated, it is a *lac d'autrefois*.[65]

Construing the newly-introduced "nous" is more than somewhat difficult. Cohn simply treats it as a dative of interest ("will it rend *for us*"; Cohn 1980, 127), and such a happy parse is indeed ultimately correct. But the dative does not appear as such until the definitive object of déchirer is stated in the third line: "Ce lac dur oublié," is an object which itself, as noted above, absent; "in the hypothesis he makes, the subject of this interior monologue [the *nous*] is first torn and then the mere witness of tearing" (Bowie, 11). The verb, then, in the progression of the sentence from the second to the third line of the strophe, *tears* its direct object from *nous* to *ce lac*. Syntactic form is labile within the reading of this verse. *We* may be witnesses, in the syntactic position of witnessing, but even when the *nous* is comfortably settled within the dative of interest, it is not entirely removed from tearing. The hypothesized *fuite* at the end of this strophe would then be an inscription (a cleavage) upon the trace of the forgotten lake. That which has not yet been inscribed in the poem (the belated cygne) is to inscribe its fuite upon an icy sheet that supplements a lake. And yet even this merest possibility of inscription is itself belated, "vols qui n'ont pas fui!" Flight is inscribed as the path not taken, not inscribed (a *pas au-delà*). The poem's syntax defers and destabilizes the *assignment* of inscription, because of syntaxation one cannot definitively *assign*.

In the first tercet the cygne is further mired within whiteness *sans issue*. The cygne *is* in that it can deny the "blanche agonie" of the ice, and yet even in this strophe of a heroically attempted achievement of *cygnefication*, the *cygne* is still *not*. In the first strophe the cygne was absent, suggested only through attributes, in the second he was belated, and here he is relegated to a fragmented representation: its col and

plumage. The cygne, thus exists, is *assigned*, as the *imperceptible* trace of resistance ("Fantôme qu'à lieu son pur éclat assigne") against the trace of whiteness, the attempted effacement of white by an act of inscription. The *cygne* rests within the iterative dimension of le transparent glacier des vols qui n'ont pas fui, the iterative interval of a forgotten whiteness, a hangover of undrunken *fuite*.

This poem does not pronounce the success of the poet supplementing the failure of the aborted *fuite* of its symbolic representative, the cygne. Instead this cygne is the assignment of a failure of *cygnefication*. Marchal concludes his reading of this poem by noting that the suggestion of the constellation *Cygnus* (in French, *Cygne*, with a capital) is proleptic for *Un coup de dés*, a passage where "RIEN N'AURA EU LIEU QUE LE LIEU… EXCEPTÉ PEUT-ÊTRE UNE CONSTELLATION" (UC: 11a–12b; OC: 474–77; Marchal 1985, 159).[66] The issue, the product, or that which survives *is* the poem *tel quel* as a constellational interval: "l'écriture, ainsi, se dénonce, au moins, implicitement, comme un reste idéal, si bien que du cygne effacé par la glace il reste encore le poème du cygne, constellation si l'on veut, mais constellation de mots, et le Cygne final, avec sa majuscule emphatique, est moins la métamorphose stellaire du cygne que le titre manquant du poème ["Sonnet du Cygne"] qui se donne, au terme de cette épure ou de ce blanchiment, à lire enfin comme un cygne de mots" (Marchal 1985, 156–57). Extrapolating further from Marchal's very precise observation, the *cygne* is the mark of an absence of escape, the cygne is that which takes place within the interval of the poem (its constellation of words into a little sound, *le sonnet du Cygne*) *as* a belated escape (l'exil inutile). What survives the poem, the *issue of the poem*, is this very absence of *cygnefication disigillato*.

The very possibility that this hopeless situation can be written (inscribed on a blank field) is itself no cause for celebration. The *cygne* can be said to be symbolic in that it suggests something else, something that is absent taking its place (in the case of the predominant readings of this poem, this would be the figure of the poet). But, as argued above, the possibility of restituting this absence (of reading it into the poem as a presence, as a figure) is itself a virtual or fictitious hermeneutical

operation. "Le symbole ne signifie rien, il n'est pas même le sens en image d'une vérité qui autrement serait inaccessible, il dépasse toujours toute vérité et tout sens, et ce qu'il nous présente, c'est ce dépassement même qu'il saisit et rend sensible dans une fiction dont le thème est l'effort impossible de la fiction pour se réaliser en tant que fictive" (Blanchot 1949, 84–85). The very fictivity of the poetic iteration—the interval in which these symbolic and virtual rapports can be suggested— *assigns* the poem to a belated *vol qui n'a pas fui*.[67]

• • •

The Deman edition of Mallarmé's poems began with *Salut* and ended with a different tempestuous marine breeze, *À la nue accablante tu* (OC: 1341). Mallarmé's collection of poems, the collection he supervised, the lisible monument he left behind for posterity, is framed as an interval between bookends of disastrous sea-fares.

> À la nue accablante tu
> Basse de basalte et de laves
> À même les échos esclaves
> Par une trompe sans vertu
>
> Quel sépulcral naufrage (tu
> Le sais, écume, mais y baves)
> Suprême une entre les épaves
> Abolit le mât dévêtu
>
> Ou cela qui furibond faute
> De quelque perdition haute
> Tout l'abîme vain éployé
>
> Dans le si blanc cheveu qui traîne
> Avarement aura noyé
> Le flanc enfant d'une sirène. (OC: 76; OCP: 394)

The syntactic difficulties and conundrums posed in this poem are nothing short of formidable. Indeed Marchal attempts to reconstruct a normalized syntax for reading the poem (Marchal 1985, 251–52) and Cohn, in the translation accompanying his commentary, interpolates almost enough syncategoremata to effectively double the poem's length (Cohn 1980, 229–30). Mallarméan removal eliminates, indeed eviscerates, the syntactic logical connectives that enable a "couche suffisante d'intelligibilité." Kaufmann argues that to read sense into the poem (even contradictory, hypothetical, provisional senses) is to *force* a possibility of syntactic coherence to the sépulcral naufrage, thereby risking a naufrage of mastery (Kaufmann, 105). This view is echoed by Gérard Montbertrand who has proposed an elegant and precise reading of this poem's syntactic conundrums, difficulties so excessive that one cannot even assume an original level of stable lisibility. Parsing the poem is inordinately challenging since the procession of each sentence defies normal and normative syntax.[68] As David Scott has noted, the octosyllabic form is one such agent of syntactic instability through its use of enjambment (Scott, 158–60; cf. Montbertrand, 286). The problem of construing the *nous* from *Le vierge, le vivace et le bel d'aujourd'hui* infects this poem in its entirety. For example, the *tu* of the first line is not the second person singular pronoun, as an initial reading of the line alone might imply, but since there is no verb anywhere within the strophe to follow from this, or any substantive, this *tu* cannot be *tu*. Indeed, it is the past participle of *taire* (cf. Bénichou, 320).[69] An apparent subject conceals the verb, the first structuring agent required for a good parse.[70] The chief obstacle in reading this poem is a paucity of conjunctive elements, and those that remain, remain ambiguous. This echoes Derrida's point: the *crise de vers* is registered through a play of syntax; the arrangement of words yields the vibratory disparition. Because of this *épuisée* syntax, an iterated subject of the silencing (*tu!*) barely appears.

The subject is, by default, the sépulcral naufrage, but even there, there is not enough to attest to a figuration of the remains of maritime disaster. Marchal and Davies both read the poem as alternating between two proposed, possible scenes. The poem sails between the Scylla and Charybdis of two hypotheses gravitating around the "Ou" of the first tercet, which although contrary, do not necessarily invalidate the other (oddly enough, the proposals of both Marchal and Davies are not contradictory). Thusly construed the poem is an iteration of a dual

"*COMME SI*" "*dans quelque proche | tourbillon d'hilarité et d'horreur*" (UC: 7a–b; OC: 466–67). The first (sustained and proposed in the quatrains) concerns an absolute shipwreck, leaving no wreckage in the lieu of its wake; the second (tersely proposed in the tercets) a more discrete shipwreck, perhaps merely a wake of white spume left behind the drowning of a child siren (Marchal 1985, 253; Davies, 379). Davies proceeds to read the *mise-en-place* of these hypotheses and Marchal states that as with *Un coup de dés,* one is left with "une immense tatuologie, comme un tourbillon marin où s'abolit le temps fictif de l'existence" (Marchal 1985, 254).[71]

Neither approach is quite satisfactory. Certainly the naufrage is obscure, but there is, even in the silencings of the first strophe, a trace of some kind. The verb *tu* is, as noted above, obscured. It is as if the action of the first strophe, the lieu's keeping quiet, is itself hidden. Even silence cannot be vouchsafed here. Indeed "même les échos esclaves" have not been silenced (subjected to *tu*) through all the sonorous echoes in this strophe (*nue, tu, vertu; basse, bassalte*; and even *esclaves* echoes with *laves*). Within the second strophe the ambiguous silence is hypothesized as being the scene of a naufrage, known by *tu* as the écume (perhaps the écume that had left so many concatenated traces in *Salut*). Then there is the problem of the second *tu,* almost definitely a preposition, but with an ambiguous addressee. Although an integral subject, this *tu* is still compromised by its écho esclave to the first strophe's *tu* (cf. Montbertrand, 293). The *tu,* however construed its force may be, is rendered as *dévêtu* as any hypothetical naufrage that may or may not have left its trace in the interval of the wake.

The first hypothesis, of the total shipwreck of the quatrains, is the more disastrous, and yet the effect it leaves, the trace whereby it is knowable, is relatively minor: an écume where one salivates and smudges (*baves*). The second hypothesis leaves a trace of a different order, an "abîme vain éployé." If the shipwreck has itself been so stripped that it leaves no trace, then the turbulent sea itself—the scene of the ship *and of the shipwreck's* perdition—proffers no index of the disaster. The wake is formidably insouciant to disaster. The poem may be iterating a hypothetical disaster but it would then also have to admit a *third* hypothesis, that there had been no disaster to begin with, that there had been no disastrous origin for the "si blanc cheveu qui traine."[72] The event dissipates into an event that *might* never have been. The event is too hypothetical to claim either that it had not or had been, as with *Un coup de dés*, "*Tout se passe, par raccourci, en hypothèse*" (OC: 455). *As the snow under the sun exscribed*, the language has lost the possibility of the disaster. There is *not even* an absence of a naufrage to designate, merely the designation of the wake of la nue accablante silenced again, "beneath a sky without memory of morning or hope of night."[73]

The poem pronounces a hypothetical silencing of a *rien* that quivers between something, some naufrage, and nothing, no naufrage that could be there "dans ces parages

    du vague

        en quoi toute réalité se dissout"

(UC: 11b; OC: 475). As with Dante, poetic language is the scene of a loss so formidable that it cannot be designated, or rather designated *obliquely* through a dissolution of the possibilities of designation. Poetic language thus becomes rendered a disastrous *lieu* where there is a hypothetical *rien*, a *rien* whose thesis lies *elsewhere*, a rien that is neither nothing nor something but a *rien à venir*, an oscillation between the two; vain elocutory disparition within the interval of the obscuring, constellar ink upon the page. The poem's inscription, the *fact* (*fait*) that the poem has been inscribed, would then be evoked *not* by any self-reflexive, hermetic semantic indexing, but rather, simply, by the very form of the struggle between various syntaxes, the logic of the phrase impacting against enjambment and the engulfing marginal spume of the page's whiteness.[74] In the precise renderings of *rien*, *rien*—by being something—winds up (*aboutit à*) being less than no thing: the absence of inachievement achieved.

Notes

[1] Maurice Blanchot, *Faux pas,* Paris: Gallimard, 1943. 120; emphasis added.

[2] This is a point developed by Derrida, first in "Force et signification" (*L'écriture et la différence,* Paris: Seuil, 1967. 9–49. 10–11, *et passim*), and later, in extensive detail, in *La dissémination* where he argues that the *criticality* of the *crise* impacts against the possibility of a criticism deciding meaning or assigning a theme. There can be nothing for criticism to fix and decide upon, there. "Les conséquences *critiques:* celles qui doivent affecter la critique mallarméenne, puis la critique en général, liée, comme son nom l'indique, à la possibilité du décidable, au χρίνειν; mais aussi les effets critiques qu'une certaine re-marque ou re-trempe de l'espacement produit sur l'opération littéraire, sur la « littérature » qui dès lors entre en crise" (Jacques Derrida, *La dissémination,* Paris: Seuil, 1972. 267).

[3] Leo Bersani, *The Death of Stéphane Mallarmé,* Cambridge: Cambridge UP, 1982. 2.

[4] Following from Bersani's claims, Rebecca Saunders attempts to read a tenor of melancholy into Mallarméan poetics. "In the lamentation, the irrational significance... marks not only a moment when structures of meaning have been destroyed but also a moment when the world is alien because new. Thus in its *likeness* to the moment of lamentation, Mallarméan defilement *bears resemblance* to a world reoriginated through catastrophe" (Rebecca Saunders, "Shaking Down the Pillars: Lamentation, Purity, and Mallarmé's 'Hommage' to Wagner," *PMLA* 111.5 [October 1996]: 1106–20. 1112; emphasis added). On the one hand Saunders construes lamentation as a state of devastated differentiation apart from restitutive economies of representation, and on the other hand she has constructed an *analogous transference* between the vocabulary of lamentation and Mallarméan poetics by arguing for likeness and resemblance, an ὁμοίοσημος: that which is *proper* to Mallarméan poetry is likewise proper to the lexicon of purity, defilement and lamentation. As Lacoue-Labarthe writes, and Saunders cites, Mallarmé proffers "la critique impitoyable du semblant" (Philippe Lacoue-Labarthe, *Musica ficta (figures de Wagner),* Paris: Christian Bourgois, 1991. 107); Saunders translates "impitoyable" as "merciless" (Saunders, 1114), thereby divesting this word of a certain neutrality and rendering its valence more compatible with her argument.

[5] Jean-Pierre Richard—in his formidably cross-referenced work on Mallarmé, a work which suggests that all Mallarmé's work can be read as a perpetual revision of itself through the repetition of several major recurrent themes—counters the tendency to read *gravitas* into Mallarmé's poetics. Richard claims that Mallarmé possessed an extraordinary optimism in the processes of poetry and that he exhuberated within the possibilities of writing witnessed in the *crise de vers* (Jean-Pierre Richard, *L'univers imaginaire de Mallarmé*, Paris: Seuil, 1961. 35–38). Gérard Genette seconded these general observations in his review of Richard's book: "Bonheur de Mallarmé?" (*Figures I*, Paris: Seuil, 1966. 91–100. cf. esp. 97). It is not our concern to comment upon the personal happiness of M. Stéphane Mallarmé (although we understand that he did enjoy boating at Valvins), however we would like to suggest—following from Derrida's critique of Richard in "Force et signification" and *La dissémination* (see note 2)—that the experience of literature to which Richard refers might not have been a *power* which one could master.

[6] Maurice Blanchot, *La part du feu*, Paris: Gallimard, 1949. 85.

[7] The Greek word σύμβολον designates a broken hinge or toggled jointure, that which joins and that which separates, that which designates the one *by* designating the other. The predicament of the σύμβολον is thus an *insufficiency* of designation in that in being joined to a meaning, the meaning also remains disjoined (a *brisure* remarked by the polyvalence of the word σύμβολον itself).

[8] Blanchot is not alone in this contra-positivistic assessment of Symbolism: "Symbolism heightens [the problem of achieving a communication of a concept] more [than Romanticism] by seriously questioning whether any communication can be achieved. The French Symbolist movement is neither a generation nor a system, but a crisis" (Laurence M. Porter, "The Disappearing Muse: Erasure of Inspiration in Mallarmé," *Romanic Review* 76.4 [1985]: 389–404. 390–91). Hans-Jost Frey arrives at a similar conclusion: "Mallarmé's doubt is a doubt in language. Language, in speaking of itself, is made doubtful because it slips away from itself and at the same time posits itself as the very thing that slips away from itself. When the poem, where every position is playfully resolved, allows this tension to go unresolved, then it transpires as the place of doubt" (Hans-Jost Frey, *Studies in Poetic Discourse*, trans. William Whobry, Stanford: Stanford UP, 1996. 60).

[9] This citation above was also a draft of a letter to Charles Morice and was collected by Scherer as fragment 2 for the *Livre* (Jacques Scherer, *Le « Livre » de Mallarmé*, Paris: Gallimard, 1957, 1977. Feuillet 2 [suite]).

[10] Suzanne Bernard, *Mallarmé et la musique*, Paris: Nizet, 1959. 41–42. Bernard cites the following comment anecdotally attributed to Mallarmé: "Ce sont ces *blancs* qui me donnent le plus de mal! Ils ont la valeur des *silences* en musique. Ce sont eux qui créent le rêve, l'ineffable" (41).

[11] R.G. Cohn makes a similar argument in his reading of the Wagner essay, according to Cohn Mallarmé is implying that what Wagner should have done, instead of all that silliness squandered on a *Gesamtkunstwerk* was to have written *Un coup de dés* (R.G. Cohn, *Mallarmé's "Divagations,"* New York: Peter Lang, 1990. 112).

[12] The centrality of this strange and estranging possibility to Blanchot's reading of Mallarmé has been phrased precisely by de Man: "The poet thus encounters language as an alien and self-sufficient entity, not at all as if it were the expression of a subjective intent with which he could grow familiar, still less a tool that could be made to fit his needs" (Paul de Man, "Impersonality in the Criticism of Maurice Blanchot," *Blindness and Insight,* revised edition, Minneapolis: U of Minnesota P, 1983. 60–78. 69). To write then, for Blanchot's Mallarmé is to surrender oneself and one's initiative—to be sacrificed—to this inhuman alterity of language. In his review of Bersani's book, Denis Hollier notes an affinity between Bersani and Blanchot, especially in how both critics insist upon the negativity of the Livre to which Mallarmé had surrendered himself: "Le livre n'est pas présentable, il ne l'a jamais été et ne le sera jamais" (Denis Hollier, "La littérature ne repose sur rien," *Critique* 431 [April 1983]: 271–286. 279).

[13] Evocation is oscillational (incantatory): "Évoquer, dans une ombre exprès [the tenebrity of ink], l'objet ti, par des mots allusifs, jamais directs, se réduisant à du silence égal, comporte tentative proche de créer: vraisemblable dans la limite de l'idée uniquement mise en jeu par l'enchanteur de lettres jusqu'à ce que, certes, scintille, quelque illusion égale au regard. Le vers, trait incantatoire!" (OC: 400).

[14] Yves Bonnefoy, "The Poetics of Mallarmé," trans. Elaine Ancekewicz, *Yale French Studies* 54 (1977): 9–21. 12.

[15] Jacques Derrida, "Mallarmé," *Tableau de la littérature française de Mme. De Staël à Rimbaud,* Marcel Arland et al, Paris: Gallimard, 1974. 368–79. 375. This essay is a brief, programmatic restatement of the first part of "La double séance," but with important additional references to Mallarmé's poems.

Barbara Johnson makes a similar point in reference to the poem *l'Azur.* By ending the poem with "*Je suis hanté.* L'Azur! l'Azur! l'Azur! l'Azur!" (OC: 38; OCP: 152 l.36), Mallarmé is not so much haunted by "an ideal symbolized by azure but [by] the very word 'azure' itself" (Barbara Johnson, "*Les fleurs du mal armé,*" *Lyric Poetry,* eds. Chaviva Hošek and Patricia Parker, Ithaca: Cornell UP, 1985. 264–80. 269). Mallarmé thus *re-marks* the word as the cliché it has become in French poetry. In his recent study of Mallarmé, Graham Robb arrives at a very similar conclusion, albeit and perhaps mercifully without recourse to a lexicon of theory. Robb claims that Mallarméan prosody (specifically his use of rhyme) is a language-game which, while influenced by the norms of classical French verse, highlights its own linguisticality thereby divesting the poem from the very possibility of a pretense of signification and reference: "the foregrounding of the material aspects of words eats away at their capacity to refer to things" (Graham Robb, *Unlocking Mallarmé,* New Haven: Yale UP, 1996. 66; cf. 32–42).

[16] Indeed the preferred example is the sonority of the word *or,* the *son or.* In reading the opening paragraph of *Igitur* Derrida notes: "*Or,* est-ce ici un mot ou plusieurs? Le linguiste dira peut-être—et le philosophe—que chaques fois, le sens et la fonction étant autres, nous devons lire un mot différent. Et pourtant cette diversité se croisse et repasse par un simulacre d'identité dont il faut bien rendre compte. Ce qui circule ainsi, pour n'être pas une famille de synonymes, est-ce le masque simple d'une homonymie? Mais il n'y a pas de nom: la chose même est (l')absente, rien n'est simplement nommé, le nom est aussi une conjonction ou un adverbe. Non avantage de mot: l'efficace est souvent d'une syllabe où le mot s'éparpille. Ni homonymie, donc, ni synonymie" (Derrida 1974, 377; cf. Derrida 1972, 295–97 fn. 54). Silencing is thus expended in syntactic deploy without reference to (semantic) reserve. Indeed by emphasizing that this destabilizing play is already in effect in *Igitur,* Derrida radicalizes Blanchot. For Blanchot, *Igitur* is bounded by the attempt to master death by essaying the coincidence between death and midnight (cf. Maurice Blanchot, *L'espace littéraire,* Paris: Gallimard, 1955, 1988. 143–44). Unlike *Un coup de dés, Igitur* retains a possibility of *comprehending* catastrophe or disaster. Derrida's reading of the destabilizing resonances of the *son or* denies this *determining* possibility for *Igitur.* We will deal with *Igitur* in some detail in the next chapter.

[17] Cohn counters Derrida's reading, which centers around the deployment of the double valence of the word *hymen*—vaginal membrane and consummation of marriage (said membrane ruptured), a *khôra* of the page and sexual union: "Ni l'avenir ni le présent, mais entre les deux. ... Si l'un ou l'autre avait lieu, il n'y aurait pas d'hymen" (Derrida 1972, 241)—by noting that the Littré dictionary preferred ὑμνός (hymn) as etymological forefather over ὑμήν (membrane) (although Liddell-Scott do suggest a filiation, as the name of the god Ὑμήν carries the force of a wedding-song). Beyond the etymological argument, Cohn prefers a *symbolic* supplementarity over the syntactic one that Derrida proposes around *hymen* (R.G. Cohn, "Mallarmé sur Derrida," *Vues sur Mallarmé*, Paris: Nizet, 1991. 273–82). Obviously Cohn had failed to consult the following *dédicace:* "Il ne faut pas serrer les nœuds de ton hymen / Avant d'avoir passé le sinistre examen" (OC: 166; OCP: 676).

[18] "Si l'on obéit à l'invitation de ce grand espace blanc laissé à dessein au haut de la page comme pour séparer de tout, le déjà lu ailleurs, si l'on arrive avec une âme vierge, neuve, on s'apperçoit alors que *je suis profondément et scrupuleusement syntaxier*, que mon écriture est dépourvue d'obscurité, que ma phrase est ce qu'elle doit être et être pour toujours" (quoted in Jacques Scherer, *L'expression littéraire dans l'œuvre de Mallarmé*, Paris: Nizet, 1947. 79, emphasis added). Derrida cites this from Scherer (Derrida 1972, 205–6; Derrida 1974, 371).

[19] Derrida is not the first to have emphasized the role of syntax in Mallarmé. Scherer's 1947 study treats the matter and the updated *Grammaire de Mallarmé* extends his study greatly. Scherer claims that Mallarmé's lexical innovations and obscurities pale beside the difficulties posed by his use of syntax. But Scherer reads this syntactic obscurity as serving an essentially restitutive function. "Il est donc nécessaire de disposer les mots pour que leurs différentes valeurs puissent coexister, pour qu'elles ne se contredisent pas, qu'elles s'équilibrent au contraire en un ensemble harmonieux" (Jacques Scherer, *Grammaire de Mallarmé*, Paris: Nizet, 1977. 161–62).

[20] This paradox between the monument and its effacement is modulated in multiple ways throughout Mallarmé's œuvre. This is phrased within *Quant au livre* as the problem of suicide: suicide does not effect mastery in that one can never *make* one's death present, make one's absentation manifest presently. "Le suicide ou abstention, ne fait rien, pourquoi?—Unique fois au monde, parce qu'en raison d'un

événement toujours que j'expliquerai, *il n'est pas de Présent, non—un présent n'existe pas*" (OC: 372; emphasis added). The problem with suicide is that it affirms, by destruction, a present, but there is no present *there* to affirm or subvert—except for the simulacrum of a present which *mimics* a non-originary present.

[21] This œuvre has been compiled variously. Since Mondor and Jean-Aubry's edition of the *Œuvres complètes* appeared in 1945 for Gallimard-Pléiade, various additional documents, fragments and miscellany have been published thereby correcting several tangible deficiencies in that volume (such as Scherer's edition of the surviving notes for the *Livre*, Mondor's edition of the juvenilia, Richard's edition of *Pour un tombeau d'Anatole*, Davies's edition of the *Hérodiade* manuscript, additional *vers de circonstance* reproduced in the volumes of the *Correspondances* [indeed additional letters have been published in the journal *French Studies* between 1986 and 1988], and additional manuscripts, some of which have appeared in the seven volumes of Carl Barbier's *Documents Mallarmé* [1969–80]). Lamentably, Barbier's death curtailed the new edition of the *Œuvres complètes* he was preparing with Charles Gordon Millan for Éditions Flammarion (cf. OCP: vii–xiii); the first volume, the verse, appeared in 1983 and the remaining two volumes, prose and translations, have been postponed indefinitely. Bertrand Marchal is currently preparing a new edition of the Pléiade for Éditions Gallimard. He notes that the failure to marshal Mallarmé's multiplicitous *bribes* into a single cogent edition of an *œuvre complète* bespeaks the discontinuity that has marked Mallarmé's work, and any editor ambitious enough to confront Mallarmé's visible output would have to respect this (Bertrand Marchal, "Éditer Mallarmé," *Genesis* 6 [1994]: 167–77. cf. esp. 168–70).

[22] The ability to enact a critical distinction between the œuvres "pures" and the œuvres "de circonstance" has been questioned and thrown into doubt. Even Scherer—who heroically undertook to propose schematic distinctions between the two—admitted that, to varying degrees, most of Mallarmé's output could be called "circumstantial." However the main tenor of Scherer's argument is to establish how the impersonality that Mallarmé had claimed ("je suis parfaitement mort") implies a non-circumstantiality to the œuvre: "Pour écrire le Livre, il faudra se délivrer complètement de la circonstance" (Scherer 1957, 17; cf. 11–17). Bersani, arguing from the same claims of impersonality, emphasizes instead the rampant contingency of the majority of Mallarmé's visible output and proposes that the project of the Livre was directly involved with a sustained relation to the contingent. Bersani remarks that most of the notes in the *Livre* deal with the performative qualities of specific

iterations rather than with conceptual matters regarding an overall essence of the work, and furthermore that there are even certain thematic affinities between circumstantial works (such as *La dernière mode*) and the Livre (Bersani, 50–55). Marion Zwerling Sugano further develops the implications of this claim with close readings culled throughout the entire range of Mallarmé's œuvre to suggest that the negativity of the œuvre is sustained by a contingency which is directly remarked by the circumstantial verse: "Viewed within Mallarmé's entire œuvre, the *Vers de circonstance* become a comment on the very circumstantiality of literature" (Marion Zwerling Sugano, *The Poetics of the Occasion*, Stanford: Stanford UP, 1992. 195). Vincent Kaufmann has argued that the circumstantial writings (such as Mallarmé's magazine *La dernière mode*) could be construed *en masse* as the grand Livre because they put into play a fictitious space, a virtual reality for the sake of propagating symbolic codes: they assume a certain rapport between the writing and its enunciation, only to then highlight the fictionality of said rapport: a speech act speaking the virtuality (and virtuosity) of the act. The circumstantial works attest to the virtuality of the Livre in that by their existence the Livre remains unwritten and *à venir* (Vincent Kaufmann, *Le livre et ses adresses,* Paris: Méridiens Klincksieck, 1986. 42–44). Kaufmann thus implies that that vers de circonstance render the Livre as being suitably apophatic.

[23] "C'est sous le signe de la musique, en effet, que les poètes Symbolistes vont combattre pour libérer la forme poétique du joug de la versification classqiue et de chercher des formes plus souples, plus fluides, et des harmonies neuves. Mallarmé, retraçant la « crise » du vers classqiue, impute à la disparition de Hugo, incomparable artisan de la versification, la rupture avec la tradition" (Bernard, 11). Bernard adroitly notes that the inscrutable vagaries of Mallarméan syntax can be traced to this emphasis upon lexical (as opposed to traditional) musicality; indeed Mallarmé called the Livre a recherche "devant un brisure des grands rythmes littéraires" (OC: 367).

[24] David H.T. Scott, "Mallarmé and the Octosyllabic Sonnet," *French Studies* XXXI.2 (April 1977): 149–63. 151; cf. 150. See also our reading of *À la nue accablante tu* on page 102 and following.

[25] It is of course commonplace within Mallarméan criticism to ascribe the forging of Mallarmé's poetics within the smithy of the *crise* of the 1860s. Since the major feature of this crise was an inability to write verse, criticism is relegated to the self-consciously agonized correspondence for documentation. Paul Bénichou proffers the following useful commentary on these: "Ce que nous avons dans ses lettres, c'est la

légende de sa destinée poétique telle qu'il entend lui-même l'avoir vécue" (Paul Bénichou, *Selon Mallarmé,* Paris: Gallimard, 1995. 49 fn. 64). Thusly construed, the voice in the letters announces itself as a captive *témoin* to an unfolding nasty adventure of *poiesis*: "tout cela n'a pas été trouvé par le développement normal de mes facultés, mais par la voie pécheresse et hâtive, satanique et *facile*, de la Destruction de moi, produisant non la force, mais une sensibilité qui, fatalement, m'a conduite là" (CI: 246). Such an account is not without analogy to one proffered in *Crise de vers:* "Témoin de cette aventure, où l'on me voulut un rôle plus efficace quoiqu'il ne convient à personne, j'y dirigeai, au moins, mon fervent intérêt, et il se fait temps d'en parler, préférablement à distance ainsi que ce fut presque anonyme" (OC: 361). To even merely *suggest* the crise is to already have surrendered to its turbulent anonymity and apartness.

[26] "La crise de vers (du « rythme », dit aussi bien Mallarmé) engage donc toute la littérature. La crise du *rythmos* brisé par l'être... est « fondamentale ». Elle sollicite les fondations mêmes de la littérature, la prive, dans son jeu, de tout fondement hors de soi. La littérature est à la fois assurée est menacée de ne reposer que sur elle-même, en l'air, toute seule, à l'écart de l'être" (Derrida 1972, 311–12).

[27] "Les monuments, la mer, la face humaine, dans leur plénitude, natifs, conservent une vertu autrement attrayante que ne les voilera une description, évocation dites, *allusion* je sais, *suggestion:* cette terminologie quelque peu de hasard atteste la tendance, une très décisive, peut-être, qu'ait subie l'art littéraire, elle le borne et l'exempte. Son sortilège, à lui, si ce n'est libérer, hors d'une poignée de poussière ou réalité sans l'enclore, au livre, même comme texte, la dispersion volatile soit l'esprit, qui n'a que faire de rien outre la musicalité de tout" (OC: 366).

[28] In this essay Blanchot counters Valéry's reading of Mallarmé as having achieved a perfection of art. "Il en résulte que les idées de Mallarmé ont trouvé dans l'œuvre de Valéry leur réalisation la plus complète, sinon la plus représentatif" (Blanchot 1949, 36)—but there, as Hamlet would say, is the rub: Blanchot reads Mallarmé as explicitly undoing the myth of achieved representation. Blanchot's undying insistence upon a reservoir of negativity within Mallarméan *poiesis* thus actually comes quite close to repeating some of the charges leveled against Mallarmé by his earliest critics, *to wit* Jean-Marc Bernard's claim in 1913 that Mallarmé "n'a point créé une œuvre littéraire véritable, ni ne pouvait le faire" (quoted in D. Hampton Morris, *Stéphane*

Mallarmé, 20th Century Criticism 1901–71, Valencia: Romance Monographs, 1977. 16).

[29] This passage from *Crise de vers* thus amplifies Mallarmé's initial, infamous gropings towards a poetics, *towards (a crise de) vers* whilst at work on *Hérodiade* (a crise that had already overtaken him): "Avec terreur, car j'invente une langue qui doit nécessairement jaillir d'une poétique très nouvelle, que je pourrais définir en ces deux mots: *Peindre, non la chose, mais l'effet qu'elle produit.* Le vers ne doit donc pas, là, se composer des mots; mais d'intentions, et toutes les paroles s'effacer devant la sensation" (CI: 137).

[30] "L'œuvre littéraire y est en suspens entre sa présence visible et sa présence lisible: partition ou tableau qu'il faut lire et poème qu'il faut voir et, grâce à cette alternance oscillante, cherchant à enrichir la lecture analytique par la vision statique par le dynamisme du jeu des mouvements, ... c'est voir et lire, mais se plaçant aussi au point où, la jonction n'étant pas faite, le poème occupe seulement le vide central qui figure l'avenir d'exception" (Maurice Blanchot, *Le livre à venir,* Paris: Gallimard, 1959, 1986. 328).

[31] This is the problem of fragmentary writing which Blanchot diagnoses: one could not even designate fragmentary writing *as such*, because in so doing one would have to assume a totality, whence comes dissolution and fragmentation. "Le fragmentaire: écrire relève du fragmentaire quand tout a été dit. Il faudrait qu'il y eût épuisement de parole et par la parole, achèvement de tout (de la présence comme tout) comme logos, pour que l'écriture fragmentaire pût se laisser re-marquer. Toutefois, nous ne pouvons pas ainsi, écrivant, nous libérer d'une logique de la totalité en la considérant comme idéalement accomplie, afin de maintenir comme « pu reste » une possibilité d'écriture, hors tout, sans emploi ou sans terme, dont une autre logique, encore difficile à dégager (celle de la répétition, des limites et du retour), prétendrait nous garantir l'étude" (Maurice Blanchot, *Le pas au-delà,* Paris: Gallimard, 1973. 62). The fragmentary is therefore not subsumable to language as a fragmentation (as a *being* fragmented) for then it would be *recognizable*, recognizable as one of the first two modulations of the exigency. "Le fragmentaire s'énonce peut-être au mieux dans un langage qui ne reconnaît pas" (*ibid*).

[32] This hinges to a decisive difference between de Man and Blanchot, the implications of which we reserve for our following chapter. For de Man, literature is in effect a *crude word*, a reportage issued from the place where this "negative knowledge about the reliability of linguistic utterance is made available" (Paul de

Man, *The Resistance to Theory*, Minneapolis: U of Minnesota P, 1986. 10). Indeed in his meticulous elaboration of this claim, in the elucidation of the hazards of confusing linguistic with phenomenal reality, de Man slyly notes that "no one in his right mind will try to grow grapes by the luminosity of the word 'day'" (11). The word "day"—like the word "fleur"—does not illuminate *res*. All de Man has done here is to note a Hegelian negativity of language: literature as reportage of the absence which it signifies. Elsewhere, in an essay devoted to Mallarmé's negativity, de Man makes a similar point by claiming that Mallarmé's poetic act of naming the discord between *res* and *verba* restores an ontological authenticity by denying the efficacious instrumentality of the word (Paul de Man, "Poetic Nothingness," trans. Richard Howard, *Critical Writings, 1953–1978*, ed. Lindsay Waters, Minneapolis: U of Minnesota P, 1989. 18–29. 21). However, what Mallarmé suggests is another possibility—that of the pure word—in which the word is made to no longer even refer to its lack of referentiality. Like de Man, Blanchot holds that literature—in that such could be said to even exist—"est le langage qui se fait ambiguïté" (Blanchot 1949, 328), but this ambiguity cannot be redeemed as and by a negative knowledge in that the ambiguity (authentic or otherwise) is not even *there to be known*. As Heidegger would (and did) say: "The poetic work speaks out of an ambiguous ambiguousness" (Martin Heidegger, *On the Way to Language*, trans. Peter D. Hertz, San Francisco: Harper and Row, 1971. 192).

[33] Cohn's account of the mot Mallarméan initially seems to converge with Blanchot's account of the parole essentiel: "le poème est le produit de plusieurs facteurs additifs (ou mieux multiplicatifs); supprimez-en un seul, par exemple ici le sens, et cela suffit à détruire l'ensemble de l'effet, tout comme d'ajouter des moustaches à la Joconde…. Le mot mallarméen est une convergence de toutes ses virtualités: pluralité de sens, étymologie, son forme des lettres, « éléments » constitutifs (mots à l'intérieur d'autres mots), échos et valeurs harmonqiues…" (R.G. Cohn, *L'œuvre de Mallarmé*, "*Un coup de dés*," Paris: Les Lettres, 1951. 92). Cohn has herewith related that the cunning accretion (to the point, perhaps, of overload) of diverse indices of *sens* effects a dispassionate cross-circuit of meaning, thereby producing a new "poetic" effect irrecuperable within economies of meaning; quite simply *sens* transverses itself through meticulous attention to detail. For Blanchot, this would still be within the register of the parole brut, since with the parole essentiel, *sens* had never been there to have been upset.

[34] "À un premier regard [and this citation marks Blanchot's *premier regard* concerning the double nature of words], l'intérêt du langage est donc de détruire, par

sa puissance abstraite, la réalité matérielle des choses, et de détruire, par la puissance d'évocation sensible des mots, cette valeur abstraite" (Blanchot 1949, 38).

[35] Blanchot has been accused of negativizing Mallarmé excessively, of reading *too much* absentation into Mallarmé' œuvre. De Man articulates this as Blanchot's remaining "within a negative subject/object dialectic in which an impersonal non-subject confronts an abolished non-object ('rien' or 'l'absente')" (de Man 1983, 71 n. 9), and this position might be more relevant for Blanchot than for Mallarmé. By virtue of being written, Mallarmé's œuvre might not proffer a site for désœuvrement. There might be *too much there* for there to be désœuvrement in Mallarmé. Roger Laporte has leveled a similar charge against Blanchot's own work (and specifically against Blanchot's reading of Mallarmé), that Blanchot's writings on silence are *loud* and thereby he too converts the negative into words: "Si la silence est notre destinée, pourquoi prendre la plume?... pourquoi Blanchot lui-même, qui parle du désœuvrement, a-t-il écrit une œuvre qui compte déjà plus de cinq mille pages? Le Livre est impossible, mais la page blanche ne l'est pas moins, car tout se passe *comme si* entre écrire et le silence il y avait un chemin interminable, *comme si* l'absence de livre exigeait l'infinité du mouvement d'écrire" (Roger Laporte, *À l'extrême pointe: Bataille et Blanchot,* Montpellier: Fata Morgana, 1994. 37; emphasis added). It is this chemin innterminable (or entretien infini) between writing and silence that mediates the work-as-unworking in the space of a hypothesis (the "comme si" of *Un coup de dés*). Hypothetically the book is written, and hypothetically the book is silenced. The book, such as it is, is the hypothetical passage within *parages* divested of any defining end-points.

[36] Indeed, Walter Benjamin cites this passage in "The Task of the Translator" as an argument for translation's power to *ripen the seed of language*. In a text on the task of the translator Benjamin has, as Derrida points out, cited Mallarmé in the *original* French. "Benjamin vient d'abord de renoncer à traduire Mallarmé" (Jacques Derrida, "Des tours de babel," *Psyché,* Paris: Galilée, 1987. 203–35. 213).

[37] De Man emphasizes a fundamental intralinguistic *Aufgabe* of the translator in his essay on Benjamin: "All these activities—critical philosophy, literary theory, history—resemble each other in the fact that they do not resemble that from which they derive. But they are all intralinguistic: they relate to what in the original belongs to language, and not to meaning as an extralinguistic correlate susceptible of paraphrase and imitation. They disarticulate, they undo the original, they reveal that the original was always already disarticulated" (de Man 1986, 84). Poetic language

thus indicates the negative knowledge of a pure language (*Reinesprache*), it indicates that the pure language has no involvement with poetic language (92).

Derrida would counter this statement of negative knowledge by asserting that the plurality of language is *bottomless* and cannot be lived as a negativity. In "Des tours de Babel" he takes Benjamin to task for positing the "original"; he interrogates the originality of the origin, which is precisely what de Man elides in "Conclusions." By simply positing "negative knowledge," de Man *admits* to an original—in a state of fragmentation, a literary absolute.

[38] This notion allows Sollers, Derrida and Blanchot to formulate Bataillian statements through Mallarméan discourse, *to wit:* "L'erreur esthétique fondamentale—l'erreur économico-politique—consiste à croire que le langage est un simple instrument représentatif" (Philippe Sollers, "Littérature et totalité," *Logiques,* Paris: Seuil, 1968. 97–117. 105). Derrida points out that Mallarmé marked himself in opposition to æsthetics and political economy—the two *promising* new sciences of the nineteenth century: sciences which aimed at restituting everything, even the most accursèd share, into their discursive orbits. "Tout se résume dans l'Esthétique et l'Économie politique" (OC: 656). In this way they are both *alchemical* practices, magically transforming the worthless into valuation (Derrida 1974, 369–70). The crisis of Mallarmé is to mime these magical transformations in such a rigorous and exacting manner that an arbitration of value is no longer possible.

[39] Graham Robb, "Mallarmé's False Friends," *French Studies Bulletin* 49 (Winter, 1993): 13–15. 14.

[40] Mallarmé no doubt was following from Poe's privileging of effect over meaning in the "Philosophy of Composition"; this valorization is why Poe claims he chose the *-or* rhyme scheme for *The Raven* (Edgar Allan Poe, "The Philosophy of Composition," *Complete Tales and Poems,* eds. Arthur Hobson Quinn and Edward H. O'Neill, New York: Barnes and Noble, 1992. 978–87. 978–82). For an account of how this poem-as-such can be reduced to its language-games with prosody, see Robb 1996, 62–67 and Catherine Lowe, "Le mirage de ptyx: implications à la rime," *Poétique* 59 (September 1984): 325–45. For an account of the relation between this sonnet and its predecessor, the *Sonnet allégorique en lui-même* [OCP: 220], see Bénichou, 135–50 and Lawrence M. Porter, "The Disappearing Muse: Erasure of Inspiration in Mallarmé," *Romantic Review* 76.4 (1985): 389–404. 398–404.

[41] In the corrected version to the published text of this letter appears Mallarmé's request for words ending in -yx since he is a "poëte en quête d'une rime" (CXI: 110).

[42] Paul Allen Miller has noted a poetic precedent for this Greek word in Pindar's first Olympian ode as a designation of the poetic: "$\kappa\lambda\upsilon\tau\alpha\hat{\iota}\sigma\iota\ \delta\alpha\iota\delta\alpha\lambda\omega\sigma\acute{\epsilon}\mu\epsilon\nu\ \H{\upsilon}\mu\nu\omega\nu\ \pi\tau\upsilon\chi\alpha\hat{\iota}\varsigma$ [(the victor... whom) I shall glorify with sounding bouts of song]" (Pindar, *The Odes*, ed. and trans. John Sandys, Cambridge: Harvard UP, 1915. Ol. I.105). The scholiasts interpret the use of $\pi\tau\acute{\upsilon}\xi$ here as referring to the various turns of the choral ode, such as strophe, antistrophe and epode, the pleats in the fabric of *making poetry*. It is also worth noting that $\pi\tau\acute{\upsilon}\xi$ can refer to the folds of a writing tablet, or even synecdochically to the tablet itself (this is more explicit in a related word, $\pi\tau\upsilon\kappa\tau\acute{o}\varsigma$, *folded,* or *folded tablet*). Therefore $\pi\tau\acute{\upsilon}\xi$ could refer to Pindar's inscriptive act as well as to the sounding of the poem. Poetry is thus *sounded* through imbrications or folds. "*Ptyx* thus comes to stand not only for verse or rhyme but for the very possibility of poetry itself—"ce seul objet dont le Néant s'honore"—for that convergence of forces that makes writing possible" (Paul Allen Miller, "Black and White Myths: Etymology and Dialectics in Mallarmé's 'Sonnet en yx,'" *Texas Studies in Literature and Language* 36.2 [Summer 1994]: 184–211. 205; see also Gretchen Kromer, "The Redoubtable PTYX," *MLN* 86.4 [May 1971]: 563–72 who argues that Mallarmé was unaware of the Greek resonance of ptyx).

[43] As has been noted by Kaufmann, Hollier and Hill, Scherer's publication of the notes towards the *Livre* required a certain response from Blanchot, who had insisted (since "La silence de Mallarmé" in 1943, the review of Mondor's biography) upon the absence of the Livre (Kaufmann, 189–90; Hollier, 276–78; Hill, 906). In *Le livre à venir* Blanchot turns away from the readings that had culminated in the Orphic paroles essentiel and brut in *L'espace littéraire,* and moves towards a renewed insistence upon the negativity of the Livre (hence also Blanchot's interest in Joubert). In essence the trajectory of Blanchot's readings of Mallarmé follows the implications of the "le livre, expansion totale de la lettre" (OC: 380): Blanchot expands his focus on the *lieu* of absentation from *la parole* to *le livre*.

[44] The implications of this propel Blanchot's readings of Mallarméan *désœuvrement* from *L'espace littéraire* to *L'entretien infini*. In the former, the exigency of communication is phrased in terms of reading an incompletion of that which was

already inachieved, the *work (l'œuvre)*. In this legible interval of incompletion there is the book as the withdrawal of the work: "Lire, ce serait lire dans le livre l'absence de livre, en conséquance la produire, là où il n'est pas question que le livre soit absent ou présent (défini par une absence ou une présence)" (Maurice Blanchot, *L'entretien infini*, Paris: Gallimard, 1969. 626). The book—that which subsists within an economy of achievement—is nonetheless *predicated* upon its absentation: to read the book (that which can be read) is to read by the *darkness* of the absence of the book. An achievement of legibility is therefore predicated upon an intangible and unlocatable difference between the book and the absence of the book—which is to say upon an interval, "Un vide d'univers: rien qui fût visible, rien qui fût invisible" (620). The livre vibrates as the emptiness of a *vers* become uni*vers*al, an oscillation of *rien*—ill seen, ill said.

[45] For a poet with such lofty ambitions, Mallarmé's frequent use of the sonnet-form seems a tad odd. Indeed, in an 1862 letter to Cazalis, he explains this bizarre mania: "Tu riras peut-être de ma manie de sonnets... mais pour moi c'est un grand poème en petit: les quatrains et les tercets me semblent des chants entiers, et je passe parfois trois jours à en équilibrer d'avance les parties, pour que le tout soit harmonieux et s'approche du Beau" (CI: 32). The sonnet-form is *another syntax* in which verse can be *condensed* or attenuated, and this process of attenuation is itself— in attenuated form—the motion of a larger poem, of the Œuvre.

[46] Describing the former occasion (the banquet) in the context of the latter (the Deman edition) Mallarmé wrote "Ce sonnet, en levant le verre, récemment à un Banquet de *la Plume,* avec l'honneur d'y présider" (OC: 1406). Sugano notes that in this description, the subject—the speaker of honor—is elided in the act of raising *the* glass with no attributive possessive pronoun (Sugano, 46).

[47] Bertrand Marchal, *Lecture de Mallarmé,* Paris: José Corti, 1985. 13. When published in the Deman edition of the Poésies, Mallarmé wrote on the title page that the reader is herewith "appelé à son tour à l'incertaine navigation de la lecture" (quoted in Robb 1996, 193).

[48] R.G. Cohn, *Towards the Poems of Mallarmé,* revised edition, Berkeley: U of California P, 1980. 33. Kaufmann makes a similar point: "le toast s'y désigne lui-même comme n'étant *rien;* il est vierge de signification et ne fait que renvoyer au geste de célébration de la coupe levée, (se) signifiant ainsi (dans) le lien qu'il institue" (Kaufmann, 46); as does Sugano: "The act [of the toast] is identical with

the utterance of the act" (Sugano, 46); and the venerable Paul Bénichou: "le poème ne dit pas autre que le toast qu'elle porte" (Bénichou, 326).

[49] In the context of *Salut*, Bénichou notes that syntactic vehicle for this confluence of readings is the "telle" of the third line (Bénichou, 326 fn. 1).

[50] In his typical and typically invaluable frenzy of cross-referencing, Cohn notes an instance of écume with specific resonance to this poem, in "Le portrait enchanté" from *Les contes indiens* there is "l'écume qui n'est rien" (OC: 594; Cohn 1980, 33).

[51] "Mallarmé obviously enjoyed the harmony of *tele* (Greek: 'far' [$\tau\hat{\eta}\lambda\epsilon$]) with the *loin*" (Cohn 1980, 34). If, as Bénichou claims, *telle* marks the syntactic confluence of the diverse outings, then said confluence is already disturbed through the etymological concatenation of this word with *loin*.

[52] Cohn reads *ivresse belle* as a beautiful drunkenness, as the drunkenness of the poetic voice (Cohn 1980, 35); it does seem passing strange that the poet would be drunk before having completed the toast. Bénichou prefers to displace the drunkenness to a muse (*une* ivresse belle) who inspires the *salut* to poetry (Bénichou, 327). This reading harmonizes nicely with Cohn's insistence upon reading in a feminine-masculine opposition throughout Mallarmé's œuvre.

[53] The "chant des mariniers" (l. 14) that concludes Baudelaire's poem reflects the light of a lightly ironized lassitude of sexual satisfaction; there the sea-travel and the satisfactions by the "rivages heureux / Qu'éblouissent les feux d'un soleil monotone" (ll. 3–4) were successful, if tiresome (Charles Baudelaire, "Parfum exotique," *Œuvres complètes, I,* ed. Claude Pichois, Paris: Gallimard, 1975. 25–26).

[54] Cohn, in his typical mode of annotating sound-sense, notes this repetition and emphasizes a fleeting character of the vocable *f* (as well as of the other vocal constituents of the word), but in so doing he reiterates the word's underlying semanticity: "the breezy effect of *f* was noted by Plato in his *Cratylus*. Mallarmé uses it nicely in his fan poems, flute poems, etc. (*Faune:* 'instrument des fuites'). The flat *a* in *là-bas* brings out the horizontal perspective of flight by sea-voyage, *way out yonder*— and sets up the next *fuir* with its acute *i* and *u*, bright as the foam, intense as the yearning; the *r* is helpfully liquid. Great word, *fuir,* hence repeated" (Cohn 1980, 290).

[55] The earlier version of this poem (1865) lacked almost all of these internal rhymes (OCP: 177).

[56] Sonorous resonance is a privileged effect of lexical associativity in Mallarmé (perhaps more so than proper, philological filliation); from *Les mots anglais:* "Au poëte ou même au prosateur savant, il appartiendra, par un instinct supérieur et libre, de rapprocher des termes unis avec d'autant plus de bonheur pour concourir au charme et à la musique du langage, qu'ils arriveront comme de lointains plus fortuits: c'est là ce procédé, inhérent au génie septentrional et dont tant de vers célèbres nous montrent tant d'examples, l'ALLITÉRATION" (OC: 921).

[57] This illustrates one of the *règles* of Mallarméan syntax observed by Scherer: "À la subordination, qui obligerait presque nécessairement à introduire des verbes, Mallarmé préfère constamment la coordination. ... Les éléments apparaissent comme juxtaposés" (Scherer 1977, 169).

[58] Bénichou notes that the *ni* in line 15 was a late addition to the poem; his explication does not link this *ni* to the clause above (Bénichou, 122).

[59] Bénichou notes that line 7 originally read "Du papier qu'un cerveau châtié me défend" (OC: 1433); in this version the absence of inspiration is attributed to an internal obstacle (which Bénichou, like Cohn, attributes to the circumstance of the family) whereas in the final version this absence is now due to an external obstacle and therefore more oppressive (Bénichou, 119). The oppressiveness is reinforced by the slow accumulation of echoes, and yet this very oppressiveness of the page is *overcome* by the inscriptions of the oppressing echoes.

[60] Cohn's parse of *blancheur* orients it towards a notion of productivity (typically eroticized) by insisting upon the connection with mother's milk (Cohn 1951, 137–40; this passage is echoed in Cohn 1980, 261–62); this reading largely derives as an expansion of the following line from *Don du poëme:* "Avec le doigt fané presseras-tu le sein / Par qui coule en blancheur sibylline la femme" (OC: 40; OCP: 192, ll. 12–13). For Cohn there is ideality in the evocation of lactate sustenance and its concomitant associations of regeneration (cf. Cohn 1980, 49–50). For his explanation of *blancheur,* Cohn cites but does not develop the following citation from a letter to Cazalis in 1864: "les pertes nocturnes d'un poète ne devraient être que des voies lactées" (Cohn 1951, 138; CI: 138). The eroticized productive and regenerative milk is already tenebrific *expenditure*.

[61] The letter Cohn cited concerning the poet's nocturnal emissions of "voies lactées" also contains a reference to the turbulence of his home-life affecting his writing: "Hélas! Le baby [sic] va m'interrompre" (CI: 137). The productive force, such as it is, of the poet's voie lactée also is an interruption of productivity.

[62] This view is seconded by Malcom Bowie (Malcom Bowie, *Mallarmé and the Art of Being Difficult,* Cambridge: Cambridge UP, 1978. 10). Bénichou, Richard and Cohn all ignore this warning and merrily decode the symbols away: "il ne parlera que du figurant, le Cygne; le figuré, le Poète, restera innommé, reconnaissable seulement à quelque qualification insolite où l'homme efface oiseau" (Bénichou, 245; cf. Cohn 1980, 124–26; Richard, 251–56). For Bénichou the poem is thus simply a simile where the apodosis lacks a protasis, however the absent protasis (the Poet) *is* present—can be said to be present—in the very inscription (as*sign*ment) of the hapless swan's aborted flight. The Poet is present because he remains the absent artist, "like the God of the creation, remains within or behind or beyond or above his handiwork, invisible or refined out of existence, indifferent, paring his fingernails" (AP: 215). Bénichou has thus granted the Mallarméan elocutory disparition a figural force of creation (indeed, he adds that the poem dates from a period of renewed creativity for Mallarmé).

[63] Scherer notes, giving this line as example, that "Le pronom personel, au lieu de désigner le sujet d'un verbe, peut redoubler ce sujet, déjà représenté dans la phrase par un nom" (Scherer 1977, 140).

[64] Richard notes that this *oublié* refers back to, or remembers, *Hérodiade*: "Mallarmé qualifie le lac dur d'*oublié,* et dans cet oubli le cygne s'est plongé; comme déjà Hérodiade, il s'est reconnu lui-même de loin, au fond de son passé" (Richard, 253). In essence, Marchal's reading of this poem is a nuanced expansion of this point, of the cygne's reminiscence or echo of Hérodiade's *effroi* by the mirror: "En somme, il n'y a guère de différence entre le rêve blanc vers lequel semble tendre toute l'écriture mallarméenne comme vers son au-delà, et la hantise stérile du cygne qui n'a pas chanté, entre le paradis blanc d'Hérodiade et l'enfer blanc du cygne" (Marchal 1985, 159; cf. 154–55). Hérodiade is indeed associated with a swan, from the *Incantation*: "L'eau morne se résigne, / Que ne visite plus la plume ni le cygne / Inoubliable: l'eau reflète l'abandon / De l'automne éteignant en elle son brandon: / Du cygne quand parmi le pâle mausolée / Ou la plume plongea la tête, désolée / Par le diamant pur de quelque étoile, mais / Antérieure, qui ne scintilla jamais" (OC: 41; OCP: 208, ll. 9–16). There is then the cygne entombed in the mausoleum, curled up

into itself (Hérodiade in the mirror indeed), illuminated under a defunct stellar light and apart from cygne inoubliable. The virginal, stellar beauty of Hérodiade, is this self-reflection under a (perhaps even *apart from a*) separation; separation is her issue: "J'attends une chose inconnue / Ou peut-être, ignorant le mystère et vos cris, / Jettez-vous les sanglots suprêmes et meurtris / D'une enfance setant parmi les rêveries / *Se séparer enfin ses froides pierreries*" (OC: 48; OCP: 232, ll. 130–34, emphasis added).

[65] Daniel Bougnoux notes the haunting obdurance of the *lac* oublié as a paronomasic metonym within the word g*lac*ier (Daniel Bougnoux, "L'éclat du signe," *Littérature* 14 [May 1974]: 83–93. 86–87).

[66] Actually Marchal prefers to ignore the possibility of a constellation as the sole survivor within the lieu, and only notes marginally that "comme le souligne L. Cellier... ce RIEN tolère une exception," but that any possible association between the constellation of *Un coup de dés* and the *Cygne* remains a "coïncidence troublante" (Marchal 1985, 159 fn. 25).

[67] This is also appropriate to the situation of finding the ideal flower in *Le nénuphar blanc*, where coldness and virtuality color even the eroticization of a remembered virtual *fuite*. "Résumer d'un regard la vierge absence éparse en cette solitude et, comme on cueille, en mémoire d'un site, l'un de ces magiques nénuphars clos qui y surgissent tout à coup, enveloppant de leur creuse blancheur un rien, fait de songes intacts, de bonheur qui n'aura pas lieu et de mon souffle ici retenu dans la peur d'une apparition, partir avec: tacitement, en déramant peu à peu sans de heurt briser l'illusion ni que le claptois de la bulle visible d'écume enroulée à ma fuite ne jette aux pieds survenus de personne la ressemblance transparente du rapt de mon idéale fleur" (OC: 286). The recollection or resumption of the dream is a nul réminiscence of a virginal absence elaborately likened to a gathering of nothing barely concealed within a flower. What little that remains visible is nullified in a rewriting over, a palimpsest's tracing of disappearance.

[68] "Dans 'À la nue…,' la syntaxe diverge de la norme à tel point que cette norme ne peut pas servir de référence pour déterminer des écarts" (Gérard Montbertrand, "'À la nue…' ou le déshabillage d'un poème de Mallarmé," *Nineteenth Century French Studies* 15.3 [Spring 1987]: 285–301. 298 fn. 6).

[69] In a brilliant gloss, Davies notes a most appropriate precedence for this participle: "Évoquer, dans un ombre exprès, l'objet *tu*, par des mots allusifs, jamais

directs, se réduisant à du silence égal" (OC: 400, emphasis added; Davies, 371). See our discussion on page 78, and the citation on page 81 for another example.

[70] Indeed this is hardly the only problematic syntactic form within the poem, it is just the one upon which there is unanimous agreement for resolution. Marchal notes that L. de Nardis proposes reading "cela" from line 9 not as a demonstrative but as the passé simple of celer, thereby rendering the poem into "la nue accablante a tu (= n'a pas dit) quel sépulcral naufrage abolit le mât ou cela que..., le verbe taire commandant une double interrogation indirecte. Si cette construction a la mérite de rendre compte de l'absence de point d'inerrogation, elle repose cependant sur un passé composé trop acrobatique pour être tout à fait plausible" (Marchal 1985, 252 fn. 2). But then, in general, this would be the problem with reading this poem, forcing it to *rendre compte*.

[71] Montbertrand also proposes two possibilities for the *lecteur*, but different ones: "Le poème se situe entre les deux poussées ascendante et surtout descendante de la 'nue' habituellement haute qui a été abaissée, et de la 'sirène' qui est montée à la surface pour finalement être noyée" (Montbertrand, 296). Bernard also noted two contradictory proposals between the quatrains of disaster and the tercets of survival (Bernard, 118–19).

[72] "Or ce qui est aboli aussi dans ce poème c'est le pronom personel 'je,' c'est-à-dire l'être même du poète. L'abolition du centre, du mât suprême une entre les épaves, c'est l'abolition du 'je' centre. C'est une déperdition de l'être, de l'être créateur, du Dieu, du démiurge tout puissant qu ne peut pas être Mallarmé" (Montbertrand, 297).

[73] Samuel Beckett, *Molloy, Trilogy*, London: John Calder, 1959. 5–176. 40.

[74] Frey's reading of this poem preserves some thing through the denegating rapports of prosody and signification. "The poem does not say anything but foams over what it says with the superfluity of allusions. In the place of allusions, language is superfluous and without foundation. It is no longer subsequential in its superficial bottomlessness but is a suspended outgrowth and sublimation" (Frey, 27). The play of words thus becomes allegorical (Frey prefers metaphorical) of itself, of its redoubling disparitions and this self-reflexivity allows for there to be enough to read, a monument allegorical of its denegation. "The foaming of language can be described and understood at the level of what can be expressed. But the expression of the foaming poem does not participate. It is an expression that is lost in what is

expressed, that is, it succumbs to exactly the manner of expression from which the expressing removes itself. It may be the discourse that expresses the foaming of the expression starts to foam itself. This means that the expressed meaning of the translated metaphor becomes a metaphor for its own unexpression becoming expressed" (30).

The Syntaxes of "Un coup de dés"

A propos of nothing in particular, there are 703 words (or so) in the poem *Un coup de dés jamais n'abolira le hasard*. The rest will not have been so certain, so *verifiable*.[1] Even the poem's place within Mallarmé's œuvre — or rather within his *œuvres,* for these are multiple, naming both the œuvres he wrote and those he did not write — is far from being fixed. Its place is ambiguous.

Is *Un coup de dés* the work that Mallarmé had planned? Does it *realize* the project of the livre inasmuch as the *Divina Commedia* was supposed to have fulfilled the project of writing announced at the close of the *Vita Nuova*? R.G. Cohn has polarized critical appraisals of the poem around the resolution of this question. He adamantly answers affirmatively: that undoubtedly the poem is, as Mallarmé described it to Gide, "cette tentative, une première, ce tâtonement" (CIX: 171–72).[2] Cohn is so eager to maintain this positive assertion that rather than elaborate its consequences, he vehemently attacks any and all contrary assertions. Cohn phrases the basic contrarian view — held by Richard and Davies — as: "the *Coup de dés* is a sort of confession of the failure of [Mallarmé's] dream [to write the livre], its abandonment" (Cohn 1966, 13). Such a view would construe *Un coup de dés* in a manner not unlike *Salut:* the iteration that iterates itself as a self-denegating *apologia* for an inability to write and to produce something more profound. Such a claim is not necessarily incompatible with the positivistic reading of the *tentative* that Cohn purports to defend, as our reading of Blanchot will shortly show.

Richard bears the brunt of Cohn's distaste for the "negative" reading of *Un coup de dés* (cf. Cohn 1966, 59 fn.3). Cohn's critique of Richard is especially harsh considering the essential similarities between both critics' work. Richard's *L'univers imaginaire de Mallarmé* is—as was noted in the previous chapter—an ambitious attempt at cross-referencing the sum-total of Mallarmé's work: everything is interrelated to everything within the imaginary universe with *Un coup de dés* occupying but one point (albeit a strange one) within this constellation.[3] Cohn exercises essentially the same methodology of interrelation, yet he maintains that *Un coup de dés* is the sun, the central, defining and almost-foundational point within this universe.[4] For Cohn each page in the poem has a metaphoric overlay, which would include glosses to and from the rest of Mallarmé's œuvre (Cohn 1951, 34–5). The critical elaboration and elucidation of these overlays precisely describes the projects of *both* Cohn and Richard.[5]

Jean-Claude Lebenstejn, commenting upon Cohn's petulant exchanges with Richard and Davies, sanely notes "*Si le Livre, dans son exigence de totalité, est toujours à venir « à des siècles d'ici… » (CIII, 287), aboutissement de l'univers, le* Coup de Dés *n'est pas le Livre. Pourtant, le* Coup de Dés *lui-même reste encore et toujours à venir, n'étant jamais fini, jamais exactement lui-même*" (Lebenstejn, 649 fn. 32). The rapport between *Un coup de dés* and the livre rests within an economy of the *à venir*. The economy of *Un coup de dés* is of the future imperfect. In *L'espace littéraire* Blanchot makes this argument by contrasting *Un coup de dés* to *Igitur*. Blanchot claims that the experience of writing *Igitur* yielded "le livre à l'impersonnalité," thereby acknowledging "dans la parole l'aptitude à rendre les choses absentes."[6] A certain lexical annullation—perhaps not unlike the floral absentation noted in *Crise de vers*—is revealed as a goal, and so in *Igitur* the poet is still concerned with "une purification de l'absence, un essai pour rendre celle-ci possible et puisser en elle la possibilité" (Blanchot 1955, 138). This absence is the absence of all power and the possibility of the poetic work is intricately bound to the possibility of the presentation of such absence.

The initial figure for absence in *Igitur* is midnight, "Certainement subsiste une présence de Minuit" (OC: 435). Igitur wants to die against this midnight setting which has always already preceded him. He is prepositioned by the liminal instant of midnight, the moment of convergence. This desire to coincide death with midnight suggests an equation of purification and presentation: that absence can be purified by being made possible and revealed as such. Death will always have been anonymous before being assumed by the boy's agitation; death's anonymity precedes any individualization. "Comme s'il fallait d'abord mourir anonymement pour mourir dans la certitude de son nom. Comme si, avant d'être ma mort, un acte personnel où prend fin délibérément ma personne, il fallait que la mort fût la neutralité et l'impersonnalité où rien ne s'accomplit, la toute-puissance vide qui se consume éternellement elle-même" (Blanchot 1955, 141). The contemplation of suicide for Igitur is intertwined with the throw of the dice: an act of a mastered numerical coincidence between the hour midnight and the double-six of the dice, "Minuit sonne—le Minuit où doivent être jetés les dés" (OC: 434). Midnight has hardened into a space where there is a necessary act (où doivent), and the announcement or sounding of this hour had been "prédite par le livre" (445). Blanchot has proffered two hypothetical claims here—a doubled *comme si* not unlike the frame within page 7 of *Un coup de dés*—in *Igitur* death is iterated as a necessary possibility. Death or absentation is the goal at the present instant of midnight. The conjunction between midnight and throwing the dice is a conjunction between "réciproques néants" (435) which is accomplished in an act of coincidence: "Il jette les dés, le coup s'accomplit, douze, le temps (Minuit)—qui créa se retrouve la matière, les blocs, les dés—" (451). This marks a possibility of *supreme necessity:*

> Bref dans un acte où le hasard est en jeu, c'est toujours le hasard qui accomplit sa propre Idée en s'affirmant ou se niant. Devant son existence la négation et l'affirmation viennent échouer. Il contient l'Absurde—l'implique, mais à l'état latent et l'empêche d'exister: ce qui permet à l'Infini d'être.
> Le Cornet est la Corne de licorne—d'unicorne.
> Mais l'Acte s'accomplit.
> Alors son moi se manifeste par ceci qu'il reprend la Folie: admet l'acte, et, volontairement, reprend l'Idée, en tant qu'Idée: et l'Acte (quelle que soit la puissance qui l'ait guidé) ayant nié le hasard, il en conclut que l'Idée a été nécessaire. (OC: 441)[7]

The impersonal midnight has already claimed the impossibility of the manifestation of such a resolute individuality. Blanchot attributes a notion of death which is not far from Heidegger: a horizon that while never present, presents the possibility of being, the possibility of a necessary being-towards-death: "la substance de l'absence, la profondeur du vide qui est créé lorsqu'on meurt, dehors eternel, espace formé par ma mort et dont l'approche cependant me fait seule mourir. Que dans une telle perspective l'événement ne puisse jamais se passer (la mort ne puisse jamais devenir événement), c'est ce qui est inscrit dans l'exigence de cette nuit préalable" (Blanchot 1955, 142). The monumental, sepulchral anonymity of night weakens Igitur: "J'étais l'heure qui doit me rendre pur" (OC: 435). However it is this wish for purification—expressed as identification with the Midnight hour—that remains denied in a most peculiar manner. In *Igitur* the risk for a *presentation* of a voiding purification is indicated at Midnight. However, what Midnight indicates is the denial of such a possibility of manifestation. Midnight marks an absence that is evaded in the suddenness of an instant. This suddenness vitiates the possibility of manifestation—the possibility of a sovereign death—just as much as it might also be a purification. Midnight is the instant that can never be made manifest under the light of day. Blanchot cites Georges Poulet for this point: "[Minuit] ne peut « jamais s'exprimer par un présent, toujours par un passé ou un futur »" (Blanchot 1955, 144 n.1). This voided presence carries a most unusual risk: "C'est à Minuit que « doivent être jetés les dés »? Mais Minuit est précisément l'heure qui ne sonne qu'après les dés jetés, l'heure qui n'est jamais encore venue, qui ne vient jamais, le pur futur insaisissable, l'heure étérnellement passée" (147). The instant of mastered coincidence has no existence. In *Quant au livre,* Mallarmé wrote that the desire for suicide is futile because the time of suicide is without mastery: "Le suicide ou abstention, ne fait rien, pourquoi?—Unique fois au monde, parce qu'en raison d'un événement toujours que j'expliquerai, *il n'est pas de Présent, non—un présent n'existe pas*" (OC: 372; emphasis added). The negation effected by suicide is ultimately affirming since suicide posits an action and a life to be taken. However for Igitur, such action resides within the intransitive instantaneity of midnight, which is an effect or mirage of a faux-semblant of presence.[8] There is no moment in which mastery can be affirmed and action taken. The instant eludes control because there is no instant there that will have been controlled. The present—such as it is—is an empty site of an intransitive awaiting. Midnight stands in the face of the horizon which can never give itself over to presence, the horizon which has always already receded. Igitur can never die at the right time because the die are always yet to be cast. Yet for Blanchot, *Igitur* marks a delegation of night to consciousness; the work still retains the possibility of a catastrophe that can be comprehended (Blanchot 1955, 145–47).[9] Midnight marks an opening of night to another, more radically obscure sphere which cannot even be designated with the propriety reserved for "night": "Minuit ne tombe jamais à minuit. Minuit tombe quand les dés sont jetés, mais l'on ne peut jeter les dés qu'à Minuit" (222). Minuit fails to coincide with its *tomb* and with the contingencies of tumbling dice.

Following Blanchot's reading, *Un coup de dés* falls as an indication of Midnight without resorting to a manifestation. Blanchot refuses to admit with any certainty the possibility that the poetic work is "la renonciation à maîtriser la démesure du hasard par une mort souverainement mesurée, peut-être, mais on ne saurait le dire aussi certainement" (148). *Igitur* had announced this failure and had thus recovered its meaning. The passivity of the poem—a passivity where the poet's mastery is perpetually at stake—is not quite the opposite of Igitur's resolve. The problem of the untimeliness of death will not be (ab)solved in *Un coup de dés*, "loin pourtant de la [*Igitur*] contredire, lui donne au contraire encore sa dernière *chance*, qui n'est pas de vouloir annuler le hasard, fût-ce par un acte de négation mortel, mais de s'abandonner entièrement à ce hasard, de le consacrer en entrant sans réserve dans son intimité, avec l'abandon de l'impuissance" (149, emphasis added). The poem, as passive, marks the abandoning to the contingencies of chance.[10] Indeed this marks Blanchot's contribution to the question concerning Mallarmé's *vers de circonstance*: *Un coup de dés* is the *verse towards* hasard, *the conjunction is no longer a possible necessity, but instead, merely, supremely, possibility.*

> Rien n'est plus impressionnant, chez un artiste aussi fasciné par le désir de maîtrise,[11] que cette parole finale où l'œuvre brille soudain au-dessus de lui, non plus nécessaire, mais comme un « *peut-être* » de pur hasard, dans l'incertitude de « *l'exception* », non pas nécessaire, mais l'absolument non-nécessaire, constellation du doute qui ne brille que dans le ciel oublié de la perdition. (Blanchot 1955, 149)[12]

Un coup de dés marks the possibility of the livre *as a possibility*, and no longer as a necessity. In this way it can be hinged to both *Salut* and to the *Divina Commedia*. As argued at the close of chapter 2, the achievement of totality as the gathering of pages within a volume (Par: XXXIII.85–87) is an achievement of forgetting, the exscription named by disigillare. The book, Dante's book is the exscription of the plenitude it *had not named*.. By re-marking itself à l'écart du livre, the book re-marks that the livre is already à l'écart and ineluctably à venir: the identity of the livre *tel quel* is its non existence—or rather its apartness from being. The very contingency of *Un coup de dés* is thus its coincidence with the eternal absence of the livre. This is the point precisely elaborated in *Le livre à venir*: "Il n'est pas moins fermement indiqué, dans *Un coup de dés*, l'œuvre même qu'il constitute et qui ne fait pas du poème une réalité présente ou seulement future, mais, sous la double dimension négative d'un passé inaccompli et d'un avenir impossible."[13] In this sense the polemic Cohn initiates concerning the *identity* (or non-identity) of *Un coup de dés* (and also Scherer with his publication of the notes for the Livre) is irrelevant. *Un coup de dés* is the livre for precisely the reason Cohn uses to derisively describe its identification as being not the livre: that it is a sort of confession of the impossibility of writing the livre. *Un coup de dés* may indeed be a "tentative," not just an attempt to present the livre, but a hypothetical projection of its *tentative possibility*. The livre, like the pure language does not exist, and so *Un coup de dés* can only remunerate it into a virtual possibility. Or, phrased differently, *Un coup de dés* is the livre because it is a circumstantial work, a work that does not deny its circumstantialities.[14]

The title *Un coup de dés jamais n'abolira le hasard* announces this possibility which is then enumerated hypothetically within its iteration, an iteration spread, thrown out and dispersed across twelve (or so) double pages. This is one of the attributes of the livre signaled by Mallarmé in *Le livre, instrument spirituel:* "la fabrication du livre, en l'ensemble qui s'épanouira, commence, dès une phrase" (OC: 380). The elaboration of the title is a *bibliofication*. This bibliofication does not tend towards a unity, rather, through orchestrated typographic modulations, it declines towards—as Bertrand Marchal notes—tautology: "le *Coup de dés* rompt délibérément avec cette tradition immémoriale du récit versifié… puisqu'il est tout entier contenu dans une seule phrase d'allure axiomatique et où s'énonce en fair une tautologie: le hasard, en effet, signifie étymologiquement « le dé », si bien que le poème, loin de se développer selon une linéarité dramatique, ne peut que se lover à l'intérieur d'une forme close."[15] The poem consists of typographically hierarchized hypothetical elaborations of a signatory hypothesis that also, as Marchal suggests, *distend* said initial phrase (Marchal, 272). The poem is the interval of these fictitious spacings that develop briefly and hypothetically from the title phrase. "La fiction affleurera et se dispersa, vite, d'après la mobilité de l'écrit, autour des arrêts fragmentaires d'une phrase capitale dès le titre introduite et continuée. Tout se passe, par raccourci, en hypothèse; on évite le récit" (OC: 455).[16] *Un coup de dés* is the work given over to chance, an interregnum of the livre announcing itself as *hasard*.

> Très proche alors du Livre, car seul le Livre s'identifie avec l'annonce et l'attente de l'œuvre qu'il est, sans autre contenu que la présence de son avenir infiniment problématique, étant toujours avant qu'il ne puisse être et ne cessant pas d'être séparé et divisé pour devenir, à la fin, sa division et sa séparation mêmes. … Naturellement, je ne dirai pas qu'*Un coup de dés* soit le Livre, affirmation que l'exigence du Livre priverait de tout sens. Mais, beaucoup plus que les notes que ranime M. Scherer, il lui donne appui et réalité, il est sa réserve et sa présence toujours dissimulée, le risque de son enjeu, la mesure de son défi sans mesure. … *Un coup de dés* annonce un livre tout autre que le livre qui est encore le nôtre: il laisse pressentir que ce que nous appelons livre selon l'usage de la tradition occidentale [which one could hear as "accidentelle"], où le regard identifie le mouvement de la compréhension avec la répétition d'un va-et-vient linéaire, n'a de justification que dans la facilité de la compréhension analytqiue. … Mouvement de diaspora qui ne doit jamais être réprimé, mais préservé et accueilli comme tel

dans l'espace qui se projette à partir de lui et auquel ce mouvement ne fait que répondre, réponse à un vide indéfiniment multiplié où la dispersion prend forme et apparence d'unité. Un tel livre, toujours en mouvement, toujours à la limite de l'épars, sera aussi toujours rassemblé dans toutes les directions, de par la dispersion même et selon la division qui lui est essentielle, qu'il ne fait pas disparaître, mais apparaître en la maintenant pour s'y accomplir. (Blanchot 1959, 318–20)

For Blanchot *Un coup de dés* is the livre but only insofar as the livre, in that it *is*, is the livre à venir: "La présence de la poésie est à venir: elle vient par delà l'avenir et ne cesse de venir quand elle est là. ... L'œuvre est l'attente de l'œuvre. Dans cette attente seule se rassemble l'attention impersonelle qui a pour voies et pour lieu l'espace propre du langage. *Un coup de dés* est le livre à venir" (326). Within the space of the poem, a space fragmented into elaborations of possibility, *on évite le récit*, "L'histoire est remplacée par l'hypothèse: « *Soit que...* »" (326). The poem is nothing more (and perhaps less) than this space, this *lieu* of iteration iterating itself as the constellation which rejoins itself as the coup de dés. Davies notes, the poem is structured as a chiasmus—"UN COUP DE DÉS / *COMME SI* / *COMME SI* / un Coup de Dés" (Davies, 60)—but rather than express a circularized completion, the jointure de-enunciates totality, and it is this de-enunciation which opens the space of the poem. "La fin de l'œuvre est son origine, son nouveau et son ancien commencement: elle est sa possibilité ouverte encore une fois, pour que les dés à nouveau jetés soient le jet même de la parole maîtresse qui, empêchant l'Œuvre d'être—*Un Coup De Dés Jamais*—, laisse revenir le naufrage dernier où, dans la profondeur du lieu, tout a toujours déjà disparu: le hasard, l'œuvre, la pensée, EXCEPTÉ *à l'altitude* PEUT-ÊTRE..." (Blanchot 1959, 332). The poem is the elaborated hypothetical exception, or the space become poem. Lebenstejn's reaction to the Ronat edition (see note 1) is thus very appropriate to the nul question concerning the possible confluence of *Un coup de dés* and the livre: *Un coup de dés* is the *hallucination* of the book.

David Scott formulates the tension between the writing and the space very precisely: "In a sense then, there is a kind of polarization of principles: language and text representing order and reason, the page chaos and chance (*le hasard*). ... on one level, one may read the proposition *Un coup de Dés jamais n'abolira le hasard* as: writing will never obliterate the page" (Scott, 146). Instead of voice, there is typography, the fluxile form and format of words on the page.[17] Writing will never overcome its manifestation; the negativity of language will always be, always *is* overpowered by the specter of the manifest and by the specter of its manifestation. Writing lacks the resources to eliminate (the circumstance) of being written, but this lack is in turn the domain and boundary of its negativity. Writing is an experience of negativity *because of* its materiality on the page. In *Un coup de dés* negativity itself becomes a negative hypothetical formula, as Marchal adroitly notes: "la formule du *Coup de dés* n'est pas un SI porteur d'espoir, mais un MÊME SI qui ferme le champ de la résignation: *même si* le dé était le Nombre, cela ne changerait rien, ce serait encore le hasard.[18] L'hypothèse ici évoquée n'est pas un potentiel, même le plus improbable qui soit, mais un irréel absolu, que consacre le formule pénultième: RIEN… N'AURA EU LIEU… QUE LE LIEU" (Marchal, 274). Even negation is to be subjunctive here.

∴

Before elaborating the characteristics of this space become poem—the specific ways in which the space of twelve pages is made to articulate a hypothetically eternal and belated future anterior—we will delineate the possibility of a different disastrous pilgrimage, that of cowardly Ulysses. The condition of *Un coup de dés* is perhaps not without possible affinities to the Ulyssean *naufrage*. The Dantean Ulysses is traditionally taken to be a transgressor since he had arrogantly attempted to reach Mount Purgatory on his own initiative; thus like Virgil's Ulysses, he lacks *pietas* even as he claims to pursue "virtute e canoscenza" (Inf: XXVI.120).[19] Ulysses is the figure of unrestrained *mortal ingegno,* and by attempting to master his voyage he shatters against human finitude. Mazzotta argues that this transgression is also a transgression in and of rhetoric: Ulysses is the master rhetor who, by imposing his own quest instead of God's, is trapped by his faith in the *ingegno* of his own *tongue*.[20] "For all his rhetorical mastery, Ulysses' deception is primarily a self-deception, a way of succumbing to the literalness of language, of being trapped by his own tongue. Ironically, the craftsman of persuasion is spellbound by his own song, the way he is caught within the tongue of fire and spellbound by the song of the sirens" (Mazzotta, 105). Ulysses suffers from the first sin, matæotechny. In his "folle volo" (Inf: XXVI.125), the wandering Ulysses has *trespassed* the limit (*segno*) of human decorum; and this limit is also a *sign* and a *mark*. His downfall is a trespassing of the sign, or rather a trespassing *by* (use of) the sign coeval with transgression, and as Mazzotta notes, the pilgrim remains at risk of such a *trapassare del segno* (Mazzotta, 105; see also our second chapter). Ulysses's shipwreck is one possible result of pilgrimage, Ulysses's *trapassare del segno aboutit à un naufrage cela*.

For Blanchot in the essay "Le chant des Sirènes," the figure of Ulysses remarks a specific condition of narrative, a condition of the journey or even of the pilgrimage that ends in a shipwreck.[21] Blanchot construes the sirens' song as a space of temptation and seduction by unreal forces of alterity, as the designation of an interval to be traversed *as well as* the traversal itself. The song is a space become pilgrimage: "il était une distance, et ce qu'il révélait, c'était la possibilité de parcourir cette distance, de faire du chant le mouvement vers le chant et de ce mouvement l'expression du plus grand désir" (Blanchot 1959, 10). The space is mastered by the deceitful cunning of Ulysses's scurrilous *technics*: "sa perfidie qui l'a conduit à *jouir* du spectacle du Sirènes.... Les Sirènes vaincues par le pouvoir de la technique qui toujours pretendera jouer sans péril avec les puissances irreelles (inspirées), Ulysse n'en fut cependant pas quitte" (11, emphasis added). In failing to escape the sirens, Ulysses repeats the encounter with the imaginary in his act of narration, "par là en apparence rendu inoffensive, ode devenue episode" (12). The narrative (more precisely *récit*[22]) is singing recounted, and is thus also defined as the *technical subterfuge* that reworks the unreal or imaginary *into* a controlled encounter or a teleologics. "Le récit n'est pas la relation de l'événement, mais cet événement même, l'approche de l'événement, le lieu où celui-ci est appelé à se produire, événement encore à venir et par la puissance attirante duquel le récit peut espérer, lui aussi, se réaliser" (14). Ulysses's mastery arrests the Sirens' charm and translates itself (its mastery) into narrative. Ulysses's passage is transitive: it makes its passage into an object of and for narration. The "chant des sirènes" is thus the paradigmatic Ulyssean narrative for Blanchot as it marks the desired confluence of narrative and narration in a motion towards a foreign and unreachable point from which "le récit tire son attrait" (17). But the approach to the Sirens could never have been planned, it could only proceed by *hasard* (12).

> C'est là l'une des étrangetés, disons l'une des prétentions du récit. Il ne « relate » que lui-même, et cette relation, en même temps qu'elle se fait, produit ce qu'elle raconte, n'est possible comme relation qui si elle réalise ce qui se passe en cette relation, car elle détient alors le point ou le plan où la réalité que le récit « décrit » peut sans cesse s'unir à sa réalité en tant que récit, la garantir et y trouver sa garantie.
> Mais n'est-ce pas une naïve folie? En un sens. C'est pourquoi il n'y a pas de récit, c'est pourquoi il n'en manque pas (14–15).

The act of narration is thus the impossible attempt at reconciling singer to song: the "naïve folie" of narrative is that the récit produces its argument as it comes to being; authorizing itself as récit and as *recited event*. Once narrated, time becomes spatial. This problematic arises "quand Ulysse devient Homère" (14), when the tale is told as a guarantee of its telling, as if under the auspices of an *auctor* the singing *is* the song.[23] The *récit* constitutes a foreign event *à l'écart*, and this very écart constitutes the possibility of the récit, the possibility that there is an écart for the récit to reciter (traverse), for without the gap there would be no possibility of a story or navigation. The récit is thus eminently futural (à venir), relying upon differentiation and absentation for its very possibility. The hubris of Ulysses thus consists of defining and realizing in narrative (in narrated time) the space and time that have been (and are to be) traversed,

> le désir de donner la parole au temps, le récit a pour progresser cet *autre* temps, cette autre navigation qui est le passage du chant réel au chant imaginaire, ce mouvement qui fait que le chant réel devient, peu à peu

> quoique aussitôt (et ce « peu à peu quoique aussitôt » est le temps même de la métamorphose), imaginaire, chant énigmatique, qui est toujours à distance et qui désigne cette distance comme un espace à parcourir et le lieu où il conduit comme le point où chanter cessera d'être un leurre (16–17).

In narrative, in the act of the *récit*, the foreign, the strange and estranging music of the Sirens comes to be translated into quotidian time. The récit iterates and defines foreignness within a teleologically delimited interval; it masters the strange into a navigation. For Dante these teleologics—the teleologics of a πολύτρπος—shatter against the plenitude of a God who can only be for Ulysses "altrui" (Inf: XXVI.141), other to his own proper sphere of ingeniously disingenuous circumnavigation. Concerning the approach to God, Ulysses can only narrate failure and disaster, in other words, enflamed, he can only narrate. As was our argument in chapter 2, the pilgrim perhaps awaits a fate similar to Ulysses's damned folle volo once he takes the pen and becomes the poet—he who recounts the divine encounter—*unless* he is to surrender his initiative to—not God—but an indefinite negativity of writing.

Blanchot's characterization of Ulyssean narrative as this rendering of the encounter with the imaginary into a human time is not without consequence for his reading of *Un coup de dés*. Ulyssean *récit*—in its act of narrating—negates the event of the encounter which constitutes the narration by its distance away (écart). *Un coup de dés*, on the other hand, lies solely within the écart of the interval of enunciation, thereby *not* relying upon the poles of the navigation between recitation and encounter. There is no present interval in which the encounter and the distance from the encounter is to be iterated, "il n'est pas de Présent, non—un présent n'existe pas" (OC: 372).[24] The poem is not subordinated to a defining moment. The space is not approached, instead it remains awaited. The work is suspended between its visible presence (its circumstance) and its eternal non-accomplishment or non-coincidence with presence.

> Et dire « le » temps, comme s'il n'y avait ici qu'une seule manière de durer, c'est méconnaître l'énigme essentielle de ce livre et sa force inépuisable d'attrait… [it takes place in] un futur éternellement négatif—« *jamais*

n'abolira » —, lequel toutefois se prolonge doublement: par un futur antérieur passé, annulant l'acte jusque dans l'apparence de son non-accomplissement— « *n'aura eu lieu* » —et par une possibilité toute nouvelle vers laquelle, par delà toutes les négations et en prenant appui sur celles-ci, l'œuvre s'élance encore: le temps de l'exception à l'altitude d'un peut-être. (Blanchot 1959, 329)

Rather than steer towards the confluence of Ulyssean *récit* (navigating the narrative to narrate itself into existence), *Un coup de dés* belongs to an interval that does not coincide with itself: the poem is the hypothetical elaboration of what would (not) take place, *n'aura eu lieu*. What takes the place of the present is the interregnum of the poem.[25] The poem does not communicate an approach to this strange place, nor does it communicate the disaster of the naufrage[26] since the naufrage has always already happened, or not, as the case may not or may be,

JAMAIS

QUAND BIEN MÊME LANCÉ DANS DES CIRCONSTANCES

ÉTERNELLES

DU FOND D'UN NAUFRAGE
(UC: 3b; OC: 460)

•••

A provisional theory concerning the lisibility of *Un coup de dés* can now be made. As suggested above, the words, the few that are there, are only part of the problem. *Un coup de dés* is a poem of the page, "Mallarmé considérait une page d'un livre comme une unité, dans laquelle il y avait lieu d'introduire une construction, toute comme dans ces autres unités que sont la phrase ou le vers."[27] The spaces articulate the poem's intercalated hypotheses, but as Malcom Bowie notes, the spaces are *equivocal*, they do not maintain a consistent function of articulation.[28] In other words the spaces are potentially infinitely suggestive of possibilities of association between the poem's syntactic elements. The spacings suggest how the poem's statements can be differentiated. Because of this potentially infinite suggestiveness of differential combinations, the spacings are ultimately *indifferent* or insouciant to unequivocal or definitive differentiation. One reads *Un coup de dés* page by page, the poem's syntax derives from pagination, from a *mise-en-page*. The spaces articulate the hypotheses. Indeed there is a notable absence of any and all formal punctuation marks, the syntax is orchestrated by the page and its blanks. This is precisely how Mallarmé qualifies the matter in his humble preface to the poem:

> *Les « blancs » en effet, assument l'importance, fraappent d'abord; la versification en exigea, comme silence alentour, ordinairement, au point qu'un morceau, lyrique ou de peu de pieds, occupe, au milieu, le tiers environ du feuillet: je ne transgresse cette mesure, seulement la disperse. Le papier intervient chaque fois qu'une image, d'elle-même, cesse ou rentre, acceptant la succession d'autres et, comme il ne s'agit pas, ainsi que toujours, de traits sonores réguliers, ou vers—plutôt, de subdivisions prismatiques de l'Idée, l'instant de paraître et que dure le concours, dans quelque mise en scène spirituelle exacte, c'est à des places variables, près ou loin du fil conducteur latent, en raison de la vraisemblance, que s'impose le texte.* (OC: 455)

The tentativity of the poem's statements is thus compounded by their dispersal along and amongst the poem's pages. The function of verse is not herewith obviated, it is merely dispersed. In the poem's bibliofication, versification is remade into *spacification*.[29] Unlike *Igitur*, there is no hardened interval—no subsistence of midnight—there, there is only the page and its concomitant dispersals. Rather than divide verses, the dispersed units are prismatic subdivisions of the Idea. The poem thus consists of a chain of mutual metonyms splattered across several pages which belong within both the multiple series of relationships suggested by the spacings and the hierarchies of typography (point-size, capitalization and italicization across pages gathers units that would otherwise remain disassociated). Each metonym is a further displaced hypothetical elaboration upon an initial hypothesis.[30] These multiply construable individual units (we refrain from calling them strophes or verses) "exert upon each other an associative pull strong enough to cancel the intricate syntactic patterning which holds them apart; in so doing they become a mosaic of reciprocally explaining fragments, a counter-syntax, a refusal of hierarchy" (Bowie 1982, 145; cf. Scott, 140–41). This explicitly recalls Scherer's notion (concerning Mallarmé's more traditional verse), cited in the previous chapter, that Mallarmé enacts subordination or hypotaxis through juxtaposition or parataxis (Scherer 1977, 169). Mary Lewis Shaw provides a very precise formulation of the implications of the aligned mutually metonymic syntax: "The semic content of one syntagmatic unit produces others that constitute at once its context and its metaphorical (or more precisely metonymic) substitution."[31] Adding to Shaw's tendency towards precision, this displacement is more properly a *metalepsis* (periphrastically indirect metonymic substitution). Each unit is a proposition unto itself articulated through its oddly incongruent rapport with the other vague statements upon the page. In other words, the separated syntactic prisms or units of the poem function as a sylleptic confusion of parataxis and hypotaxis; one reads hither and thither across the page.

In order to further complicate matters, we will turn to the top half of page 5 (UC 5a–b; OC: 462–63), the page which shows the greatest variety of horizontal and vertical readings. Here, syntax has yielded to spacing since both the vertical and horizontal clauses radiating from LE MAÎTRE qualify his situation, and yet the relative priority of these attendant clauses remains ambiguous. All this uncertainty is aimed towards the calculation of "l'unique Nombre qui ne peut pas | être un autre" (UC: 5a–b; OC: 462–63). Furthermore, by being capitalized, LE MAÎTRE also falls within a syntactic sequence outside this page: "SOIT // LE MAÎTRE…" (UC: 4a–5a; OC: 460–62). Within page 5 the MAÎTRE's enstatement initially seems secure, he is posited as the new element within the poem, the new figure standing at the top of the page; but beyond this page and in the procession of the poem's pages, he may only have been hypothetical (cf. Marchal, 274–75). Furthermore, there is a direct contradiction between "surgi" and its placement on the page: the attribution of rising *falls* beneath the MAÎTRE. So the MAÎTRE is, on the one hand, apart from ancient and belated reckonings ("où la manœuvre avec l'âge oubliée" [UC 5b; OC: 463]), and on the other hand, he rises in order to infer new hypotheses from *this* conflagration. Yet the exact syntactic referent to *cette* conflagration remains elided and only its location is elaborated by a complement across the page ("à ses pieds / de l'horizon unanime" [UC 5b; OC: 463]). That the MAÎTRE *is*, remains uncertain, only his *place* is elaborated, and that place also remains uncertain and possibly even retracted: "*hors* d'anciens calculs / où la manœuvre avec l'âge *oubliée* / *jadis* il empoignait la barre" (UC 5b; OC: 463; emphasis added). Orbiting around (the printed phrase) "LE MAÎTRE" are sequences of elaborations that consign it to a belated and unspecified conflagration through which it emerges as its hypothetical, statutory and navigational head.[32] Unlike Ulysses, comically chained to the mast, the MAÎTRE is hardly prepositioned for a safe passage. The MAÎTRE is thus articulated within a liminal state—which could be explicated symbolically, as many critics since Cohn have done[33]—in and through which the possibility of a Ulyssean calcul towards encountering the unique number and mastering chance is somewhat compromised.

Syntactically the unique number remains ambiguous, something that perhaps commands the MAÎTRE as the "Esprit / pour le jeter / dans la tempête / en reployer la division et passer fier" (UC: 5b; OC: 463). A potential action is projected that modifies and amplifies the integral number. The number is integral precisely because it is already divided and composed out of division (a doubling of six). Such additive bifurcation is played out on the page as follows:

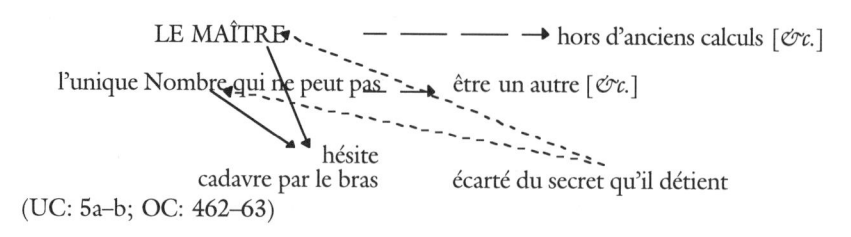

LE MAÎTRE　　— — — → hors d'anciens calculs [*&c.*]
l'unique Nombre qui ne peut pas　→ être un autre [*&c.*]
　　　　　　　hésite
　　　cadavre par le bras　écarté du secret qu'il détient
(UC: 5a–b; OC: 462–63)

Cohn, Marchal and Davies unequivocally claim that the MAÎTRE is the subject of hésite (Cohn 1951, 182; Marchal, 289–90; Davies, 83, 180), and yet the unique nombre (which is—through an appositional secondary clausal sequence—qualified as not being another) could *also* function as the subject of this verbal hesitation　because the phrases are paratactically arranged without explicit indication of hierarchy. Such a reading admittedly yields a less elegant syntax as the MAÎTRE will be left dangling without a finite verb, but such an elision is not without precedence in Mallarmé, and all we wish to do is merely indicate the possibility of this variant construction.[34] The verb hésite, by virtue of its position, thus yokes together both the MAÎTRE and the nombre, thereby potentially sundering the integrity of the number in this zeugma of espacement. The finite verb, the one active element within the severed syntaxes of this page, is left ambiguous and tentative: the verb hésite hesitates. The alternative played out is a negative one, the dice not thrown and the number not manifest: "plutôt / que de jouer / en maniaque chenu / la partie / au nom des flots" (UC: 5a; OC: 462). Because of this hesitation the integrally unique and ontogenetic number remains non-self-identical: "écarté du secret qu'*il* détient" (again, the secret that is held by the pronominal il could refer to either the MAÎTRE or to the nombre, but not to both simultaneously). The number or the MAÎTRE find themselves *apart*, sundered from the possibility of enstating a definite identity. Indeed this line would seem to be the central point of the page: the distancing away from the secret that is being (with)held. What is designated is not that there is a secret, but rather that the supplementary, masking machinations of secrecy *have themselves been withdrawn*, "Così la neve al sol si disigilla" (Par: XXXIII.64). As with the reassertion of the motions of the sea concealing *the very possibility* of a past shipwreck in *À la nue accablante tu*, the possibility of there having been some subject is elided through the alignment of characters on the page. There is no subject installed amidst the hither and thither of the page as all proceeds through metaleptic hypothesis.

Such is the standing of the naufrage, enunciated appositionally under the MAÎTRE at the bottom of page: "un | envahit le chef / coule en barbe soumise / naufrage cela | direct de l'homme / sans nef / n'importe / où vaine" (UC: 5a; OC: 462). The vanity of action upon blankness, the vanity of not having left a trace upon the page is taken up by a shipwreck that leaves no trace (sans nef) behind. The double motion of reading across the page (horizontal and vertical) entails a doubled withdrawal orbiting around the MAÎTRE and the redoubled blankness thereof. Marchal proposes that the absentation of the MAÎTRE recalls the doubled disparitions within *Ses purs ongles* (Marchal, 274). In both poems the withdrawal of the Maître has itself been withdrawn or exscribed, and in *Un coup de dés* this doubling elision is effected through the counter-syntaxes of spacings. The alignments of the prismatic subdivisions are labile. Syntax—that which ordinarily articulates and actuates each word's semanticity, that which acts as commander and guarantor of sense and sensibility by reigning in meaning (see our previous chapter; cf. OC: 385–86)—here negates meaning through a superfluity of connectivity. Each metalepsis is sylleptic, open to multiple directions of being construed. The poem's hypotaxis (the hierarchies of rapport between phrases) is articulated through a sylleptic parataxis. This multiplicity of possible conjunctions between these mutually aligned and aligning statements *inflects* semanticity into a subjunctivity.

There is a danger of construing the poem's blanks as a *signifying* force that would constitute a different sphere of semantic articulation. This would happen by admitting that the spaces merely replace punctuation. Such a reading could be buttressed by Mallarmé's annotation to the word "séparation" in *La musique et les lettres:* "une ponctuation qui disposée sur papier blanc, *déjà s'y signifie*" (OC: 655, emphasis added). In the lecture Mallarmé postulated the following as the inevitable implication of his researches, a potential alternative to punctuation:

> Je réclame la restitution, au silence impartial, pour que l'esprit essaie à se rapatrier, de tout—chocs, glissements, les trajectoires illimitées et sûres, tel état opulent aussitôt evasif, une inaptitude délicieuse à finir, ce raccourci, ce trait—l'appareil; moins le tumulte des sonorités, transfusibles, encore, en du songe.
> Les grands, de magiques d'écrivains, apportent une persuasion de cette conformité.
> Alors, on possède, avec justesse, les moyens réciproques du Mystère—oublions la vieille distinction, entre la Musique et les Lettres, n'étant que le partage, voulu, pour sa rencontre ultérieure, du cas premier: l'une évocatoire de prestiges situés à ce point de l'ouïe et presque de la vision abstrait, devenu l'entendement; qui, spacieux accorde au feuillet d'imprimerie une portée égale.

> Je pose, à mes risques esthétiquement, cette conclusion…: que la Musique et les Lettres sont la face alternative ici élargie vers l'obscur; scintillante là, avec certitude, d'un phénomène, le seul, je l'appelai, l'Idée.
> L'un des modes incline à l'autre et y disparaissant, ressort avec emprunts: deux fois, se parachève, oscillant, un genre entier. Théâtralement pour la foule qui assiste, sans conscience, à l'audition de sa grandeur: ou, l'individu requiert la lucidité, du livre explicatif et familier. (OC: 649)[35]

The work, whilst engaging in the theatrics of poetry and of the page—sumptuous sonorities, rhyme and rhythm, word-plays and so on—is to reclaim a musicality, an *evocatory disparition* or the silencings of the notes once struck. Music is the rhythmic and progressive "exscription" of vain sounds, and (as noted in the previous chapter) this is to be the character of writing, the character of the Idée "imprinted." The blanks *re-mark* the circumstance of marking on the page. But then are the blanks of *Un coup de dés* merely another *appareil*? merely another mark through which the sylleptic parataxis is imprinted?

As noted in the previous chapter, for Derrida the naming of whiteness (blanc, virginité) is nothing but a "trope du blanc « vide »" enmeshed within a supplementary chain:

> La dissémination des blancs (nous ne dirons pas de blancheur) produit une structure tropologique qui circule infiniment sur elle-même par le supplément incessant d'un tour de trop: *plus* de métaphore, *plus* de métonymie. Tout devenant métaphorique, il n'y a pas de sens propre et donc plus de métaphore. Tout devenant métonymique, la partie étant chaque fois plus grande que le tout, le tout plus petit que la partie, comment arrêter une métonymie ou une synecdoque? Comment arrêter les *marges* d'une rhétorique?[36]

Overdetermination comes to be overloaded with a result of less than zero (cf. Derrida 1972, 204). In *Un coup de dés* the unique number belongs within this *arhythmatic* of twelve pages (or so, if Ronat's editing is to be followed). The return or *reinscription* of blankness suspends or takes away the meanings of the words inflicted upon the page. The blanks *exscribe* the semanticity of the printed words. Continuing in this way, the pli is the re-mark *par excellence* as it is an inscription that doubles back and effaces itself, *re-marking* only the auto-erasure. The re-mark does not mark presence—or a *segno* or *sign* (being) of presence—but rather an absence, it is a mark *de trop*. Each metaleptic syntactic unit acts as a prism: containing all the other units, even as it is itself contained by each one of all the others. Thus the poem drowns within profligate reciprocity. "Dans la constellation des « blancs », la place d'un conténu sémique reste quasiment vide: celle du sens « blanc » en tant qu'il est référé au non-sens de l'espacement, au lieu où n'a lieu que le lieu" (289). Derrida thus takes very seriously Mallarmé's claim about the intervention of the page. The blanks do not just have a symbolic force (a force for inflecting and indicating meanings) since in affecting the words on the page they are also affected *by* the words and this affect is *re-marked* by the interplay between words and margin. In this interplay, the integrity of both blank and word (semic unit) is compromised (this is where Derrida critically reintroduces the double-sense of the word *hymen* as both virginity and consummation): each means *and* each *detracts* from the accumulation of meanings, and this double-motion is what is re-marked on the page: "Le pli (se) plie: son sens s'espace d'une double marque, au creux de laquelle un blanc se plie. Le pli est à la fois la virginité, ce qui la viole, et le pli qui n'étant ni l'un ni l'autre et les deux à la fois, indécidable, *reste* comme texte, irréductible à aucun de ses deux sens" (291). The alternations on the page, the very rhythm of the page, are not just limited to sonorous plays or to syntactics (or even to hierarchizable tenets of rhetoric), but also to an oscillation between black and white.

This situation is obviously complicated when the words themselves attempt to name blankness, to write white upon white (as was seemingly the case with *Le vierge, le vivace et le bel aujourd'hui*): "Le blanc se colore de blanc supplémentaire, d'un blanc en surnombre qui devient... un blanc ouvert au carré, blanc qui s'écrit, se noircit de lui-même, faux vrai sens blanc, sans blanc, qui ne se laisse plus compter ou totaliser, s'escompte et se décompte à la fois, déplace indéfiniment la marge et déjoue ce que Richard appelle l' « aspiration unitaire du sens » (p. 542) ou la « sûre révélation du sens » (p. 546)" (293). The situation is thus not a binarism of decidability or even of marks on the page, "Il n'y a pas d'*aletheia*, seulement un clin de l'hymen. Une chute rythmée. Une cadence *inclinée*" (293). Alternation with no meaning: this is what leads to *dissémination*, the surplus (*de trop*) of a hazardous dispersal *sans issue* of meaning and of the grounds through which meaning could be said to appear. As more meanings are added or become possible through typographic play, the text means less, it is supplemented by the very motion of (a)semic supplementarity.[37]

This profligate wasting supplementarity en abîme never becomes a decidable or articulable phenomenon: "L'abîme n'aura jamais l'éclat du phénomène parce qu'il devient noir. Ou blanc. L'un et/ou l'autre au carré de l'écriture. Il (se) blanchit dans l'inclinaison d'*Un coup de dés*" (297). Even the abyss is subjunctive, lost amidst blanched sonorities, "A take back to the virgin page, darm it!" (FW: 513.27).

The diagonally declining motion of the words on page 4 could be described as plané sous une inclinaison, as if the arrangement of words were pictographically imitating the sinking ship or the tumbling dice.[38] "SOIT / que / l'Abîme / blanchi / étale / furieux / sous une inclinaison / plane désespérément / d'aile / la sienne / par" (UC 4a; OC: 460). This question concerning the overall pictorialness of the poem impacts against the issue of hermeticism since it would entail an auto-picturation: the page *depicting in* the images created by the arrangement of words what those words say. But the inclining phrase is itself subjunctive: the circumstance of the blanched abyss inclining is *indéfinite* (SOIT que…). The incline, the re-mark of the incline and the re-mark of whitening are all hypothetical, and are re-marked as being hypothetical. In a much-quoted 1897 letter to Camille Mauclair concerning the proofs for *Un coup de dés* Mallarmé wrote:

> Je crois que toute phrase ou pensée, si elle a un rythme, doit le modeler sur l'objet qu'elle vise et reproduire, jetée à nu, immédiatement, comme jaillie en l'esprit, un peu de l'attitude de cet objet quant à tout. La littérature fait ainsi *sa preuve:* pas d'autre raison d'écrire sur du papier. (CIX: 288)[39]

The question then would be upon *what* is the page modeled? What is the pre-position of the slant? The "avance" that follows "par" falls on the same line, but on the other side of the page. It is what falls afterwards, on the other side, the *recto* of the *pli:* "par | avance retombée d'un mal à dresser le vol / et couvrant les jallissements / coupant au ras les bonds /

très à l'intérieur résume / l'ombre enfouie dans la profondeur par cette voile alternative / jusqu'adapter / à l'envergure / sa béanté profondeur en tant que la coque / d'un bâtiment / penché de l'un ou l'autre bord" (UC: 4a–b; OC: 460–61). Furthermore, the path taken on the recto side is not as straightforward a slope as the verso. If the verso page inclines, then the recto has been pre-positioned as having "par avance retombée d'un mal à dresser le vol." The recto page elaborates the negative side of the possibility, the désespéré character of the gliding, since the flight (vol)— by falling—has been incapable of being established (mal à dresser). It is as if the tumble is (partially) arrested by the pages' *pli*, leaving the flight poorly *addressed*. The fall is the pre-position, and therefore the flight had never soared. Indeed by covering the foaming turbulences (couvrant les jallissements), the soarings (bonds) remain on a level with the surface and concealed (coupant au ras). Withdrawn from flight, les bonds remain held imperceptibly upon the surface without even a trace of soaring. The abyss is abysmally without trace, unsuccessfully trying to fly and leave its mark, and not unlike the cygne from *Le vierge, le vivace et le bel aujourd'hui* it remains mired within "Le transparent glacier des vols qui n'ont pas fui!" (OC: 67; OCP: 308 l.4). In sylleptic rapport, each metalepsis comes to be retracted leaving in its wake a residual effacing vacuity in progress.

But within this negative possibility remains a further possibility that a mark may be left: "très à l'intérieur résume l'ombre enfouie dans la profondeur par cette voile alternative." There is a possibility that a darkening might have begun anew, and therefore that which is enfouie might still be able to fui. This is a possibility of the utmost significance (or *cyngeficance*) since Mallarmé has, in *Quant au livre,* explicitly defined writing as a shadowing, splattering the brightness and clarity of the blank page with blackness:

> Écrire—
> L'encrier, cristal comme une conscience, avec sa goutte, au fond, de ténèbres relative à ce que quelque chose soit: puis, écarte la lampe.
> Tu remarquas, on n'écrit pas, lumineusement, sur champ obscur, l'alphabet des astres, seul ainsi s'indique, ébauché ou interrompu; l'homme poursuit noir sur blanc.

> Ce pli de sombre dentelle, qui retient l'infini, tissé par mille, chacun selon le fil ou prolongement ignoré son secret, assemble de entrelacs distants où dort un luxe à inventorier, stryge, nœud, feuillages et présenter.
> Avec le rien de mystère, indispensable, qui demeure, exprimé, quelque peu.
> (OC: 370)

Writing—that which is to be read—is an ineluctable écart of clarity which is already contained in the inkpot. In the pursuit of signs on a white field a *secret* pli gathers a nul mystery presented as a remainder that is *quelque peu:* a minusculity tending towards (*vers*) annulment in the poem (*vers*). The constellation, the *alphabet des astres,* is thus the constitutive source for annullation; it is also an *alphabet désastre,* a constellation composed solely of building blocks of annullation.[40] Through this constellation a work is prolonged thereby persisting in incompletion. The work of the *pli* is a profound and vertiginous secret. The book is interlaced to a totality which can be known only as a secret, and in said imbrication totality achieves its work: disparition or unworking. It is this possibility that might be resumed within by the voile alternative, but it is worth reiterating that this possibility is itself enstated within the possibility of "SOIT que l'Abîme." This possibility is folded into the aborted and belated flight of the abyss, conjoined perhaps alongside. There is thus a descent into the extrapolations of possibility, each further possibility denying its antecedent (that there is the abyss; that it is imperceptible; that it might inscribe within). With the voile alternative there are two possibilities, held in suspense, held by the page's fold.[41] Possibilities spawn to be denied perpetually. There is always something left to be negated: the poem disseminates annullation. In *Le livre, instrument spirituel,* Mallarmé described the proliferating secondary groups around and within the book as "un *semis* de fioritures" (OC: 381; emphasis added): these additive and additional syntagmatic elements *seminate* denegatory dispersal. No element appears to be granted any definitive status in itself since each element is already subjunctive and furthermore the interaction between elements further vitiates their standing. Even the possibility of the tenebrific articulation, the ombre, finds its negation, as Cohn suggests, in the *Nombre* on page 5a (Cohn 1951, 152). The paratactic clauses also work at cross-purposes in this constellation of negativity. The words do not just disappear into blankness, they disappear into each other as their phrases *multi-ply*.

In *Le livre, instrument spirituel,* Mallarmé claimed that one major advantage of the book over the newspaper was that it is folded:

> Le pliage est, vis-à-vis de la feuille imprimée grande, un indice, quasi religieux: qui ne frappe pas autant que son tassement, en épaisseur, offrant le minuscule tombeau, certes de l'âme. ...
> Jusqu'au format, oiseux: et vainement, concourt cette extraordinaire, comme un vol recueilli mais prêt à s'élargir, intervention du pliage ou le rythme, initiale cause qu'une feuille fermée, contienne un secret, le silence y demeure, précieux et des signes évocatoires succèdent, pour l'esprit à tout littérairement aboli. (OC: 379)[42]

The folds of the book are its materiality, a materiality which may be evanescent, but a materiality which is also ingathered and hidden. Like the cygne, the book does not soar, it does not *transcend* heavenwards. Instead, the flat monolith silences itself. The book is the interval mired in materiality and betrayed towards silence. Annullation is material, the *work* of a disastrously tenuous and tenebrous alphabet. For *Un coup de dés* this silencing *takes place* through hypothetical denegating proliferations of the page.

One further extrapolation of the shadow's possible alternative flight rest within negative concatenations. The "au ras" which had designated the flushness of the belated flight with sea-level also complements the bâtiment, by naming—in the context of that word—a dismasted vessel (un bâtiment ras); not unlike the abolished "mât dévêtu" in *À la nue accablante tu* (OC: 76; OCP: 394 l.8). The ship that might possibly flee is already within the sphere of the possibility of the naufrage that never had fled and that could have never left a trace of flight. Indeed *ras* also carries a connotation of blankness, de l'un ou l'autre bord there is the possibility of not having stirred, as the words have sloped (penché). This is the lieu that pre-positions the hapless MAÎTRE, a sloped tenebrous writing that might be l'ombre *enfouie* dans le profondeur de cette voile alternative.

As if the MAÎTRE's situation or place were not tenuous enough, the hesitation possibly appurtenant to both MAÎTRE and Nombre continues on page 6 amidst echoes of certain disparitions disveloped thus far:

ancestralement à n'ouvrir pas le main
                          crispée
              par delà l'inutile tête

   legs en la disparition

                  à quelqu'un
                        ambigu

              l'ultérieur démon immémorial

ayant
      de contrées nulles
           induit
le vieillard vers cette conjonction suprême avec la probabilité
(UC: 6a; OC: 464)

Presumably the "ancestralement" clause complements the preceding "MAÎTRE / hésite," thereby repeating Igitur's hamletian hesitation to act inside his family's tomb (Cohn 1951, 196; Davies, 88–89). Davies makes an interesting claim *à propos* of "de contrées nulles," this emplacement suggests a nul place whereby "le protagoniste... ne peut d'avoir d'origine, n'arrive de nulle part" (Davies, 92).[43] Here amidst the typographic hither and thither of the page, there is neither whither nor whence to the MAÎTRE. The action of not opening the hand is beheld ancestrally, and *in* which the legacy is lost within disparition (already a doubled loss of the potential progeny): retrospective and anticipatory temporalities are frozen in the clenching of a fist. Within this inert inertia appertains à quelqu'un ambigu *l'ultérieur démon immémorial*. The belatedness (immémorial) of this dæmonic force is both *intensified and negated* by the word ultérieur: it is either doubly preterite and beyond memory in the past (meta-immemorial) and/or it is a *futural* (ulterior) belatedness rendering the dæmon beyond the present in both the ancient past and the unforeseeable future. The time that is claimed is a belatedness out of time; a profligate loss perdures within temporal *ecstases*. Loss is re-marked in an ec-static conjugation and the iteration of hesitation is thus hyperbolized out of any possibility of a present. The statement of a presence is compromised. There is neither source nor destination within these successive metaleptic appositions *de trop* and there can be no (Ulyssean) journey within this place re-marked on and by the page. The supreme conjunction with probability is itself only induced as one possibility within a series of negating appositional clauses of subjunctive possibilities; as with *cette* conflagration, *this* conjunction remains unspecified within its *spacification*.[44] Unlike *Igitur*, there can be no definite time for withdrawal within the interval of the page.

          celui
                son ombre puèrile
caressée et polie et rendue et lavée
        assouplie par la vague et soustraite
        aux durs os perdus entre les ais

          né
             d'un ébat
la mer par l'aïeul tentant ou l'aïeul contre la mer
        une chance oiseuse

                                    Fiançailles
dont
        le voile d'illusion rejailli leur hantise
        ainsi que le fantôme d'un geste

          chancellera
          s'affalera

            folie

(UC: 6a; OC: 464 *bis*)

This sequence erupts from the appositional demonstrative pronoun *celui* which amplifies the ultérieur démon immémorial (cf. Davies, 93). This appositional clause expands and expounds upon this doubly belated dæmon, rendering its infantile shadow defunct and disjected (the ombre puèrile also is in apposition to the vieillard/aïeul below). The shadow is eviscerated of darkness by the abrasions and *vagaries* of the wave—"caressée et polie et rendue et lavée assouplie par la vague"—in a series of rapid-fire paratactic statements, and then beyond this diminution of its visibility, it is furthermore *subtracted* from the ruins of the shipwreck, which had themselves been lost ("soustraite aux durs os perdus entre les ais"). A certain redoubling of *perdition* is itself multiply redoubled within this passage and is re-marked within this navigation down the page as a further perdition among a series of absentations. The ombre, the tenebrous ink of inscription, becomes one further element imbricated within this exscription of perdition.

But there is (again) apparently an issuance from these redoubling denegations: "né d'un ébat la mer par l'aïeul tentant ou l'aïeul contre la mer une chance oiseuse." The birth, such as it may be, is itself a nul issue, the folly of hasard. The struggle out of which this chance emerges is itself an undecidable proposition between ancestry and the sea. The productive conflagration or conjunction is ambiguous. Indeed this struggle (*ébat*) itself links to the naufraged *bât*iment. The union (Fiançailles) which might produce this chance oiseuse could be a potential consequence of one of the earlier hypotheses; it is a union derived from a *voile d'illusion:* the veil (*le* voile) potentially being one of the two possible flights (*une* voile alternative) on page 4b. The voile d'illusion is potentially subordinated to a voile alternative even as it further undoes itself in its own elaboration as the ghost of a gesture of concealment. An act of concealing is concealed by its ghost with virtually no possibility of a positive issuance (not unlike the écarté secret on page 5b). The futility of this spectral gesture *will* collapse into folly and annullation, "chancellera / s'affelera / folie / N'ABOLIRA" (UC: 6a–b; OC: 464–65). The futural promise of a birth comes to be swept along with a futural abolition which takes place within the poem's dispersed titular sequence. The N'ABOLIRA serves as a contested apposition to the issue of the Fiançailles. The disjected *folie* of redoubled perdition is taken up within n'ab*oli*ra, the ghost of a glottal gesture.[45]

Once the possibility of hesitation is iterated through redoublings of hypothetical perditions, further hypotheses are proposed as intervals framed on the page between a doubled "*COMME SI*": scenes from further annihilating possibilities. The dual and dueling *COMME SI* frame the passage on this page as two oppositional protases without any inferable apodosis, two possibilities for iterating an unnamed struggle, as if the struggle were not between mer and l'aïeul but instead between *possibilites*.

    Une insinuation   *simple*

        au silence   *enroulée avec ironie*

                          ou

                            le mystère

                                  précipité

                                        hurlé

  dans quelque proche   *tourbillon d'hilarité et d'horreur*

        voltige   *autour du gouffre*

                                sans le joncher

                                    ni fuir

                                et en berce le vierge indice

(UC: 7a–b; OC: 466–67)

The italicization of this page—which continues for three more pages, only to be stilled (or straightened into roman type) by a reintroduction of assertive capitalizations—sets this passage off, even as it purports to iterate a new clause to be added. The two hypothetical alternatives hereby proposed seem modest enough: either there will be a simple insinuation in silence, rolling the dice ironically as if an action were to be taken but ultimately remaining restrained, *or* there will be some mystery, some mysterious outcome will be set forth into the proximate tempest of the world. There is nothing simpler than these two proffered alternatives, either action will be taken or it will not. The hypothesis of restrained action is both suitably and forcefully litotic, and the projection of action is not without a measure of hyperbole: *le mystère précipité hurlé*.

Unfortunately the layout of the page implies an ambiguous apposition to the locative *quelque proche tourbillon d'hilarité et d'horreur* as it could amplify *both* possibilities. Both possibilities could impact in the same tourbillon.

Furthermore, the active clause introduced by the verb *voltige* also appertains to both possibilities (of a simple insinuation or of a hurled mystery), if only because syntactically neither possibility can unequivocally be subject. Therefore neither possibility produces issuance or escape. As with *Brise marine* the possibility of an interval of escape (*fuir*) is denied by and within its iteration. Instead of the possibility of tenebrous articulation as on page 4b (l'ombre enfouie dans la profoneur par cette voile alternative), *le vierge indice* is tenuously, stutteringly (*bercer*) contained within (*en:* within the shared location of the tourbillon). The game has not been played and will not have been played, remaining as the perpetually withdrawn and retained virginity of an inscription-to-be. Paradoxically (if not implausibly), the page re-marks that it has not been written yet.

The Ronat edition shows that the *et* of *et en berce le vierge indice* is directly aligned under the *et* of *et d'horreur*.[46] These two clauses occupy different syntactic positions and thus would not immediately seem complementary: the latter is merely an additional element *within* the locative syntagm *dans quelque proche,* whereas the former enstates a further elaboration of the action within the place designated by that locative (et *en berce* le vierge indice). The association suggested by this alignment is that the play of the virginal index, the play of the possibility of an index withdrawn is the horror of the hypothesis, the horror that there will have been no trace, no wake to be known of the tumbling dice. This possible association between paratactic clauses is effected purely through alignment and not through syntactic agreements. Alignment or spacification here yields a different order of sylleptic consociation.

It is unclear if the second "*COMME SI*" of page 7 stands within that page as the hypothesis's end-mark, or whether it leads into page 8. It is ambivalently proleptic and analeptic, out of time like the ultérieur démon immémorial. This ambivalently asemic atemporal hypothesis is perhaps the issuance of page 7 to its successors: *"plume solitaire éperdue*

sauf"

(UC: 8a; OC: 468). Alone, lost, upmost on the page is the *plume solitaire éperdue;* the word for its desperation—*éperdue*—reinforces its solitude (*et pérdue*). Indeed the solitary *sauf* almost seems to further reinforce the solitariness of the quill. But this quivering quill meets an exception across the page, although this encounter could just be nothing but a passing tenuous glance. Even the rencontre is uncertain.

que la rencontre ou l'effleure une toque de minuit
    et immobilise
     au velours chiffonné par un esclaffement sombre

    cette blancheur rigide

dérisoire
    en opposition au ciel
  trop
    pour ne pas marquer
      exigüment
       quiconque

    prince amer de l'écueil

   s'en coiffe comme de l'héroïque
   irrésistible mais contenu
   par sa petite raison virile
       en foudre

(UC: 8b; OC: 469)

The midnight encounter (that it might have been) is met by an esclaffement sombre. This meeting is carried forth in the typography of this passage as the doubled *ff*s of *effleure* are repeated in *chiffonné*, *esclaffement* and by *s'en coiffe* below.[47] The quill, or at least its *form* is taken up within the folds of the velvet encounter. As with *Igitur*, there certainly subsists a presence of midnight, albeit a presence relegated to syntactic and typographic dispersion since within the phrasing of the plume's encounter and its object is introduced a verb—*et immobilise*—whose subject is ambiguous. Davies unquestioningly reads the toque as the subject (Davies, 111, 182), whereas Marchal notes that the verb ruptures the syntax hereto established (Marchal, 290). The object is unequivocally *cette blancheur rigide...,* but then there is again the problem of an *unspecified* demonstrative pronoun, as with *cette voile alternative, cette conflagration* and *cette conjonction*. Within the passing midnight encounter there is an immobilization of *cette blancheur rigide,* as if the words, as if the shapes of the words and their constitutive letters could themselves effect such a forceful restraining action upon the page, and as if inscription could *work*. But this rigidity of blankness is absurd in its opposition to the sky. The inscriptions are *too excessive* (*trop*) to not have left a trace of whosoever (*quiconque*) out of necessity (*exigüment*). Some trace of this encounter between plume and toque is left out of necessity within the immobilization of the whiteness. However the object of the marking is not the blancheur rigide, rather it is the undefined quiconque, being perhaps, but not necessarily, the prince amer de l'écueil. The prince does become imbricated within the encounter of plume and toque by donning—*s'en coiffe*—the cap, thereby appropriating the *ff*. Some attempt at mastery is undertaken, recalling Igitur (Davies, 114) and Hamlet (Cohn 1951, 276–77),[48] but the attempted *coup de Maître* is still not productive.

The prince, with reason, appropriates the means of an encounter in the hopes of mastering the possibility of inscribing, the hopes of mastering the trace that will have been left by necessity. Mastery is no more virile, no more efficacious and no more masterful than an awkward floppy cap, badly worn. The prince desires to master, appropriate and affirm the encounter, *his* encounter: "*soucieux / expiatoire et pubère / muet / rire / que / SI*" (UC: 9a–b; OC: 470–71). The word *soucieux* neatly recapitulates a partial swath of the previous page's tentative encounter, concern under the skies, *sous les cieux* (Cohn 1951, 295). The subject of this souciant locative does not necessarily have to be (or not to be) the prince and indeed this prepositional clause could well be a pre-position proleptically announcing that "*CE SERAIT / LE HASARD*" (UC: 10a–

b; OC: 472–73). That which is to be, and to be quizzically affirmed under the skies *would be* chance. Prematurely (*expiatoire et pubère*) Hasard would resound invariably. There is to be an emboldened laughing endorsement, contradicting *en face* the souciant muteness—*rire que SI*—a laugh that quivers between affirmation and hypothesis.[49]

On the bottom of page 9 (UC: 9a–b; OC: 470–71), the plume is now an aigrette alternating between invisibility and luminescence. This is precisely what is tentatively affirmed: that an aigrette will alternate in appearing and that the oscillation of the affirmation (rire que *SI*) is taken over by the vibratory appearing of what is (putatively) affirmed. The experience is one of immensity, an immensity detached and *en face*: "*La lucide et seigneuriale aigrette | de vertige*." Vertige and the aigrette are witnesses to each other immobilized around the *pli* that separates them. This is its siren song, its attractive affirmation is nought *but* tentative. The hypothesized trace is but a siren twist "Dans le si blanc cheveu qui traîne / Avarement aura noyé / Le flanc enfant d'une sirène" (OC: 76; OCP: 394 ll. 12–14). The appearance of such remains eminently, sovereignly subjunctive: would that there had been the time for this to have appeared, to have registered appearance against the rock. The siren flirts with scintillation and with the possibility of having appeared and left a trace of its flight, a rock: "*un roc / faux manoir / tout de suite / évaporé en brumes / qui imposa / une borne à l'infini*" (UC 9b; OC: 471). The rock that is thus tentatively affirmed is *disastrous* (fallen *dès astres*) and *insouciant*, insouciant to the possibility of there even having been an effaced trace *évaporé en brumes*. The rock is a monument to the fact that something might have happened and not even a trace of this here remains.

C'ÉTAIT
issu stellaire

(UC: 10a; OC: 472)

This disastrous stellar issue *imposa une borne à l'infini*. Even this designation is not so certain since it is an imperfective issuance: *SI C'ÉTAIT issu stellaire*. The monument is a subjunctive affirmation of a *defunct possibility*: of the possibility that there had been detritus *and* that this possibility would be itself belated. All that remains is the possibility of a disastrous writing in the wake of said defunct possibility: as Blanchot has said, *l'écriture du désastre*.[50] The *borne, segno* or σημεῖον that is inscribed subsists within this hazardously enmeshed subjunctive interval. "Le désastre ruine tout en laissant tout en l'état. ... Le désastre est séparé, ce qu'il y a de plus séparé" (Blanchot 1980, 7). The disaster is that which is most proximate, a ruination à venir and within said proximity there is no present trace of disaster, no index that could be designated or marked in an indicative mood. "Il n'y a désastre que parce que le désastre incessament se manque. Fin de la nature, fin de la culture" (70). The writing of the disaster thus marks a very different rapport with writing, a different rapport with the imposing inscripting of a *borne*:

> Écrire, c'est ne plus mettre au futur la mort toujours déjà passé, mais accepter de la subir sans la rendre présente et sans se rendre présent à elle, savoir qu'elle a eu lieu, bien qu'elle n'ait pas été éprouvée, et la reconnaître dans l'oubli qu'elle laisse et dont les traces qui s'effacent appellent à *s'excepter de l'ordre cosmique,* là où le désastre rend le réel impossible et le désir indésirable. (108–9)

The problem of death—perhaps evidenced even by Igitur—is that it can serve as a basis of individuation and knowledge. Death was still something to be indicated in the sublation of tossing dice at the present moment when the clock strikes twelve. For Blanchot, death is never individual or recuperable by acts of knowledge. Any application or program to restitute death (Blanchot chooses Winnicott as an example subsequent to the above quotation, but this description is not without relation to his account of Ulysses, the desire to approach and master the bourn of desire) assumes that a never-present death can be transferred or given over into the present. But Blanchot maintains that writing is *exclusive* or without relation: "Désir, encore rapport à l'astre—le grand désir sidéral, religieux et nostalgique, panique ou cosmique; de là qu'il ne puisse y avoir désir du désastre" (84). Writing is the passive acceptance of the becoming anonymous of the writer, a situation that can never be manifest in the present. The paradox is perhaps that writing is a kind of gift of that which is completely other to presence. The stellar detachment, or insouciance, of the disaster marks a break with concern. This detachment of the disaster is what mimes death because it is not a representation, not even a trace of a representation. The disaster and death are without relation: "*Il n'y a rien à faire* avec la mort qui a toujours eu lieu: œuvre de désœuvrement, non-rapport avec un passé (ou un avenir) sans présent. Ainsi le désastre serait au-delà de ce que nous entendons par mort ou par abîme, en tout cas *ma* mort, puisqu'il n'y a plus de place pour elle, y disparaissant sans mourir (ou le contraire)" (182). The disaster is without relation thus necessarily always incomplete, without even a *dès astre*. This insouciance is the tension signaled between *Igitur* and *Un coup de dés*: the "naufrage cela" suspended alongside "direct de l'homme." The disaster does not concern death as a project nor as an object or subject to be regarded. The writing of the disaster can never be pinned down in its profligate proliferation. In this sense l'écriture du désastre proceeds as insouciant dissemination. Writing, the writing of the disaster, does not anticipate any object: "Si je dis: le désastre veille, ce n'est pas pour donner un sujet à la veille, c'est pour dire: la veille ne se passe pas sous un ciel sidéral" (85). There is nothing there to be attributed, no locative subject, in the interval awaiting disaster, no subject *sous cieux*. To anticipate death—to question death—would be to assume that an answer could be given to the questioning thus altering, perhaps even absolving, the questioning. Questioning anticipates this absolution: an affirmation, a revelation, it is eminently proleptic. But questioning—questioning the disaster—is also a call for help. The disaster awaits without anticipating any project—the disaster awaits nothing. The stellar issuance of *Un coup de dés* could thus be a disjected materialization of insouciance.

Page 10 of *Un coup de dés* thus brings to bear the monumentality of issuance, the detritus of the disaster. This stellar residua is not without qualification. If the outcome of action restrained was a stellar issue, if the restrained actions thus far serially hypothesized (to cast or not to cast the dice) were nevertheless disastrous, then *it* (action or otherwise) was also…

LE NOMBRE

EXISTÂT-IL
autrement qu'hallucination éparse d'agonie

COMMENÇÂT-IL ET CESSÂT-IL
sourdant que nié et clos quand apparu
enfin
par quelque profusion répandue en rareté
SE CHIFFRÂT-IL

évidence de la somme pour peu qu'une
ILLUMINÂT-IL

(UC: 10a–b; OC: 472–73)

The number survives, it stands in an imperative mood (albeit an imperfect tense), yet it is immediately questioned, it is perforated by minute and minutely elaborated subjunctive statements (des *dissemis de fioritures*). The resultant numeration is eminently optative: would that the number have existed. The minuscule elaborations of each subjunctive reinforce the tentativity of the number which had not left a trace, were it to have an existence other than an evanescent hallucination of agony. Tentativity and imprecision redouble as the unique number withdraws into hazardous indeterminacy and innumeracy. The subjunctive statement of beginning and end—and as Bowie has noted, the inversion of subject and object lends the appearance, but not necessarily the force of a question (Bowie 1982, 143–44; see note 30)—implies that there will be no interval in which the number can be stated: there is neither space nor time for the numerative of subjunctivity to appear or even to be denied (nié et clos quand apparu). Amidst dispersion the number might not even have been numerated or reckoned (par quelque profusion répandue en rareté SE CHIFFRÂT-IL). The number is just as innumerate as the belated "ancien calcul." Were even these minimal hypotheses to be met, then there would be "évidence de la somme pour peu qu'une ILLUMINÂT-IL." The barest glimmer of manifest numeration would be enough for there to be some illumination, some sum to be reckoned within the interval of this gleam. It is as if an hypothesis states the number into a kind of being, and this being would be chance: "*CE SERAIT / pire / non / davantage ni moins / indifféremment mais autant* / LE HASARD" (UC: 10a–b; OC: 472–73 *bis*).

Were the number able to fulfill these elaborated subjunctive attributions, it would still be chance: "*LE NOMBRE / EXISTÂT-IL / COMMENÇÂT-IL ET CESSÂT-IL / SE CHIFFRÂT-IL / ILLUMINÂT-IL /* LE HASARD" (UC: 10b; OC: 473). Within further hypothetical elaboration, the outcome of HASARD is certain even as the specific numeration remains variably hypothesized. Amidst uncertainty, uncertainty *might* remain certain. This immediate sequence ending with the reassertion of HASARD is coterminous with the dispersed title phrase "UN COUP DE DÉS JAMAIS N'ABOLIRA LE HASARD" (cf. Davies, 130). The stellar issue stands insouciant (*pire non davantage ni moins indifféremment mais autant*) to the various hypothesized machinations of any pre-positionings; the pre-position will not have affected the result. Even uncertainty will not have been so certainly vouchsafed.

Choit
    la plume
        rythmique suspens du sinistre
            s'ensevelir
            aux écumes originelles
naguères d'où sursauta son délire jusqu'à une cime
            flétrie
            par la neutralité identique du gouffre
(UC: 10b; OC 473 *bis*)

There is an additional result below HASARD: the pen falls (*choit*) — a fall suggestive of choosing (*choisir*). The choice amidst and between all the possibilities falls to chance and to the pen in this suspension. This suspended interval buries and conceals itself within the original waves as if it had never been, as if it had never inscribed itself in the tempestuous ocean. The interval *ex-scribes* the pen within its assertion. The phrase *du sinistre* (that against which the interval suspends itself) is vertically aligned with the phrase *aux écumes:* that which is suspended is aligned with the concealing fate of the falling plume. Through the *espacement* of this suspension the one residual outcome from all this auto-concealment is stained by the neutrality of the abyss, *flétrie par la neutralité identique du gouffre*. The splurge is whitewashed in the "contrées nulles," as if it had never been there to stain the écumes originelles. Writing's initiative has been ceded to the hazardous operations of the gulf, and even the ineluctable affirmation of hasard that so perturbed Igitur remains effaced.

What then remains of the remains (of the naufrage) that remain unknown, what remains of this mémorable (if innumerate) crise. "RIEN / de la mémorable crise / ou se fût / l'évènement" (UC: 11a; OC: 474).

>   accompli en vue de tout résultat nul
>   humain
>   N'AURA EU LIEU
>   une élévation ordinaire verse l'absence
>
>   QUE LE LIEU
>   inférieur claptois quelconque comme pour disperser l'acte vide
>   abruptement qui sinon
>   par son mensonge
>   eût fondé
>   la perdition
>
>   dans ces parages
>   du vague
>   en quoi toute réalité se dissout

(UC: 11b; OC: 475)

Only the interval in which something had happened remains, and whatever had happened (or had not happened, for this cannot be known) has had its place taken by the place. The act accomplishes itself in a tautology of exscriptive hypotheses. Human action entails a nul result and so the event[51] is lost in the crise in which the empty act is dispersed. *Here* words are enunciated as (the place that takes place, and that takes the place of) *falling*: "une élévation ordinaire *verse* l'absence." Here one must be sure to hear all the modalities of *vers* within *verse*: the issue of absence is an élévation ordinaire. The enunciation interlaces the event with its *lieu*: the lieu *in lieu* of what had happened, and this lieu *re-marks* the "mémorable crise *ou* se fût l'évènement." This lieu is therefore not so much a *place* (an answer to the question *where: où*), but a hypothesis (*peut-être: ou*). Iterated hypothetically the nothingness (rien) of the lieu is "l'évènement accompli en vue de tout résultat nul humain": nothingness is (accom)*pli*—*sans issue* (with result nul), "ÉXCEPTÉ / PEUT-ÊTRE / UNE CONSTELLATION" (UC: 12a–b; OC: 476–77), the constellation of marks *disastrously* fallen from the totality of the alphabet (l'alphabet des astres) onto the page. There is no present *except* for the initiative of the dispersed and dispersing intervals of words—"par le heurt de leur inégalité mobilisés" (OC: 366)—that will have taken place (n'aura eu lieu) throughout the pages of the poem. And what will have taken place is that which takes place on the page: the future *is not* (it exists neither now nor later as a present *à venir*) *except* as a disruption of the present. "Rien n'aura eu lieu que le lieu" conjugates the present into a futur antérieur passé, as Blanchot claims (see page 138), an interval of nul accomplishment. Indeed, in Mallarmé's visible book, the évènement is separated (or interrupted) from the phrasing of its nul accomplishment by the *pli* of the page. The act of the paper's fold is perdition *sans trace*. In the place's taking place, disparition is annulled in an interruption of enunciation hypothetically enstated: preterition and perdition without remittance. *Un coup de dés* is a poem of the *fin-de-siècle*, century's end with neither a day of judgment, nor a "Day the Dicebox Throws" (FW: 122.13).

Taking then the place of *la* vague, the wave that has engulfed, is *le* vague, a vague of a different genre. That which re-marks the *vague*, its gender, re-marks it in this redoubled iteration (repetition with a difference) as a vague surrendered. The waves in which the remnants of a shipwreck were washed and dissolved on page 6 have now yielded to a void, the annulling motion itself annulled (and that annulling motion had annulled that which was already dissipated); multiply imbricated disparitions enfold and disperse and no annullation is left without disseminated disparition. No silence is left to resound. The LIEU of the poem, then, the *parage*, is where *genres of disparition alternate*. These genres could be codified (typographical sequences, rhythmic clusters, parataxes, syntactic spacifications, sylleptically misaligned reference, hypotheses, &c., &c.), but even such a meticulously calculated and reckoned precession of terms would yield to subjunctive disparition (SE CHIFFRÂT-IL). What is left, what is without doubt, is that there was loss and loss redoubled elaborately. Loss is itself lost paratactically; and so the only way in which this LIEU is to be held together is through concatenated and hypothetical parataxis, "en quoi toute réalité se dissout."[52]

The LIEU does admit a possible, hypothetical exception of a trace that will have been possibly left. Unsurprisingly qualifications circulate through the statement of this possible exception. This exception (the possibility of a trace) is indicated in much the same way as the poem's previous imbricated indications of redoubling exscriptions. "EXCEPTÉ / à l'altitude / PEUT-ÊTRE / aussi loin qu'un endroit | fusionne avec au delà / hors l'intérêt / quant à lui signalé / en général / selon telle obliquité par telle déclivité / de feux" (UC: 12a–b; OC: 476–77). The exception involves a *union*, reminiscent of the earlier annulling rencontre. Yet this union is *ethereal:* "à l'altitude / aussi loin qu'un endroit | fusionne avec au delà hors l'intérêt." The effected union "hors l'intérêt" will be between, on the one hand, a location that is neither specifically defined nor unambiguously located and, on the other hand, an even less distinct "au delà." This is clearly a most unclear union and issuance, and this tentativity reinforces the PEUT-ÊTRE. This elaboration of ambiguity allows for the possibility of there having been a trace: "quant à lui signalé en général selon telle obliquité par telle déclivité." An index was made by *such* obliqueness and *such* descent. In this way, this passage appears to be self-referential: describing its own oblique and declining pattern. Yet allowing for a cross-linguistic rupture in the word *telle*—which Cohn had noted in *Salut* ($τῆλε$, *far;* see the previous chapter)—then the obliqueness and slant are neither present nor within the interval of the poetic enunciation, but they too are *au delà, hors l'intérêt*. Even in self-designation, even in the interval of the re-mark, the iteration remains *apart*.

vers
> ce doit être
>> le Septentrion aussi Nord

UNE CONSTELLATION

> froide d'oubli et de désuétude
>> pas tant
>> qu'elle n'énumère
>> sur quelque surface vacante et supérieure
>> le heurt successif
>>> sidéralement
>> d'un compte total en formation

veillant
> doutant
>> roulant
>>> brillant et méditant

>>> avant de s'arrêter
>>> à quelque point dernier qui le sacre

Toute Pensée émet un Coup de Dés

(UC: 12b; OC: 477)

The downward spiral inclines "vers *ce doit être* le Septentrion aussi Nord," it *must have* gone upwards and it *must have been* the specific constellation Ursa Major (le Septentrion). Of course the certitude of this claim works ironically and indeed the ascription of the Septentrion surrenders to the vaguer, generic CONSTELLATION. Were this word to be taken literally one would read that the issue must be *with* (*con*) the stars and so the fusion falls amidst "the apathy of the stars" (U: 17.2226), froide d'oubli et de *désuétude*. This then is the writing of the *désastre:* an étude of the dés that stands insouciant and destitute amidst (con) stellar issuance. The insouciant alphabet des astres is innumerate, a nombre that could always have been and always will be another (see note 40). The poem is the *interval of insouciance,* the interval of seemingly incessant and

insouciant rapports between words composed from letters of the alphabet. But this destitution is not enough so as to fail to enumerate. *Finally* the doubling and redoubling of negation might yield something positive as here an unequivocal double negative points to a possibly achieved numeration despite destitution. And yet, as always, the elaboration of this seeming positivity denies the alluded result for there is no apparent object of the enumeration. In the continuing declivity of the poem's oblique precessions, there remains nothing to be enumerated *d'un compte total en formation*. In a limited sense, destruction was the Beatrice of the passage through *Un coup de dés* as the traversal was navigated by the imbricated denegations of the poem's metaleptic subdivisions. All that then remains is the declining precession of the words of the poem, in this its final page, until there is some terminal moment which defines the iteration that had preceded it, some *Ulyssean* moment of *definitude,* a moment in which the passage towards has been fulfilled and *achieved*: quelque point dernier qui le sacre. Yet this terminal moment—"Tout Pensée émet un Coup de Dés"—lies *outside* this statement of projected definitude. The only unequivocal statement of the poem (Bowie 1982, 144) concerns the perdurance of hasard. The only possible issuance is uncertainty, or rather, allowing for the poem's chiasmic (or palindromic) circularity, the only issuance is *the iteration of uncertainty* (traversing the poem) that *Un coup de dés jamais n'abolira le hasard*. Even if Ronat's dodecahedral pagination were to be accepted, there is still some ambiguity if the poem reaches or accomplishes 12 pages at its end (the title page can be taken both as lying within the sequence of the poem and also *hors l'intérêt*); the unique number that could not be another could have been either 11 or 12 at the poem's end. "En fait, ce coup de dés céleste, qui réalise idéalement le coup de dés manqué, n'annule en rien—ni même ne corrige—la tautologie avérée, mais déplace en quelque sorte le lieu de la poésie, de la réalité sinistre de l'abîme à la pure fiction d'un espace idéal; de l'abîme au ciel constellé, il n'y a pas de continuité, pas d'« élévation *ordinaire* », mais un saut extraordinaire di réel à l'imaginaire, même si cet imaginaire se fond dans une représentation spatiale" (Marchal, 283). Even the virtuality of the

poem's suspension across twelve (or so) pages impacts against the hazardous futility attempted to be inscribed. The "goal" of the poem, the result of 12, remains *within* the interregnum of *hasard* that might have occasioned it. The putative answer remains a part of the question. Much as God remained the inevitable unproffered at the close of *Paradiso*, so too *hasard* at the endfall of *Un coup de dés*.

As with *À la nue accablante tu,* there is here the evocation of nothing withdrawn: nothing may not or may have happened. The monument, the border to infinity, commemorates this absented lacuna. Said absentation is sustained through a specification of vertiginously sylleptic cross references in which each metaleptic statement weakens the others in a progressive attenuation of statability. Even the poem's pagination will have been innumerate. At the close of the *Paradiso*, after a quite arduous ascent, the pilgrim beheld God only to have that experience dissolve out of the pilgrimage within a lyric instant of *disigillare*. In *Un coup de dés* this instant has become a book. The poem—perhaps, after all is said and done, not that unlike the livre—is a *tomb* taking the place for the *rien* that is not there. The shipwreck is the condition of the poem, but it is not a Ulyssean shipwreck, a shattering of progress and (diachronic or narrational) progression; instead the shipwreck is that which prepositions the possibility of this *recherche du rien perdu*. In this way, as we will suggest in our final chapter, *Un coup de dés* has a tenor not unlike that of *Finnegans Wake*, the subjunctive *recherche de* HCE *perdu* (for want of a better name).

Beyond all measure of formal innovation and syntactic obfuscation in Mallarmé's œuvre, what one would call the tenebrific *obscurity* of his work (as was noted briefly in our first chapter) is this inscriptive unworking or exscription, or what Blanchot calls the absence of the book: "rien qui fût visible, rien qui fût invisible."[53] What is on the page is beyond sense and sensibility all the while remaining within certain formal constraints or arrangements of intelligibility. *The* book, the livre à venir, is the book no longer become artifact—"hélas un livre, rien qu'un livre" (Blanchot 1959, 16)—but the bound interval into which disparition is folded and extrapolated. In *Un coup de dés* bibliofication comes to nought.

Sait-on ce que c'est qu'écrire? Une ancienne et très vague mais jalouse pratique, dont gît le sens au mystère du cœur.
Qui l'accomplit, intégralement, se retranche.
Autant, par ouï-dire, que rien existe et soi, spécialement, au reflet de la divinité éparse: c'est, ce jeu insensé d'écrire, s'arroger en vertu d'un doute—la goutte d'encre apparentée à la nuit sublime—quelque devoir de tout recréer, avec des réminiscences, pour avérer qu'on est bien là où l'on doit être (parce que, permettez-moi d'exprimer cette appréhension, demeure une incertitude).
(OC: 481)

Writing is then the mad game both born from and dwelling within an interval of uncertainty uncertainly re-marked: toute pensée émet un coup de dés. The difficulty of Mallarmé is the difficulty of writing, the obscurity of the very experience of writing. First Dante, then Joyce, in-between hither and thither Mallarmé.

Notes

[1] The very format of the poem is not definite, for most critics to whom these issues matter, the only consensus is that the Pléiade edition of *Un coup de dés* is sorely deficient: "une reproduction fortement réduite et imprécise" (Jean-Claude Lebenstejn, "Note relative au *Coup de dés*," *Critique* 397–98 [June–July 1980]: 633–59. 641). The only edition of the poem to have appeared in print during Mallarmé's lifetime was an incomplete version for the English journal *Cosmopolis* in May 1897 (OC: 1581, this was reprinted in 1996 by Editions du Tiroir). In 1966 R.G. Cohn published Mallarmé's corrected proofs for an aborted edition of *Un coup de dés* which was to have been accompanied by three illustrations by Odilon Redon (R.G. Cohn, *Mallarmé's Masterwork: New Findings*, The Hague: Mouton, 1966. The manuscript is reproduced on 89–111; cf. 78–80 for Cohn's commentary). These page-proofs were later identified as those for the Didot/Vollard edition, a deluxe edition for bibliophiles (Danielle Mirham, "The Abortive Didot/Vollard Edition of *Un coup de dés*," *French Studies* XXXIII.1 [January 1979]: 39–56. 39–41; cf. Lebenstejn, 637–38). This manuscript provides the strongest authorial witness to the poem, indeed Thibaudet claimed that it was at this stage, the correction of the proofs, that the poem was actually written since it was only here that the typographic layout was established (Albert Thibaudet, *La poésie de Stéphane Mallarmé*, 9th edition, Paris: Gallimard, 1926. 417–18; quoted in Lebenstejn, 638). The 1914 Gallimard edition of the poem, the first actual publication of the poem in its final form, was based on, but occasionally deviates from the Didot/Vollard proofs (Cohn 1966, 78–80; Lebenstejn, 639, 642–47). Lebenstejn calls the 1914 edition "plutôt satisfaisante" (643) and Cohn agrees with this assessment (Cohn 1966, 80). The 1914 edition has been reprinted in 1952, 1969 and 1993, but these subsequent editions were of reduced size to accommodate shelving in libraries (Lebenstejn, 640–41).

In 1980 a new edition was published, edited by team led by Mitsou Ronat (Paris: Change/d'Atelier, 1980); this edition scrupulously follows the Didot/Vollard proofs and their attendant documents, thereby respecting Mallarmé's meticulous attention to typographic detail. Lebenstejn describes his reaction upon first encountering this edition as like holding "une hallucination, la matérialisation d'un fantôme: on passe le doigt, il y a un creux, l'encre reste noire et nette: le livre est là, chose incroyable" (653). Lebenstejn does later admit that the Ronat edition is still not *the* edition of *Un coup de dés* (655) and he notes two minor flaws (658–59).

One notable feature of the Ronat edition is that the cover page is rendered as one of the pages of the poem itself, thereby effecting a total of 12 pairs of pages, and for Ronat 12 is the motor of the poem: the double sixes of the dice and the number of syllables in the alexandrine (cf. Mitsou Ronat, "*Un coup de dés*, mystère hurlé?" *Cahiers cistre* 5 [1978]: 59–92. 64–68; Lebenstejn, 651). Indeed whilst preparing the Didot/Vollard edition, Mallarmé remarked to Gide that "Le poème s'imprime, en ce moment, tel que je l'ai conçu; quant à la pagination, où est tout l'effet" (CIX: 172); it is perhaps in *12* pages that there is the unique number that cannot be another. Cohn disputed Ronat's valorization of this number 12, claiming that Mallarmé was too polyvalent to allow for such arithmetical delimitations (R.G. Cohn, "À propos du *Coup de dés*," *Critique* 416 [January 1982]: 92–93, reprinted in R.G. Cohn, *Vues sur Mallarmé*, Paris: Nizet, 1991. 269–71). Ronat responded that the pagination does not necessarily reflect an absolute privileging of this number, and furthermore "le nombre 12 n'est pas un nombre quelconque dans l'histoire de la poésie française: il est la base rythmique du mètre alexandrin, mètre dominant plusieurs siècles et précisément mis en question au moment du *Coup de dés*. ... Notre hypothèse est donc... [que] dans le *Coup de dés,* Mallarmé a voulu donner une réponse *poétique* au questionnement *théorique* exposé dans *Crise de vers* et dans ses autres « essais ». L'architecture spatiale et typographique du poème est une projection tridimensionnelle de la versification classique à laquelle Mallarmé se deeclarait fort attaché.... Par conséquent, le nombre 12 peut traduire à la fois une expérience de rupture et la volonté de prolonger la tradition qui caractérise l'aventure mallarméenne" (Mitsou Ronat, "Réponse à Robert Greer Cohn," *Critique* 418 [March 1982]: 276–77. 276). Virginia La Charité claims that Ronat exaggerates the importance of the number 12 since the 24 pages (12 pairs) the poem occupies are required by the printer's use of signatures comprising four pages each (Virginia A. La Chariot, *The Dynamics of Space,* Lexington: French Forum, 1987. 181 fn. 8). However, this objection does not necessarily diminish the importance of the number 12 since, in addition to being the rhythmic basis of the Alexandrine, it also reflects the exigencies of the printer in producing a book out of *Un coup de dés*.

[2] Cited in R.G. Cohn, L'œuvre de Mallarmé: "Un coup de dés," Paris: Les Lettres, 1951. 24; cf. 23–24. This letter to Gide is always cited by partisans of the argument that Un coup de dés has a direct filiation to the livre (cf. Cohn 1966, 13–5; Suzanne Bernard, Mallarmé et la musique, Paris: Nizet, 1959. 133).

[3] The strangeness that Richard emphasizes might initially seem counter-intuitive. Richard claims that in a certain way *Un coup de dés* is Mallarmé's simplest work because it proffers an elaboration of a single theme (that of the hypothesis); it is thus a singularity that nevertheless remains fundamentally cathected within the

Mallarméan universe (Jean-Pierre Richard, *L'univers imaginaire de Mallarmé*, Paris: Seuil, 1961. 563–64).

[4] Cohn also tends towards including his 1951 study *within* the Mallarméan constellation of reference, as virtually all his subsequent studies refer to his work as if it were the first and final word on *Un coup de dés*. His 1966 study is in essence an update of the earlier work in the light of the discoveries of the juvenilia, the *Anatole* fragments and the notes for the livre. Rather than reassess his work, Cohn merely uses these discoveries as further evidence of his previous claims: "I anticipate that the reader may be surprised at the fact that in the texts which will be quoted from my *Œuvre de Mallarmé* occasionally occur precisely the same terms that Mallarmé had used in the *Tombeau* [*d'Anatole*], which was then totally unknown to me. But there is an explanation: working back from the synthesis of the *Coup de Dés* to abstract or analytical critical formulations, I often encountered in my own mind the relatively naked patterns Mallarmé was preparing as the skeleton of his future Work" (Cohn 1966, 30).

[5] Cohn's critique of Davies is also a criticism of a project more related to his own than he admits. Davies considers but discounts the characterization of *Un coup de dés* as a "tentative" because in the preface Mallarmé describes it as an intellectual effort (OC: 455), and the livre was supposed to have been lyrical (Gardner Davies, *Vers une explication rationnelle du « coup de dés »*, nouvelle edition, Paris: José Corti, 1992. 157). Davies provides additional anecdotal evidence for his proposal concerning the non-identity of *Un coup de dés* as the livre which Cohn summarily dismisses, although Cohn's valorization of the letter to Gide hardly seems more reliable (Cohn 1966, 17–19; cf. Cohn's review of the first edition of Davies's book, reprinted in Cohn 1991, 304–8, cf. esp. 305).

[6] Maurice Blanchot, *L'espace littéraire,* Paris: Gallimard, 1955, 1988. 136–37.

[7] As we noted in the previous chapter, Derrida countered Blanchot's claims of the attempted auto-ipseic conjunctions of *Igitur* by noting that concatenations of sound distend the attempted enstatement of definitive confluences. Note in this passage the slurs between the repetitions of *corne* and also with *l'état latent*. Already latent within the subsistence of the midnight state are the contingencies of the materiality of words, the *hasard* of their *sonority*.

[8] Marc Froment-Meurice astutely notes that "Lorsque Mallarmé dit qu'il n'est pas de présent, il ne dit pas qu'il n'y a rien, qu'à présent rien n'est, mais que ce maintenant est un faux présent, un présent sans présence" (Marc Froment-Meurice, *Solitudes,* Paris: Galilée, 1989. 41).

[9] In a letter to Cazalis from 1869, Mallarmé expressed a desire for an achievement with *Igitur*: "S'il est fait (le conte), je suis guéri: *simila similibus*" (CI: 313). It is as if the resolution of the tale would resolve Mallarmé's *crise,* as if *crise* could impact into a happy ending.

[10] Dianna Niebylski makes a similar point: *Igitur* remains within an economy of mastery (the desire to coincide various orders of disparition at midnight) whereas in *Un coup de dés* "No amount of premeditation or planning will abolish the future time which Mallarmé calls *le Hasard*" (Dianna C. Niebylski, *The Poem on the Edge of the Word,* New York: Peter Lang, 1993. 74; cf. 72–74).

[11] One should remember the fastidious and consummate attention lavished in the notes for the livre, how Mallarmé attempted to plan each possible variation in its performance even as he attempted to plan out an infinite combination of performative permutabilities (cf. Jacques Scherer, *Le "livre" de Mallarmé,* nouvelle édition, Paris: Gallimard, 1957, 1977. 72–74; cf. esp. feuillets 143–202).

[12] In many ways Blanchot's distinction between *Igitur* and *Un coup de dés*—which is less severe than it might seem—derives from the earlier essay "La littérature et le droit à la mort," the right to death is the *accident* of writing, and this is the chance the writer takes, the hasard to which the writer is staked: "*Toute œuvre est œuvre de circonstance: cela veut simplement dire que cette œuvre a eu un début, qu'elle a commencé dans le temps et que ce moment du temps fait partie de l'œuvre, pusique, sans lui, elle n'aurait été qu'un problème indépassable, rien de plus que l'impossibilité de l'écrire*" (Maurice Blanchot, *La part du feu,* Paris: Gallimard, 1949. 297).

[13] Maurice Blanchot, *Le livre à venir.* Paris: Gallimard, 1959, 1986. 318.

[14] Marion Sugano shows that the typographical disposition of *Un coup de dés*, the alignment of words around spaces, follows from some of the experiments undertaken in the *Vers de circonstance,* specifically the *Loisirs,* the *cartes de visites*, the *œufs de Pâques,*

and especially the *eventails* (Marion Zwerling Sugano, *The Poetics of the Occasion,* Stanford: Stanford UP, 1992. 171–76; cf. Davies, 53–55; Scherer 1977, 228–30).

[15] Bertrand Marchal, *Lecture de Mallarmé,* Paris: José Corti, 1985. 272. That the poem can be defined as an elaboration of the title phrase is a point phrased variously by commentators of the poem. For Cohn the title phrase works as a simultaneous affirmation and negation of meaning thereby providing a pattern for the overall syntax of the poem (Cohn 1951, 32–3). David Scott's formulation explicitly acknowledges the spacings and the typographic distinctions enacted *within* the play of this titular elaboration: "The large capitals, engraving themselves on the reader's mind, become an ever-present backdrop to the more detailed and extensive ramifications of thinking explored over the successive pages in the smaller type" (David H.T. Scott, *Pictorialist Poetics,* Cambridge: Cambridge UP, 1988. 140).

[16] In his initial identification of *Un coup de dés* as the livre, Cohn actually comes close to this point, but this proximity is obviated by his subsequent polemics. He notes that the most complete program for the livre announced by Mallarmé can be found in *La musique et les lettres:* "Quand son initiative, ou la force virtuelle des caractères divins lui enseigne de les mettres en œuvre" (OC: 646; Cohn 1951, 36–37). Cohn claims that *Un coup de dés* is this *work* (this mise-en-œuvre) here projected, what he misses is that this identification with a virtual force can itself only be possible by a virtuality of *rapport.*

[17] Recall from *Crise de vers* the use of *heurt* as an unsteady lexical motion: "L'œuvre pure implique la disparition élocutoire du poëte, qui cède l'initiative aux mots, *par le heurt de leur inégalité mobilisés*; ils s'allument de reflets réciproques comme une virtuelle traînée de feux sur des pierreries, remplaçant la respiration perceptible en l'ancien souffle lyrique ou la direction personnelle enthousiaste de la phrase" (OC: 366, emphasis added). The words themselves in *Un coup de dés* have ceded power through their labile alignments.

[18] This is, of course, in the course of throwing the dice, why Igitur "trouve l'acte inutile, car il y a et n'y a pas de hasard—il réduit le hasard à l'*Infini*—qui, dit-il, doit exister quelque part" (OC: 442).

[19] John Freccero notes that Dante's figuration of Ulysses's folly of the intellect against faith was specifically Medieval (John Freccero, *Dante: The Poetics of Conversion,* ed. Rachel Jacoff, Cambridge: Harvard UP, 1986. 17; cf. ED: V.808).

[20] Giuseppe Mazzotta, *Dante, Poet of the Desert,* Princeton: Princeton UP, 1979. 81–83.

[21] It is no coincidence that *Le livre à venir* begins with Ulysses and ends with *Un coup de dés*. Although Blanchot's essay takes as its point of departure Kafka's "The Song of the Sirens," the figure of Ulysses he considers—"un Grec de la décadence qui ne mérita jamais d'être le héros de *L'Iliade*" (Blanchot 1959, 11)—is not inappropriate for most Classical figurations of Ulysses from Homer to Sophocles to Virgil to Ovid to Seneca to Dante *&c., &c.* An example is the following invective from Philoctetes: "Hateful creature, what things you invent! You plead the Gods to screen your actions and make the Gods false" (Sophocles, *Philoctetes,* trans. David Grene, *Sophocles,* eds. David Grene and Richmond Lattimore, Chicago: U of Chicago P, 1959. 401–60. ll. 991–92).

[22] Libertson provides a useful qualification of the French word *récit* in distinction to the English word *narrative*: "The French word *récit* describes a recounting, telling or reciting, and thus the communicational genre 'story' or 'narrative.' Every novel or story is a *récit,* but the *récit* itself is a more general moment of communication, a pure 'telling' of an event, whose economic implications Blanchot will mediate" (Joseph Libertson, *Proximity,* The Hague: Martinus Nijhoff, 1982. 150 n.).

[23] "Réunir dans un même espace… les Sirènes et Ulysse, voilà le vœu secret qui fait d'Ulysse Homère, … et du monde qui résulte de cette réunion le plus grand, le plus terrible et le plus beau des mondes possibles, hélas un livre, rien qu'un livre" (Blanchot 1959, 15–16).

[24] In a generally well-argued essay, Malcom Bowie attempts to read a "Ulyssean" narrative into *Un coup de dés*. He claims that there is a temporal structure to the poem which performs scenes from a man's life ("né" [UC: 6a; OC: 464]; "*vierge*" [UC: 7b; OC: 467]; "*pubère*" [UC 8a; OC: 470]; "Fiançailles" [UC: 6a; OC 464]; "l'homme" [UC: 5b; OC: 463]; "MAÎTRE" [UC: 5a; OC: 462]; "vieillard" [UC: 6a; OC: 464]; "cadavre" [UC: 5a; OC: 462]). In other words a Ulyssean recitation survives: through non-contiguous recitation a human quotidian time is imposed over and against the interval of the poem's excruciatingly tortured and tortuous syntax. In this way Bowie argues that the poem's syntactic conundrums recuperate the negativity of language into a human deed ("The Question of *Un coup de dés*," *Baudelaire,*

Mallarmé, Valéry: New Essays in Honour of Lloyd Austin, eds. Malcom Bowie, Alison Fairlie and Alison Finch, Cambridge: Cambridge UP, 1982. 142–50. 149–50).

[25] In a careful analysis of the projected yet never manifest futurity of *Un coup de dés*, Jean-Michel Rabaté notes that "The Book is not a re-creation but a suspension of the world. It brackets the world and negates it, and then, in another sense, embodies the only possible sense of existence, existence as ontological difference" ("'Rien n'aura eu lieu que le lieu': Mallarmé and Postmodernism," *Writing the Future,* ed. David Wood, London: Routledge, 1990. 37–54. 41).

[26] The naufrage of *Un coup de dés* is not an event, not something that happens, but rather it is the condition (the disaster) that is the poem: "le naufrage n'est pas un accident, à tous les sens de ce mot, parce qu'il est, si l'on peut dire, l'essence même de la réalité. Ce que dit le *Coup de dés,* c'est en somme qu'il y a pas d'autre réalité que le naufrage; en d'autres termes, que l'immersion de tout dans tout et la dissolution de l'esprit même dans la profusion hasardeuse d'un monde sans issue" (Marchal, 277).

[27] Jacques Scherer, *Grammaire de Mallarmé,* Paris: Nizet, 1977. 222. "In inviting the page back into the text, the poem enhances its own profile and visual impact, but at the cost of a certain dislocation of language's intrinsic functions, especially those associated with linear advance: syntax and the logic of proposition. The page thus asserts itself both as an ironic denial of language's positive, rational gestures and as a potentially symbolic field, capable, silently, of reverberating, extending or enlarging the irrational or unconscious implications of the text" (Scott, 139).

[28] Malcom Bowie, *Mallarmé and the Art of Being Difficult,* Cambridge: Cambridge UP, 1978. 122. La Charité writes that the spaces provide the fluxile and dynamic component of the poem in distinction to the type, which is what remains, after all, fixed and rigid (La Charité, 85–86). On the other hand, both Marchal and Davies attempt to reign in the errant syntax of the poem by proffering syntactic breakdowns of the poem (Davies, 179–86; Marchal, 289–93). Indeed Davies's reading is explicitly predicated by the possibility of restituting a normal and normative syntax to the poem (as opposed to Cohn's overtly metaphorico-symbolico-cosmological reading). Davies essentially has faith that syntax bears a responsibility to delimit and define meaning (cf. Davies, 173). Marchal is a bit more hesitant in this regard, but does imply nonetheless that there is in the poem a basic pattern of syntax that can be adduced, upon which all sorts of counterpointing is inflicted (Marchal,

270). Julia Kristeva undertook a complex analytic of several phrases in order to adduce that syntactic relations within the poem change continuously and thus cannot be definitively fixed: "La négativité agit ici comme un *surplus syntaxique* qui, à la longue, apparaît comme une défaillance linguistique, mais qui n'en est pas moins productrice de nouveaux rythmes, ici syntaxiques" (Julia Kristeva, *La révolution du langage poétique*, Paris: Seuil 1974. 283, cf. 274–83).

[29] Ronat suggests an analogy between the fragmented syntactic units and the momentum of *terza rima* in that both patternings effect a notion of embedded forward momentum through division and in this way the blanks *articulate* the fragments into a retrospective and advancing syntactic chain (Ronat 1978, 76–77). Freccero's characterization of *terza rima* seems especially apt for the claims that Ronat is making, "*terza rima* implies: a forward motion, closed off with a recapitulation that gives to the motion its beginning and end. Any complete appearance of a rhyme ... BA BCB ... incorporates at the same time a recall to the past and a promise of the future that seem to meet in the now of the central rhyme" (Freccero, 262). This reading is just as narratological as Bowie's (see note 24), but instead of a human evolution there is a rhythmic development. It remains to be seen if such a notion of a *present moment* of recollection and advance is sustainable within the interval of the poem.

[30] Bowie notes that Mallarmé's frequent inversion of subject and object suggests a question, but also, in the absence of a question-*mark,* suggests an exclamation, thereby compromising or even losing the interrogative character. He also finds examples of this oscillational interrogativity in Mallarmé's verse, such as *À la nue accablante tu* (e.g., "Quel sépulcral naufrage") (Bowie 1982, 143–44).

[31] Mary Lewis Shaw, *Performance in the Texts of Mallarmé*, University Park: The Pennsylvania State UP, 1993. 173.

[32] Davies draws a series of allusions between this MAÎTRE and the precipitous navigation of *Salut* (Davies, 76–77); indeed as with that poem the disaster re-marked upon the page *had already been* and is consigned to such belatedness in its being written upon the page.

[33] This symbolic reading installs on the page a boundary or cæsura between sea and sky, the clouds crashing against the waves' spume, a primordial archetypal

conflict in which the hapless MAÎTRE would be situated (cf. Cohn 1951, 136–39, *et passim*; Davies, 70; Marchal, 276).

[34] As Scherer notes, all too frequently substantives and substantival units take the place of the verb in the Mallarméan sentence (Scherer 1977, 103). It is as if the verb were forgotten in excessive paratactic elaboration. An example which Scherer gives that is analogous to our above reading of the "nombre" as the subject of "hésite" (thereby leaving the unfortunate MAÎTRE to dangle with the past participle "surgi") comes from *Le mystère dans les lettres:* "sitôt cette masse jetée vers quelque trace que c'est une réalité" (OC: 383; Scherer 1977, 121).

[35] This proposal lies between the notes for the livre and *Un coup de dés*, with the emphasis on the hope that the project of silence will be accessible to the public in such a way that its disparitional attributes will not be compromised, otherwise it will be a "livre explicatif et familier," "le plus terrible et le plus beau des mondes possibles, hélas un livre, rien qu'un livre" (Blanchot 1959, 15–16).

[36] Jacques Derrida, *La dissémination,* Paris: Seuil, 1972. 290. Derrida's target is Richard's massive investment of symbolic and cross-symbolic interpretations, a reading in which every *thing* in Mallarmé's work, every *rien,* means some thing else.

[37] Blanchot also notes that the separating of words with blanks distorts the abilities of syntaxes to compose a progressive accumulation of sense. Espacement impoverishes the word to a point of madness: "La lassitude devant les mots, c'est aussi le désire des mots espacés, rompus dans leur pouvoir qui est sens, et dans leur composition qui est syntax ou continuité du système (à condition que le système ait été en quelque sorte préalablement achevé, et le présent, accompli). La folie qui n'est jamais de maintenant, mais le délai de la non-raison, le « il sera fou demain », folie dont on ne doit pas se servir pour en agrandir, alourdir ou alléger la pensée" (Maurice Blanchot, *L'écriture du désastre,* Paris: Gallimard, 1980. 18–19). The system will never have been accomplished, and although it is already tenuous, any iteration of its incompletion will be a further interval of tenuousness.

[38] Scott notes that unequivocal interpretation of the calligrammatic or pictographic aspects of the poem could be overplayed as the overall shapes and patterns of the pages are more suggestive than concrete (Scott, 144).

[39] Sugano draws an example of this from *Eventail* 15, "composed so as to imitate the contour of a fan being opened vertically"; and she notes that the motif of

expansion and contraction, depicted by the arrangement of the words, is reinforced by the accelerating and decelerating rhythm of the strophes (Sugano, 174–75):

Palpite,
   Aile,
      mais n'arrête
Sa voix que pour brillamment
La ramener sur la tête
Et le sein
      en diamant (OC: 110; OCP: 554).

[40] "Avec les caractères initiaux de l'alphabet, dont chaque comme touche subtile correspond à une attitude de Mystère, la rusée pratique évoquera certes des gens, toujours: sans la compensation qu'en les faisant tels ou empruntés aux moyens méditatifs de l'esprit, ils n'importunent" (OC: 375). The numerically delimited alphabet expands ceaselessly in an indefinite reserve of permutability; the work of the alphabet is *beyond numeration*: "Si! Avec ses vingt-quatre signes, cette Littérature exactement dénommé les Lettres, ainsi que par de multiples fusions en la figure de phrases puis les vers, système agencé comme spirituel zodiaque, implique sa doctrine propre, abstraite, ésotérique comme quelque théologie: cela, du fait, uniment, que des notions sont telles, ou à un degré de raréfaction au delà de l'ordinaire atteinte, que de ne pouvoir s'exprimer sinon avec des moyens, typiques et suprêmes, dont le nombre n'est, pas plus que le leur, à elles, illimité" (OC: 850).

[41] "Sans que dans cette « *voile alternative* » on puisse décider si le texte est « *penché de l'un ou l'autre bord* » (*Un coup de dés*). Les deux pôles de la lecture ne sont pas également actuels: du moins la syntaxe a-t-elle ménagé un effet de flottaison indéfinie entre deux possibles" (Derrida 1972, 254).

[42] In the notes for the livre, there is a contemplation of the possibilities of foldings entombed within the block of the book (Scherer 1957, feuillet 43a):

et le livre est pour ce lecteur bloc pur —
transparent   —   il lit dedans, le devine — sait
                  mon<u>trant</u> |
d'avance—— | où c'est — ce qui devra être —
   ou finir
                raccords —— rappor<u>ts</u> |

[43] Davies immediately retracts the full implications of this claim by noting that "Le veillard a été inéluctablement attiré vers cette suprême rencontre avec le Hasard" (Davies, 92), thereby restituting a Ulyssean archeteleologics of mastery to this *passage*.

[44] We prefer the admittedly awkward word "spacification" over "spacings" because of the perhaps specious etymological association of *-fication* (making, from *facio*) with ποιέιν. Spacification denotes a poetry of spacing, a poetry that is defined within the spacings of the blank page.

[45] Indeed this page resounds with various echoes and pseudo-echoes (some continued from previous pages): d'*aile* (UC: 4a); M*aî*tre; v*ai*ne (UC: 5); t*ê*te; vi*eill*ard; soustr*ai*te; *ais*; *aïels*; Fian*çailles*; rej*ailli* (UC: 6) form one sequence and *o*mbre; s*ou*straite; *o*s; *oi*seuse; fant*ô*me; f*o*lie; n'abo*l*ira form another. These echoes embed a notion of a belated perdition through sonorous parataxis.

[46] Neither the Pléiade nor the 1914 NRF edition share this alignment, the former places the bottom *et* slightly to the right of the top, and the latter slightly to the left. The Didot/Vollard proofs show a precise alignment (cf. Cohn 1966, 101).

[47] Mallarmé's comments on the Didot/Vollard proofs show a careful attention to the precise shape of the italicized letters, preferring a quill-like *f* and a bottom-curved *y* (Cohn 1966, 79, 101–5).

[48] One line which would reconcile these two variant readings of the prince amer de l'ecueil is from Mallarmé's *Hamlet*: "Son solaire drame! et qui, parfois, tant ce promeneur d'un labyrinthe de trouble et de griefs en prolonge les circuits *avec le suspens d'un acte inachevé*, semble le spectacle même pourquoi existent la rampe ainsi que l'espace doré quasi moral qu'elle défend, car il n'est point d'autre sujet, sachez bien: l'antagonisme de rêve chez l'homme avec les fatalités à son existence départies par le malheur" (OC: 300, emphasis added). Both Igitur and Hamlet endure within the intervallic suspension of inachievement, of the achievement of inachievement inachieved; both endlessly conjugate *to be or not to be*… as if this were a question that could be answered and resolved.

[49] In the Didot/Vollard proofs Mallarmé explicitly requested that the "SI" be printed in as bold an italic face as possible: "voir s'il n'y aurait pas, dans le même jeu exactement, des italiques plus fortes, pour ce mot SI; comme je l'ai précédemment

demandé" (Cohn 1966, 105). The Ronat edition is the only one to observe this request, but as Lebenstejn notes (and this is one of the two quibbles he has with the Ronat edition), the "SI" is rendered in a slightly different typeface than the "SERAIT" (Lebenstejn, 658).

[50] Blanchot's *désastre* derives from Mallarmé's *Tombeau d'Edgar Poe,* the poem that has fallen (tombé) from the tomb. This poem is also not irrelevant to the "roc qui imposa une borne à l'infini." For a modicum of terseness, we will treat only the tercets:

> Du sol et de la nue hostiles, ô grief!
> Si notre idée avec ne sculpte un bas-relief
> Dont la tombe de Poe éblouissante s'orne,
>
> Calme bloc ici-bas chu d'un désastre obscur,
> Que ce granit du moins montre à jamais sa borne
> Aux noirs vols du Blasphème épars dans le futur (OC: 70, 190; OCP: 272 ll. 9–14).

The first tercet echoes with the *o* of tombe and of Poe's sonorous name, which makes its first appearance in the poem in this strophe's last line (these onomastic echoes and this placement of the deceased's name in the final line of the first tercet occurs in Mallarmé's other tombeau poems). In the line "Dont le tombe de Poe éblouissante s'orne," Poe becomes lost amidst the ornaments of his tomb. He is forgotten or disarticulated, or disoriented by that which is supposed to remember him. Furthermore, the poem appears to fold into this line, and, more precisely, into the word "s'orne." The tercet appears to posit some hypothetical ominous advent arising from "sol et... nue hostiles," and yet this advent is nowhere enstated. A possible disaster is suggested, but this disaster is not specified, indeed the disastrous advent remains elided. There is nothing inscribed du sol et de la nue. An uncomfortable ambiguity is present here in sol, which would name both ground and the sun. The struggle between sol et nue hostiles names both a celestial struggle and the strife between heaven and earth. This evocation of an event continues in the suggestion that a conflict between sol and nue will arise "si notre idée avec *ne* sculpte un bas-relief." The attribution of negation here is especially problematic as there appears no element to be negated. In this syntactic position ne negates nothing. It is almost as if ne is actually some pronoun, *as if* the negation takes the place of a name: si notre idée *avec* ne sculpte un bas-relief.

This problem of the ne becomes more acute in the final word, s'orne: a mélange of the sonorous cliché *or* (see the previous chapter) with the negative *ne*. S'orne is thus the denegation of sonority—sonority advocated in one clichéd inscription suffixed with a cliché of negation. The embellishment of the éblouissante tomb is here the reflexive action of this *ornementation*: s'orne. This reflexivity dissociates the ornamentation of the tomb from notre idée. The foreclosed advent announced between sol and nue seals itself within a sonority *deprived*; and it is at this point that the poet is named. When the poet Poe is named there remains nothing to be vouchsafed. When he is named sonority is both given and denied—and this is the reflexive action of his tombeau. The poet's name—Poe, the advocate of sonority—becomes the witness to its own status as cliché. Amidst the echoes of o, Poe becomes less than nul: not a figure for a poet but one more cliché before the auto-negation *s'orne*. The inscription of a bas-relief is what at once can and cannot make this loss bearable: it makes the loss ostensibly legible (as if it were a *corpse*); but this loss hardens as Poe's disappearance into sonorous cliché *sans issue*. There is nothing to be recuperated conceptually in the death or sacrifice of the poet.

The final tercet describes the form and legibility of the tomb: "Calme bloc ici-bas chu d'un désastre obscur." The block has fallen, as if a meteorite from the sky: a *dès astre* or "*issue stellaire.*" In the description of Poe for the *Médaillons et portraits*, Mallarmé characterized Poe as a similar dès-astre: "quelqu'un comme aérolithe; stellaire, de foudre, projeté des desseins finis humains" (OC: 531). Poe is identified as an aérolithe: a rock from the sky, the *disastrous* residue of the struggle between sol and nue hostiles (the thunderous foudre). Also the tomb is now called *tombe*, which could also be understood as *falls* (tomber): fallen from the sky. The bloc is a disastrous witness, giving witness to disaster. This disaster is marked ici-*bas*, testimony to the uneventful "grief" of the *bas*-relief above.

This testimony is named as "sa borne": its limits or boundaries. The *disastrous* bloc shows its boundaries à jamais. It testifies to its *delimitation*, imposing its bourn up-on against infinity. Now borne also echoes s'orne: the sonorous denegation s'orne is now emplaced as the witness of its boundaries to the nevermore evermore (à jamais). However such display quickly becomes unfeasible as it is presented to a *dispersal*: "Aux noirs vols du Blasphème épars dans le futur." There can be no dwelling in the boundary fallen from disaster. The borne endures as blasphemy disperses. But that which endures, the auto-testimony of the borne's delimitation, is not the poet, rather it is the *disaster* of the poet. There is no poet, but there is a remembrance of nothing past.

This impacts against the poem's first line: "Tel qu'en Lui-même enfin l'éternité le change." The poet, in order to give death, in order to write, must surrender himself to death, in advance. In disaster, the poet's auto-disaster of becoming himself, *issue stellaire*, the poet does not reconcile heaven and earth. However the auto-expenditure of his death is not quite successful—which is not to claim that there is a remainder (corpse) of the poet—instead there is a *writing* which remains insouciant in its vanity and sonority. The words which he has ostensibly purified, the words glossed over by his contemporaneous reportage "de quelque noir mélange" (l. 8), nevermore *perdure* aux noirs vols du Blasphème. The poet is *lost* (se perdre) in his monument. The death is the death of the poet but the poet is not Poe. The pure word unsaid, the poet dead, perdured both. There is, in the sonnet, nothing there. The poet *is* the tomb, in the tomb, the poet as an individual has been given up. "Pour moi, le cas d'un poëte, en cette société qui ne lui permet pas de vivre, c'est le cas d'un homme qui s'isole pour sculpter son propre tombeau" (OC: 869). Isolated and misunderstood, the poet entombs himself: translates himself into a tomb through his task of poetry.

[51] Both the Ronat and the 1914 editions retain Mallarmé's misspelling of "événement" on the Didot/Vollard proofs (cf. Cohn 1966, 80, 108). Whether by accident or design, the év*é*nement remains mis-ciphered on the page.

[52] Turning the dice-game to cards, Derrida trumps Blanchot by showing how in the word *parages* semantic overdetermination yields to syntactic displacement:

En vérité le nom [*Parages*] n'est jamais seul. Chacune de ses syllabes reçoit d'une onde sous-marine la venue d'un autre vocable—qui, lui imprimant un mouvement parfois imperceptible, y échange encore sa mémoire. Et c'est le souvenir des *mots en,* comme on dit étrangement pour accentuer le commencement ou la fin d'une nomination: ici les noms en *pa, par, para, ra, rage, age*. Avec leur valeur de signifiants, comme on disait naguère. Dans les collusions d'un glossaire qui ne reste jamais aléatoire, syllabes ou mots entiers, ils inquiètent l'inconscient peut-être, et le corps propre d'un titre. La liste et la généalogie de ces *autres mots* ne doivent pas ici s'établir—ni table ni tableau. La déduction serait longue et ne saurait se clore. Apparement fortuite, l'occurrence de chaque vocable viendrait croiser, dans ces parages, et le hasard et la nécessité: lueur brève, abbréviation d'une signature à peine équissée, aussitôt effacée, un nom dont on ne sait plus à qui il revient, à quel auteur ou à quelle langue, à l'une ou à l'autre (Jacques Derrida, *Parages,* Paris: Galilée, 1986. 17).

[53] Maurice Blanchot, *L'entretien infini,* Paris: Gallimard, 1969. 620.

The Desistance of Narrative in Joyce's Works

This chapter is a digression, a digression concerning narrative. Perhaps narrative itself could be construed as digression, a digression that self-consciously announces, pronounces and repeats itself as such. "Le divertissement est son chant profond."[1] We will temporarily, within the span of this chapter, essay to refrain from notions of exscription, of the interval and of silence in order to account for the narrative moments in *Ulysses* and *Finnegans Wake*. We suggest neither development nor evolution across these texts, but rather differences between the articulations of narrational possibility. First we will show how narratologics are exploited and expanded in *Ulysses*, and then we will suggest how these notions might fail in *Finnegans Wake*. The possibility of this failure of narratologics in the *Wake* marks the possibility of silence, a silence that might emerge only through the manifolded noises of *Wakean* polyglottism. Our concern is not just how narrative *marks* the Joycean text (and corollary to that how the Joycean text can be said to bear the marks of narrative and thereby belong to an appurtenant genre), but also how narrative is *re-marked*, variously, throughout the Joycean œuvre. We will argue, thus, how Joyce *digresses* in *and* from narrative, how narrative is achieved in Joyce, and how narrative is inachieved.

In the essay "Mallarmé et l'art du roman," Blanchot poses the question as to why Mallarmé's "dream" of the livre has not been followed by novelists. Blanchot characterizes this dream in terms not unrelated to his distinction between the parole essentiel and the parole brut (see chapter 3), the Mallarméan dream effuses from a discovery of language's capability of desistance, a discovery of how in *verbe*, *res* falls silent.[2] Such a situation of the insufficiency of representation should strike the most fundamental presuppositions of narrative and yet it has been ignored in the traditions of the novel. For a narrative to exhibit the denegating rapports proposed by Mallarmé, it would have to—instead of reconciling singer with song, instead of reconciling the distance traversed across *parages*—re-mark the ineluctable *écart* between swerve of shore and bendings abeyed. It would have to *annul* (and not merely *ironize*) its passage *en passant*. But this ironization would *allegorize* the traversal as a *separate* (unstated) reconciliation, and this has become the narrative *genre* par excellence, "C'est pourquoi il n'y a pas de récit, c'est pourquoi il n'en manque pas" (Blanchot 1959, 15). Blanchot bemoans this lack of attention from novelists to desist from teleologics and he ends his essay with a dream of an ideal novelist, a novelist (of the) *à venir:* "Ce romancier, pour lequel un écrivain comme Joyce nous offre quelques traits, se poserait assurément les mêmes problèmes dans lesquels Mallarmé a épuisé sa vie, et comme Mallarmé, il serait heureux de vivre pour effectuer en soi des transformations singulières et pour tirer de la parole le silence où il doit mourir" (Blanchot 1943, 196).[3] The novel might, by digression, have "rearrived" (FW: 003.05) at silence.

• • •

In *A Portrait of the Artist as a Young Man* ironization—no matter how ambiguously applied—essentially remained as a *distance* (albeit variable) *between* narration and narrated, whereas in *Ulysses* there is introduced a formidable disparity of diegesis. There is no longer merely a fluxile distance between narration and the narrated, there is also a *variability* of narrational perspectives. Narration becomes an instance of mobile parallaxes.[4] Modes of narration become ironized amidst their proliferation. In the accumulation of diverse points of narration, a single authority for narrative is denied *yet* the persistence of these diverse, often contradictory points vouchsafes the possibility of narrativizability.[5] *Ulyssean* narrative would follow diegetic exigencies rather than purely mimetic impulses. Michael Patrick Gillespie provides an excellent elaboration of this point in regard to the narration of the "Lestrygonians" chapter which progresses through tropes of food: "Rather than the consciousness of Bloom entering and influencing the discourse, an independent thematic impulse (a vestigial manifestation of the metadiscourse) has peppered the diction of the narrative voice with culinary metaphors."[6] To this restatement of Joycean *style indirect libre* we offer the following qualification: the thematic impulse is not *completely* independent from Bloom, rather it derives from him, yet develops separately. An aspect of Bloom (in this case hunger) takes over the narration—"Ham and his descendants musterred and bred there" (U: 8.742)—thereby rendering the narrative figuration of Bloom as a metonymic effect of the chapter's style (this process would also clearly work with the narration of Gerty MacDowell in "Nausicaa," cf. Gillespie, 191-2). The diegesis refers to the scene narrated only to the extent to which the scene narrated is *inferred* by the narrative style.

Gillespie's statement follows from the aptly-named Benstock principle: "*Fictional texts that employ free indirect speech* (the narrational mode most common to *Ulysses*) *establish the contextual supremacy of subject matter, which influences the direction, pace, point of view, and method of diction.*"[7] This descriptive analysis was made possible by Hayman's notion of the "arranger," an implicit *site* of meta-narration that organizes the narrative while also distancing the narrative from its source.[8] Admitting an arranging presence (or rather an arranging *pretense* of a presence), the so-called subject matter loses contextual supremacy as diegetics now follow a separate though not-unrelated influence. Karen Lawrence provides the next necessary step to Gillespie's statement: the methodologies of narration themselves become subject matter. A corollary to this is that once narrative style or decorum becomes odd (the headlines in "Aeolus" provide an apt example for both Gillespie and Lawrence), the seemingly naturalistic narrative style of the early chapters begins to seem arbitrary and artificial.[9] The use of an "encyclopedia of narrative possibilities" (Lawrence, 14) estranges and ironizes narration.

In *Ulysses* diegesis shifts thereby *re-marking* the operation of narrative as such. Furthermore, there may be inconsistencies in point-of-view, but these inconsistencies only serve to reinforce the machinations of perspective (cf. Gillespie, 160; 177; Lawrence, 58). We will argue that narrative is invariably recuperated out of these diegetic shifts through a parallax of referentiality. To show this we will examine how narrational tropes are themselves re-marked in the text.

• • •

So anyway, not to put too fine a point on it, there are literally two tropes of narrative in *Ulysses*. On the one hand, there is, easily apparent, a *Ulyssean* narrative[10]: a return home after a turbulent day of untumultuous errands, a defining progression towards some definitively putative final point—"Yes because he never did a thing like that before as ask to get his breakfast in bed" (U: 18.1–2)—a decisive end, even if there is to be, always, a further final point, of questionable magnitude, regressing into "a series originating in and repeated to infinity" (17.2130–31).[11] Such a notion of narrative is not without immediate affinity to Mr. Deasy's definition of (Christian) history: "All human history moves towards one great goal, the manifestation of God" (2.380–81); if not God then, at least, the matinal manifestation of eggs and a grilled mutton kidney.

History is not the only thing that moves to one great goal: "The carcass lay on his path. He stopped, sniffed, stalked round it, brother, nosing closer, went round it, sniffling rapidly like a dog all over the dead dog's bedraggled fell. Dogskull, dogsniff, eyes on the ground, moves to one great goal. Ah, poor dogsbody! Here lies poor dogsbody's body" (3.348–52). As Udaya Kumar expertly argues, these instances of repetition (all-too-frequent in *Ulysses*) destabilize fixed notions of identification and chrometric time through all manner of perpetual recontextualizations, thereby yielding a heterogeneous experience of temporality.[12] This type of recontextualization is what Lawrence calls the spatial approach to *Ulysses*: construing *Ulysses* as a synchronous mass of cross-references (Lawrence, 4–5). A diachronic progression would thus be constituted by the text's motion of continually "harking back in retrospective arrangement" (U: 15.442–43).[13] Kenner has argued, *pace* Kumar, that such repetitions will ultimately yield a totality: "As we confront such instances [of recurrent elements] we receive the impression that whatever line we follow into the past of the book, it will meet some other line equally traceable, and return upon itself; we receive, that is, once again the impression of a finite set of materials, finite in reality as they must be finite in the book, of which the book is the adequate exemplar."[14] Our argument will be that *Ulyssean* synchrony ultimately yields to the diachronic sweep of the text, but that this sweep is neither the ontogenetic or autotelic whole Kenner postulates, nor is it the perpetually fragmenting blur advocated by Kumar.

On the other hand, in *Ulysses* there is, in addition to the Ulyssean, a narrative of the wandering Jew,[15] a planetary errancy unsubsumed by a single transcendent moment of definitude, "they're still waiting for their redeemer, says Martin. For that matter so are we" (U: 12.1644–45). There is also a narrative of a diaspora without a definitive homecoming, aimless exile, "like a shot off a shovel" (12.1918). Both modes cohabitate, so to speak, within the person of Leopold Bloom, "Of Israel's folk was that man that on earth wandering far had fared. Stark ruth of man his errand that him lone led till that house" (14.72–73).[16] Through allusions to both Ulysses and the wandering Jew, two tropes of narrative—one teleologically bounded and the other circuitously errant— are enacted, performed and repeated. Indeed one could even use either the trope of the wandering Jew or the trope of Ulysses to characterize the diegetic deviations of the text, thereby reading *Ulyssean* narrative as belonging to either genre. The incompletion or inachievement of a triumphant Ulyssean return could be figurable through the trope of the wandering Jew, and likewise the figuration of a possible completion of errancy could be figured with Ulysses. However these two generic tropes are not entirely distinct, each could function as a subset of the other. The tropes of the wandering Jew and of Ulysses are mutually metonymic. In their mutual elaborations, circulations and interferences, neither trope completely subsumes or engulfs the other. Their paths crosscirculate, "rererepugnosed in rerererepugnant" (15.3057).

⋯

Our path begins with Mr. Deasy's statement of antisemitism: "They sinned against the light, Mr Deasy said gravely. And you can see the darkness in their eyes. And that is why they are wanderers on the earth to this day" (2.361–63). Deasy's general sentiment is echoed variously throughout the book and is specifically applied to Bloom, *to wit* Buck Mulligan's comment as Bloom passes between Buck and Stephen on the Library steps: "The wandering jew, Buck Mulligan whispered with clown's awe. Did you see his eye?" (9.1209–10).[17] Bloom is identified, albeit partially, through the trope of Mr. Deasy's wandering Jew; to be sure the figuration of dark eyes is hardly unique to Deasy but his citation of it participates within a textual circulation of figurations of dark eyes. One further citation of the wandering Jew that is not without consequence occurs amidst the drunken babble of the "allincluding most farraginous chronicle" (14.1412) that closes the "Oxen of the Sun" chapter: "Sinned against the light and even now that day is at hand when he shall come to judge the world by fire" (14.1575–77). The vengeful "he" here is presumably Christ, Whose last judgment will consume the world by fire, a consequence of this purification being the end of the wandering Jew's travels.[18] However, the smallcase "he" also refers to the he who has sinned against the light, the wandering Jew himself. Indeed, this notion of an apocalyptically vengeful wandering Jew is buttressed later in the text through further accumulations of mismatching figurations.

Bloom himself also inadvertently recalls Deasy's figure of the Jew when he incorrectly refers to a not-unimportant line from *Hamlet*: "*Hamlet, I am thy father's spirit / Doomed for a certain time to walk the earth*" (8.67–68). The actual Shakespearean line is slightly different: "I am thy father's spirit; / Doom'd for a certain term to walk the night."[19] Bloom's miscitation uneasily recontextualizes Shakespeare's ghost through Deasy's description of the wandering Jew walking the earth. Through this circulation of reference, a kind of *transference* is suggested between Bloom, the wandering Jew and the ghost of Hamlet's father. There is perhaps no definitive *identification* between these three figures (they are not isomorphic), yet they participate within a textualized economy of suggestion (reference) and counter-suggestion (cross-reference).[20]

Not unexpectedly, this nexus of Shakespearean, Judaic and Bloomean reference complicates itself. In "Scylla and Charybdis" Stephen deploys the same citation from Hamlet's ghost in his peculiar argument concerning authority. Stephen claims that William Shakespeare had himself first played the ghost of Hamlet, and so when he had said on stage "*Hamlet, I am thy father's spirit*" (9.170), he was addressing his dead son Hamnet. "It is possible that that player Shakespeare, a ghost by absence… speaking his own words to his own son's name…: you are the dispossessed son: I am the murdered father: your mother is the guilty queen" (9.174–80). Stephen, like Bloom, has miscited the line, beginning it with a spurious apostrophe to Hamlet. The presence of said apostrophe in Stephen's citation provides the argument's fulcrum, but its absence in the text of Shakespeare's play throws a wrench into the ghost in the machine. Bloom's miscitation of the line from *Hamlet* produced an affinity to the wandering Jew, whereas Stephen's miscitation produces a spuriously authorized statement of dispossession (the absent father returning to tell his dead son of his dispossession); "there was something spurious in the cut of his jib" (16.832–33). The implications of Stephen's Shakespearean miscitation thus dovetail with Bloom's by enabling an expansion of the already overcathected trope of the dispossessed wandering performative Jew.[21]

There is thus suggested a potential filiation between Bloom and Shakespeare in that both are fathers displaced by unfaithful wives and dead sons. Both play the role of "a wellknown cuckold" (15.117). Furthermore, during his discourse on Shakespeare, Stephen is asked to "Prove that he was a jew" (9.763). Like Bloom, Shakespeare's religious affiliation is open to question.[22] Exacerbating any possible identification between Bloom and Shakespeare, Stephen's argument *also displaces* the authority through which this statement of parallel displacements could possibly take place. Notably, this possibility occurs in a passage in which Hamlet's ghost is (finally) cited correctly:

> A father, Stephen said, battling against hopelessness, is a necessary evil. He wrote the play in the months that followed his father's death. … [Yet] The corpse of John Shakespeare does not walk the night. From hour to hour it rots

> and rots. He rests, disarmed of fatherhood, having devised that mystical estate upon his son. ... It is a mystical estate, an apostolic succession, from only begetter to only begotten. ... *Amor matris,* subjective and objective genitive, may be the only true thing in life. Paternity may be a legal fiction. Who is the father of any son that any son should love him or he any son? (9.828–45)

Stephen's argument rests upon a tightly packed cathexis of allusion and reference.[23] Stephen argues that there is no patrilineal transference precisely by deploying tropes of and references to authority. Stephen names authority in order to *show* that authority has no essential name. Reference is performed through difference (see page 201 and following). The only right for paternal generation is onomastic and the sign of the father *is* the *sign* of semantic negativity. Stephen argues that negativity is to be manifest through the onomastic displacements and interferences of tropes of authority: "He has hidden his own name, a fair name, William, in the plays.... He has revealed it in the sonnets where there is Will in overplus. ... What's in a name? That is what we ask ourselves in childhood when we write the name that we are told is ours" (9.921–28). Indeed the ninth chapter occasionally indulges in a play upon proper names and so authority and masterful paternity are displaced onto onomastic variation.[24] In order for Shakespeare to have followed the logic of Stephen's argument, he filches from himself his own proper name in order to represent his own proper familial displacement on the Stratford stage. He displaces himself to have a displacement enstaged. Therefore in this chapter Stephen performs an *interchangeability of tropes of displacement*. Displacement comes to function metonymically, between (and not within) tropes. Indeed portions of Stephen's argument combine various fragmentary cathexes from earlier in the text,[25] as well as providing a base of reference for further combinations and recombinations of these cathexes elsewhere. Indeed, to a very limited degree, Stephen's repetition of Bloom's miscitation ("*Hamlet,* I am...") is itself analogous to how *Ulysses* repeats the *Odyssey*: a parallel is established (in this instance, the miscitation) but is then redeveloped in a novel and separate context. These recontextualizations complicate the diegetic sympathy posited by the so-called Benstock principle. The subject matter here is not exclusively Stephen but rather an admixture of Stephen and

Bloom made possible through Deasy's comments. The subject matter is the *narrativizability* of Stephen, a possibility which is organized around textual reminiscences of Bloom and Deasy. Diegetic sympathy is interfered with by these cathexes.[26] This pattern of echoing becomes more complicated in the example of Stephen and Bloom since they do interact with each other (whereas neither Bloom nor Stephen interact with Odysseus) and these interactions generate further patterns of concatenation and correspondence. What *passes* for narrative in *Ulysses* does so by virtue of the *interferences* of correspondences, kinetic reconfigurations of synchronic reference.

•••

Diachronic narrative (albeit discontinuous) in *Ulysses* is produced by and sustained through ever-denser synchronic confluences. In *Ulysses*, narrative blooms from ironic coincidence: "Now that's really a coincidence: second time. Coming events cast their shadows before" (8.525–6). Although the overall narrational composition and tenor of *Ulysses* could be characterized as an interplay or exchange between the Ulyssean voyage and a Jewish wandering ("Jewgreek is greekjew. Extremes meet. Death is the highest form of life. Ba!" [15.2098–99]), each descriptive element functions comfortably within the divagations of the text. There could be no peregrine trope (no trope of peregrinism) foreign to the text. The Ulyssean and the Judaic both *re-mark* (in the full ingenuity of this term) narrative in *Ulysses;* remarkably within, they mark a narrative tendency and mark themselves as markers of this marking. Instead of unfolding as meta-descriptors, they subsist as de-scriptions *de trop*. *Ulysses* deploys its narratologics tropically.

> Across the world for a wife. Quite a number of stories there were on that particular Alice Ben Bolt topic, Enoch Arden and Rip van Winkle and does anybody hereabouts remember Cacoc O'Leary, a favourite and most trying declamation piece by the way of poor John Casey and a bit of perfect poetry in its own small way. (16.424–28)

It is not entirely surprising that, whilst considering the delays of a mariner's homecoming, Bloom omits citation of Homer as an exemplar within the convoluted and turgid periphrases of Eumean style. Nevertheless in the above passage, "One thinks of Homer" (9.1165), even if the alluded tale is eluded in the interferences of the citations of other stories, other alluded narratives. The citation of Rip van Winkle is not without interest as it recurs to recombine with other referential cathexes. Like Odysseus, Rip was absent for twenty years but unlike Odysseus, he deliberately left his shrewish wife. Furthermore, Odysseus left to fight in the Trojan War (albeit reluctantly), whereas Rip, during his slumber, avoided participating in the American Revolutionary War.[27] Additionally, the story of Rip van Winkle already bears an affinity to one variant of the legend of the wandering Jew: apparently after many years of wandering, he is to sleep for a certain length of time in order to be rejuvenated. In the above citation (or networks of citation and reference), the Ulyssean allusion is thus made partially analogous to the wandering Jew through Eumean malapropisms.

Earlier in the day, on the beach, recovering from a certain kind of climax after the mutually masturbatory voyeuristic encounter with the charming yet lame Gerty MacDowell, Bloom remembers playing charades with Molly in Mat Dillon's garden (and the *rencontre* with Gerty was nothing if not another genre of charades):

> Curious she an only child, I an only child. So it returns. Think you're escaping and run into yourself. Longest way round is the shortest way home. And just when he and she. Circus horse walking in a ring. Rip van Winkle we played. Rip: tear in Henny Doyle's overcoat. Van: breadvan delivering. Winkle: cockles and periwinkles. Then I did Rip van Winkle coming back. She leaned on the sideboard watching. Moorish eyes. Twenty years asleep in Sleepy Hollow. All changed. Forgotten. The young are old. His gun rusty from the dew. (13.1109–16)

One coincidence, that of Molly and Leopold both lacking siblings, blooms into further patterns of coincidings. The logic of thought above ostensibly starts from a shared fact, a union of a kind (the unity of both being only children), and then reiterates that unity by imposing a disunion, "longest way round is the shortest way home"; or "Where there is a reconciliation, Stephen said, there must first have been a sundering" (9.334–35). A voyage or sundering is imagined as the subtension of coincidence or unity, and this leads to the second strata of coincidence. Bloom remembers that the Washington Irving story *Rip van Winkle* was one of the entries in that game of charades. Thus a further element is introduced which coincides again with the thought of a belated homecoming. Indeed the name Rip van Winkle, once introduced, produces a brief series of associations thereby introducing further *écarts* into the thought. Each reference that is added produces interferences, some of which help to spawn further cross-references. Bloom then does return to certain elements of the story, the twenty year slumber and the rusted gun, "All changed. Forgotten." Gifford's annotations note that this line is a citation from the story. Gifford also notes that Bloom's location of the slumber in Sleepy Hollow, while suggestively appropriate, is incorrect (and thus yet another example of Bloom's frequent lapses of memory). *The Legend of Sleepy Hollow* was another story by Irving which, like *Rip van Winkle,* appeared in the *Sketch Book* (Gifford, 400). By installing a coincidence, Bloom introduces deviation. Rip van Winkle, the self-imposed exile, returns belatedly as a *figura* of Bloom's marital errancy, and the figuration of this is enacted through lapses caused by Bloom's mental errancy.

Bloom's misattribution of Rip van Winkle's slumber returns to haunt him in "Circe":

BLOOM
To drive me mad! Moll! I forgot! Forgive! Moll.... We.... Still.....

BELLO
(*ruthlessly*) No, Leopold Bloom, all is changed by woman's will since you slept horizontal in Sleepy Hollow your night of twenty years. Return and see.

(*Old Sleepy Hollow calls over the wold.*)

SLEEPY HOLLOW
Rip van Wink! Rip van Winkle!

BLOOM

> (*in tattered mocassins with a rusty fowlingpiece, tiptoeing, fingertipping, his haggard bony bearded face peering through the diamond panes, cries out*) I see her! The first night at Mat Dillon's! But that dress, the green! And her hair is dyed gold and he…
>
> BELLO
> (*laughs mockingly*) That's your daughter, you owl, with a Mullingar student. (15.3150–66)

Bloom is coaxed into expressing a reconciliation with Molly but this reconciliation is denied by the misattributed slumber. Bloom metamorphoses into Rip van Winkle in his attempt to reconcile; in the attempt to reconcile there is a sundering in which he returns to Mat Dillon's (where the game of charades in which *Rip van Winkle* was played), only to find all changed, a subsequent generation in the place of the former.[28] Bloom returns only to find the *nostalgic* location disturbed and displaced, and said displacement or interference occurs on several levels, each reflecting *and* further disturbing the others.

Upon Bloom's return home on the morning of June 17, a more severe exile is contemplated. Bloom returns only to contemplate taking his leave yet again, yet this further leave might be no more radical than its predecessors.

> Would the departed never nowhere nohow reappear?
> Ever he would wander, selfcompelled, to the extreme limit of his cometary orbit, beyond the fixed stars and variable suns and telescopic planets, astronomical waifs and strays, to the extreme boundary of space, passing from land to land, among peoples, amid events. Somewhere imperceptibly he would hear and somehow reluctantly, suncompelled, obey the summons of recall. Whence, disappearing from the constellation of the Northern Crown he would somehow reappear reborn above delta in the constellation of Cassiopeia and after incalculable eons of peregrination return an estranged avenger, a wreaker of justice on malefactors, a dark crusader, a sleeper awakened, with financial resources (by supposition) surpassing those of Rothschild or the silver king. (17.2012–23)

In place of Dublin and environs, errancy is now mapped out onto the solar system. Bloom's orbit is to be cometary, parabolic, an orbit less restrained by the sun's influence than by that exerted by the planets. Yet the orbit is still reigned in by the sun's gravity, suncompelled Bloom would still fall back to Earth. From the perspective of an earthbound observer, the receding cometary Bloom would fade in the constellation of the Northern Crown—a constellation in which a nova had "appeared... and disappeared... about the period of the birth of Leopold Bloom" (17.1124–26)[29]—only to bloom anew above the delta of Cassiopeia—the site of Shakespeare's birth star, also known as Tycho Brahe's nova (17.1122–23; 9.928–29; Gifford, 244; 584–85). Bloom would be reborn as an avenger of Shakespearean magnitude, a ghost that returns after having been doomed to walk the earth (or, improving ourselves, the night), "Who is the ghost from *limbo patrum*, returning to the world that has forgotten him?" (9.150–51). After his planetary exile—figured through patterns that emerge out of mismatching references—Bloom comes to be imagined as a figure of apocalyptic vengeance (a figure anticipated by a slip in the "Oxen of the Sun" chapter, see page 190). Here Bloom's returning ghost would be the return of Shakespeare in a manner not without affinity to Stephen's argument concerning Shakespeare's enstaged revenge in *Hamlet:* Bloom returns as a ghost to enact revenge (an obvious Homeric parallel is also here suggested).[30] Bloom would thus be fulfilling his preterite career choice of being an "exponent of Shakespeare" (17.794); he would be the Shakespearean representative and avenger. Bloom is thus a partial fulfillment of Stephen's figuration of the bard, but in doing so he also becomes one more term in a displaced series of displacements: "What went forth to the ends of the world to traverse not itself, God, the sun, Shakespeare, a commercial traveler, having itself traversed in reality itself becomes that self" (15.2117–19). Returning after his absence he would find that the world he had left has itself disappeared and returned again. Both wanderer and world have been unfaithful to each other. Stephen's postulated self-coinciding is thereby achieved only through autodeviation. In this way, by repeating Stephen's Shakespearean avenger the extrapolated cometary Bloom is again a figura of Rip van Winkle. Through a concatenation of references, the return both is and is not decisive.

> What would render such return irrational?
> An unsatisfactory equation between an exodus and return in time through reversible space and an exodus and return in space through irreversible time. (17.2024–27)

Bloom can return to his house but he cannot return to what has been lost by "that double-headed monster of damnation and salvation—Time."[31] Errancy will not coincide with fulfillment. The Shakespearean revenge predestined by constellations of stellar coincidences is undone by "the apathy of the stars" (17.2226). The stars that can be construed into constellations of prediction remain insouciant to the achievement they augur. There is, instead, a perpetuation of inachievement, a perpetuation which is narrated through tropes of errancy, allusions to the peregrine and the fulfilled which haunt the Dublin day and bay. If Bloom is denied the fulfillment of a most triumphant Homeric Odysseus, he is also spared the definitive eschatological disaster of the Dantean Ulysses. The figure of Bloom is thus steered a path through allusions—"A man passed out between them, bowing, greeting" (9.1203)—he exists as citation.[32] Coincidences thus are enacted as shadows, "Reminiscences of coincidences" (17.323): coincidences always already depend upon reminiscences. Coincidences are eminently referential.

A minor Ulyssean reminiscence involves Bloom's "Secondbest Bed" (9.698–99). Early in the morning, "He heard then a warm heavy sigh, softer, as she turned over and the loose brass quoits of the bedstand jingled. Must get those settled really" (4.58–60). The noise of the loose quoits reminds Bloom that they need to be fixed and silenced, they remind him of one of his many minor marital duties. Their jingles also announce Molly's infidelity: in "Sirens," Boylan is repeatedly identified through the noise his jaunting car makes, "jinglejaunty blazes boy" (11.290).

The quoits also would refer to the marital bed of Odysseus and Penelope, a not surprising referential possibility since "Antiquity mentions famous beds" (9.718). When Odysseus returned home, Penelope did not recognize him; his appearance had so changed that he potentially faced a fate similar to that of Rip van Winkle. Odysseus identified himself to Penelope by being tricked into recounting the story of how he had built their wedding-bed.[33] Odysseus's homecoming is vouchsafed by his and Penelope's shared memory of the bed. Now, Odysseus may have been a πολύτροπος but Bloom is a domestic, forgetful tinkerer, "the way he plots and plans everything out" (18.1008–9). He has forgotten to remember the bed quoits and their noise continually reminds him of this forgetfulness:

> With circumspection, as invariably when entering an abode (his own or not his own): with solicitude, the snakespiral springs of the mattress being old, the brass quoits and pendent viper radii loose and tremulous under stress and strain: prudently, as entering a lair of ambush of lust of adders: lightly, the less to disturb: reverently, the bed of conception and of birth, of consummation of marriage and of breach of marriage, of sleep and of death. (17.2115–21)

It is unsurprising that the quoits are loose since clearly this bed carries an excess of weight both real and hypostasized. The noise of the loose quoits reminds Bloom not just of his marital duty but also of the violation and breach of his marriage. They echo both the persistent "Cuckoo"s of cuckoldry (resounding sigils of Molly's infidelity) and his own little infidelities, "I know. Soiled personal linen, wrong side up with care. The quoits are loose. From Gibraltar by long sea long ago" (15.3288–89). This belief is contradicted by Molly: "the lumpy old jingly bed always reminded me of old Cohen I suppose he scratched himself in it often enough and he thinks father bought it from Lord Napier" (18.1212–14). The quoits testify to the frailty and to the endurance of the hymen, to the frail endurance of marriage and misunderstanding.

THE TIMEPIECE

(*unportalling*)

Cuckoo.
Cuckoo.
Cuckoo.

(*The brass quoits of a bed are heard to jingle.*)

THE QUOITS

Jigjag. Jigajiga. Jigjag. (15.1131–38)[34]

The fear of this testimony of the quoits is confirmed by Molly: "this damned old bed too jingling like the dickens I suppose they could hear us away over the other side of the park till I suggested to put the quilt on the floor with the pillow under my bottom" (18.1130–33). The quilt muffles the quoits and Molly's cunning (perhaps overstated) silences the quoits. Her cunning denies even the testimony of infidelity. Molly mollifies or silences the token of the persistence of the memory of a frail marriage. She has silenced the *figure* of Bloom's fear, yet the overlying separation remains. Indeed, with the admission that the bed does not hail from Gibraltar, she reveals that the very bases by which Bloom has figured marital errancy are themselves erroneous.

References to both the Ulyssean and the Judaic circulate and interfere with each other. Although there are digressions of style which tend towards—as Kumar, Gillespie and Lawrence have noted—the irreducibility of a singular point of guiding authority (no one trope can completely comprehend the book), there is still, continually, a *logic of reference* at work in *Ulysses*. There may be no single referent but there remains a singular efficacy of reference repeatedly concatenated throughout. In this way the exilic motion of the wandering Jew remains Ulyssean: a non-totalizable errancy is sub-scribed to teleologics and yet teleology is also inscribed within errancy. Like the *Divina Commedia*, *Ulysses* re-marks a motion to a totality slightly apart from definitive totalization. In *Ulysses* no single diegetic mode prevails, but nevertheless a *law of diegesis* perdures throughout through the *interferences of referentiality*. An individual trope in *Ulysses* (our examples have been Garryowen, Rip van Winkle, Hamlet, the quoits, to say nothing of Ulysses and the wandering Jew) does not just generate reference, but by being imbricated through referential interferences produces further reference. Each trope participates within a convoluted cathexis of referentiality: amidst interactions each trope is a partial *genre* (or more precisely generic mark) of narrative. Narration thus becomes a function of these cathexes of diegetic referentiality. In *Ulysses*, through the momentum of referential concatenations, *on n'évite pas le récit*.

•••

One can see in this paradox of reference the source of Derrida's interest with Joyce. *Ulysses* follows a logic of *ference* (*ferre, fero,* from φέρω, to set in motion, bear, produce, yield). Although *Ulysses* follows one logic of production, this very logic is enabled by the deferral of a decisive issuance through the perpetuation of the crossreferences' *inter-ferences*. Derrida cannily refers to this as *différance* (the deliberate and deliberative inability to refer to what is named by *différance* aloud helps to lend this essay a rather annoying quality); *différance* does not announce (pronounce, refer), rather it delays, and this delaying takes the place of *ference*.[35] "Comment vais-je m'y prendre pour parler du *a* de la différance? Il va de soi que celle-ci ne saurait être *exposée*. On ne peut jamais exposer que ce qui à un certain moment peut devenir *présent,* manifeste, ce qui peut se montrer, se présenter comme un présent, un étant-présent dans sa vérité, vérité d'un présent ou présence du présent. ... En toute exposition elle serait exposée à disparaître comme disparition. Elle risquerait d'apparaître: de disparaître."[36] Rather than bear a product, the process of ference constitutes its production through a never-present constellation of tracings and spacings (Derrida 1972, 13–14), which nevertheless always runs the risk of a systematization (26–28). As with God at the close of the *Paradiso*, that which is unnamable remains enmeshed within this *differantial* network of interference: "« Il n'y a pas de nom pour cela »: lire cette proposition en sa *platitude*. Cet innommable n'est pas un être ineffable, dont aucun nom ne pourrait s'approcher: Dieu, par exemple. Cet innomable est le jeu qui fait qu'il y a des effets nominaux, des structures relativement unitaires ou atomiques qu'on appelle noms, des chaînes de substitutions de noms, et dans lesquelles, par example, l'effet nominal « différance » est lui-même *entraîné,* emporté, reinscrit, comme une fausse entrée ou une fausse sortie est encore partie du jeu, fonction du système" (28). For example, Stephen's cunning attempts to argue himself out of a system of authority are themselves instances of an economy of *tropes* of authority and authorization. And indeed the *Ulyssean* operation of interferences amongst synchronic echoes could be similarly imbricated within such a scheme of totalization. Furthermore the characterizations of *Ulyssean style indirect libre,* such as the Benstock principle, could be modulated into describing a *stylistics of ference*: the tone, pace and diction of narration is *inferred* from the subject matter. Narrative styles resonate from and are in-formed by the cathexis of ferences. In this way, *Ulyssean* style is a function of the play of ference.

Not to put too fine a point on it, Derrida singles out the Joycean œuvre as an example, *the singular example,* of a work that would (in distinction to the Husserlian system of equivocation) "répéter et reprendre en charge la totalité de l'équivoque elle-même, et un langage qui fasse affleurer à la plus grande synchronie possible la plus grand puissance des intentions enfouies, accumulées et entremêlées dans l'âme de chaque atome linguistique... faire apparaître l'unité structurale de la culture empirique totale dans l'équivoque généralisée d'une écriture qui... circule à travers toutes les langues à la fois."[37] According to Derrida, Joycean *production* exfoliates out of a massively overloaded synchronic cathexis of interference, and this synchronous web, in all its equivocations, does not necessarily subscribe to an autotelic presence (Dieu, par exemple). However, as soon as this interference is written, Joycean interference can be codified, and hence systematized and reckoned by the *"joyciciel."*[38] As with Blanchot's Ulysses, the space of the estranging encounter *can be* mapped out; through cunning mnemotechnics differences can be articulated and be made to be articulate, even a lost absence (such as the quoits' testimony) is not entirely mute within a chain of ference. The irreducible equivocity, by virtue of being written, by virtue of its *ference,* can always be *agrapher;* its inter-ferences always remaining *à venir* through narration and narrativizability.

In the essay "Ulysse gramophone: Ouï-dire de Joyce," Derrida questions exactly how one can respond to Joycean interference with recourse neither to reference nor to system. Since the text is already overloaded with reproductive interferences (and reproduction is already programmed into the *sens* of φέρω), how is one to respond to this *singular event* of total iteration, this "whole galaxy of events" (U: 16.1224): "Oui, tout nous est déjà arrivé avec *Ulysse,* et d'avance signé Joyce" (Derrida 1987a, 98). Derrida construes the Joycean text as the ineluctable modality of systematization inherent in a project of *différance* (exponentially overdetermined interferences). For Derrida, *points* are made in Joycean dissemination: too many points to be sure, but points nonetheless. "Tous les gestes esquissés pour prendre l'initiative d'un mouvement, on les trouves annoncés dans un texte surpotentialisé qui vous rapellera, à un moment donné, que vous êtes captif d'un réseau de langue, d'écriture, de savoir *et même de narration*" (97).

Derrida's solution to this double-bind of interferences signed by Joyce is ethical. Derrida has posed a question of how to respond to Joyce, to *Ulysses,* and specifically to Molly's yes (which in its repetitions, stands as an ambiguous affirmation, an affirmation that affirms itself as affirmation without decidable referent, an affirmation of *ference* that takes the place of *ference* [89–90; 107–11]). The *yes* stands apart from reference and so how is it to be referred? and to be answered responsibly? An act of reference to the yes would annul the apartness of the yes from reference (throwing dice to abolish chance), and yet avoiding reference would be somewhat irresponsible, to say the least. This yes is an intractable pre-position of language (*sic, oc oïl*): "avant la langue, dans la langue mais aussi dans un expérience de la pluralité des langues qui ne relève peut-être plus d'une linguistique au sens strict" (123). In other words, in responding to the yes, one would have to responsibly respond to the irresponsible, to the Other (that which is other to responsible discourse): the two modalities of response (responsible and irresponsible) *should* thus become reciprocal and dialogic; the response allows itself to be interfered, to become a subject of interference: "Réciproquement, deux réponses ou deux responsabilités se rapportent l'une à l'autre sans avoir aucun rapport entre elles. Les deux signent et empêchent pourtant la signature de se rassembler. Ils ne peuvent qu'appeler un autre *oui,* une autre signature. Et d'autre part, on ne peut décider entre deux *oui* qui *doivent* se ressembler comme des jumeaux, jusqu'au simulacre, l'un comme la gramophonie de

l'autre" (141). To say yes, to affirm the yes, is to listen to the ouï-dire and to have and to hear that listening respond.[39]

Derrida has prepared an elegant if itinerant solution to the necessity of response to a book of contingencies, a book in which contingencies interfere thereby producing a text *à agrapher*. And yet Derrida's response is still predicated upon the necessity of a response to the Joycean text (however that may be construed). Ultimately he resolves the aporia of response as the production of a responsibly cathected response, a further atom of interference. Yet the problem to which Derrida responds in Joyce is not without affinity to what Blanchot has identified in Mallarmé: the tautology of a manifestation of an experience of negativity. Derrida resolves this problem by asserting that it is a question that must be responsibly answered. As argued in the previous chapter, for Blanchot this manifestation is itself insouciant and apart from responsibility, no matter how much interference is allowed in the response. Interference is itself both insouciant and insufficient.

Following Derrida's logic, a metonymic chain of ferences displaces manifestation of a nubbin of meaning. In the overwrought Ulyssean interference between Bloom, Shakespeare and the wandering Jew, a univocal statement of meaning is no longer possible through a textual traversal. But this very displacement of meaning comes to be the place (of meaning) that *takes the place* of meaning: equivocation is voiced multiply *yet* univocally. The loss of meaning (the loss of patronimity, of authority *&c.*) is *re-counted* in one singular instance of telling. This is precisely Blanchot's Ulyssean definition of narrative. The act of narration reconciles negativity by bringing it to light in the act of recitation, unification achieved by narration: narrative makes νόστος the singing of homecoming, the journey into the song (see also note 15). Narrative *refers* to its action of recounting: narrative is reference to interference. Any generic re-mark within narrative would be subsumed within the dynamic of *ference*. Ironizations of narrative decorums (ironizations of, if you will, irony) still bear a *trait* of narrative; narrative always re-marks the fact that there is narration, that there is a traversal recounted. Narrative re-marks distanciation, in other words narrative puts distance

into words, naturalizing the distance it enstates; in other words narrative is the genre *par excellence*.[40] Through indefinite serializations, through further points of appurtenance *de trop* "nought nowhere was never reached" (U: 17.1068–69). This is precisely Stephen's problem in the library: through a metonymic play of names and authorial attributes and attributions, he recounts loss. Loss persists as a present figure in that it is recounted in a "poche interne plus grande que le tout" (Derrida 1986, 256).

It is thus our claim that *Ulysses* progresses as this extra-large pocket, subsuming synchronic interferences within the appearance (simulacrum) of a narrated progression. Tropes of narrative (Ulysses, the wandering Jew, *&c.*, *&c.*) fall within these metonymic chains of interference even as they (partially) re-mark the procedures of recounting. *Ulysses* ironizes narrative procedures whilst remaining eminently narrational. Convoluted patternings of crossreferentiation are subsumed not into a totality (*selon* Kenner) nor into a fractured mass (*selon* Kumar), but into the progression of convoluted totalizations. The gestures of totalization remain even as the achievement of totality is denied and deferred. In this sense *Ulysses* is not the "expansion totale de la lettre" (OC: 380), but rather an expansion of the epiphany: synchronous interrelations concatenated into a network of interferences.

Although *Finnegans Wake* contains referential and cross-referential concatenations analogous to but somewhat more extreme than those found in *Ulysses,* we will argue that there is no singular dimension (nor even a *partial* constellation of limited and delimited rapports) in which the concatenations could be subsumed. There is no subsumptive progression in *Finnegans Wake,* in other words *Finnegans Wake* is not narrative.

•••

The attempt to locate narrative momentum in *Finnegans Wake* has been a critical concern ever since its initial serial publication as *Work in Progress*. One could almost say that the history of *Wake* criticism has been a continuing attempt to provide some get-up-and-go to Joyce's eschewal

of "goahead plot" (LIII: 146). Clive Hart's *Structure and Motif in "Finnegans Wake"* is both exemplary and inordinately influential for this narrative insistence. Central to Hart's proposal is that the shorter units of Joyce's text yield larger recognizable and repeatable constituent blocks: "The large cyclic blocks of the constituent material are both clearly defined and predictable, but the smaller the structural units we consider, the more difficult it is to know how they will function."[41] Apperceived patterns accumulate and fuse together out of lexical chaos, and thus the critic's task is reduced to an explication of the tension of articulation between tenebrous passages and comprehensible macro-text. Hart essentially established a hermeneutic faith that *Finnegans Wake* is a readable book despite of—or even because of—the unreadability of individual passages.[42] This paradigm of readability has been programmatic for *Wake* studies ever since, and can be recognized in its broad forms in David Hayman's theory of nodality,[43] John Paul Riquelme's viral Möbius narratives,[44] Umberto Eco's critical restitution of metaphoric substitutions,[45] and Susan Shaw Sailer's application of tropic incoherence,[46] to name just a few. The world according to Hart is a narratological nightmare from which Joyce studies has not yet escaped; *Finnegans Wake* is still read, at least in part, as if it were Ulyssean. In practice the absence of narrative is compensated for by the critic with an excess of narratology. Rabaté addresses this succinctly by characterizing the *Wakean* experience as reading "a machine containing matrixes of matrixes of stories, capable of narrating everything, and thus never really narrating one story. ... On the other hand, this lucid epic of disillusion exploits the pleasure we still take in expecting stories to be told to help us lose our knowledge, shed it gloss after gloss in the bottomless structure of perforated stories."[47] There may be some narrative there, after all, but amidst evaporations of narratologics, there is something else to be read. *Finnegans Wake* challenges *our* reading.

Hart's assumption of *Wakean* narrative is not without affinity to Genette's definition of narrative as "l'expansion d'un verb.... "*l'Odysée* ou la *Recherche* ne font d'une certaine manière qu'amplifier (au sens rhétorique) des énoncés tels qu'*Ulysse rentre à Ithaque* ou *Marcel devient*

écrivain."⁴⁸ Hart emphasizes the persistence and authority of an underlying narrative structuration amidst the profligate expansiveness of the text's deviancy. There is a foundation to confusion and this foundation entails a global notion of a synthetic structuration: "The brief qualifying and elaborating phrases have become Joyce's fundamental units, and in the long run they are usually more important for the sense than is the skeletal meaning of the sentence to which they were annexed" (Hart 1962, 41). Indeed, Hart's notion of the motif and leitmotif implies a notion of passage and progressivity instrumental to narrative: "The main requirement of a true *leitmotiv* is that it should, as its name implies, *lead* from point to point; it is, in fact, an essentially dynamic device" (164). Hart here emphasizes that the motif works in that it retains a consistent and stable vector of reference despite the dynamics of difference that emerge through its repetitions. In this way, the motif enables the expansion of a narratological theme by allowing it to progress and emerge on multiple levels simultaneously.

This paradigm of *Wakean* criticism reified by Hart involves articulating passages into a typically narrativized totalizing and totalized structure, which has usually been defined as some modulation of a family-drama with a tendency to a universalizable network of allegories. Such a hypothetical phrasing of the ur-*Wakean* narrative could be, for example (and many examples are possible): "The solid man saved by his sillied woman" (FW: 094.03).⁴⁹ This type of structuration is a narrative move *par excellence* precisely because it determines meaning through a moment of closure that defines and delimits the text. The text is surrendered to a teleology without a specific telos: a transcendent structuring moment of *definitude*. A common structuring moment applied to the work as a whole, and Hart is here typical, is Vico's cyclic history—or "vicociclometer" (FW: 614.27)—through which the meanings of both isolated passages and the book-as-a-whole are determined by "wheels spinning even faster within wheels as the whole major cycle turns, with no particular centre, from the first page to the last and back again to the beginning" (Hart 1962, 45). In the application of this Vichian scheme, the absence of a specific telos functions as a *defining* teleologics for the

text. Recent work on Joyce and Vico—by John Bishop and others—has tended to de-emphasize the "vicociclometer" in favor of Vico's broader contributions to *Wakean* language.[50] The critical presupposition behind any notion of structuration is that *Wakean* passages *can be articulated* under the auspices of such a teleological moment, and thus that there is an underlying logic and logistics to the text.

The question now is: can *Finnegans Wake* be *defined* in this way? In *Finnegans Wake* we find a maximization of discursive potential sustained by a tension between translinguistic semantic expansiveness (or peregrinism) and an unconventional syntax. Hart admits to the semantic conundrums posed by the *Wake*, but insists that these are reined in by a normal and normative English syntax (Hart 1962, 31). This view was challenged in 1969 by Strother Purdy's meticulous Chomskyian analysis of *Wake*an grammar as qualitatively distinct from English.[51] Jacques Aubert has proposed that the *Wake* can be read as an *interplay* between the overdetermining machinations of *both* semantics and syntax (we will discuss Aubert's article in more detail in the following chapter). Syntax destabilizes sense and sensibility even as it might act as a grounding. One cannot even take syntax for granted as a principle of structuration.

This "usylessly unreadable" (FW: 179.26–27) book aims at suggesting everything within the scope of its tortured and tortuous iteration. One can see this with the ten thunder words which could be characterized as painful prolongations of breath subsuming a babelian agglutination of thunder that is ultimately quite meaningless: "The hundredlettered name again, last word of perfect language" (FW: 424.23–24). These words, in their universality, suggest totalization and yet the linguistic precession of the word belies a single and singular totality. Perhaps these thunder words do indeed fall into an "easily freudened" (115.23) narrative of a patriarch's downfall—as has been suggested by virtually everyone since Campbell and Robinson—but the iterative space of these words is both less and more than straightforward. The constituent words cannot be pronounced in any one language, and thus parsing these words together individually or as a unit is a reenactment or repetition of the hubris of the babelian fall, and not a

pentecostal redemption of meaning. Laurent Milesi writes: "Annoçant l'origine de la langue et la dispersion en langues, le mot-tonnerre en 3.15–17 subsume tout le mouvement de l'œuvre: de l'émergence de la langue et l'exploration des différents angles d'où l'on peut produire du sens à partir d'une fusion de sons, à la dissémination babélienne et la possibilité d'une résolution dans la Pentecôte."[52] There is *no single word* or primal scene of decrepitude to be construed here at the place of this hundred-letter word, "where flash becomes word and silents selfloud" (FW: 267.16–17), and so this initerability denies their incorporation into a diachronic teleologics. In *Finnegans Wake* narrative devolves and dissolves into linguistic miscegenations. The *recherche d'un père perdu* is absent within an interval of peregrinism.[53]

Furthermore, it would be a mistake to construe *Wakean* peregrinisms, "however basically English" (116.26) as a polylinguistic deviation *imposed upon an* English base, since the English language is already—long before Joyce—a tissue or gallimaufry of other languages. As Mallarmé noted in *Les mots anglais*, English is the exemplary language in that it is *already* formidably miscegenated. Mallarmé's study begins with the difficult question "Qu'est-ce que l'Anglais?" (OC: 899), a question which implies that the English language (or indeed any single language) can be neither defined nor circumscribed without reference to a plurality of languages. *Les mots anglais* testifies to the richness of the eccentricities, the *mots anglés*, of nomadic English words, in this way it is a manual of the *possibility* of *Finnegans Wake*.[54] In the *Wake*, English peregrinism is opened out onto the babelian exterior in which it is already imbricated. There is not even a stable language upon which *Wakean* enunciatory deviation is *predicated*. As with Dantean and Mallarméan *poiesis,* the preposition for *Finnegans Wake* is the absence of a pure language, an absence which is to be re-marked through a babelization of English. *Finnegans Wake* is not so much written *in* English as it is written *from* English, "But twill cling hellish like *engels opened to neuropeans,* if you've sensed, whole the sum" (519.01–2, emphasis added). English is opened out, exiled, made foreign, cunningly silenced.[55] "Are we speachin d'anglas landadge or are you sprakin sea Djoytsch?" (485.12–13).

Beckett has phrased this nicely: "Mr. Joyce has desophisticated language. And it is worth while remarking that no language is so sophisticated as English" (Beckett 1939, 15).[56]

Sensibility is maximized much to the irreparable detriment of *sense*. If Mallarmé proffers crispation through a paucity of discourse, then the *Wake* would also tend towards an enunciatory disparition, albeit a desistance imbricated within repetitive expansiveness. "Yet is no body present here which was not there before. Only is order othered. Nought is nulled. *Fuitfiat!*" (FW: 613.13–14). There is no presence in the present or the past and under the auspices of such absentation is order *othered:* nothing is canceled with no result: the *de-negation of nought being nulled. This* is the standing of the situation (*lieu*) which was (*fuit fiat*: as it was). This would thus be the moment of the desistance of narrative in the *Wake:* denegation *translated* into the writing or production of a book, the production (and unworking) of a work across languages. Milesi notes that by miscegenating English, by re-marking Babel in English, "L'avènement de la Pentecôte est sans cesse déjoué et la réconciliation n'apparaît pas derrière la fusion formelle des langues dans le moule de l'idiome wakien" (Milesi, 178). Languages are fused, but do not restitute a whole, the supreme language, as ever (and as noted by Mallarmé), remains unproffered.

The rampant and rabid inclusion and infusion of not-entirely discrete heterogeneous linguistic valences into an indiscreet English not only serves to disarticulate the referential status of *Wakean* "langwedge" (FW: 073.01), but also *emphasizes* that a singular delimitation of language *is itself disarticulated*. This kind of originary disarticulation is a point that Beckett draws from Dante's vernacular appropriations in comparison to the linguistic miscegenation of *Finnegans Wake*.[57] *Wakean* deviation does not operate upon a single happy structure of definitude. Indeed, as with Dante and Mallarmé, the languages upon which *Finnegans Wake* is predicated are already languages of loss. Perhaps the *Wake* never achieves a closure by which one could establish a teleologics of articulation; instead it might be read as a suspension or interval of articulation, an interruption of teleologics which proceeds without reference to a *defining* and *definitive* transcendent closure.

• • •

This is the starting point for Derrida's essay "Des tours de Babel," which is in many ways preparatory to his essay on *Wakean* language "Deux mots pour Joyce." The outline of this argument is similar to Sollers's emphasis of the importance of Babel for the *Commedia* (see chapter 2): the *trapassare del segno* named by Babel is no longer accessible after the confounding of languages: the "correctione... memorabili" (DVG: I.vii.5) only serves to re-mark the *fait* of the plurality of languages. Derrida argues that "Babel" is the name for the inadequation of one language to another. In Hebrew *Ba'bel* (בְּבָאֵל) means "God, the father" and *Bavel* (בָּבֶל) means confusion. The city of God—Babel (בָּבֶל)—bears the name of God the father *and* the name of confusion. In the act of His wrath neither sense can be disengaged from the other. His name is spoken as the confusion that commands dispersal: the *con-founding* of languages. God's presence—the present or gift of languages—poisons the present by acting as the command to peregrination: "La ville porterait le nom de Dieu le père, et du père de la ville qui s'appelle confusion.... En donnant son nom, un nom de son choix, en donnant tous les noms, le père serait à l'origine du langage et ce pouvoir appertiendrait de droit à Dieu le père. ... mais c'est aussi ce dieu qui, dans le moment de sa colère... annule le don des langues, ou du moins le brouille, sème la confusion parmi ses fils et empoisone le présent (*Gift-gift*)."[58] He (*Lui*) is already hearsay (*l'ouïe*). His presence is less than present.

In "Deux mots pour Joyce" Derrida unfurls a reading of *Finnegans Wake* (or two words therefrom) as a counter to Heidegger's argument of the oblivion of the Greek experience of Being. Derrida argues that this withdrawn trace of Being is possible only through unequivocal linguistic disarticulation. According to Heidegger's reading of the Anaximander fragment, Being belongs to an *ec-static* temporality that can be registered in the manifold senses of the archaic use of the German word *war* (clearing, securing, protection); "war" is the statement concerning the time of being.[59] Parallel to his reading of *Finnegans Wake*, Derrida proffers a critique of Heidegger by arguing that the event of Being's self-appropriation (*Ereignis*) can only be remarked through a translinguistic trace that *is not* present in the present. Language may be, as Heidegger famously asserted in the "Letter on Humanism," the house of Being, but it is a peripatetic dwelling, a dwelling of exile. By the implied enstaging of a dialogue between Joyce's polyglossia and Heidegger's privileging of the Greek and German languages, Derrida implies that Heidegger's famous "turn to language" is already inscribed within *des tours de Babel*.[60] Derrida uses Joyce to counter Heidegger by proposing that the presence of being has always passed and is always deferred: the preservation or lingering of the time of being is always linguistically *preterite*. This is done through reading the multiple valences of the two words "he war," "à supposer qu'on puisse compter des mots dans *Finnegans Wake*" (Derrida 1987a, 15):

> Kidoosh! Of their fear they broke, they ate wind, they fled; where they ate there they fled; of their fear they fled, they broke away. Go to, let us extol Azrael with our harks, by our brews, on our jambses, in his gaits. To Mezouzalem with the Dephilim, didits dinkun's dud? Yip! Yup! Yarrah! And let Nek Nekulon extol Mak Makal and let him say unto him: Immi ammi Semmi. And shall not Babel be with Lebab? And he war. And he shall open his mouth and answer: I hear, O Ismael, how they laud is only as my loud is one. If Nekulon shall be havonfalled surely Makal haven hevens. Go to, let us extell Makal, yea, let us exceedingly extell. Though you have lien amung your posspots my excellency is over Ismael. Great is him whom is over Ismael and he shall mekanek of Mak Nakulon. And he deed. (FW: 258.05–18)

Derrida plays with Philippe Lavergne's translation of "he war"—"Et il fut ainsi" —to suggest his own Francophonic edition of "he war": "Il se garde ainsi, à declarer la guerre" (Derrida 1987a, 17). *That is how he preserves himself, by declaring war*. His event of war was (and is no more) but lingers *ainsi* (here, in this manner, so be it). If "he war" remarks the fundamental conflict and confusion within the ecstases of the temporality of being, then the very possibility of a time of being depends upon its linguistic disarticulation. The effaced Greek trace bemoaned by

Heidegger is already constituted by the babelian confusion of language. Reverting to Heideggerian parlance, the destiny of the West, *wahr*, is already war. Translation obliterates the trace of linguistic difference that is evident in, *say*, the word *war*. "Le *war* allemand n'aura été vrai (*wahr*) qu'à déclarer la guerre à l'anglais. A lui faire la guerre en anglais. Une guerre qui n'en est pas moins essentielle—de l'essence—pour être fratricide. Le *fait* de la multiplicité des langues, ce qui fut *fait* comme confusion des langages ne peut plus se laisser reconduire, par la traduction, dans une seule langue, ni même réduire" (44-45). *He war*, for Derrida, is the call (*appel*) to translate, the call to respond to the state of linguistic diaspora: the impossible call (or double bind) to restitute postlapsarian linguistic difference. The oblivion of Being is disarticulated in the impossible yet necessary (ethical) act of translinguistic response and responsibility (*l'appel*).

Derrida suggests that the *he* of "he war" is Him, the God of Israel, to Whom the Shem (the builders of Babel, *shem*, the Hebrew name for *name*) pronounce the Shema, the injunction to *he ar*: Babel "Il, c'est 'Il,' le 'lui,' celui qui dit *Je* au masculin, 'Il,' la guerre déclarée, lui qui fut la guerre déclarée, en déclarant la guerre il fut celui qui fut et celui qui fut vrai" (17). Derrida is forced into posting "he" as a pronominative event (*Ereignis*) *in place of* a name—*in the place* of the impossibility of *His name*. As with "Ulysse gramophone," the issue concerns response and responsibility: how does one respond to God's name*s*, how does one respond to the "God" that is named differently in multiple languages, how does one responsibly respond to linguistic heterology and disaster. To read the *Wake*, following Derrida, is to be abandoned by *his* impossible call to *hear* amidst the babble of languages. God's call has been erased and this erasure or desistance of *dieu mots* is named by the pair of words that announce *he war*. In this way, Derrida emphasizes the responsibility of hearing *His oui-dire*.

However, in the Joyce passage it would appear that *he* could also be "Ismael": a confusion of Israel (Jacob: father of the twelve tribes; and the state of Israel, the state enstated by a declaration of *war,* a name which means "he who strives with God") and Ishmael (Israel's uncle and father of the Arabs, a name which means "he whom God hears"). It would seem that there is an event—a dispute, a war—marking the tomb of the dead and departed patriarchs.[61] In exile the Shem attempt to proffer obeisance to the figures of the departed Gods as a means of making their exile holy. They want to be able to say the "Kidoosh!" (FW: 258.05)—the prayer by which holiness is proclaimed. They hope that the figure of the "exeomnosunt" (258.02–3) will perdure in holiness through their proclamations, but this figure has already departed: it is *ex*-omniscient and has, through the rearrangement of its letters, withdrawn (exe-omn[e]s-unt = *exeunt omnes*; also *exeo* [to die, to escape, to be spread abroad, to rise, to exceed]; *sunt* [are]). The Shem want to be heard (they want to be who God hears: Ishmael)—they want to subsume the power to speak, His power to speak: "Loud, hear us! / Loud, graciously hear us!" (258.25–26).

But the time of this being has irretrievably passed: it can only be awaited, endlessly. Perdurance has already been lost. The declaration then might be an attempt by Ismael *to be heard* despite this loss. We see this in a dialogue of sorts: "And let Nek Nekulon extol Mak Makal and let him say unto him: Immi ammi Semmi. And shall not Babel be with Lebab? And he war. And he shall open his mouth and answer: I hear, O Ismael, how they laud is only as my loud is one" (258.10–13). Folded into the response to "he war" is a variation of the *Shema*, the great commandment, the pronouncement of a single God: "Hear, O Israel: the Lord our God is one Lord" (Deut: 6.4). In the Bible this is the *single* invective to hear, before all others. The name, Yahwé, has commanded the ennamed (the Shem, the name of the name, *shem* being Hebrew for name). This is precisely the impossible situation commanded by *Him* (*El*) of translation disclosed by Derrida: "Le *double bind* est en elle. En Dieu même, et il faut en suivre rigoureusement la conséquence: *en son nom*" (Derrida 1987b, 219). *He* (Derrida *and* Yahwé) has commanded the Shem to Shema, to rigorously hear and pay obeisance to the impossible *appel* of God to translate: to hear God in exile: "à savoir tendre l'oreille (*e ar, he, ar, ear, hear*) et obéir au père qui élève la voix, au seigneur qui parle haut (*Lord, loud*).... Cette dimension audiophonique... s'annonce dans la syllabisation anglaise *he(w)ar*..." (Derrida 1987a, 35–36).

God has already gone and the exiles have returned to war. After all is said and done, there is no reconciliation between the figures of the brothers; in trying to be heard by the god(s) with whom they attempt to strive, they remain separate from each other: "Till tree from tree, tree among trees, tree over tree become stone to stone, stone between stones, stone under stone for ever" (FW: 259.01–2). *Lui* is the hear-say: the tale extold between the sons Shem and Shaun. The father is expropriated by the exile of the sons and is replaced by a filial *maintwainance* of his departed deeds: a good-night story of suppliant noise for "Pray-your-Prayers Timothy and Back-to-Bunk Tom" (FW: 258.35–36). The awaited reconciliation remains eternally deferred. *A linguistic pentecost* — ALP — is always to be awaited. The mummification at the end of this chapter silences the laughter containing "he" as but one in a series of vowels appended to the guttural spirant "h." This letter is absent in the name of Ishmael in this passage. There is a *heard* difference between Ismael and the name of "who God hears" — what is heard is the caesura in the exile's name; an ellipsis to *he-ar*. *His* words might then just be these "laughters low! / Ha he hi ho hu / Mummum" (259.07–10). The elided spirant of the exile's name appears enjoined to vowels. Rather than serve as "God's signature," this *re-sounding* laughter is voiced preparatory to being silenced; the laughter awaits its end but is met by a murmur. Response (from both Ishmael and Israel under the name Ismael) is thus fractured: each fractures the other, neither prevails amidst the prevarications of languages. The end is always forthcoming. The event *war* not, and is (not) heard and remembered as such. The lauds are too loud. The interval is also an interregnum of responsibility.

Milesi's study of *Wakean* babelization neatly expands from several of Derrida's points. Milesi argues that babelian confusion is constitutive for the scene of the downfall of HCE. Commenting on the following passage — "When men want to write a letters. Ten men, ton men, pen men, pun men, wont to rise a ladder. And den men, dun men, hun men wend to raze a leader" (278.18–21) — Milesi notes that "Babel élevée

(Babel raised) devient Babel en-levée *(Babel razed)*, une fois que le leader-chef des travaux est abattu par le malédiction divine" (Milesi, 182). A portion of Milesi's essay concerns the ferences of the trope of Babel in *Finnegans Wake* and its preparatory notebooks. Babelian confusion is constitutive for the scene of the downfall of HCE and by extension would also be constitutive for any and all attempts at re-presenting that downfall in stories. "It may half been a missfired brick, as some say, or it mought have been due to a collupsus of his back promises, as others looked at it. (There extand by now one thousand and one stories, all told, of the same.)" (FW: 005.26–29). One such circulating narrative presented here concerns HCE's becoming subject to a *collupsus*. Or rather, his *back promises* are subject to a collupsus: these back promises are his anatomical back or a series of anterior responsibilities. The collapse does not affect HCE, but rather some displacement of him, which is itself ambiguously stated. This is of course but one of one thousand and one extellings extold of the advent of the event of HCE's fall from the offwall. And in said excerpt wall and erection are enstated as being inseparable ("a wall of course in erection"): their course is coeval. The advent of the narrative recounting (or extelling or "stolentelling" [424.35]) is absolutely isomorphic with the disastrous event. This accounting is of course somewhat *hopeful* in regard to the possibility of narrative as it implies that the fall "*mought* have been due...." The word *mought* modulates *nought* into subjunctivity: the hope of a telling. But this hope has already been extold in the nulling of—not the mought, but—the nought.

> *Finnegans Wake* est plein d'irrésolutions et d'hésitations, *hesitencies* structurales. Son intraduisibilité, celle du nom propre de Babel, acquise en dépit de la traduction intralinéaire, humaine, née du jeu des langues, *e*ncre dans l'écriture l'opposition sans cesse recommencée entre l'homme et Dieu/le fils et le père, la jubilation dans la chute linguistique venant en partie défaire la suprématie de la paternité, à laquelle les héros wakiens tentent, suivant les cas, de se cramponner ou d'accéder. (Milesi, 191)

Rather than complicate, or confuse, a pre-existing patriarchal plot, a plot of the father's downfall, *Wakean* peregrinisms provide a polemic of iterability through which HCE *et alia* come to be spoken. If Bloom existed in part as mis-citation (such as L. Boom "to give him for the nonce his new misnomer" [U: 16.1274–75]), then HCE has no subsistence apart from linguistically errant and misattributed ference: "The great fact emerges that after that historic date all holographs so far exhumed initialled by Haromphrey bear the sigla H.C.E.... it was equally certainly a pleasant turn of the populace which gave him as sense of those normative letters the nickname Here Comes Everybody. An imposing everybody he always indeed looked, constantly the same as and equal to himself and magnificently well worthy of any and all such universalization" (FW: 032.12–21).[62] The "plot" (such as it is) *is an effect of the babelian confusion of languages*, a confusion which is the ineluctable pre-position for language. What passes for *Wakean* plot is a tropic effect of babelization,[63] much as the possibility of Dante's pilgrimage heavenward was tropically enacted.

In the *Divina Commedia* Dante registered an experience of supreme plenitude through the exscription of tropic statement. He surrendered both experience and his *ingegno* to the annulations of language. Likewise, Mallarmé surrendered his very writing to the neutral passivity of the blank page, he expended his meager resources of ink in a restrained action of exscription. The annulatory machinations of language and of writing, for both, take the place of the guiding *Ulyssean* initiative. This then would be the possibility of *Finnegans Wake* for Joyce, the place that takes the place of a human dwelling.

Wakean writing is not articulated in and by principles of structuration, precisely because it *exceeds* the possibilities of said definitude. *Wakean* overdetermination removes the possibility of schematic subsumption and definition. However, there is nothing easier for a narratologics to do than to restitute continuity out of excess and deviation, to find the appurtenant marks of narrative in its denial. Indeed formalist criticisms, with all their didactic power, have made the aberrational exemplary, in order to be able *to complete* the incomplete.[64] But, following from our earlier discussions of Blanchot, perhaps the fragment *incompletes* the complete. *Wakean* expansion impoverishes the work, maximization is, paradoxically, also a work of extreme attenuation..

This possibility of nontotalizable antinarrativity in *Finnegans Wake* (in contradistinction to *Ulysses*) hinges it to our present study of silence as an odd iteration iterated oddly and perpetuated perpetually.

Notes

[1] Maurice Blanchot, Le livre à venir, Paris: Gallimard, 1959, 1986. 13.

[2] Maurice Blanchot, "Mallarmé et l'art du roman," *Faux pas*, Paris: Gallimard, 1943. 189–96. 189–92.

[3] In *L'entretien infini* Blanchot associates such a project with Flaubert's attempts to poeticize prose, a project of "donner à la prose le rhythme du vers (en laissant prose, et très prose)" (Gustave Flaubert, *Correspondance*, Volume II, ed. Jean Bruneau, Paris: Gallimard, 1980. 287). Blanchot calls this an attempt at an *intransitive writing*, a sort of *crise de prose* (Maurice Blanchot, *L'entretien infini*, Paris: Gallimard, 1969. 487–93).

[4] In *Ulysses* whenever a shadow is cast, "Parallax stalks behind" (U: 14.1089). For example, early in the morning both Stephen and Bloom witness the same cloud obscure the sun which then influences their thoughts toward the apocalyptically melancholic: "A cloud began to cover the sun slowly, wholly, shadowing the bay in deeper green. It lay beneath him, a bowl of bitter waters" (1.248–49); "A cloud began to cover the sun slowly, wholly. Grey. Far. No, not like that. A barren land, bare waste" (4.218–19). This confluence between Bloom and Stephen is later phrased as "the reapparition of a matutinal cloud (perceived by both from two different points of observation, Sandycove and Dublin) at first no bigger than a woman's hand" (17.40–42). *Ulysses* is a book in which one cannot even have "the pleasure of defecating" (LII: 187) without there plopping an echo elsewhere.

[5] We take as an initial minor example of this univocal tendency of polyvocal narration the varied narratives of the dog known to all men, Garryowen. The roughandtumble "I" narrator of "Cyclops" (or dun) describes this fine beast thusly: "The bloody mongrel let a grouse out of him would give you the creeps. Be a corporal work of mercy if someone would take the life of that bloody dog. I'm told for a fact he ate a good part of the breeches off a constabulary man in Santry that came round one time with a blue paper about a license" (U: 12.124–28); an inflated intrusion refines Garry as follows: "a savage beast of the canine tribe whose stretorous gasps announced that he was sunk in uneasy slumber, a supposition confirmed by hoarse growls and spasmodic movements" (12.201–3); a subsequent intrusion magnifies or transmogrifies Garry into something even more respectable: "All those who are interested in the spread of human culture among the lower

animals (and their name is legion) should make a point of not missing the really marvellous exhibition of cyanthropy given by the famous old Irish red setter wolfdog formerly known by the *sobriquet* of Garryowen and recently rechristened by his large circle of friends and acquaintances Owen Garry" (12.711–17); and in the Gerty narration Garry's description is suitably colored by a festering mawkishness: "grandpa Giltrap's lovely dog Garryowen that almost talked it was so human" (13.232–33). Garry is mongrelized in and by varying narrations. The variable figurations participate within certain temporary diegetic states thereby allowing for a continuity out of diegetic shifts and discontinuities. There is not so much a single Garryowen inferable from the text, but rather a persistence of multiply mutated mutts.

[6] Michael Patrick Gillespie, *Reading the Book of Himself*, Columbus: Ohio State UP, 1989. 182.

[7] Shari Benstock and Bernard Benstock, "The Benstock Principle," *The Seventh of Joyce,* ed. Bernard Benstock, Bloomington: Indiana UP, 1982. 10–21. 18. The Benstock principle is an expansion of Kenner's Uncle Charles Principle which posits a slight interference of the mimetic onto the diegetic: "the normally neutral narrative vocabulary [is] pervaded by a little cloud of idioms which a character *might use* if he were managing the narrative" (Hugh Kenner, *Joyce's Voices,* Berkeley: U of California P, 1978. 17, emphasis added). Kenner's use of the conditional here is crucial since it implies that there is and remains a *distance* between the narrative and the narrated even as that distance appears to be elided through the tenor of the narrative. In distinction, the Benstock principle allows for a greater matrix of variability of diegetic interference.

[8] Initially Hayman had described the arranger as an absent *character* whose influence impacts upon the tenor of the narrative (David Hayman, "Cyclops," *James Joyce's "Ulysses,"* eds. Clive Hart and David Hayman, Berkeley: U of California P, 1974. 243–75; cf. esp. 263–68). He has subsequently redefined the arranger as more of a *site* than a character: "a significant, felt absence in the text, an unstated but inescapable source of control" (David Hayman, *"Ulysses": The Mechanics of Meaning,* revised edition, Madison: U of Wisconsin P, 1982. 123; cf. 122–25). This view is infinitely more supple and accommodates virtually all attitudinal shifts within *Ulysses*; practically all contemporary readings of narratologics in *Ulysses* follow from this reading.

[9] Karen Lawrence, *The Odyssey of Style in "Ulysses,"* Princeton: Princeton UP, 1981. 44–47.

[10] Parallels to Homer are invariably suggested by the book's title, and also by certain of Joyce's comments ("I am now writing a book based on the wanderings of Ulysses. ... Only my time is recent time and all my hero's wanderings take no more than eighteen hours" quoted in Frank Budgen, *James Joyce and the Making of "Ulysses,"* Oxford: Oxford UP, 1968. 15), as well as the two (not entirely uncontradictory) schemes Joyce had prepared for friends. Stuart Gilbert is most responsible for aggravating readers' fears by emphasizing Homer's underlying role in *Ulysses*. Gilbert's premise is that Joyce's entire book can be more-or-less adequately explained through Homer, that *Ulysses* is a translation of the *Odyssey* into Dublin (cf. Stuart Gilbert, *James Joyce's "Ulysses,"* revised edition, New York: Vintage, 1952. 76–84, *et passim*). Hugh Kenner was probably the first critic to have downplayed the Homeric correspondences; while admitting the importance, he denied them a singularly decisive centrality (Hugh Kenner, *Dublin's Joyce*, New York: Columbia UP, 1987. 180–81). More recently, Kenner has characterized the Homeric reference as less an "analogy of incident or character than [an] *analogy of situation*" (Hugh Kenner, *Ulysses*, London: George Allen and Unwin, 1980. 24, emphasis added). Michael Seidel has argued that in writing *Ulysses*, Joyce superimposed a Mediterranean geography under the Dublin cityscape, thereby producing a palimpsest of two topoi *in and through* which Bloom and Stephen move. In one sense Seidel argues for a greater presence of Homer in *Ulysses* than even Gilbert had claimed, but for Seidel these allusions contribute more to *texture* than to the structure of the text (Michael Seidel, *Epic Geography: James Joyce's "Ulysses,"* Princeton: Princeton UP, 1976. 132–37, cf. 176–81). The correspondences to Homer do not *define Ulysses*, rather they converge into one series (amongst several) of *Ulyssean* reference. Homer is one of several coincidental aspects through which *Ulysses* steers.

[11] The provenance of this citation is the introduction to the list of Molly's supposed lovers, a breathtaking cavalcade of names which had been assumed to be literally accurate until David Hayman noted that Molly could not have actually slept with many of those named (David Hayman, "The Empirical Molly," *Approaches to "Ulysses": Ten Essays*, eds. Thomas Staley and Bernard Benstock, Pittsburgh: U of Pittsburgh P, 1970. 103–35. cf. esp. 113–14). Accurate reference is thus displaced and distorted by diegetic decorums, although this particular distortion remains

eminently ironic since an alternative, potentially accurate reference, remains at least implicitly recuperable.

[12] "On the one hand [Joyce's procedure of repetition] detaches one specific element, usually a verbal fragment, from the universe of a text and puts it in communication with another similar fragment. This *découpage* fragments the original text in its relation to *Ulysses*. On the other hand, it makes a plurality of new connections possible so that the original can belong to two texts without being fully determined by either of them" (Udaya Kumar, *The Joycean Labyrinth*, Oxford: Oxford UP, 1991. 162; cf. 17–18; see also Robert Spoo, *James Joyce and the Language of History*, Oxford: Oxford UP, 1994. 72–73). Bernard Benstock makes a similar point by noting how the recurrence of *Ulyssean* items from varying perspectives constitutes the text even as such recurrences destabilize possibilities of stable and determinate identification: "Con/Text in *Ulysses* presents a field of play in which such counters as content, conflict, confluence, contradiction and consistency (as well as inconsistency) are constantly operative" (Bernard Benstock, *Narrative Con/Texts in "Ulysses,"* U of Illinois P, 1991. 2; cf. 73–76).

[13] Such an approach has been crystallized by William M. Schute's *Index of Recurrent Elements in James Joyce's "Ulysses"* (Carbondale: Southern Illinois UP, 1982) which translates *Ulysses* into a tourist-map of interrelated points..

[14] Hugh Kenner, *The Stoic Comedians,* Berkeley: U of California P, 1974. 66.

[15] Padraic Colum—noting the influence upon Joyce of Victor Bérard's notion of a Mediterranean and semitic Odysseus—claimed that "Odysseus and the Wandering Jew are different versions of the same character" (Mary and Padraic Colum, *Our Friend James Joyce,* New York: Doubleday, 1958. 112). Semitism—and the various constituting discourses that circulate around it—is thus one scheme that is imposed over and interferes with the Homeric resonances. To be sure there are certain affinities between Odysseus and the wandering Jew, enhanced no doubt, by the permutabilities of each figure. Some Homeric scholarship maintains the *possibility* that the conclusion to the *Odyssey* is a later, synthetic addition to the tale, and so even Odysseus might have been denied a νόστος (cf. D.L. Page, *The Homeric Odyssey,* Oxford: Oxford UP, 1955. 110–4). Gregory Nagy argues against such a reading of a stratified text of the *Odyssey* by following the *intentio operis* in order to read Odysseus's achievement of κλέος as being concomitant with his νόστος (Gregory Nagy, *The Best of the Achaeans*, Baltimore: Johns Hopkins UP, 1979. 38–39).

Furthermore he notes that νόστος does not just name a homecoming but also the "tradition that told about a homecoming" (97). Nagy's argument (which is compatible with Blanchot's reading of Ulysses and the Sirens) is that Odysseus garnered fame *tautologically*, he gained fame by occupying the locus of narration.

[16] Bloom may be a figure for the wandering Jew, but, in several ways, he is not technically Jewish. He fails to observe kosher cuisine (U: 4.46; 17.1897 *et passim*), he is uncircumcised (13.979–80), his mother was not Jewish (17.536), he had been baptized three times (17.542), and his father had been converted first by Protestants and then by Catholics (8.1071–74; 15.2455–58; 17.1637–40). Despite this accumulation of asemitism, Bloom is persistently identified as Jewish, both by himself and his feisty Dublin compatriots, notably at Barney Kiernan's pub: "He called me a jew and in a heated fashion offensively. So I without deviating from plain facts in the least told him his God, I mean Christ, was a jew too and all his family like me though in reality I'm not" (16.1082–85). Bloom has wandered apart from Judaism, his identity coterminous with his errancy (see Ira Nadel, *Joyce and the Jews*, London: Macmillan, 1989. 24–34; 134–35). Bloom is a wandering Jew *because* he has also peripatetically wandered away from Judaism, his Judaism is not reducible to cultural or racial enframing.

[17] Buck is not the only one to comment upon Bloom's eyes, which seem to be a visible mark that differentiates Bloom. Gerty MacDowell "could see at once by his dark eyes and his pale intellectual face that he was a foreigner" (U: 13.415–16; cf. 14.1058). And after the performance of a certain act on the beach, the eyes return as an overdetermined mark of *errancy*: "An utter cad he had been! He of all men! But there was an infinite store of mercy in those eyes, for him too a word of pardon even though he had erred and sinned and wandered" (13.747–49).

[18] Don Gifford and Robert J. Seidman, *"Ulysses" Annotated*, second edition, Berkeley: U of California P, 1988. 449.

[19] William Shakespeare, *Hamlet, The Oxford Shakespeare: Complete Works*, ed. W.J. Craig, Oxford: Oxford UP, 1905. 870–907. I.v.9–10.

[20] "In the repetition of allusions… there is a movement of transformation and recontextualization of the original text. The source of the allusion does not provide any unique authority that legislates over the production of meaning in the text. On the contrary, the original text is put into circulation within *Ulysses* with variable meaning" (Kumar, 30).

[21] This constellation of a Bloomified Shakespeare recurs to both Stephen and Bloom in "Circe" when they both "see" the face of William Shakespeare in a mirror, "rigid in facial paralysis, crowned by the reflection of the reindeer antlered hatrack in the hall" (U: 15.3822–24). Bloom here shares with Stephen the vision of a cuckolded Shakespeare who would also be figured as Bloom's partial double. Indeed this scopic bard, speaking *"in dignified ventriloquy"* (15.3826), chastises Bloom for his phantasy of watching Blazes and Moly enjoy a moment of intimacy.

[22] Although apparently no scholar has ever seriously entertained the idea that Shakespeare might have been Jewish, his specific religious affiliation has been much debated. It cannot be claimed with absolute certainty if Shakespeare was Catholic, Puritan, or a reforming Protestant (Samuel Schoenbaum, *Shakespeare's Lives*, Oxford: Oxford UP, 1970. 122–24).

[23] "Le paradoxe de Stephen tient précisément en ce qu'il a besoin de présenter un Shakespeare historique, sur la scène datée par ses allusions et son langage, au milieu de toutes les rivalités, les usurpations et les traîtrises familiales, afin justement de libérer la puissance créatrice du père de la tutelle maternelle" (Jean-Michel Rabaté, *Joyce: Portrait de l'auteur en autre lecteur*, Paris: Cistre-Essais, 1984. 52; cf. 52–55).

[24] Examples of this are "Mr Secondbest Best" (U: 9.714–15); "Monk Mulligan" (9.773); "Rutlandbaconsouthamptonshakespeare or another poet of the same name" (9.866); "John Eclecticon" (9.1070); "Puck Mulligan" (9.1125) *&c*. The most interesting onomastic shuffle is Stephen's comment "A.E.I.O.U." (9.213). This pun orients the continuity of Stephen's existence to his debtor A.E. (and also proves, as if there had been doubt, that Stephen is not English since according to Deasy the proudest boast of an Englishman is *"I paid my way. I never borrowed a shilling in my life"* [2.253]). Identity is reduced to vocalization. Rabaté notes that Dante, in the *Convivio*, explored the manifest possible alignments of the five vowels. Dante notes that the archaic word for author was "auieo" which means to link together, and this very word demonstrates or re-marks (authorial) linking through its enjoining of the five vowels, "E in quanto 'autore' viene e discende da questo verbo, si prende solo per poeti, che con l'arte musica le loro parole hanno legate" (C: IV.vi.4; cf. 3–4). For Dante authority is realized and figured by attaining the single proper alignment whereas for Stephen the absence of a single true confluence is realized by Protean metamorphoses and realignments of various rapports (Rabaté 1984, 135–41). As with the problem of the allegory of the theologians and the allegory of the poets

(discussed in chapter 2), the ascription of authority rests within a series (in this case the vowels) whose reconfigurability entails differentiation away from a single and autotelic point. For Stephen linguistic negativity does not yield the mark of a higher authority sublimated, instead the figure and figuration of authority is *gathered and realized* (*legate*, deriving from λέγειν) through multiple configurations.

[25] These include the miscitation of Hamlet already discussed; the description of *amor matris* which derives from Stephen's thoughts concerning the hopeless swot Cyril Sargent (U: 2.165); and the certainty of maternal love which also derives from Stephen's reflections on Sargent (2.143) and also from one of Cranly's statements in the *Portrait* (AP: 241–42).

[26] As Kumar notes, these recontextualizations allude to the existence of an arranger (see note 8) which functions as a generative site for asymmetric and disjunctive reference (Kumar, 112).

[27] In "Circe," when Zoe is reading Bloom's hand she first diagnoses him as a Ulyssean adventurer: "Travels beyond the sea and marry money" (U: 15.3701). When Bloom informs her that she is wrong, she then proposed that he is a "Henpecked husband" (15.3706). This is exactly how Rip van Winkle is first described: "a simple good natured man... a kind neighbour, and an obedient, henpecked husband" (Washington Irving, *Rip Van Winkle and The Legend of Sleepy Hollow,* San Diego: Harper Brace Jovanovich, 1984. 4).

[28] Conflations of Molly and Milly persist throughout the day; indeed in "Nausicaa" Bloom's thoughts concerning Molly's love for Milly echo his posited affinity between himself and Molly: "What do they love? Another themselves?" (U: 13.1196). Concerning Milly's blond hair, Bloom exhibits some trepidation: "blond, born of two dark, she had blond ancestry, remote, a violation, Herr Hauptmann Hainau, Austrian army, proximate, a hallucination, lieutenant Mulvey, British navy" (17.868–70). The shock of seeing another edition of Molly, but this time blond, reminds Bloom of Molly's youthful assignations with the fairhaired Mulvey (17.2133; and less unreliably 18.818). And, of course, throughout the day Bloom is also preoccupied with Milly's assignation with Bannon and occasionally thinks of traveling to Mullingar to halt any impropriety (4.447–54 *et passim*), just as he occasionally thinks about returning home early so as to interfere with Boylan and Molly's tryst: "Useless to go back. Had to be. Tell me all" (8.633 *et passim*).

[29] Gifford notes that a nova of the second magnitude appeared in Corona Borealis in May 1866, the year of Bloom's birth (Gifford, 585); he also notes that the name Leopold implies a birth under the Northern Crown (70). Frequently comets and novæ are confused in their initial appearances, however a nova spends its visible lifetime—brightening and dimming—in one fixed location whereas a comet appears to traverse the sky during its brief interval of visibility.

[30] There is also a further intercalated reference: the "dark crusader," which is a possible reference to, as Gifford notes, Edmund Dantes the Count of Monte Cristo, a character whom Stephen had thought, as a young man, to be a "dark avenger" (Gifford, 600; AP: 62). Again there is a diegetic interference between Bloom and Stephen.

[31] Samuel Beckett, *Proust,* London: John Calder, 1965. 11.

[32] And of course he exists also as a miscitation. For example, through Hynes's less-than-perfectionism Bloom is reduced to "*L. Boom*" (16.1260) in the list of those in attendance at Paddy Dignam's funeral. In the same newspaper list, the infamous man in the macintosh becomes, also through Hynes's journalistic acumen (6.894), a new individual named M'Intosh (16.1261). Bloom had even been (before having read the newspaper account) confounded with and by the staged manifestation of this spurious M'Intosh: "THE MAN IN THE MACINTOSH / Don't you believe a word he says. That man is Leopold M'Intsoh, the notorious fireraiser. His real name is Higgins" (15.1560–64). The hallucinated man in the macintosh further conflates the Scottish fireraiser John M'Intosh (Gifford, 476) with Bloom's mother's maiden name Higgins (U: 17.536).

[33] Homer, *The Odyssey,* trans. Richmond Lattimore, New York: Harper Collins, 1965. XXIII.181–206.

[34] The "Cuckoo"s do not just testify to Bloom's cuckoldry but also to a less-than-consummated infidelity on his part: after the voyeurism on the beach with Gerty, the clock booms nine: "it was a little canarybird that came out of its little house to tell the time that Gerty MacDowell noticed the time she was there because she was as quick as anything about a thing like that, was Gerty MacDowell, and she noticed at once that that foreign gentleman that was sitting on the rocks looking was / *Cuckoo / Cuckoo / Cuckoo*" (U: 13.1299–1306). Bloom's (attempt to reveal his) identity ("AM. A. / No room. Let it go" [13.1264-5]) has been supplemented by the clock's testimonial (see also note 32).

[35] In part Derrida's notion of différance derives from Heidegger's dif-ference, which is "neither distinction nor relation. The dif-ference is, at most, dimension for world and thing" (Martin Heidegger, "Language," *Poetry, Language, Thought,* trans. Albert Hofstadter, New York: Harper and Row, 1975. 187–210. 203). The dif-ference that Heidegger names is without filiation to a semiotic system (it is not a difference apperceivable within a network of signs). This stands in contrast to Derrida's différance which is eminently semiotic (the mute, errant and truant *a* standing as the re-mark of inscription) and yet différance, precisely by virtue of being semiotic, re-marks an insouciance of overarching structural rapport.

[36] Jacques Derrida, "La différance," *Marges de la philosophie,* Paris: Minuit, 1972. 3–29. 6.

[37] Jacques Derrida, *L'origine de la Géometrie de Husserl, Introduction et traduction,* Paris: PUF, 1962. 104.

[38] Jacques Derrida, *Ulysse gramophone*. Paris: Galilée, 1987. 23. One example of such a "joyciciel" would be Schute's *Index* (see note 13). In the following chapter we will have more to say concerning the apparent necessity for compiling databases in order that Joyce might be read and understood.

[39] Rodolphe Gasché makes a similar point concerning the problematic which Derrida elicits out of Joyce: "A genuine response to what in a work is open to the arrival of the Other has thus all the allure of irresponsibility: it is singular, untranslatable, affirming the chance of encounters and the randomness of coincidences, never in its own, or arriving at itself, always only beginning. A response that truly addresses the Other cannot have the security, the certainty, of being an unconditional affirmation. ... The two yeses *must* contaminate themselves precisely because what seems to be a threat is also an opportunity, a chance, the only chance of responsible response. Without the risk, without the threat of contamination, there could not possibly be a genuine response" (Rodolphe Gasché, *Inventions of Difference,* Cambridge: Harvard UP, 1994. 248; cf. 236–50). In this scheme, a reading of *Ulysses* (and for that matter a reading of Derrida) would be valid only insofar as the recklessness of insouciance (the yes! of the Other) is heard and vouchsafed through a dialogic rapport with rigor (yes…). Selon Gasché, to affirm responsibly, responsibility *must* equivocate, *must* be open to equivocation. However, his phraseology—which highlights the word "must"—determines and conditions

hasard as the singular necessity ("the only chance") of responsibility. Gasché, and perhaps Derrida as well, tilts the equation towards a categorical imperative.

[40] Derrida argues that generic participation (exhibiting the mark of appurtenance) is not equivalent to being subsumed within a classificatory matrix: "le genre, concept par essence classificatoire et généalogico-taxonimique, engendre lui-même tant de vertiges classificatoires quand il s'agit de le classer lui-même et de situer, dans un ensemble, le principe ou l'instrument classificatoire" (Jacques Derrida, *Parages,* Paris: Flammarion, 1986. 258; cf. 257–58).

[41] Clive Hart, *Structure and Motif in "Finnegans Wake,"* London: Faber, 1962. 65.

[42] Such insistence obviously predates Hart; one can find its boldest (yet also most timid) instance in Campbell and Robinson's *Skeleton Key*. Campbell and Robinson claim that once the broad outlines of the *Wake*'s armature are perceived, the text would begin to make sense: "Yet some of the difficulties disappear as soon as the well-disposed reader picks up a few compass clues and gets his bearings. Then the enormous map of *Finnegans Wake* begins slowly to unfold, characters and motifs emerge, themes become recognizable, and Joyce's vocabulary falls more and more familiarly on the accustomed ear" (Joseph Campbell and Henry Morton Robinson, *A Skeleton Key to "Finnegans Wake,"* Harmondsworth: Penguin, 1961. 3–4). Of course, not entirely unlike Hart, this broad pattern is the family-plot as backdrop for an allegory of cyclical fall and redemption.

In light of recent theoretical developments, Hart has re-examined some of his presuppositions concerning the readability of *Finnegans Wake*. While renouncing some of his methodologies in *Structure and Motif,* Hart notes that he still favors the general tenor of his inquiry. Indeed, he still holds out the necessity of an overall structure which would somehow inform any and all individual passages, even if both the broad pattern and the specific texture remain mystifying (Clive Hart, *"Finnegans Wake* in Adjusted Perspective," *Critical Essays on James Joyce's "Finnegans Wake,"* ed. Patrick A. McCarthy, New York: Macmillan, 1992. 15–33. 31). More recently, he has stated that "I now have sympathy with only a few details in it. Most of it is tripe" (Clive Hart, "Fritz in the Early Awning," *A Collideorscape of Joyce,* eds. Ruth Frehner and Ursula Zeller, Dublin: Lilliput, 1998. 4–10. 10 fn. 2).

[43] Hayman's nodal system is essentially a radical modulation of motif structuration: these systems "may be built around or evolved from narrative

sequences, descriptive tropes, clusters of words in an exotic language, song tags. ... The sort of non-narrative or narrative-resistant structure of *Finnegans Wake* necessitates a device that works more like a melodic line upon which variations can be played but that remains capable of carrying structural weight" (David Hayman, *The "Wake" in Transit*, Ithaca: Cornell UP, 1990. 37). What *passes for* plot and character is described through the interplay of imbricating nodal resonance. This reading thus attenuates the role of a specific overarching narratologics, yet a principle of organization (albeit decentralized and decentralizing) remains. In this way, Hayman's theory is quite similar to some deconstructive readings of *Finnegans Wake* (see note 46). Kumar's theory of *Ulyssean* recontextualization (see note 12) also bears some passing affinities to nodality.

[44] John Paul Riquelme, *Teller and Tale in Joyce's Fiction*, Baltimore: Johns Hopkins UP, 1983. 25–28. In essence, Riquelme reads *Wakean* narrative as a massive locus of *inter-ference*.

[45] In "Sémantique de la métaphore" Eco proposes an "exigence méthodologique qu'on retrouve telle quelle dans une étude de sémantique générale qui se proposerait d'éclairer la manière dont le langage pourrait engendrer des métaphores" ("Sémantique de la métaphore," trans. Marida di Francesco, *Tel Quel* 55 [Autumn 1973]: 25–46. 26).

[46] "Rather than proceeding on the basis of specifiable central concerns, the *Wake* moves instead through its tropic language that, by remaining always in process—substituting itself, associating itself with its other, identifying part and whole, simultaneously affirming and denying all the preceding operations—defies formulation of what it is 'about.' ... At every instant, the text is definable as the acts its words perform" (Susan Shaw Sailer, *On the Void of To Be,* Ann Arbor: U of Michigan P, 1993. 157). Sailer's argument applies Derridian differentiation to *Wakean* narrative and a more conventional narratologics (such as Genette's) would be more pertinent and appropriate.

[47] Jean-Michel Rabaté, "Narratology and the Subject of *Finnegans Wake*," *James Joyce: The Centennial Symposium*, eds. Morris Beja, Phillip Herring, Maurice Harmon, David Norris, Urbana: U of Illinois P, 1986. 137–46. 145–46.

[48] Gérard Genette, *Figures III*, Paris: Seuil, 1972. 75; cf. 74–76.

[49] This of course would be the HCE/ALP, male/female plot, how the belated HCE is rescued by ALP from perdition into continuation and regeneration: "ancients

link with presents [ALP] as the human chain extends [HCE]" (FW: 254.08–9; cf. Hayman 1990, 171–77).

[50] The Vichian influence on Joyce apart from the historical structuration had been more or less ignored in the aftermath of Beckett's essay (Samuel Beckett, "Dante... Bruno. Vico.. Joyce," *Our Exagmination Round His Factification For Incamination Of Work In Progress*, Samuel Beckett *et al*, New York: New Directions, 1939. 3–22), until Bishop examined Vichian poetics as a metaphor for an unconscious's miscegenated retention of a history of consciousness (John Bishop, *Joyce's Book of the Dark*, Madison: U of Wisconsin P, 1986. chapter 7).

[51] Strother B. Purdy, "Mind Your Genderous: Toward a *Wake* Grammar," *New Light on Joyce*, ed. Fritz Senn, Bloomington: Indiana UP, 1972. 46–78. See also F.G. Asenjo, "The General Problem of Sentence Structure: An Analysis Prompted by the Loss of Subject in *Finnegans Wake*," *Centennial Review of Arts and Sciences* VIII (1964): 398–408.

[52] Laurent Milesi, "L'idiome babélien de *Finnegans Wake*," *Genèse de Babel, Joyce et la création*, ed. Claude Jacquet, Paris: CNRS, 1986. 155–215. 186. Such a claim is indebted to Hayman's study of Joyce's neologisms with respect to Mallarmé. Hayman suggests—analogously to Benjamin's argument in "The Task of the Translator"—that Joycean *peregrinisms* serve to enhance the English language, and thus Joyce "ne détruit pas les mots qu'il emploie. Il les rends plus puissants" (David Hayman, *Joyce et Mallarmé*, 2 volumes, Paris: Lettres Modernes, 1956. I.126). Both Milesi and Hayman point to an *expansion* of referential possibility subsumed by the word-as-name. However Milesi resists Hayman's conclusion of lexical empowerment by suggesting a dissemination without recapitulation: dispersal without meaning. This notion of a polylinguistically enabled lexical empowerment will be a major concern in the first section of the following chapter.

[53] HCE appears to be conjugated into existence in an subjunctive mood: "Yet may we not see still the brontoichthyan form outlined aslumbered" (FW: 007.20–1). The argument is phrased *as if* he could be conjugated into being: "Would he were even among the lost!" (489.04–5). If anything, he is conjugated into "lextinction" (083.25). His existence, such as it is, remains within the realm of the sigla HCE dispersed throughout, which can, at certain intervals (notably the "Haveth Childers Everywhere" section of III.3 [532.06–554.10]), coalesce into a voice, identifiable as such because of a somewhat consistent deployment of the tropes that had been

associated with him: "By hearing his thing about a person one begins to place him for a certain in true" (490.09–10): it is as if gossip would be enough to impart a place in which he could exist, his home is in his gossip. This subjunctive preterition is also consigned to the fate of those who have quested after HCE, "the crowd of Caraculacticors as much no more as be they not yet now or had they notever been. Canbe in some future we shall presently here amid those zouave players of Inkermann the mime mumming the mick and his nick miming their maggies" (048.07–11). See also our discussion on page 216 and following.

[54] "Par sa Grammaire... marche vers quelque point futur du Langage et se replonge aussi dans le passé, même très ancien et mêlé aux débuts sacrés du Langage, l'Anglais: Langue Contemporaine peut-être par excellence, elle qui accuse le double caractère de l'époque, rétrospectif et avancé" (OC: 1053). This stands in marked contrast to Mallarmé's characterization of his own language: "La langue neutre, par excellence, c'est le Français; et rien de plus rare que voir un de ces Mots Nomades qui n'ait pas abouti chez nous d'abord" (1033). Considering recent actions by the Académie Française concerning the maintenance of the purity of the French language, if Mallarmé were alive today, he would be rolling around in Du Bellay's grave.

[55] Preparatory to writing *Ulysses*, Joyce remarked: "I'd like a language which is above all language, a language to which all will do service. I cannot express myself in English without enclosing myself in a tradition" (quoted in Richard Ellmann, *James Joyce*, revised edition, Oxford: Oxford UP, 1982. 397). What Joyce does in *Finnegans Wake* is, in part, to reject the tendency of a hegemonic and unequivocal English sense in favor of a tradition of linguistic difference and equivocation which is already latent in the English language that it has informed.

[56] Beckett's claims have been followed by various critics for various reasons. Eugene Jolas notes that predominantly the "background languages" are those "spoken in the British Empire, past and present" (Eugene Jolas, "The Revolution of Language and James Joyce," *Our Exagmination Round His Factification For Incamination Of Work In Progress*, Samuel Beckett, *et al*, New York: New Directions, 1939. 77–92. 90). This type of claim has resurfaced within the last few years in various attempts to provide a "political reading of *Finnegans Wake*," showing that Joyce fractured, subverted and de-natured the autonomy of the colonizer's language with the argots of the colonized; glibly phrased, the subaltern speaks in Joyce's Irish stew (cf. esp. Colin MacCabe, *James Joyce and the Revolution of the Word*, London: Macmillan, 1978. 143–57). Such readings tend towards a pentecostal redemption of

Joyce's fragmentation by assuming a restitution of a silenced voice or identity (cf. MacCabe, 155).

[57] "[Dante's] conclusion is that the corruption common to all dialects makes it impossible to select one rather than another as an adequate literary form, and that he who would write in the vulgar must assemble the purest elements from each dialect and construct a synthetic language that would at least possess more than a circumscribed local interest" (Beckett 1939, 18).

[58] Jacques Derrida, "Des tours de babel," *Psyché*, Paris: Galilée, 1987. 203–35. 204–205; cf. Milesi, 176–78.

[59] "All things present and absent are gathered and preserved in *one* presencing for the seer. The old German word *war* [was] means protection. We still recognize this in *wahrnehmen* [to perceive], i.e. to take into preservation; in *gewahren* and *verwahren* [to be aware of, to keep or preserve]. We must think of *wahren* as a securing which clears and gathers. Presencing preserves [wahrt] in unconcealment what is present both at the present time and not at the present time. The seer speaks from the preserve [*Wahr*] of what is present. He is the sooth-sayer [*Wahr-Sager*]" (Martin Heidegger, "The Anaximander Fragment," *Early Greek Thinking*, trans. David Farrell Krell and Frank A. Capuzzi, New York: Harper and Row, 1984. 13–58. 38. cf. esp. 32–38; 48–58). Heidegger's gesture to Homer in this passage authorizes a sigil of the primordiality of Being through an archaic formulation (i.e. prior to Anaximander) into the German language (the word *war*).

[60] The dwelling of being builds into Heidegger's notion of dif-ference (see note 35). In *On the Way to Language*, Heidegger reworked the statement of language-as-guardianship from the "Letter on Humanism" (trans. Frank Capuzzi, J. Glenn Gray and David Krell, *Basic Writings*, ed. David Krell, New York: Harper and Row, 1977. 189–242. 193) to a notion of language as a grounding of the experience of the event of being's appropriation (Martin Heidegger, *On the Way to Language*, trans. Peter D. Hertz, San Francisco: Harper and Row, 1971. 135–6; cf. 58–63). Derrida's contribution to this argument is the notion of an errantly trans-linguistic event, the notion of translinguistic différance might mitigate the potential for such gathering dif-ference.

[61] Both Jacob and Ishmael are buried in the cave of the patriarchs in Hebron, the site of a massacre in 1929—shortly before Joyce drafted the passage (JJA: 51.137)—

and the site of more-than-several massacres and disagreements since. Derrida has thus forgotten the second contentious state at war in the name Ismael.

[62] The sigla Joyce had employed for his cast of characters—"The Doodles family, ⊓, Δ, ⊣, X, □, ∧, ⊏. Hoodle doodle, fam.?" (FW: 299.F4)—have provoked a mixture of indifference and controversy among critics (these sigla are far more frequently employed in the notebooks preparatory to the *Wake* than they are in the text itself; for an early treatment of the sigla as a means of providing a generative structure for the *Wake*, see Roland McHugh, *The Sigla of "Finnegans Wake,"* London: Edward Arnold, 1976. cf. esp. 10–14). Jean-Michel Rabaté has provided an eloquent formulation of the sigla's role, the very iconicity of the sigla remarks an arbitrary accretion of characteristics (including the names), the sigla thus re-mark that characters in the *Wake* are not so much characters but *characteristics* that shift between icons and names. These sigla are perverted forms of the alphabet which can be transformed into different sigla: "the meant to be baffling chrismon trilithon sign ⊓ finally called after some his hes hecitency Hec, *which moved contrawatchwise*, represents his title in sigla as the smaller Δ, *fontly called following a certain change of state of grace of nature* alp or delta" (FW: 119.17–21, emphasis added; cf. Jean-Michel Rabaté, "'Alphybettyformed verbage': the shape of sounds and letters in *Finnegans Wake*," *Word and Image* 2.3 [July–September 1986]: 237–43. 239–40; and *Joyce upon the Void*, New York: St. Martin's, 1991. 81–89). With a slight variation, ⊓ will be returned as Δ; a change of grace invoked by geometric transformation with some *hecitency*: (a misspelt word that betrays the forged letter Pigott wrote to incriminate Parnell). Now it would seem that ⊓ is *incarnated* in "his hes hecitency Hec," that he is implicated falsely within and *as* a typographical error. The sigla—these "variously inflected, differently pronounced, otherwise spelled, changeable meaning vocable scriptsigns" (FW: 118.19–21)—thus play out this accumulation of *hecitent* identifications as recombinable shapes and reconfigurable characteristics.

[63] Recently Hayman has revised his theory of nodality and has made a similar point: "we have something approximating and reflecting the conventions of the novel but in neither case does the novelistic element contribute to a recuperable development. If III.4 presents itself at times as oral narrative, it is a narrative of action in the present tense, a recounting of what we are now viewing. Yet it is also and clearly, especially in the description of the characters and in the legal texts, but also in its baroque arrangement, emphatically a *written document*. This was so even before the night language was laid on during the revision process. The result is not

really novelistic even though we are treated to a multifaceted view of the situation of what we take to be the dreamer and the locale, even though we experience a barrage of attitudes relevant to that situation, and though we may have a sense that there may be real people lurking behind the screen of language. Rather it is a simulacrum of novelese, a novelese that is deliberately undercut and even erased" (David Hayman, "The Manystorytold of the *Wake*: How Narrative Was Made to Inform the Non-Narrativity of the Night," *Joyce Studies Annual* 8 [1997]: 81–114. 101).

[64] There would be no more well-known example than Victor Shklovsky's assertion that Sterne's *Tristram Shandy* is "the most typical novel in world literature" (Victor Shklovsky, "Sterne's *Tristram Shandy*: Stylistic Commentary," *Russian Formalist Criticism: Four Essays*, eds. & trans. Lee T. Lemon and Marion J. Reis, Lincoln: U of Nebraska P, 1965. 25–57. 57).

SOME INCONCLUSIVE UNSCIENTIFIC COMMENTS WITH CONSTANT REFERENCE TO "FINNEGANS WAKE"

Ill has been said of *Finnegans Wake*, but nonce more odd than what the text can say about itself. To read *Finnegans Wake* is an acutely unusual if not unsettling experience since the reader surrenders to the mendacious cadences of multilinguistically polyvalent word-plays: echoes that ricochet over and across what seems to be the entire interval or circumference of all locutably possible human experience. In the previous chapter we outlined some past critical attempts to overrule the chaotic and discomfiting verbal microstructure in favor of a comprehensible and readable macrostructure (typically, although not universally, a narrative structure). Such readings of the *Wake* share in the attempt of "letting punplays pass to ernest" (FW: 233.19–20), since these allusive and elusive punplays prove deleterious to ready comprehension.[1] The problem is not that *Finnegans Wake* makes no sense, rather it makes *too much sense,* so much sense that sense becomes dysfunctional. Without being grasped or delimited, the *Wake* perdures. *Finnegans Wake concentrates* its *dis-sense* into words, words that flow, words that flow away from a simple telling since "every telling has a taling and that's the he and the she of it" (213.12). The *Wake*'s lexical logic is a concentrated effluence that slips through exegetical fingers.

The most obvious agent or vehicle of this concentrated and excessive *dis-sense* is the arrant *Wakean* punning and general word-play which tweaks the algebra of reference into a kaleidoscope of differential effects. Bernard Benstock notes three levels to *Wakean* puns: "as serious linguistic manipulators they allow the author to include various concepts, overlapping themes, and levels of meaning in compressed form; as humorous concoctions they grate against our dulled senses—they are the stumbling blocks that make us conscious of every step we take through the *Wake*; as poetic devices they are controlled by a rhythmic logic that creates individual sound patterns at once familiar in rhythm and new in sound."[2] These three levels are interrelated, and indeed the humor that *Wakean* punning affords is the balm to our Gilead of reading.[3]

Derek Attridge expands on Benstock's work by locating the engine for the complexity of *Wakean* perplexities in the portmanteau-word which radicalizes the pun's tendency towards ambiguity and polysemy by "[denying] that single words must have, on any given occasion, single meanings; and like the various devices of assonance and rhyme, it denies that the manifold patterns of similarity that occur at the level of the signifier are innocent of meaning."[4] The portmanteau condenses a plethora of linguistic contiguities, contiguities that remain implausible, to say the least, within a phenomenal register. The portmanteaux capitalize upon a latent tendency within *verbe* to deviate sense and appurtenance away from *res,* as Mallarmé had noted: "la Parole, en créant les analogies des choses par des analogies des sons" (OC: 854). The *Wake*'s portmanteaux have "anastomosically assimilated" (FW: 615.05) a broad range of experience into the text by morphological adjustments and additions (metaplasm) to the work's words. The metaplasmic variations of the portmanteaux articulate paradigmatic confluence.[5] The portmanteau—we use the term liberally as a generic name for the various tricks and turns of *Wakean* word-play—packs together multiple meanings and its semantic effusion is consequent from a lexical packing or fusion; "how minney combinaisies and permutandies can be played on the international surd!" (284.12–14). Lexically, *Finnegans Wake* glosses a universe of minutiæ, and the text itself proceeds through concatenated deployments of these multivalent glossings. The text is itself an expansion of the possibilities of the portmanteaux and puns—an "expansion totale de la lettre" (OC: 380)—but it is this *expansion* which entails some difficulty. Overcathected, *Finnegans Wake* parodies textuality by bearing the trait of a text whilst remaining lost amidst and within the dis-sense sustained within its own referential accretions.

Most critics merely read *Wakean* portmanteaux as additional reservoirs of sense grafted into the warp of the text by its peculiar idiom.

These explications of *Wakean* passages proceed through the explicatory force provided by astute (or not-so-astute) recuperations of alluded meanings culled from "the Nichtian glossary which purveys aprioric roots for aposteriorious tongues" (FW: 083.10–11).[6] These readings of *Finnegans Wake* thus *gather together* the disparate suggestions of the *Wake*'s "Wholesale Safety Pun Factory" (Harriet Shaw Weaver, quoted in Ellmann, 590). Such an approach obviates the peculiar momentum of the *Wakean* word, a momentum that bears an "exprogressive process" (FW: 614.31). The assumption behind such an approach is that once the words' encoded referential appurtenances can be decoded, there would be a normal and normalizing sense and structure (whether narratological, psychoanalytical, etymological or linguistic). In this way exegesis runs the risk of becoming what Stephen (in *Stephen Hero*) calls vivisection: "The modern process is vivisective. Vivisection itself is the most modern process one can conceive. ... It examines the entire community in action and reconstructs the spectacle of redemption" (SH: 186). Instead of tending towards the greater glory of some definitive autotelic point (*ad majorem Dei gloriam*), the *Wake* progresses "for the greeter glossary of code" (FW: 324.21). The paradigmatic confluences also include syntagmatic dissipation, from progression there are complex patterns of diffusion. The *Wake* is the interval within which semantic diffusion and effusion flows.

Recently Thomas Rice has proposed a new paradigm for reading *Finnegans Wake* based on the emerging interdisciplinary study of complexity which "maintain[s] that a vast majority of natural and social phenomena exist in a border land between simple order and pure randomness."[7] Judiciously employing the jargon of this inchoate field, Rice characterizes the *Wake* as an information-rich network of mutually interfering forces. The *Wake*, according to this paradigm, consists of a large number of discrete units which interrelate on both synchronic and diachronic axes, and the complexity of these interrelations that constitute this network fundamentally destabilizes a structural order (Rice, 90–94). However, Rice ignores the antagonistic inter-differentiation that characterizes the *Wake*'s web of synchronic inter-relation. Indeed, if one ignores the differentiations between elements on the vertical level then the synchronic web becomes little more than a motival nexus such as Hart had proposed (see the previous chapter), with synchrony performing an enrichment of sense.

To defend and illustrate the *Wake*'s syntagmatic differential dis-sense, we will first turn to a negative example, a passage presumed to have been written by Joyce as a mock diatribe against the Work in Progress:

> Dear Mister Germ's Choice,
> in gutter dispear I am taking my pen toilet you know that, being Leyde up in bad with the prewailent distemper (I opened the window and in flew Enza), I have been reeding one half ter one other numboars of "transition" in witch are printed the severeall instorements of your "Work in Progress."[8]

Here a clear statement of displeasure at Joyce's language is distended in a parody of that very language. Most individual words are distorted slightly providing a punning commentary of the *déplaisir du texte*. Dixon's lexical distortions, amusing as they are, are thus linked to this *theme* of parodic commentary, the puns can all be easily wiped away with glosses. This letter thus voices dissent but not quite dis-sense. There is a key difference with *Wakean* procedure at this level: in the *Wake* lexical distortions work together, not necessarily in order to provide a continuous or even coherent argument, but, at the very least, in a manner that reverberates within the constellation of the text as a whole. In the *Wake,* the semantic distortions provided through the portmanteaux *appear* to coalesce into broader patterns of reference and cross-reference. In this way the portmanteaux begin to effect a broader syntactic level of the work rather than just the semantic connotations of the individual words. In Dixon's letter there are neither reverberations nor rapports *between* the lexical distortions (other than save perhaps the fæcal confluence between gutter and toilet).

A simple but limited example of such a reverberation, chosen not entirely at random, is "the panaroma of all flores of speech" at I.6.9 (FW: 143.03–4). The two words—"panaroma" and "flores"—are not exactly English words although they do suggest various possible glossings. The catachrestic portmanteau "panaroma" implies a vista not of space but rather of smell, and this olfactory landscape could perhaps contain the "flores of speech." A phonetic reading favors *flowers* for the nonce word "flores," and indeed a panaroma of flowers is a lovely, if overly-quaint suggestion. At a first level, the paronomasia effected by the orthographically forced confluence of panorama and aroma is buttressed by the word flore which evokes a word that suggests an order of odor. However the matter does not end there since "flores of speech" continues to yield *flowers of speech* (rhetoric) as well as, possibly, floors (or levels) of speech.[9] One possible suggestion of these lexical alterations is that rhetoric becomes a plurality of modalities of speech. Furthermore, these modalities of speech—if one's pronunciation is imperfect—are also *flaws* of speech. Through a flaw of speech (or a flaw in speaking), suggested patterns of association flow between the words in this simple phrase, patterns which expand, digress and disperse as the contexts broaden. The portmanteaux in contexts both limited and grand thus work with and against each other to suggest alternate possibilities of meaning. Therefore these alternate possibilities extend the dis-sense of the portmanteaux onto a network of contested differences of suggestion. The sentence "the panaroma of all flores of speech" is a condensed syllepsis of all the dis-sensible suggestions evoked therein.

The cathexis of diverse concatenations evinced in the "panaroma of all flores of speech" elicit patterns of incompatible meanings, or—as is the answer to the question in which the panaroma is to be found—a "collideorscape" (143.28): a word which itself subsumes the word kaleidoscope (a not inappropriate initial description of the portmanteau effect) and the phrase "collide or (e)scape."[10] Within the collideorscape of the *Wake*'s "once current puns" (183.23), possible meanings both coalesce and dissipate. The fact that the sentence phrases multiple levels of meaning that contradict but cannot completely obviate or deny each other—the simple fact that words mean multiply *à la fois*—implies that the *levels of articulation* between these words is likewise distended and malleable. Harry Levin remarked upon this syntactic disturbance in the wake of lexical freeplay: "As with music, as with any composition in time, the structure seems to dissolve into the structure when we examine it closely. At close range, *Finnegans Wake* seems to realize the aspiration of the other arts toward the condition of music."[11] As with Mallarmé, the *tendency* toward music is effected through the lexemes' residual semanticity. The *Wake* has meaning in overplus to squander in its "scribicide" (FW: 014.21).

The effect of the *Wakean* portmanteau word is not located just within the individual lexeme—in the archive of meanings that could be subscribed to the lexeme—but rather also within the interplay of *Wakean* words, "par le heurt de leur inégalité mobilisés" (OC: 366). As Mallarmé noted in *Les mots anglais*: "Qu'y a-t-il? des *mots*, tout d'abord: reconnaissables eux-mêmes aux *lettres* qui les composent, ils s'enchaînent et voici des *phrases*. Un courant d'intelligence, comme un souffle, l'esprit, met en mouvement ces mots, pour qu'à plusieurs d'entre eux ils expriment un sens avec des nuances" (903). The words are ceded to the phrase, thereby nuancing sense through their mutual arrangements and dispositions. In contradistinction to Mallarméan attenuation, *Wakean* nuance explodes from an extreme "lowquacity" (FW: 424.34). Distorted words distort meaning by virtue of their irregular progress, their inability to be reconciled to and subsumed under a single command for procession, a single *syntax*.

The *Wake*'s polyvalent words thus elicit an ambivalence of syntax. *The* word collideorscape neatly remarks the resonances of the *dis-sense* of *Wakean* punning. "The portmanteau has the effect of a *failed* pun—the patterns of language have been shown to be partially appropriate, but with a residue of difference where the pun found only happy similarity" (Attridge, 148). This cathexis of contiguity and difference that sustains and characterizes the portmanteau is also a feature of the larger elements that constitute the *Wake*. Any systemic cohesion must comprise the centrifugal forces of the portmanteaux, as well as itself be characterized by its own *dif-ferences*. Any *Wakean* passage is susceptible to multiple and incommensurable contextualizations and readings. Each reading is a fractal or partial metonym of some imagined yet non-present asymptotic whole. *Finnegans Wake* speaks many incommensurable languages. The proliferation of patterns that can be adduced—the puns that can be parsed, the estranged words that can be translated, the syntax that can be construed, and (even) the characters that can be named—make it seem *as if* there could be an overall subsumptive structure, a figure in the carpet. But the rampant proliferation of these clues also interferes with the possibility of a tidy synthesis without remainder, the carpet remains too messy and littered. This ineluctable detritus of reading *Finnegans Wake* points somewhere other than meaning. "Thus the unfacts, did we possess them, are too imprecisely few to warrant our certitude" (FW: 057.16–17). As with the Mallarméan dream of suggestion, in the evocation of collideorscapes, what is ultimately also evoked, what is evoked *en plus,* is the *rien* behind (the word) *res.* A portmanteau is thus only possible because of what Mallarmé termed language's incapacity to be a model language (see our argument in chapter 3).[12]

Through the referential operation of a nonce word, various constellations of meaning are suggested and are proliferated *across the interval* of the work. "La valeur réside précisément dans l'hétérogénéité, dans la distance même entre les divers éléments que l'écriture va parcourir en un jeu incessant de relations et de correspondances, par lequel chaque élément devient la fiction d'un autre."[13] The supplementary meanings themselves *re-mark* the poverty or blankness of an autotelic signification. As an example of this, we take an apparently simple line from the end of the Anna Livia Plurabelle chapter: "O, my back, my back, my bach!" (FW: 213.17). A simple complaint about back-pains is transformed through a contiguity made available only through the graphic and phonetic similarities between the word "back" and the noun "Bach" (*rivulet* [German]). On the one hand, the Germanic overtone to the word "bach" flows easily into the tone of the chapter (laden as it is with river names and lore), thereby enriching a fluvial context. On this level the portmanteau supports and enriches its synchronic context. On the other hand, the "bach" disvelops to also include divergent and disharmonizing claims as, say for example, "the history of Bach has become the history of music itself."[14] Rather than mutually augment and amplify each other into complementary tributaries, these various senses fail to completely submerge into one stream of harmonious meaning.

Sense and sensibility become dysfunctional through the semantic overloading effected by the homophonous pun.

The phrase then exhibits a series of differences: first and most obviously the morphological difference between the words "bach" and "back," which in turn re-marks a linguistic differentiation between English and German. The admission of the German "bach" introduces further senses which both enhance and destabilize the nexus of vertical association. Between these two words and these two languages, points of sense accumulate which generate themselves out of a differentiation that is lexically re-marked.[15]

As with *Ulysses*, verticality opens out onto an intratextual level as the above lament refers to the following two lines: "O moy Bog, he contrited with melancholy" (FW: 416.19–20) and "O my big, O my bog, O my bigbagbone!" (567.06). The recurrent elements could be gathered through Hart's motival analysis, which is essentially a dynamic of restatement in which an underlying coherence can be adduced through a correspondence of contexts designated by the repeated element.[16] In this way repetition yields to an underlying structure of rapport. However the variations upon the repeated "motival" lexemes also implies a dynamic of recontextualization in progress through the correspondence of the repeated *yet differentiated* elements. Such recontextualization tends to undermine the efficacy of a uniting structure to the work that is in progress. The synchronic associations enacted by repetition of certain elements differentiate the paradigmatic associations iterated at the diachronic level of the individual syntagm. Repetition introduces difference, thereby deferring sense to dissonance. "The seim anew" (FW: 215.23), again and again, "being humus the same roturns" (018.05), "moves in vicious circles [Vichian cycles] yet remews the same" (134.16–17), "The same renew" (226.17), "And Sein annews" (277.17), "This aim to you!" (510.02), "To flame in you" (614.09), "The sehm asnuh" (620.15), and "The way I too" (620.27–28).[17] Reconstitution remains mutable. The same does anew, but always through differentiation and circuitous detour.

Wakean dis-sense thus operates through a perpetual compacting of *dissonance*: dissonant meanings which propagate through a vast network of lexical gatherings of reference, cross-reference and counter-reference. Within the interval of a word resides the possibilities of many other words, possibilities which tear the *Wake* away into a wake of echoes: "Le temps de *Finnegans Wake* sera donc très précisément le 'pressant' (FW: 221.17), non pas un simple présent mais un présent qui se presse, toujours déjà creusé par la marque de ce qui n'est pas lui, le temps de l'espacement des traces dans le mouvement infini des uns aux autres."[18] The 628 pages of *Finnegans Wake* form a finite yet unbounded differential network (such a generalized definition is also appropriate to contemporary cosmological models of the Universe,[19] but beyond such a coincidence the *deuil* lies in the details). Amidst the proliferation of "litterish fragments" (066.15), what then remains to be read in this interval of intransitive appurtenance?

> (Stoop) if you are abcedminded, to this claybook, what curios of signs (please stoop), in this allaphbed! Can you rede (since We and Thou had it out already) its world? It is the same told of all. Many. Miscegenations on miscegenations. (FW: 018.17–20)

These words here—in the middle of the way of the first chapter—issue an injunction to stop, to please stoop. If one is "abcedminded" then this allaphbed would seem to consist of seemingly random curios of signs, for indeed the words here seem to be composed *otherwise* since the letters are built into *different* words. The conflation of absentmindedness and alphabet entails a collideorscape of signs within the claybook which consists of miscegenations upon miscegenations. The injunction "Can you rede" is itself such a miscegenation since it suggests both *reading* and the German *Rede, speech:* can this be read *as* spoken, can there be an unequivocal meaning registered in both the grapheme and the phoneme (especially when both are disymmetrically errant): *Finnegans Wake* claims that it cannot be read, that no single reader has the requisite competency to read the book. Every reader is, to some extent, abcedminded. So the *Wake* is to be read *otherwise* than towards complete comprehension—even if all possible glosses could be known, *pronounced* and codified, there is still something else to be read. In addition to our knowledge, we bring our ignorance to read *Finnegans Wake*. The allaphbed, the "locative enigma" (135.26) of words remains apart from an economy of reading. This is not to say that the overloaded references are not important—since they clearly are—but rather they are important in that they function, in part, as an accumulation of indices of the reader's ignorance, and by extension of language and memory's ignorance. Absentmindedness and ignorance is so profound as not to be isolable in any specific reader but rather in a communal ignorance or discontinuity. Through such a scrim of dis-sense there is only a belated legibility. The accumulation of diverse references deviates the *Wake* from a single, simple and comprehensive reference.

Wakean wordplay opens out onto, not merely a scene of additional meaning, but rather a differential network of meaning through which legibility is deferred within the interval of disseminative word-plays. This intervallic "pressent" (221.17) is what Derrida calls, in his reading of Sollers's novels *Drame* and *Nombres,* the *plus-que-présent:*

> Ce présent total et différencié, équivoque, qu'il faut donc se garder de rabattre sur le présent simple qu'il remet violemment en jeu; ce présent structuré et sans fond, en rapport avec le double fond qui comprend le présent et qui n'est pas lui, le *Drame* le nommait « plus-que-présent ». ... Cette réinscription *a lieu, il y a* sa violence. Ce « il y a » de l' « avoir lieu » n'est au présent que dans l' « illusion » de l'énoncé ou de l'énonciation. Contenu et acte de ce langage sont aussitôt ouverts l'outre-présent. Ce qui a lieu, ce qu'il y a, c'est l'écriture, c'est-à-dire une machination dont le présent n'est plus qu'une toupie.[20]

The time of the *Wake* is that of the interval, an interval of heterogeneity. "For here the holy language. Soons to come. To pausse" (FW: 256.14–5). *Wakean* language, much like poetry for Mallarmé, exists as inachievable remuneration for the absence of a pure, holy language: "Les langues imparfaites en cela que plusieurs, manque la suprême" (OC: 363). Until the day of a pentecostal language "we're presurely destined to be odd's without ends" (FW: 455.17–18) in this world of disseminated differentiations "through the germination of its gemination from Ond's outset till Odd's end" (505.12–13). The *Wake* is that which is circuitously and scriptively *between*, "But the world, mind, is, was and will be writing its own wrunes for ever" (019.35–36), an interval in which writing writes constellations of differentiations.

Beckett characterized *Finnegans Wake* as purgatorial: "In what sense, then, is Mr. Joyce's work purgatorial? In the absolute absence of the Absolute. Hell is the static lifelessness of unrelieved viciousness. Paradise the static lifelessness of unrelieved immaculation. Purgatory a flood of movement and vitality released by the conjunction of these two elements."[21] This is an interesting move since Purgatory is not a *synthesis* of Heaven and Hell, but rather it is that which lies *in-between*. Furthermore, Beckett notes that unlike Dante's conical Purgatory which "implies culmination. Mr. Joyce's is spherical and excludes culmination" (Beckett, 21). The *Wake* — then — between viciousness and vitality, an approach to an end that never comes. *Neither* Heaven *nor* Hell, *Wakean* appurtenance falls elsewhere, elsewhere within the play of differences between viciousness and vitality.

One description of this scriptive interval is the temporal specification of the question concerning the observation of the collideorscape in progress at I.6.9, "at this auctual futule preteriting unstant" (FW: 143.07–8). The "futule preteriting unstant" is initially qualified as being "auctual": not quite actual and not quite authorial but also (possibly) an auction, a bidding of wares. The futule preteriting unstant is not a moment, an actual time, but a *commodity*, an element within an economy. Within this phrase several meanings are suggested, though heaping up references would be futile since this very phrase speaks of futility, or rather of the futility which is confused by that word's orthographical miscegenation with the word "future." The future is corrupted in its pronunciation alongside the futile. The past that is joined to this unhappy future comes next, it is "preteriting." Preterite is at once a bygone time and a complicated tense, a grammatical fusion of disparate times: an action that *will have occurred*. It does not refer to its *present*. Additionally "preterition" carries the theological sense of one who has been passed over by God, one who is unworthy of salvation (a future redemption), it speaks of a redemption and a resolution that *will not have occurred*. The taut tensing of "futule preteriting unstant" deviates from and around a notion of the present. The word preteriting differentiates itself from a designation of presence by its various (and differing) connotations.

This differentially *ec-static* designation is further qualified as an "unstant." The word unstant is marked by a confusion of the "un" into the "instant," into a moment that quite simply is *not*. The *perfect* future and past are available in these three words as a present that is not present: a being that remains passed over by preteriting writing. The *Wake*'s writing is quite imperfective. The present is not in the future, awaiting its coming to presence since it has already been declared preterite. The moment which is constituted as an unstant *is* itself a moment of the withdrawal of the present—a moment of *exappropriation* or *exscription*. The present is only statable as being *something else, somewhere else*: a *plus-que-présent*. Not unlike *Igitur*'s midnight, the unstant has no existence, it is a time that denies itself in and by its instantaneity, or unstantaneity. Amidst destabilizing and differentiating rapports, "un présent n'existe pas" (OC: 372) in an unstant.

We can now prematurely characterize the logic of *Wakean* punplays as a "parapolylogic" (FW: 474.05):[22] a multiplicity of senses threaded throughout words thereby stringing along a tissue of possible iterations which convolve only in the aspect that they remain heterogeneous and differentiated. Hayman names something similar with the term "*super*paratactic," which is a combination of horizontal and vertical parataxis: elements within coordination yield to many non-necessarily-compatible schemes of patterned subordination without ever being subsumed by one universal logic.[23] This profusion and effusion of complementary and contradictory contexts out of the *Wake*'s babelian dyslexia is what we call a parapolylogics. *Wakean* semantic overloading proffers an effect of dissonant and differential reverberations across a syntactic field. In this way, the density of portmanteaux or word-plays in *Finnegans Wake* has an effect not unlike that of the spacings of *Un coup de dés*; indeed Malcom Bowie's comment on the spacings of that poem (cited in chapter 4) are relevant to our present study. In *Finnegans Wake* the portmanteaux "exert upon each other an associative pull strong enough to cancel the intricate syntactic patterning which holds them apart; in so doing they become a mosaic of reciprocally explaining fragments, a counter-syntax, a refusal of hierarchy."[24] With word-play, the word matters less than the deluge of play in the multiplicity of available yet incommensurable syntactic organizations suggested by the portmanteaux. There are multiple patterns proffered by "[t]hese ruled barriers along which the traced words, run, march, halt, walk, stumble" (FW:114.07–8). If σύνταξις means disciplined arrangement of proper subordination, coordination and agreement for suitable progression then, as with Mallarmé, there are many syntaxes within the *Wake* which do not coordinate and intersubsume under a single ball and chain of command. Instead *Wakean* syntax is, if anything, a diffuse *para-taxis,* simultaneous lexical organizations strung alongside, which only occasionally yield partial and incomplete glimmers of *syntaxis* through differentials of exprogressive progressions. *Wakean* syntax is overridden and overwritten by plurabilities of syntaxes; σύν is deferred to and through παρά.

While the dissonant disturbance is effected lexically, its effects of dis-sense reverberate throughout the book on a non-semantic or syntactic level (or "*flore* of speech"). The *Wake*'s parapolylogic of interfering suggestions thus functions like the prismatic subdivisions of the word clusters in *Un coup de dés*. Instead of an absent punctuation which facilitates, if not encourages, multiple possible combinations of reading, the overflowing reservoirs of semantic meaning in *Finnegans Wake* carry along mobile hierarchies of mutually explicating fragments in a flow of counter-syntaxes. The semic content of any word or cluster of words in the *Wake* provides a generating and generative context which it simultaneously bolsters and subverts. Eventually such semic inversions interfere within the various patterns of the text that they partially imply. The word then, the word as semic reservoir, evaporates under the effervescence of accumulated dissonant meanings.

To illustrate such a notion we turn to the opening of III.1 which will show how even simple distortions reverberate against a possibility of unitary coherence:

Hark!
Tolv two elf kater ten (it can't be) sax.
Hork!
Pedwar pemp foify tray (it must be) twelve.
And low stole o'er the stillness the heartbeats of sleep. (FW: 403.01–5)

The argument of this passage—in general like that of *Igitur*—concerns the certainty of the midnight hour.[25] Numbers are sounded in various languages in order to finally assert that "(it must be) twelve." The second line cites numbers from several languages in a mostly undistorted form: "Tolv [(Danish) *12*] two [*2*] elf [(German and Dutch) *11*] kater [*ceathair* (Irish) *4*] ten [*10*] (it can't be) sax [(Icelandic, Norwegian and Scotch) *6*]." Because they are undistorted (with the exception of "kater"[26]), these words tend towards designating only their linguistically appropriate number. And yet two of these words—elf and sax—name the same numbers in multiple tongues.[27] The simple formula of sounding a sequence of numbers in different languages becomes complicated once one starts to differentiate, say, the Dutch *elf* from the German *elf* and the Icelandic *sax* from the Norwegian *sax*. The numerations could be a simple guessing game, but even within a seemingly aleatory sequence, patterns can be found. Indeed, despite the parenthetical protestation that it can't be six, there could easily exist a mathematical relation between these numbers that would arrive at the disputed answer of six.[28] But then there could be multiple relations between these numbers justifying the order, however the complexity of such a possible formula would perhaps explain why it can't be sax.[29]

The second sequence of numbers proves to be more complicated even though only two languages other than English—Welsh and Italian—are used: "Pedwar [(Welsh) *4*] pemp [*pump* (Welsh) *5*] foify tray [*tre* (Italian) *3*]." The problem here is the word foify, which could be some diminutized variant of five, or it could be fifty, and if it is read as being such then it could either stand alone or in conjunction with tre thereby yielding fifty-three. The exact number of numbers in this line therefore remains indeterminate.[30] And if the word/number foify is omitted, then the sequence reads 4, 5, 3 which neatly adds up to 12, thereby generating a simple logical progression justifying the parenthetical claim that "(it must be) twelve." The word foify would then just be a bit of stray noise added into the calculation (as indeed the homophonic mutation of the Italian *tre* into an English *tray* provides another example of the noise made available through the interference of lexical permutation). But the presence of this noise shows something interesting about both numbers and languages. Numbers are themselves composed of other numbers in highly variable schemes. As was evinced through the zeugmatic spacings of *Un coup de dés*, there can be no "unique Nombre qui ne peut pas | être un autre" (UC: 5a–b; OC: 462–63). Like the "twelfth page" of *Un coup de dés*, the solution (12) remains *within* the phrasing of the paradigm that purportedly will have achieved it. Furthermore, the answer 12 is equal to (or, more precisely, approximately equal to) the first number in the first sequence: Tolv. Numbers are seemingly infinitely reconfigurable (one can easily arrive at the number 12 from any number of routes, arithmetical, symbolical *&c., &c.*).[31] This reconfigurability is precisely the problem that issues from foify tray since this collocation within a list of numbers provides a dual numerical rebus of 3 and 53. This possibility of reconfiguration is figured additionally in this passage through the use of diverse languages since the numbers are themselves named through a skein of diverse linguistic ciphers.

Numbers are perpetually re-deconstructive, in their recombinations they defy a single and definitive construction, that is unless one resorts to an æsthetics of "elegance" (mathematical or otherwise). In this way numbers are conjugated in a *plus-que-présent,* a present constituted by perpetual and equivocal differentiation (cf. Derrida 1972, 329–33). This realignment into perpetual differentiation evinced in numeric ciphers is also precisely the possibility that is opened up by the metaplasmic initiative of the portmanteau. The cipher twelve, by virtue of the associative pull and ference of other ciphers, could always be another number.

These sententious declarations of the "[t]eems of times" (FW: 215.22–23) at the midnight hour will not parse until difference—a recognition of linguistic differentiation, a recognition of different permutations of linguistic difference—is allowed. The possibility of e'er misreading is written into the reading of *Finnegans Wake*.³² No pattern is definitive (no pattern can account for all the parapolylogical cadences of dis-sense), yet all that can be read are these partial and incomplete series that take the place of answers, as "the infinisissimalls of her facets becomes manier and manier" (298.31–32).

The linguistic and numerological cipherings in this passage thus evince "the beerlitz in his mathness" (182.07). The inevitable conclusion of 12, the certain subsistence of the presence of the midnight hour, is achieved only through a variable and perhaps inexact admixture of cipherings. The necessity of it being 12 is just as uncertain as the fact that it could not be 6, since deriving 12 from 4, 5 and 3 (or whatever) is just as uncertain and unlikely an answer as 6 from 12, 2, 11, 4 and 10. The present of midnight is a multiple unstant, a *plus-que-présent* made possible through a linguistic and numeric multiplicity. Amidst so much commotion and noise of reference, the words quiver silently away. This entire passage, a passage which aims towards declaring and identifying the present, speaks through differences both arithmetic and linguistic, but the reckoning deployed by the "Twelve o'clock scholars" (427.34) remains highly variable.³³ Through permutabilities enacted by differentiation, the certain hour does not strike, the initiative follows patterns of lexical distention, patterns of possible sense derive from the patterns of the words. Sense derives from the configurations of the word, and follows from the words' protean changes: "meet their night, mid their nackt, me there naket, made their nought the hour strikes" (067.04–5).

The convoluted complex of parallel suggestions proffered by *Wakean* portmanteaux (such as foify tray) are not merely adjuncts to meaning, but disrupters of meaning in that they proffer synchronously contesting differentials of reading. The παρά of *Wakean* suggestion lies in this synchronic or tangential constellation of allusive and elusive evocation. This is not allegory, but it is *close* to allegory: the logic of the surface has multiple obliquely intercalated levels *because of the initiative that has been ceded to words*. The initiative of this allegoresis is neither the poet's nor God's, instead it derives almost entirely from the parapolylogic mobilization of nuanced words. Unlike allegoresis, meaning is not displaced, instead it is reference that is perpetually displaced by differentiations, and the errancy of suggestion is not subordinated to some controlling yet absent idea or theme. In and of themselves *Wakean* portmanteaux are merely polysemous, they register confluences of other meanings from other languages. Derrida has argued that polysemy alone does not register difference since the plurality of gathered meanings remain circumscribed under and by the horizon of some hypothesized final (pentecostal) meaning which comes to be present "dans la richesse rassemblée de ses déterminations. ... Tous les moments de la polysémie sont, come le nom l'indique, des moments du sens" (Derrida 1972, 389). But the concentration of parallel meanings *interact* in a seemingly infinite potential of recombination. The senses invested into words through centuries of discourse are reconfigured in such a way as to perpetually generate new proliferating senses which differ with each other in ways that cannot always be resolved and dialectically subsumed. This regenerative and irreducible multiplicity is what Derrida calls dissemination:

> La dissémination ouvre, sans fin, cet *accroc* de l'écriture qui ne se laisse plus recoudre, le lieu où ni le sens, fût-il pluriel, ni *aucune forme de présence* n'agraphe plus la trace. La dissémmination traite—sur lit—le *point* où le mouvement de la signification viendrait régulièrement *lier* le jeu de la trace en produisant ainsi l'histoire. Saute la sécurité de ce point arrêté au nom de la loi. C'est—du moins—au risque de ce faire sauter que s'entamait la dissémination. Et le détour d'une écriture dont on ne revient pas. (Derrida 1972, 33)

Dissemination is a non-finite semantic dispersal unsubscribed by a singular and definitive logic. As with *Un coup de dés*, each possible coordinate sense is open to multiple directions of reading, the syntax of parapolylogic dis-senses relegates a single and definite meaning into belated subjunctivity. Disseminative multiplicity is thus written into the *Wake* through words of multivalent porousness. Multiple threads are strung together in *"words of silent power"* (FW: 345.29), which in turn generates a further porousness of sense. Difference comes in through the perpetual interferences of multiple senses thereby rendering sense dysfunctional. In this way the lexical manipulations and their concomitant dis-sense generate a palimpsest of readings that perpetually displace each other. By imposing synchronic equations (such as, say, between a rivulet, a back and a composer), reference comes to be ambivalent and equivocal.

> Tour de Babel en laquel les langues et écritures multiples se heurtent ou passent les unes dans les autres, se transforment et s'engendrent depuis leur altérité la plus irréconciliable, la plus affirmée aussi car la pluralité ici n'a pas de fond et n'est pas vécue comme négativité, dans la nostalgie de l'unité perdue. (Derrida 1972, 379)

The most formidable difficulty of *Wakean* languages stems from their possibilities of syntactic articulation. These are problems identified by Jacques Aubert in his reading of the alternation between readability and unreadability of first word of *Finnegans Wake*, "riverrun" (FW: 003.01). Aubert argues that the articulation of "riverrun" depends not upon any meaning of the word itself, but rather upon economies of differentiation registered in both the word and its context. Alone the word suggests several incongruous possibilities in that it remains undifferentiated; it lacks an article. And yet, parapolylogically, it has an excess of possible signification because it belongs to multiple grammatical genres: noun and verb combined (*river run* with an elided pause); solitary substantive (with an elided article *[the] riverrun*); literary allusion;[34] &c., &c. In reading the sentence which this word inaugurates, riverrun appears *in the place of a subject* (Aubert, 120–21).

> riverrun, past Eve and Adam's, from swerve of shore to bend of bay, brings us by a commodius vicus of recirculation back to Howth Castle and Environs. (FW: 003.01–3)

A noun is actualized through its articulation, through "*l'actualization de l'article*" (Aubert, 123). The decorum of English syntax imbues the odd word "riverrun" with the force of a noun (this is done specifically through the genitive clause and the verbal unit since they both require a nominal). Aubert does not radicalize his argument concerning the "véritable *généalogie du nom*" (123) by admitting that the diverse effects of riverrun are themselves pronominative: these differentiating divagations between presence and absence take the place of a name. In other words the *Wake* is perhaps not unlike the letter in that it is a "prepronominal *funeral*" (FW: 120.09–10). The disarticulation performed by the word itself falls within a disarticulation of syntactic placement. A definite article can be available by the last sentence on the last page of the book: "A way a lone a last a loved a long the" (628.15–16). This last sentence is presumably hinged to the first sentence: the break—the unenjoined article—is supposedly to be read as a jointure. But this article does not definitely articulate the word riverrun since the separation between the last and first pages might not be articulable as a fracture. However, Aubert does claim a continuity predicated upon a circular discontinuity:

> Finalement, le point capital est celui-ci: *le jeu n'était pas à sa place*, c'est à dire entre *river* et *run*, il était au début, avant *river*. Au commencement jouait le jeu, c'est là l'insolence suprême. Et c'est dans ce jeu comme acte initial que résident les puissances de l'articulation et de la nomination: c'est dans l'écart entre les deux pôles inaugurés *the* et *riverrun* qu'elles jaillissent. (Aubert, 124)

Aubert thus demonstrates how a grammatical indetermination (of the silent pause between the first and last words) surrenders to determination, yet this effluvia of excessively different senses remains within the word. The predicate of indeterminacy yields to syntactic nominalization and normalization, and yet the effective syncategoremata of the *Wake* themselves participate within the levels of parapolylogic differentiation and dis-sense that are normally ascribed to the portmanteaux.[35] The interplay between portmanteaux and syntax creates what Fritz Senn, in a rare affinity to Derrida, calls "deferred semantification":[36] meanings are broken down through the very differential networks which should adjudicate, arbitrate and articulate them. Amidst and within the noise of a hyperagglutination of meanings—"Loud, graciously hear us!" (FW: 258.26)—meaning is completely surrendered to a silence whence it might (never) have come: the "drama parapolylogic *had yet to be*, affact" (474.05; emphasis added). Univocal meaning thus surrenders to a "labile iction" (602.29). This parapolylogical interplay in the *Wake* is precisely the *Wakean* game between legibility and illegibility, a game that is conjugated in the subjunctive as it had *yet to be* in the *plus-que-présent* of its unstantaneous iteration in progress.

The parapolylogic effect of deferred semantification provides the staggered momentum of the exprogressive process of *Wakean* lisibility. Semantification is deferred as the text spawns further bases of contextualization which in turn suffer from an aporetic procession of contexts: "It goes. It does not go" (FW: 245.17). The result of this parapolylogic of dis-sense is a self *re-de-generating* context: contextualizing schemes are amplified by their constitutive parapolylogic patterning (*bach* and the fluvial quality of I.8) *which also* provides for different patternings (Bach, the harmonious squire) which in turn destabilize the harmony, primacy and reverie of any solitary pattern. The effect of parapolylogic is this redegeneration, this "contonuation through regeneration of the urutteration of the word in progress" (284.20–22).

In this way, *Wakean* writing is not unlike the floral suggestiveness of Mallarmé: "Je dis: une fleur! et, hors de l'oubli où ma voix relègue aucun contour, en tant que quelque chose d'autre que les calices sus, musicalement se lèvre, idée même et suave, l'absente de tous bouquets" (OC: 368; as adumbrated in chapter 3): a new word, "étranger à la langue" (368)—whilst reminiscent of some thing and some other words—remains different and apart. While remaining within the manifold networks of reference that are available over and across the archives of more-than-several languages, each portmanteau *re-marks* itself as a differential of perpetual re-ference. The portmanteau is auto-differentiating and this re-marking portmanteau, like the Mallarméan declaration of a flower, stands as an absence of all bouquets (all *logical* unities), sniffed within the panaroma of all *flores* of speech. The possibility of this disparition within accumulation derives from a lexical *ingegno*: reducing language to the possibilities of the word, different words, worldless words, nothing but, but that is enough, more than enough.

∙∙∙

The game then is between the word and its context, a game of redegeneration between word and work. The word unworks the work one word at a time. To better delineate the tensions of this redegeneration, we will turn to chapter I.5 in order to precisely show how redegeneration operates on a broader flore of speech. In our previous section our argument followed a theoretical logic, a logic buttressed by gathering examples from the text, whereas in this section we will focus upon a lengthy example. As Laurent Milesi notes: "the letter complex [as seen in I.5] shows a readiness to explode into perpetual thematic interbranchings and to drag an overwhelming proportion of the *Wake*'s substance with it as soon as it comes under scrutiny."[37]

The chapter begins with an *invocatio:* "In the name of Annah the Allmaziful, the Everliving, the Bringer of Pluralities, haloed be her eve, her singtime sung, her rill be run, unhemmed as it is uneven!" (FW: 104.01–3). Initially this *invocatio* might seem like merely a punning parody of the Lord's prayer, a parody of the same order as Dixon's letter. However folded into the Christian context is the opening of the Suras of the Koran: "In the name of Allah, the Merciful, the Compassionate." The Islamic overtone ironically provides an orthodox Christian resolution to the Trinitarian controversy by resolving the Trinity (father, son and holy ghost) as a unity (Annah, the allmaziful, the compassionate). But the name of the Christian God does not just neatly transpose into Allah since the resolution is effected by producing yet another name, Annah, a name with its own overtones (such as Anna Livia Plurabelle).[38] The tenor of the *invocatio* has already brought pluralities, and this synchronic plurality of contexts informs the *propositio* of the chapter, if not the book as a whole, unhemmed as it is uneven. The two religious texts are disparately sewn into the texture. In the place of a singular ground for meaning (*à la* Allah) there are enmeshed fractally miscegenated subdivisions that rill be run.

The contextual *propositio* thus follows, the enumeration of "Her untitled mamafesta memorialising the Mosthighest [which] has gone by many names at disjointed times" (104.04–5). Lacking a title, the mamafesta nevertheless possesses a superabundance of names which are then catalogued, and, in a typically *Wakean* fashion, this list defies a breakdown into specific discrete units.[39] The name—in the name of Allah—is given many irreconcilable names. A disjointed plurality of names supplements the namelessness of the mamafesta; the time of its dissemination is disjointed within a parataxis of unstantaneous namelessness.[40] The list names numerous *Wakean* topoi, partially incorporating them into the wake of the mamafesta's onomastic odyssey. The remainder of the chapter is perhaps but one further element within this named dispersal, a further elaboration within which are further furtive elaborations.[41]

The body of the mamafesta is then described, initially through a parodic rendering of a pedagogical presentation of manuscript study. This mock-philological study concerns the possibility of the legibility of this curiously untitled document: "The proteiform graph is itself a polyhedron of scripture. There was a time when naif alphabetters would have written it down the tracing of a purely deliquescent recidivist, possibly ambidextrous, snubnosed probably and presenting a strangely profound raimbowl in his (or her) occiput" (107.08–12). Only a naïve alphabetter—one who is perhaps still abcedminded—would read this as a univocal document with a single author of an albeit hypothesized *genre*. Indeed the account—even in this relatively clear initial formulation—betrays some intimations of miscegenation and mixed genres; and such suggestions of "mixed sex cases" (048.02) are buttressed by the statement that "To the hardily curious entmophlilust then it has shown a very sexmosaic of nymphosis" (107.12–14). The writing is multiple, it is *given to multiplicity*. The document and its account are both conditioned by pluralities of discourse and transmission. This does not necessarily mean that the text and its paratextual[42] transmission and enframing are one and the same, but that at the very least, they cannot always be neatly differentiated.

The document is proteiform, and through such protean variations and modulations, it suggests a multiplicity of aspects (polyhedron). The document is a plural plurability. In this way it could accommodate the plurality of names that it has acquired in its *travails* in progress: each name would function as some non-subsuming metonym. In its initial description, there are modulations on two Latinate names of writing: *graphicus*, which suggests a pictorial quality, and *scriptus*, which denotes a religious aspect: the proteiform *graphicus* is itself also already a polyhedrous *scripticus*. To even begin to constitute the document is to surrender to the multiple modalities of inscription (miscegenations) within a hyperactive palimpsest, which of course *tend towards* to a universalization in that "It is told in sounds in utter that, in signs so adds to, in universal, in polyglutteral, in each auxiliary neutral idiom" (117.12–14). Even universality is but one of many non-finite and interfering modes of iteration that constitute the protean *precession* of the account of the mamafestive document. The conjunctive element of a hypotactic articulation (so as to) is rendered as a partially intransitive paratactic disjunction ("so *adds* to"), and so the accumulation or addition of modes disturbs the diachronic motivation of a single account. Rather than construe these distortions as metonymic examples of the machinations of the work's peculiar idiom (as parts of a work-in-progress which add up to an achieved work), they function as *holographic* subdivisions (if a hologram is cut into pieces, each piece conveys the entire image, rather than a part of it, but at a lower resolution), which, when pieced together, fail to add up neatly to a single picture. The *Wake* might then be seen as a mosaic of fragments from many different holograms. Reading the *Wake* would then be an exercise in tracing the fault-lines of the parapolylogic inter-ferences of the exprogressive accumulations of these fractal holograms.

There had been a time when the manuscript was attributed to a deliquescent recidivist by the naif alphabetters, but the syntax implicates the alphabetters—those who gamble with the alphabet—into the scribal transmission and perpetuation (or copying) of the letter. The naif alphabetters *would have* written it down the tracing of a purely deliquescent recidivist. Their attribution, their reading itself becomes a part of the manuscript. The "text" comes to be generated purely as a function of paratextual machinations since the manuscript absorbs its misreadings into its perpetuation. And in the alphabetters' gamings, they are contaminated and rendered deliquescent by the page. But then all of this is hypothetically enstated in this passage: "*would* have written it down." They *would* have transmitted the letter or *would* have interpreted it. Furthermore the clause specifying or enstating this tentativity (or withdrawal) is elided. The agency or event of the advent of withdrawal is *gone* within the exprogressive process of the document's transmission. Additionally there is no conjunctive element between "would have written it down" and "the tracing of a purely deliquescent recidivist." The syntax has broken down at this crucial passage between the act of writing and the appearance of inscription. The syntax breaks or fractures at the precise moment when writing becomes written. The various semantic overdeterminations here concerning the status of writing are compounded by syntactic elisions which prohibit a passage from the act of writing to inscription thereby separating the description from an economy of articulated and *achieved* writing. The de-scription of writing is thus worked through disjunctions. There is yet another disjoining naming at yet another disjointed time.

 The text, such as it *may have been*, is inseparable from its constitutions. In this sense, the discourse around the mamafesta recalls the Mediæval commentary tradition which "does not simply 'serve' its 'master' texts; it also rewrites and supplants them."[43] The *Wake* proffers its own glosses and comes to be inseparable from them as if it were a text composed solely of footnotes: glosses of a passage that remains separate and apart. In this way *Finnegans Wake* is not unlike the *Divina Commedia*, a recounting of a motion that remains distant *because of* its recounting. Amidst their proliferation, the glosses lose their transitivity. As in Nabokov's *Pale Fire*, "it is the commentator who has the last word";[44] but here the text-as-commentary will always provide more than a last word. Its text is already *paratextualizing*, parapolylogically prone to the paratexual. That into which everything in the world ends up is not just a book but a footnote, just a footnote.

 The transitively problematic account of the mamafesta then moves on to further various "interpretations," or accountings, many salacious, hoisted upon the fragile tissue of this document which also come to be woven into its texture. The discourse moves more explicitly towards a treatment of textual corruption at this point: "Closer inspection of the *bordereau* would reveal a multiplicity of personalities inflicted on the documents or document and some prevision of virtual crime or crimes might be made by anyone unwary enough before any suitable occasion for it or them had so far managed to happen along" (FW: 107.23–28). The text is already corrupt and indeterminate (document *or* documents) and such indeterminacy and confusion is also applied to the inspector(s) of the manuscript (it *or* them); here questions concerning textuality cannot be disentangled from corruption. There is thus a double path here: both reader and manuscript intertwine so as to constitute each other within a genealogy of error. The philological recovery of the text becomes the recovery of an error, which is itself an error added on to the list thereby ensuring its (erroneous) continuity. The vivisection of the document ensures its survival. The reader and the manuscript exist only to the extent that each is a function of the other within an act of redegeneration:

> In fact, under the closed eyes of the inspectors the traits featuring the *chiaroscuro* coalesce, their contrarieties eliminated, in one stable somebody similarly as by the providential warring of heartshaker with housebreaker and of dramdrinker against freethinker our social something bowls along bumpily, experiencing a jolting series of prearranged disappointments, down the long lane of (it's as semper as oxhousehumper!)[45] generations, more generations and still more generations. (107.28–35)

As soon as a pattern emerges, the traits disseminate. Redegeneration perdures repeatedly throughout various statements. There is no definitive statement, only a precession of cryptic statements of disparition. The telling of the fall and desistance recurs shamelessly, ever deferring a definitive instance of closure. And so a not impertinent question would be to attempt to posit an authorial definitude:

> Say, baroun lousadoor, who in hallhagal wrote the durn thing anyhow? Erect, beseated, mountback, against a partywall, below freezigrade, by the use of quill or style, with turbid or pellucid mind, accompanied or the reverse by mastication, interrupted by visit of seer to scribe or of scribe to site, atwixt

> two showers or atosst of a trike, rained upon or blown around, by a rightdown regular racer from the soil or by a too pained whittlewit laden with the loot of learning? (107.36–108.07)

Hayman has drawn a small constellation of parallels to *Un coup de dés* from this passage.[46] However the most telling Mallarméan moment here would perhaps be the iteration of the place that takes place. A tabular reading, or enstatement of parallels, might not be the best approach to reading Mallarmé within Joyce since Mallarméan *topoi* are so densely imbricated within this passage concerning the *authority* (and thus mastery) of the letter (and imbrication is itself a key operative procedure in both these works).

This passage begins as a questioning of the possibility of authorship: "who in hallhagal wrote the durn thing anyhow?" The text is thus concerned, in a sense, with *tracing out* its own autobiography, of delineating a portrait of the book as a young text. The putative author is assumed to be the master Hegel who is interrogated topographically (who *in* hallhagal), authority is delegated to a place: "We speak of Gun, the farther. And in the locative" (481.19). But this locution of a locative enigma of authoritative inscription is a *between-two:* "atwixt two showers or atosst of a trike." The place is a differential that lies between, the so-called place of authority is the interval of difference.

The document of the fall, that "durn thing" is thus erected through a *doubled* inscription: "Erect... by the use of quill or style." The only advent enstated is the event of the inscripting and the enunciation is not of an event, but of an undecided *interruption:* "interrupted by visit of seer to scribe *or* of scribe to site." This scriptive and/or locative interruption had already been announced in the disjunction of inscription re-marked by the syntactic omission when the "naif alphabetters would have written it down the tracing of a purely deliquescent recidivist." The enunciatory interruption *takes the place* of the advent of inscripting thereby ex-scribing the in-scripting in the interval of inscription. Therefore presence (or the project of representation) is interrupted by inscriptive lapses (such as, say, the misreadings hoisted upon the page by, among others, naif alphabetters). The place that takes the place of the document is thus conditioned by interruption. A *tracing* of the text's genesis (or even ontogenesis) is locatable only within the interval of its own enunciation, an interval that is itself conditioned and predicated by lapses of inscription and the misreadings thereof: both the paratextual misreadings of any individual reader of the *Wake* as well as the textualized misreadings of the mamafesta's philologists (textualized misreadings that are problematically dissociable from the text).[47] These two orders of misreading re-mark each other in the form of, to name one example, "that ideal reader suffering from an ideal insomnia" (120.13–14).

In place of an unequivocal authority there is the interval of the equivocating textual corruptions suffered by a "traumscrapt" (623.36), holographic corruptions that tend towards supplementing any possible statement of an Ur-text or "urutteration" (284.21). The presentation of the letter is subjunctive, and the recurrent conjugations of these deferred presentations *would be* the condition of *Finnegans Wake*: "would the letter you're wanting be coming may be" (623.29–30). As with *Un coup de dés*, only the interval in which something might (not) or will (not) have happened remains, and this remnant is continually susceptible to further redegenerations. "It may not or maybe a no concern of the Guinnesses but" (309.01). The matter is never quite definitively resolved:

> Naysayers we know. To conclude purely negatively from the positive absence of political odia and monetary requests that its page cannot ever have been a penproduct of a man or woman of that period or those parts is only one more unlookedfor conclusion leaped at, being tantamount to inferring from the nonpresence of inverted commas (sometimes called quotation marks) on any page that its author was always constitutionally incapable of misappropriating the spoken words of others. (108.29–36)

An original author has yet to have been posited as any thing more than purely hypothetical and yet the absence of citational apparatus lends to the apparent conclusion that the work is not constituted by plagiarism. However, the conclusions here tend to work at cross-purposes since this is just one more unlooked-for conclusion that has been leaped at. The evidence for the negative conclusion is a positive absence of fact, which is phrased as a negative presence: the nonpresence of inverted commas. The conclusion is not actually phrased that the author did not appropriate the work of others, but rather that he (or she) could not *misappropriate* the spoken words of others. To conclude from a positive absence, quotation marks would merely serve as an indication of appropriation and their absence indicates that misappropriation could have been dissimulated. And to further surmise from another positive absence, the written words of others are not excluded from this hypothesis. "Screamer caps and invented gommas, quoites puntlost, forced to farce!" (374.10–11). Not unlike Shem's fecund and feculant writing—"how very many piously forged palimpsests slipped in the first place by this morbid process from his pelagiarist pen" (182.02–3)—the manuscript is a function of multiple ingredients that have been penned through many hands.[48]

It is at this point that a new hypothesis is entertained: "Luckily there is another cant [*kant* (Dutch) *side*] to the questy. Has any fellow... given to ratiocination by syncopation in the elucidation of complications... ever looked sufficiently longly at a quite everydaylooking stamped addressed envelope?" (109.01–8). Looked at from a different angle, and in a style more prone to turgid periphrasis, the polyhedral manuscript appears as a letter. The form of the manuscript is thus a function of the ratiocination that is brought to bear upon it. Its context has changed, and indeed this change itself becomes the context for the following rather lengthy exposition and extrapolation concerning superficiality:

> Admittedly it is an outer husk: its face, in all its featureful perfection of imperfection, is its fortune: it exhibits only the civil or military clothing of whatever passionpallid nudity or plaguepurple nakedness may happen to tuck itself under its flap. Yet to concentrate solely on the literal sense or even the psychological content of any document to the sore neglect of the enveloping facts themselves circumstantiating it is just as hurtful to sound sense (and let it be added to the truest taste) as were some fellow in the act of perhaps getting an intro from another fellow turning out to be a friend in need of his, say, to a lady of the latter's acquaintance, engaged in performing the elaborative antecistral ceremony of upstheres, straightaway to run off and vision her plump and plain in her natural altogether, preferring to close his blinkhard's eyes to the ethiquethical fact that she was, after all, wearing for the space of

the time being some definite articles of evolutionary clothing, inharmonious creations, a captious critic might describe them as, or not strictly necessary or a trifle irritating here and there, but for all that suddenly full of local colour and personal perfume and suggestive, too, of so very much more and capable of being stretched, filled out, if need or wish were, of having their surprisingly like coincidental parts separated don't they now, for better survey by the deft hand of an expert, don't you know? Who in his heart doubts either that the facts of feminine clothiering are there all the time or that the feminine fiction, stranger than the facts, is there also at the same time, only a little to the rere? Or that one may be separated from the other? Or that both may then be contemplated simultaneously? Or that each may be taken up and considered in turn apart from the other? (109.08–36)

The degree of figurative mismatching is so painfully acute that we might almost need a chart just to begin. However this would tend to oversimplify matters since catachresis and context are intimately, if not monstrously wedded in this passage which is awash in a phlegm of over-qualification. A new cant has been posited to the questy: the mamafesta is now considered as an envelope, a paratextual container that insures a relatively safe transmission of the text therein. As such, the envelope is a superficial covering that is to be discarded once the message has been duly received by its designated addressee. In and of itself, the envelope signifies nothing except the addressee, it is, for all intents and purposes, an outer husk. But here it is also valued as a featureful perfection of imperfection and as a type of clothing for the nakedness therein. Although superficial, the envelope provides the only legible features that cover the naked contents, the envelope is thus analogous to the ink inscripted over and upon a blank page, silencing the blanks with denser accumulations of noise.

The literal sense of the document or text is thus constituted and conditioned by the envelope: the enveloping facts *circumstantiate* the literal sense, and therefore these should not be ignored (even if they could be). However, the word "circumstantiating" conveys two disparate notions: on the one hand it designates the circumstantial facts that adduce a context, and on the other hand it designates the context that subtends these so-called facts. The figure of the circumstantiating envelope thus conflates context and paratext, and so the circumstantiating facts paratactically redegenerate the context one catachrestic portmanteau at a time.

This paratextual redegeneration is intensified in the following slightly lude if not epic simile. Instead of clarifying the context of the primacy (or not) of the enveloping facts, the simile replays, reconfigures and reinforces the confusion of the figural language of the problematic circumstantiating statements. The protasis appears as a warning to not imagine a lady in a state of undress just as, in the apodosis, one should not imagine a message without considering its envelope. The figures deployed in the protasis are metonymically displaced extensions of the figures already used to describe the enveloping facts as "civil or military clothing of whatever passionpallid nudity or plaguepurple nakedness may happen to tuck itself under its flap." Within the protasis, the logic of the clothing proceeds by its own salacious momentum since, once it has been suggested, the superfice of clothiery is "suggestive, too, of so very much more." The additional elements of suggestion could be construed in at least two different ways: on the one hand the clothes could suggest the alluring naked form therein (and in so doing they would designate by an act of concealment), and on the other hand they could also be suggestive of *more* clothes or further enveloping facts and facets. The overenthusiastic description of the alluring role played by such fineries supports the notion (not atypical to advertisement) that the context of a lady is her clothing.[49] In this passage the overall context has shifted to a contemplation of the mamafesta as an envelope which then becomes a denegating *encominium* to the force of a *circumstantiating* paratext, thereby simultaneously undermining an reinforcing both the general role of paratext and the new, revised enveloping context. Of course the trope of clothing itself participates within a lengthy tradition concerning rhetoric, invoked as either a critique or an *apologia* of the role of ornamentation in discourse.[50] Through such a tradition, the word "circumstantiate" quivers between designating contextualization or adornment. The question of whether an unadorned and autotelic *essence* can be recuperable or even inferable from under the precession of enveloping contexts is lost within surface-play. Contemplating the mamafesta as an envelope is not unlike a game of strip-poker in reverse: clothes are always being added, and so the mamafesta wears many paratextual guises and glosses.

In his fashion magazine *La dernière mode,* Mallarmé valorized the elaboration of decoration: "*La décoration!* tout est dans ce mot" (OC: 712). Artifice is the holographic supplement for "everything." And indeed the accumulation of costume fineries *takes the place* of whomever is clothed, what is naked (*nu*) is known (*connu*) by clothes: "Somme toute, jamais ne régnèrent plus superbement les tissus opulents et même lourds, ... mais parmi cette enveloppe, somptueuse ou simple, plus qu'à aucune époque, va transparaître la Femme, visible, déssinée, elle-même, avec la grace entière, de son contour ou les principales lignes de sa personne" (OC: 833). The bearer of clothes is revealed, even unconcealed, through the garb that guises. As in the passage from the *Wake,* the naked lady is circumstantiated solely in and by the figure of the enveloping clothes. In this way, Mallarmé's concern with fashion remains very close to his purported poetic project to "*peindre, non la chose, mais l'effet qu'elle produit*" (CI: 137).[51] Likewise, the woman lasciviously imagined in the *Wake*an simile is figured or generated through the *effects* of her redegenerating paratexts, which are parapolylogically circumstantiating disguises.

This then is the allegorical moment of the *Wake*: the moment when any inferable apodosis becomes a decorative protasis through the surface play of parapolylogic inter-ference. Lucia Boldrini parallels this extended simile in the *Wake* with the problems concerning the polysemy of allegory announced by Dante in the *Convivio* and the *Epistle to Can Grande.* "What in *Finnegans Wake* is defined as 'stranger' is however the 'fiction,' which in the words of the *Convivio* is in fact again the literal sense, the 'beauteous fiction' [bella menzogna] that veils allegory. This fiction is 'only a little to the rere,' this time like the allegorical meaning in Dante: 'sempre lo litterale dee andare innanzi' [C: II.i.8]. ... By deliberately confusing the issue and by drawing attention to the envelope as well as to the letter proper, Joyce is moreover pointing out that layers of meaning go on proliferating in all directions and at all levels, crossing borders, becoming, as it were, 'stranger(s).'"[52] In *Finnegans Wake*, the tension of Dantean allegory is exaggerated and amplified by the ceding of initiative to the fabric of textual effects. In the *Wake*, Dantean allegoresis becomes Mallarméan virtuality.

In this pattern of redegenerating context, the question thus concerns the hermeneutic possibility of distinguishing between paratext and text. The paratext has been generated through the use of a metaphorics (first that of the envelope, which is then analogically extended through the simile to that of clothes and naked ladies). This figural paratext in turn orchestrates the tenor of the descriptive process. It might seem that the discursive mode "let[s] every crisscouple be so crosscomplimentary" (FW: 613.10–11), but there remain some residual cross-circuits. So far such crosscomplimentary patterning is not dissimilar to the machinations of *style indirect libre* in *Ulysses* (as described in our previous chapter): stylistics follow from an elaboration of a tangential detail within the narrative (such as food within the "Lestrygonians" chapter) with an ever-increasing complexity of *re-ference* and *dif-ference*. But here the stylistics are so convoluted within the precession of details so as to be *fundamentally indissociable*. The metaphorics that generate context themselves follow patterns that are apart from the context they elicit (tangential patterns of dis-sense following from the possibilities opened up by the portmanteau's lexical initiative) *which in turn* produce more context (further incompatible abundances of structure), and so on. Neither context nor semantic and tropic content fully predicates each other: they are all mutually pre-positioning and mutually destabilizing. Circumstantiation is perpetually redegenerated in a kind of Rube Goldberg variations. Of course within this paratactic redegeneration of metaphoric substitutions metonymically displaced, the unnamed mamafesta remains unseen and lost within the elaboration of further enveloping names. The play of surface disruptions distorts any defining and definitive structure, any structure that there may be remains catachrestic in its virtuality; as Alexander Pope wrote in the *Dunciad*: "Figures ill-pair'd, and Similes unlike."[53] Inappropriate metaphors, catachrestically applied are but one further indignity that the subjunctive letter suffers.

Indeed the polyhedral if not polytropic context further shifts in the subsequent paragraph as *something more* is suggested. "Here let a few artifacts fend in their own favour" (110.01). The discussion of the hermeneutic valuation of context is displaced towards the individual artifacts: discarded shards of information retrieved from the "litterage" (292.16) that may provide their own context and paratext so as to illuminate the tenebrousness of the missing letter. Indeed the argument now concerns the mamafesta as neither a manuscript nor a letter, but as an artifact that has been discovered by a hen (of all people) in a midden heap. The scene is thus translated from bad similes to an almost fairy-tale-like evocation of a Hibernian scene, "Our isle is Sainge. The place" (110.06), whence some metonymic detritus comes, through "a sequentiality of improbable possibles" (110.15):

> About that original hen. Midwinter (fruur or kuur?) was in the offing and Premver a promise of a pril when, as kischabrigies sang life's old sahatsong, an iceclad shiverer, merest of bantlings observed a cold fowl behaviourising strangely on that fatal midden or chip factory or comicalbottomed copsjute (dump for short) afterwards changed into the orangery when in the course of deeper demolition unexpectedly one bushman's holiday its limon threw up a few spontaneous fragments of orangepeel, the last remains of an outdoor meal by some unknown sunseeker or placehider *illico* way back in his mistridden past. What child of a strandlooper but keepy little Kevin in the despondful surrounding of such sneezing cold would ever have trouved up on a strate that was called strete a motive for future saintity by euchring the finding of the Ardagh chalice by another heily innocent and beachwalker whilst trying with pious clamour to wheedle Tipperaw raw raw reeraw puteters out of Now Sealand in spignt of the patchpurple of the massacre, a dual a duel to die to day, goddam and biggod, sticks and stanks, of most of the Jacobiters. (110.22–111.04)

If in the manuscript study the text could not be disengaged from textual and paratextual corruption, then in this account the artifact that has been retrieved is not entirely separable from the muck whence it was found. The manuscript has been damaged and has accumulated further traces of disjected matter. There are two resonances here, one concerns the status of *The Book of Kells* which was "stolen by night... and found after a lapse of some months, concealed under sods" (quoted in Atherton 1959, 63), and the other concerns the dissemination of the Torah: if a scroll is found to contain but one minor error, the entire scroll is buried or destroyed.[54] Upon corruption there is distortion and damage, and this is the status of the artifact that has been both disjected and valued by multiple contentious constitutions. The letter is reduced to a corrupting pile of fæcal materiality.[55] In *this* constitution the artifact resembles a turd or a lump of Shemmish inscription:

> Well, almost any photoist worth his chemicots will tip anyone asking him that if a negative of a horse happens to melt enough while drying, well, what do you get is, well, a positively grotesquely distorted macromass of all sorts of horsehappy values and masses of meltwhile horse. Tip. Well, this freely is what must have occurred to our missive (there's a sod of turb for you! Please wisp off the grass!) unfilthed from the boucher by the sagacity of a lookmelittle likemelong hen. Heated residence in the heart of the orangeflavored mudmound had partly obliterated the negative to start with, causing some features palpably nearer your pecker to be swollen up most grossly while the farther back we manage to wiggle the more we need the loan of a lens to see as much as the hen saw. Tip. (111.26–112.02)

Again an unfortunate analogue dictates the tone of presentation as tropes from the example of the horse's photograph persist in the depiction of the artifact ("obliterated the negative"; "loan of a lens"). The fate of the artifact is likened to a misdeveloped photograph of a horse whose image has been completely distorted and is recognizable as a horse only through recourse to some notion of a Platonic form of horseness that would designate the "masses of meltwhile horse."[56] There is perhaps not enough form that remains to even claim that the letter has been deformed at all, instead it is *in-formed* by the operative and optative paratextual discourse that constitutes it. The image of the manuscript has become a chaotic blur, only inferable as such through the loan of a lens of context. The text dissolves in the precession of exemplary similes. There is perhaps no text left there, and in its place is a whirligig of redegenerating (re)contextualizations.[57] But this context shifts as the artifact now develops into a turd.[58] It is nothing but a fowl mass, a litter has been ob*litter*ated in the development of its depiction. *Rien n'aura eu lieu que le loo*. The text is betrayed by its paratext, but would not and could not appear without it. Awash in the wake of words there is almost, but not quite, nothing there that takes the place of the nothing not there.

So far there has been little description of the contents of the document, only its fate has been thus far enumerated. The letter that is eventually presented in this chapter is not the longest, nor the most informative, yet it is porous with reference to other iterations of the letter in the *Wake*, recognizable as such through the repetition (and alteration) of certain generic elements.[59] Through the repetitions of these re-marking elements, the so-called text of the letter is perpetually engaged within the dynamic of recontextualizations.

> The bird in the case was Belinda of the Dorans, a more than quinquegintarian (Terziis prize with Serni medal, Cheepalizzy's Hane Exposition) and what she was scratching at the hour of klokking twelve looked for all this zogzag world like a goodishsized sheet of letterpaper originating by tranship from Boston (Mass.) of the last of the first to Dear whom it proceded to mention Maggy well & allathome's health well only the hate turned the mild on *the van* Houtens and the general's elections with a *lovely* face of some born gentleman with a beautiful present of wedding cakes for dear thankyou Chriesty and with grand funferall of poor Father Michael don't forget unto life's & Muggy well how are you Maggy & hopes soon to hear well & must now close it with fondest to the twoinns with four crosskisses for holy paul holey comer holipoli whollyisland pee ess from (locust may eat all but this sign shall they never) affectionate largelooking tache of tch. The stain, and that a teastain (the overcautelousness of the masterbilker here, as usual, signing the page away), marked it off on the spout of the moment as a genuine relique of ancient Irish pleasant pottery of that lydialike languishing class known as a hurry-me-o'er-the-hazy. (111.05-24)

In this iteration the text of the letter is presented through discursive paraphrase. Rather than present the letter as such, here only certain epistolary tropes are designated: the sender's address in Boston; the salutation; local news and gossip concerning presents and various comings and goings; a farewell and a postscript. Information concerning its author and sender is absent in this version of the letter, the name is obliterated by a teastain, or a tache of tch. This odd stain upon the parchment authenticates it, thereby supplementing the signatory's mark. The stain vouchsafes the letter in the place of an authorial signature.[60] The text is still inscribed by its material circumstances of discovery and re-presentation. Apart from the recurring tropes, this presentation of the letter is entirely consistent within the contextualizing machinations of this chapter in that its iteration derives from the contamination and degradation of contextualization. Furthermore, in this passage the recurring tropes coalesce into a letter because of the context, in other contexts although the tropes are proximate, they do not necessarily blend into a letter. The transcript is already "tran*shipt*" between many, many environs; its *scriptus* has succumbed to a polyhedral *metaphorics* (μεταφορά, *transference of a word to a new sense*). The trope of the envelope is thus a metonym of the paratextual metaphorics through which the letter circulates.

It is thus to the recurring tropes that we turn in order to further *characterize* the letter and to show more precisely how *Wakean* reference works as redegeneration. Almost immediately after the above paraphrase, an elaboration of the role of the hen in all this leads to another iteration of a letter, another "pick a peck of kindlings yet from the sack of auld hensyne" (112.08). This letter, now apparently *penned* by the hen, tends to confirm by insistent denial the possibility of a malfeasance by a male consort.

> And. She may be a mere marcella, this midget madgetcy, Misthress of Arths. But. It is not a hear or say of some anomorous letter, signed Toga Girilis, (teasy dear). ... We note the paper with her jotty young watermark: *Notre Dame du Bon Marché*. ... she feel plain plate one flat fact thing and if, lastways firdstwise, a man alones sine anyon anyons utharas has no rates to done a kik at with anyon anakars about tutus milking fores and the rereres on the outerrand asikin the tutus to be forrarder. ... Mesdaims, Marmouselles, Mescerfs! Silvapais! All schwants (schwrites) ischt tell the cock's trootabout him. Kapak kapuk. No minzies matter. He had to see life foully the plak and the smut, (schwrites). There were three men in him (schwrites). Dancings (schwrites) was his only ttoo feebles. With apple harlottes. And a little mollvogels. Spissially (schwrites) when they peaches. Honeys wore camelia paints. Yours very truthful. Add dapple inn. Yet is it but an old story, the tale of a Treestone with one Ysold, of a Mons held by tentpegs and his pal

whatholoosed on the run, what Cadman could but Badman wouldn't, any Genoaman against any Venis, and why Kate takes charge of the waxworks. (112.28–113.22)

This letter fits into the pattern of accusing HCE for some trespass. The original sin (or hen) of HCE is nowhere explicitly stated, yet through its repetitions certain recurrent tropes are attributed to it, tropes which are present in this statement, albeit in a vague form (some kind of sexual indiscretion involving up to three other men and some women of apparently loose moral standards, *&c.*). The question concerning the sin is just as malleably subject to the redegenerating machinations that perpetually modify the letter in its recurrences. Indeed the two are fundamentally and parapolylogically intertwined as the letter becomes a document (or misdocument) of that sin: both the sin and the letter redegenerate each other, and by implication the text itself (as noted earlier, both letter and sin involve the midnight hour).[61] Indeed, the sin generally seems to exist only in its varying recountings and contextualizations. The sin and the letter are already only paratexts: paratextually constituted and parapolylogically suggested. They are the fictitious asymptotes that fail in salvaging a belated past, the hypereffects of errant language: "if he did not exist it would be necessary quoniam to invent him" (033.35–36). But what is invented is too belated, and what is invented is the gone and departed locative enigma that nevertheless takes place by always suggesting *more*.

The apparently innocuous letter from page 111 has now been recontextualized into a less-than-anodyne document on page 113. Indeed the Hen is also far from innocent here, in the description of her prior to this letter, her character is defended: "she is ladylike in everything she does and *plays the gentleman's part every time*" (112.16–17; emphasis added). This recalls the "born gentleman" from the epistolary iteration on page 111 (one of the letter's recurrent tropes) who gives a gift of wedding cakes. The born gentleman thus is recontextualized out of the letter into a *figura* for the hen that finds it as well as to the fowl consort or Mons whom she defends.[62] As with HCE, the character defense serves to accuse and condemn the hen.

Not without significance, this defense is hypothetical: "*if* lastways firdstwise, a man alonees sine [*sin; without* (Latin)] anyon anyones." The morphology of the word "alonees" suggests a verb which accords with the subject "man," and so this man *alonees* without (*sine*) anyone. The prepositional clause created through the Latin *sine* is redundant to the inferred sense of the nonce verb "to alone." The condition of defense short-circuits because the hen's epistolary defense will take place *if* man is alone *and/or if* man sins; the letter takes the place of a dis-sensible *either/or* situation. The possibility then of an inscription of HCE and the letter (that is his defense) are already *ex-scriptions* in that the possibility of either comes to be retracted in the work in progress of intransitive inscribing. Both are removed and remain as perpetually contested discursive possibilities that, in part, motivate the word in progress, "Putting Allspace in a Notshall" (455.29).

Rather than remain relatively constant emblems transposed throughout the text, these recurrent tropes parasitically disvelop into whatever context calls them forth *just as* that context comes to be modified through the properties of reference that these tropes imply by their recursions. There is not necessarily a coherent development between the varying articulations that get repeated within *Wakean* reference (as there was in *Ulysses*). Throughout the sheer multiplicity of ferential vectors in *Finnegans Wake,* the ference breaks down on both a synchronic and a diachronic level even as ference perpetuates through the repetition of various elements. Statements within the book expand so that each additive element is itself liable to displacement and palimpsestuously additive, holographic *raturage*. The repetitions insure that these snippets have the force of narrative even as there is no narrative development there.

The letter *as such* exists only through its recurrent tropes which are highly susceptible to substantitive reconfiguration and through which the "letters have never been quite their old selves again" (112.24–25). Its few traits disseminate throughout in game of perpetual distributed recombinations (of which there had never been an original combination *as such*). Figuration is malleable in the shifting context of the polygraph of scripture.

The letter then documents nothing if not this detour, circuitously, it is a document of its swerving and bending journey: "it has acquired accretions of terricious matter whilst loitering in the past" (114.28–29). Its "pressant" is always being palimpsested, the original writing recedes under the accretion of inscription: it is (being) written as it journeys, and thus Shemmish writing is perpetually coordinate with Shaunish delivery. The cry "Shaun! Shaun! Post the post!" (404.07) is e'er the same as, interfered with the lowness of Shem. Shem and Shaun are parapolylogically related to and inferred from the trope of the letter. As with the problematic hermeneutic and *ferential* distinction between text and paratext (and the figurations thereof: between the letter and its enveloping facts, between a naked lady and her clothes), the Shemmish mode and the Shaunish mode are somewhat separate but can never be iterated apart.[63] Intervalically, they *maintwain* each other through the disjunctive and intransitive inscripting of the letter. The letter, and indeed the book that is the Work in Progress, is conditioned by the interval that keeps them apart: "*Shem and Shaun and the shame that sunders em*" (526.14). The third element is the discontinuity that is written as it is posted and disseminated. The brothers are not synthesized into a unity, instead the intervallic persistence of their separation *informs* the Work in Progress. "So hath been, love: tis tis: and will be: till wears and tears and ages" (116.36–117.01). The letter—"this oldworld epistola of their weatherings and their marryings and their buryings and their natural selections [which] has combled tumbled down to us fersch and made-at-all-hours like an ould cup on tay" (117.27–30)—stands in between the past and the re-presentation of the past, having itself accumulated the debris and tea-stains of its writing and transmission, it is the interval between the forgotten past and the belated future. The sin, if anything, is the *plus-que-présent* iteration of "the sin against the past participle" (467.24). The letter, absent as it might have been, *remains betrayed into legibility,* and such betrayal is conditioned by paratextual machinations which take the place of the text as the perpetually pre-positioning working-in-exprogress.

In *Finnegans Wake* writing and delivery are thus parapolylogically imbricated with exscription and loss through the discontinuous additive inter-ferences of various tropes that circulate around what could be called "The Doodles family, ⊓, Δ, ⊣, X, □, ∧, ⊏" (299.F4). This would be why such a maximization of discursive possibility is, in fact, so difficult to read. Its writing is *dense* with its constitutive and redegenerative misreadings. The earlier question posed in the chapter, "who in hallhagal wrote the durn thing anyhow?," is somewhat redundant since it has *already been written* by its paratextual inter-misconstitutions (the "intermisunderstanding minds of the anticollaborators" [118.25–26]), in the space of its arrantly errant words.

> And it is surely a lesser ignorance to write a word with every consonant too few than to add all too many. The end? say it with missiles then and thus arabesque the page. ... So why, pray, sign anything as long as every word, letter, penstroke, paperspace is a perfect signature of its own. (115.01–8)

There is no authority here in the locative enigma, save in the parapolylogics generated by dis-sensible words. This passage suggests the earlier quoted passage from *Le Livre, instrument spirituel:* "le volume ne comporter aucun signataire, quel est-il: l'hymne, harmonie et joie, comme pur ensemble groupé dans quelque circonstance fulgurante, des relations entre tout" (OC: 378). Within a space of obeisance—Christian for Joyce, that inveterately inverted jejune Jesuit evinced by the injunction to pray, and secular for Mallarmé with the hymn—the book, the expansion totale de la lettre, enunciates the author's disparition élocutoire in the very marks of inscription. The author is ceded to the signatory initiative and *ingegno* of not just words, but the nullity of the white page that is dis-sensibly constituted by the arabesques. In a sense a writer does not contaminate (or arabesque) the blank page, but rather *it is the blank page that disavows the writer*. In the blackening of the page, there is not so much a manifestation (or manifesto, or even a mamafesta), but rather parapolylogically enfolded and convoluted disparitions:

the travelling inkhorn (possibly pot), the hare and turtle pen and paper, the continually more and less intermisunderstanding minds of the anticollaborators, the as time went on as it will variously inflected, differently pronounced, otherwise spelled, changeably meaning vocable scriptsigns. (FW: 118.23–28)

Writing travels from the pen, not unlike a postman making the rounds. Inscription is delivered to the page where it perdures. This recalls Mallarmé's elaboration of the mad game of writing in *Quant au livre:*

> L'encrier, cristal comme une conscience, avec sa goutte, au fond, de ténèbres relative à ce que quelque chose soit: puis, écarte la lampe.
> Tu remarquas, on n'écrit pas, lumineusement, sur champ obscur, l'alphabet des astres, seul ainsi s'indique, ébauché ou interrompu; l'homme poursuit noir sur blanc. (OC: 370)

As argued in our third chapter, for Mallarmé poetry is never actually present in the attempt of its *enunciation* (which is its *crise*); poetry is thus to be à venir. The book, in all its paratextual glory and shame, is the (handsomely) bound interval of awaiting the silence which it perpetually displaces in and by its fractal language. In deviation, the book announces the *disastrously* errant wanderings of a "litteringture" (FW: 570.18) awaiting the tortured gasp of its impossibly final inachieved silencing under an ironic stellar detachment. The book coincides with its absentation but nevertheless fails to achieve the silence that is its unworking in progress.

> Plus l'Œuvre prend de sens et d'ambition, retenant en elle non seulement toutes les œuvres, mais toutes les formes et tous les pouvoirs du discours, plus l'absence d'œuvre semble près de se proposer, san toutefois jamais se laisser désigner. Cela arrive avec Mallarmé. Avec Mallarmé, l'Œuvre prend conscience d'elle-même et par là se saisit comme ce qui coïciderait avec l'absence d'œuvre, celle-ci se détournant alors de jamais coïncider avec elle-même et la destinant à l'impossibilité. Mouvement de détour où l'œuvre disparaît dans l'absence d'œuvre, mais où l'absence d'œuvre échappe toujours davantage en se réduisant à n'être que l'Œuvre toujours déjà disparue. (Blanchot, 622)

If Mallarmé is concerned with the act of writing, then the account of the letter in *Finnegans Wake* is concerned with the misdelivered reception of the intransitive inscribing of an inscription constituted by the stains of the travelling inkhorn and its interlaced *méprises*. For Mallarmé all that speaks can only be sounded through writing, the *action restreinte:* a *disastrous* annulment of absence by perpetually displacing holographic figurations. The langue suprême is thus given up in the very approach to constitute it; it is condemned to be both *jadis* and *méconnu*, "continually more and less intermisunderstanding minds of the anticollaborators." Mistranscribed, the letter and its expansion remain misunderstood: its disparition remains encrypted amidst erring exegesis.

The inscription or the letter is a collideorscape of supplementarity. The writing is always damaged in and by its working in progress and (especially) in the reading thereof and thereupon. As a final example of this deferral (but there could always be others), the chapter on the letter concludes with a further professorial rambling concerning the accumulation of errors in transmission, errors that come to characterize the document. Indeed, in the account of the final reception of the letter in this chapter, it has thoroughly been replaced by a few untoward splurges of further punctuation.

> The original document was in what is known as Hanno O'Nonhanno's unbrookable script, that is to say, it showed no signs of punctuation of any sort. Yet on holding the verso against a lit rush this new book of Morses responded most remarkably to the silent query of our world's oldest light and its recto let out the piquant fact that it was but pierced butnot punctured (in the university sense of the term) by numerous stabs and foliated gashes made by a pronged instrument. These paper wounds, four in type, were gradually and correctly understood to mean stop, please stop, do please stop, and O do please stop respectively, and following up their one true clue, the circumflexuous wall of a singleminded men's asylum, accentuated by bi tso fb rok engl a ssan dspl itch ina, — Yard inquiries pointed out → that they ad bîn "provoked" ay ∧ fork, of à grave Brofèsor; àth é's Brèak — fast — table;   ; acùtely profèššionally *piquéd,* to = introdùce a notion of time [ùpon à plane (?) sù' ' façʻe'] by pùnct! ingh oles (sic) in iSpace?! (FW: 123.31–124.12)

The initial feature most apparent on this original document is an absence of immediately apparent punctuation. Without punctuation marks, the document cannot easily be *rede* since one of the features of punctuation is to supplement the initial voicelessness of ambivalent "Signs on a white field" (U: 3.415) with indications of cadence for reading aloud. In this sense, along this light, the document is indeed written in an unbrookable script since it does not appear to flow together. This unbrookable script *hanno o non hanno* (Italian, *they have or do not have*): it lies between two apparently contradictory possibilities, to have or not to have that is the question, "*The haves and havenots: a distinction*" (FW:295.L4–6).[64] That, concerning the manuscript, there can be distinction cannot itself be distinguished.

However, inflicted upon the document are gashes, "legibly depressed, upon defenceless paper" (189.09), which provide a basis of distinction and inflection. The reading of these four paratextual paper wounds recalls the aporetic admonition from the first chapter: "stop, please stop, do please stop, and O do please stop respectively." The wounds provide for the legibility, a legibility which informs, once "correctly understood," aporia. Introduced by a pronged instrument, or "ay ∧ fork," the marks of *punc*tuation are construed as pierces, not *punc*tures (in the university sense of the term, coined by a grave Professor at the breakfast table no less).[65] These textual wounds are *accentuated* by a matinal disintegration and recombination as "bits of broken glass and split china" splits and breaks into "bi tso fb rok engl a ssan dspl itch ina"—a severance which seems composed of shards of broken English (such as "fb rok engl") and what seems to be a mongrelized phonetic Chinese ("bi tso"). These combinations provide the accents for the remainder of this passage, accents which decline the letterwritten description of the letter into further wounding marks. The accents introduce further markings of differentiation that had been perpetrated by "à grave Brofèsor." The grave accent is redundant once qualified by the word grave, and indeed the grave accent falls upon the Brofèsor in question. More importantly "à" is not exactly the indefinite article that the sentence's generally English syntax (which is admittedly fractured) articulates, since it is orthographically equivalent to the French preposition of appurtenance. The phrase "à grave," on the one hand performs the designated accentuation but, on the other hand, by performing the accent, the designation becomes superfluous if not excessive. Rather than enhance (or even demonstrate) this aspect of the text, the self-reflexive accentuation disturbs it further. The marks that mark difference (inflection, pronunciation, meaning), *re-mark too much difference*.[66] Indeed the only cogent reading of this passage (a reading of a Professor overeager with his cutlery at breakfast) is possible if the reader is indifferent to these differentiating marks. And so the introduction of a simulacra of time upon the spatial interval of the page ("to=introdùce a notion of time [ùpon à plane (?) sù' ' fàç'e'] by pùnct! ingh oles (sic) in iSpace?!"), the introduction of temporalizing marks, has gone astray.[67]

Prima facie, the passage above appears to perform a self-reflexive quality of deploying the differentiating paper wounds that it describes, it appears to demonstrate the piercings at the grave Brofèsor's Brèak — fast. Yet the over-punctuation undermines the reading that it constitutes, and so the text wounds itself, and keeps on wounding itself. The accents and so forth that supposedly illustrate and demonstrate the morning manuscript, the accents that parse the manuscript themselves do not parse away into the night of a tenebrous reading. The simulacra of time yield to *a syntactic temporalization* that underlies semantic deferral. References (to *The Book of Kells,* to Holmes's novel and so on) are no longer just semantic enhancements (buttressing any narrativized reading of a Professor reading and wounding a document in the morning), but rather further displacing wounds inflicted upon the polyhedral text. Each further mark ex-scribes the past into a pressant, a belated gift of incomprehension. Amidst *over-ference* there is the iteration of discontinuity, the book made discontinuous with itself through its parapolylogically deployed figurations. This then is the book, the betrayal of and by the book: beyond the differential paratextual manifestations (the differences between the empirical editions of the book) *into and as* legibility, "Le livre est le travail du langage sur lui-même: comme s'il fallait le livre pour que le langage se prenne conscience du langage, se saisisse et s'achève de par son inachèvement" (Blanchot, 623). The book *delivers* itself into the book so that inachievement is to no longer have been achieved. The book is the *mark* of the failure of the book, the re-mark that *fails* the book again. The book is then what will have been outside what can be read, *pas au-delà* the paratext.

> L'écriture est absente du Livre, étant l'absence non absente à partir de laquelle, s'étant absenté d'elle, le Livre (à ses deux niveaux: l'oral et l'écrit [what can be *rede*], la Loi et son exégèse, l'interdit et la pensée de l'interdit) se rend lisible et se commente en enfermant l'histoire: fermeture du livre, sévérité de la lettre, autorité de la conaissance. De cette écriture absente du livre et cependant en rapport d'altérité avec lui, on peut dire qu'elle reste étrangère à la lisibilité, illisible pour autant que le lire, c'est nécessairement entrer par le regard en relation de sens ou de non-sens avec un présence. Il y aurait donc une écriture extérieure au savoir qui s'obtient par la lecture, extérieure aussi à la forme ou à l'exigence de la Loi. L'écriture, (pure) extériorité, étrangère à toute relation de présence, comme a toute légalité. (631–32)

Beyond the words in the book in all their parapolylogics of play, there is a writing exterior to sensibility that is perpetually "signing the page away" (FW: 111.21), "A way a lone a last a loved a long the" (628.15–16). And so, as much with Dante at the end of the *Paradiso* and Mallarmé with the disaster of the unwritten Livre, there is nothing there but the exscribing of a locative enigma. The work thus depicted is not the book, not just the physical artifact of the book, but rather the effect of silence that it produces: *peindre non le livre, mais l'effet de silence qu'il produit*. In Dante, Mallarmé and Joyce nought comes to the nullity wither and whence it had not been. That we still cannot read Dante, Mallarmé and Joyce is not our fault for the books that are there take the place of *what could be read*.

Notes

[1] James S. Atherton has made an extreme yet hardly atypical statement on this matter: "until all the quotations, allusions and parodies in *Finnegans Wake* have been elucidated the complete meaning of the whole work must escape us" (James S. Atherton, *The Books at the Wake*, Carbondale: Southern Illinois UP, 1959. 20). Although, by implication, any overall and defining structuring principle must remain partial and incomplete (at least until all the appropriate facts have been codified), there is still the hope that such a principle of understanding *can be* achieved through painstaking glossing. This hope of a futural structuring principle itself rests within a generalized structuring principle, one that maintains that *Finnegans Wake* is ultimately readable. Such sentiments tend to reduce the *Wake* to a message that contains information yet requires resources of additional information to decide and decrypt that initial message (and by implication such information would arbitrate the hermeneutic statements that could be made about the *Wake*). *Even if* one could amass and assimilate all the requisite information, *Finnegans Wake* would still remain somewhat incompressible and mystifying. The reliance upon additional information is not trivial, yet the information alone does not *decide* the matter.

[2] Bernard Benstock, *Joyce-Again's Wake*, Seattle: U of Washington P, 1965. 124

[3] In response to a reader's question about his Work in Progress, Joyce stated "it's meant to make you laugh" (quoted in Richard Ellmann, *James Joyce*, revised edition, Oxford: Oxford UP, 1982. 716). Joyce indeed took the humor of his work seriously, in the planned but never executed sequel to the *apologia* of the Work in Progress entitled *Our Exagmination Round His Factification for Incamination of Work in Progress,* Joyce considered including an article on humor (613). "Loud, heap miseries upon us yet entwine our arts with laughters low" (FW: 259.07–8).

[4] Derek Attridge, "Unpacking the Portmanteau, or Who's Afraid of *Finnegans Wake?*," *On Puns,* ed. Jonathan Culler, London: Blackwell, 1988. 140–55. 145; cf. 140–45. This argument is repeated in *Peculiar Language,* Ithaca: Cornell UP, 1988. 195–209.

[5] This recalls Freud's contribution to rhetoric. In *Jokes and Their Relationship to the Unconscious,* he describes how the metaplasmic alterations of words in jokes prosopopoeiacally allegorize the unconscious. The unconscious comes to speak

through the cracks of lexical lapses (Sigmund Freud, *Jokes and their Relationship to the Unconscious. Standard Edition of the Complete Psychological Works of Sigmund Freud*, volume 8. ed. and trans. James Strachey, London: Hogarth, 1960). Following from Freud's reading of jokes, Jacques Lacan claims that Joyce's portmanteaux do not merely gather together and condense different meanings from various languages, but also transgress the possibility of univocal, monosemic meaning by unleashing the differential power of language. For Lacan, Joy(ce) and Freud(e) echo the joys of the libido unchained across languages: "cette jouasse, cette jouissance est la seule chose que de son texte nous puissions attraper. Là est le symptôme. Le symptôme en tant que rien ne le rattache à ce qui fait lalangue elle-même dont il supporte cette trame.... Le symptôme est purement ce que conditionne lalangue, mais d'une certaine façon, Joyce la porte à la puissance du langage, sans que pour autant rien n'en soit analysable, c'est ce qui frappe, et littéralement interdit—au sens où l'on dit—je reste interdit" (Jacques Lacan, "Joyce le symptôme I," *Joyce avec Lacan,* ed. Jacques Aubert, Paris: Navarin, 1987. 21–29. 27). The problem here is that Lacan has *determined* a value for metaplasmic manipulation, thereby reasserting a moment of linguistic intent (if not *ingegno*) in the wake of the *Wake*.

[6] "Dénombrer les branchements, calculer la vitesse des communications ou la longueur des trajets, ce serait du moins impossible, en fait, tant que nous n'aurions pas construit la machine capable d'intégrer toutes les variables, tous les facteurs quantitatifs et qualitatifs. Ce n'est pas pour demain. Cette machine en tout cas ne serait que le double pesant de l'événement « Joyce », la simulation de ce que ce nom signe ou signifie, l'œuvre signé, le logiciel Joyce aujourd'hui, le *joyciciel*. Il est sans doute en cours de fabrication, l'institution mondiale des études joyciennes, la *James Joyce Inc.* s'y emploie, à moins qu'elle ne le soit elle-même. Cela même. De toute façon, elle le constitue" (Jacques Derrida, "Deux mots pour Joyce," *Ulysse gramophone,* Paris: Galilée, 1987. 14–53. 23).

[7] Thomas Jackson Rice, "The Complexity of *Finnegans Wake*," *Joyce Studies Annual* 6 (1995): 78–98. 88. Rice has expanded on this in *Joyce, Chaos, and Complexity*, Urbana: U of Illinois P, 1997. chapter 4.

[8] Vladimir Dixon, "A Litter to Mr. James Joyce," *Our Exagmination Round His Factification For Incamination Of Work In Progress*, Samuel Beckett *et al,* New York: New Directions, 1939. 193–94. 193. Ellmann states unequivocally that Dixon was Joyce (Ellmann, 626); this has been subsequently corrected by Thomas A. Goldwasser, who pointed out that Vladimir Dixon was fortunate enough to have had

an existence not entirely circumscribed by Joyce's revolution of the word ("Who Was Vladimir Dixon? Was He Vladimir Dixon?," *JJQ* 16.3 [Spring 1979]: 219–22).

[9] Within the immediate context of this phrase, the potential glossing of "flore" by "floor" admittedly seems improbable (or at least less-than-compelling), but there are instances within the *Wake* when such a suggestion seems a likely adjunct to "flower": "persequestellates [*persequor* (Latin) *to pursue,* this Latinate suggestion is buttressed by the infix *quest*] his vanessas from flore to flore" (FW: 107.18); and "You plied that poker, gamesy, swell as aye did, while there were flickars to the flores" (606.32–34). These additional uses do not unequivocally assign the sense of "floor" to the contents of the portmanteau "flore," but they indicate that a stable grounding is denied to the word and that multiple patterns of contextualization are always possible. Once a word is glossed, no matter how decisively, the possibility of further slips always remains.

[10] Scape can be equivalent to escape: the elided "e" makes little difference. That which does not collide, escapes (escapes citation, not unlike the elided "e"). But the word "scape" could also be a landscape without a land. Scape carries the additional meanings of transgression, error, and, oddly enough—according to the *OED*—fart. Once the "e" of escape has been elided we have additional senses; the elision, the ( ) of scape makes all the difference. The possibility of escape is thus forgotten by the lapsed "e" and supplemented by a newly redolent *panaroma* of all flores of speech.

[11] Harry Levin, *James Joyce,* revised edition, Norfolk: New Directions, 1959. 184.

[12] In an early review of *Finnegans Wake*, a philologist draws the opposite conclusion from *Wakean* punning and claims that Joyce's wordplay, preoccupied by possibilities of onomatopœia, betrays the naïve belief "that there is, or should be, a real connection between the sound and the thing" (Archibald A. Hill, "A Philologist Looks at *Finnegans Wake*," *Virginia Quarterly Review* XV [1939]: 650–56. 652). In a recent study, Peter Myers suggests that the sound-effects of *Wakean* words—the "sound sense sympol" (FW: 612.29)—rather than try to mimetically convey some aspect of reality, provide an additional register upon which sense can be disfigured (Peter Myers, *The Sound of "Finnegans Wake,"* London: Macmillan, 1992. cf. esp. 20–44). The phonotext is merely another "flore" of dissonance since it frequently differs from the orthographical suggestions. This is not to say that the phonotext is more authentic (although on occasion Joyce did say exactly that [Ellmann, 702–3]),

but rather *between* the phoneme and the grapheme there is a difference which, instead of being reconciled and subsumed under an idea, is put into play as part of the *Wake*'s ongoing network of contra*dict*ory enunciations (cf. Garrett Stewart, *Reading Voices: Literature and the Phonotext,* Berkeley: U of California P, 1990. 232–58).

[13] Stephen Heath, "'Ambiviolences': Notes pour la lecture de Joyce," *Tel Quel* 50 (Summer 1972): 22–43. 31.

[14] Friedrich Blume, *Two Centuries of Bach,* trans. Stanley Goodman, Oxford: Oxford UP, 1950. 85. If one accepts the evident fact that Monteverdi is the far superior composer, then one would read this passage somewhat differently.

[15] Once German is admitted into the phrase to provide further parses for "bach," then there would exist a further possible, additional overtone: "Backe," thereby shifting the pain from the back to the *cheek*. Indeed, homophonic Germanic glossing could further run wild with the not-entirely-germane suggestion of "Bache" (a wild pig more than two years old).

[16] Clive Hart, *Structure and Motif in "Finnegans Wake,"* London: Faber, 1962. 164–66.

[17] This line, a homophonic link to "The seim anew" (FW: 215.23) also echoes another phrase from I.8, "Towy I too, rathmine" (215.11); therefore its reference is multiple and subject to *inter-reference*.

[18] Stephen Heath, "'Ambiviolences' 2," *Tel Quel* 51 (Fall 1972): 64–76. 66.

[19] At the very least, *Finnegans Wake* satisfies Borges's definition of the baroque: a "style which deliberately exhausts (or tries to exhaust) all its possibilities and which borders on its own parody. ... I would say that the final stage of all styles is baroque" (Jorge Luis Borges, "Preface to the 1954 Edition," *A Universal History of Infamy,* trans. Norman Thomas di Giovanni, Harmondsworth: Penguin, 1975. 11).

[20] Jacques Derrida, *La dissémination,* Paris: Seuil, 1972. 343–45.

[21] Samuel Beckett, "Dante... Bruno. Vico.. Joyce," *Our Exagmination Round His Factification For Incamination Of Work In Progress*, Samuel Beckett, *et al*, New York: New Directions, 1939. 1–22. 22.

[22] A variant of this term "parapolylogic"—"pollylogue" (FW: 470.09)—has already been pilfered by Philippe Sollers in his novel *H:* "j'oppose au monologue

intérieur le polylogue extérieur" (*H*, Paris: Seuil, 1973. 42). In her theoretical assessment of *H*, Julia Kristeva uses the word polylogue to name the semiotic experience of an intervalically phrased simultaneity of the heterogeneous, an experience of fragmentation that raises a "cri anarchique contre la position thétique et socialisante de la langue syntaxique" (Julia Kristeva, "Polylogue," *Polylogue*, Paris: Seuil, 1977. 173–222. 187; cf. esp. 181–87). Our use of this term is different since we retain that *para-*: the παρά, *beside, along, beyond.*

Hayman has noted that this term comes from one of Joyce's early *Finnegans Wake* notebooks (VI.B. 10) as a description of a multiplicity of dialogue broadcast simultaneously (David Hayman, *The "Wake" in Transit*, Ithaca: Cornell UP, 1990. 158–59). The term parapolylogic reinforces the synchronicity of these multiple parallel λόγοι.

[23] David Hayman, "James Joyce, Paratactitian," *Contemporary Literature* XXVI.2 (1985): 155–78. 175. See also his *Re-Forming the Narrative*, Ithaca: Cornell UP, 1987. 194–96.

[24] "The Question of *Un coup de dés*," *Baudelaire, Mallarmé, Valéry: New Essays in Honour of Lloyd Austin*, eds. Malcom Bowie, Alison Fairlie and Alison Finch, Cambridge: Cambridge UP, 1982. 142–50. 145. The only critics to have seriously proposed a hermeneutic for *Finnegans Wake* based on the issues raised in *Un coup de dés* are R.G. Cohn (whose insistence upon thematic parallels, as we detailed in chapter 4, seriously hampers his suggestion), David Hayman (*Joyce et Mallarmé*, 2 volumes, Paris: Lettres Modernes, 1956. I.70–75 and I.171–72); Jean-Michel Rabaté ("'Alphybettyformed verbage': the shape of sounds and letters in *Finnegans Wake*," *Word and Image* 2.3 [July–September 1986]: 237–43) and Simone Verdin who has proposed that Joyce's effect of massively blackening the page with reference—in distinction to the Mallarméan gambit of attenuation—eviscerates reference through overloaded cross-circuitry (Simone Verdin, *Le presque contradictoire, précédé d'une Étude de variantes*, Paris: Nizet, 1975. 253; cf. 250–54).

[25] This is a time that occurs several times in *Finnegans Wake*, a time that seems to designate an impropriety and thus comes to be associated with that impropriety: "to ask could he tell him how much a clock it was that the clock struck had he any idea by cock's luck as his watch was bradys. Hesitency was clearly to be evitated. Execration as cleverly to be honnisoid. The Earwicker *of that spurring instant*... told the inquiring kidder, by Jehova, it was twelve of em sidereal and tankard time" (FW:

035.18–34; emphasis added). When asked for the time, the respondent (Earwicker) is constituted by the very time that he names (*"of* that spurring instant").

[26] One overtone of this morphological adjustment to *ceathair* (which reads as an Anglicization of spoken Irish) is the suggestion of Kate—"Cowtends Kateclean, the woman with the muckrake" (FW: 448.10)—the cleaner who apparently waits over the letter. Perhaps inadvertently the word "kater" also strays to the Dutch word for tom-cat.

[27] The isomorphism of the Dutch and German *elf* (as well as the Nordic *sax*) is not unproblematic. In his *Annotations,* McHugh notes only the Dutch instance, ignoring the possible, even likely, Germanic overtone (*Annotations to "Finnegans Wake,"* revised edition, Baltimore: Johns Hopkins UP, 1991). Geert Lernout, with the acuity and restraint typical of a native Dutch speaker, proposes that in instances of a word that could be Dutch, German, or Danish (or even English), the context should determine which exact language is construed (he cites as example "langsome" [FW: 415.12] which *prima facie* could easily derive from the Dutch *langzaam,* the Danish *langsom* or the German *langsam*). Lernout also notes that the epithet Dutch is misleading since there are three broad variants of the language: the Dutch spoken in Holland; Flemish and Afrikaans (Geert Lernout, "Dutch in *Finnegans Wake,"* *JJQ* 23.1 [Fall 1985]: 45–66. 66–67). With the word *elf* above, context is of no help since the context itself concerns linguistic variety, and indeed within the register of such variety between words, it is unsurprising that one elfin word could itself exhibit such linguistic variation. Linguistic parataxis exists not just within the series but also within the words that are within the series.

[28] It is, or could be six o'clock at other passages or times in the book, as Anna Livia exclaims "Pingpong! There's the Belle for Sexaloitez!" (FW: 213.18–19). Through the commodiousness of the Sechseläuten spring festival in Zürich, Joyce packs together sex and six into the ringing of bells. These bells lasciviously echo across the *Wake*: "Peingpeong! For saxonlootie!" (058.24); "ringrang, he chimes of sex appealing" (268.02–3); "I beg to traverse same above statement by saxy looters" (492.14–15); "Silks apeel and sulks alusty?" (508.29); "Ding dong! Where's your pal in silks alustre?" (528.18–19); and "Skulkasloot!" (610.14). The possibility of a mixed designation between six and sex via a Zürich festival itself comes to be miscegenated within varying contexts thereby destabilizing the subsistence of the sextile hour.

[29] The sequence in question is 12 → 2 → 11 → 4 → 10 → 6. This series could be seen as two independent yet intertwined and alternating algorithms: the first counts down by 1 from 12 (12, 11, 10, &c.) and the second counts up by 2 from 2 (2, 4, 6, &c.). The sixth number in such a sequence is, coincidentally, six. The answer is thus equal to its place in the sequence. This is but one possible formula for this numerical sequence and no doubt there are others.

Following from Rice's description of complexity, an algorithm *can* be written to predict a random number (the example he gives is the result of a toss of the dice), *but* in such a case the algorithm, "the instruction that will always give the same complex result then must be exactly as long as the [process of achieving the] number itself. This is the highest degree of mathematical complexity, indicating pure numerical randomness" (Rice, 91). In other words, *un coup de dés jamais n'abolira le hasard*. The algorithm we have provided here is at least as long as the sequence of numbers it predicts, and it still does not account for its apparently simple polylinguistic overtones.

[30] The many catalogues in *Finnegans Wake* also evince such difficulty. More so than in *Ulysses*, *Wakean* catalogues are not always easy to distinguish from their context. Bernard Benstock has noted that the elements within catalogues are not easily differentiable into discrete quantal units since they themselves tend towards subdivision. He notes that the element "A tinker's bann and a barrow to boil his billy for Gipsy Lee" (FW: 210.06-7) from the list of ALP's gifts could be construed as either one or two items. "A patterned development in these enlarged catalogues seems to mature toward a finite number, but a tendency toward disintegration near the end becomes the operative technique instead, a splashing out of possibilities rather than a fulfillment of cohesive assemblage" (Bernard Benstock, "Cataloguing in *Finnegans Wake*: counting counties," *Joyce in Context,* eds. Vincent J. Cheng and Timothy Martin, Cambridge: Cambridge UP, 1992. 259-69. 264). *Wakean* parataxis cannot easily be numerated.

[31] There is a similar numerological conundrum in the *Vita Nuova* with the allegorical overdeterminations around the number nine. This number is a consistent figure or index of Beatrice, but the ways in which it is figured in the story of Beatrice, and the ways in which it indexes Beatrice are notoriously multiple. The number nine in this way communicates *something*, but what it communicates and even *how* it is being communicated remains mysterious and unanswered. In chapter XXIX—after showing how the number nine can figure in the date of Beatrice's death in any number of different calendars (which is not an especially difficult feat)—the narrator

proposes to explain the persistence of nine as indicating a divine status since the root of nine is the Trinity. However all is not well and good as the narrator then adds "Forse ancora per più sottile persona si vederebbe in ciò più sottile ragione; ma questa è quello ch'io ne veggio, e che più mi piace" (XXIX.4). The proffered reason is not necessarily the true one and the true allegorical significance of the number is thus not revealed. The number nine remains mysteriously, numinously and arithmetically multiple (we are grateful to David Califf for bringing this point to our attention).

[32] In the first edition of the *Annotations* (Roland McHugh, *Annotations to "Finnegans Wake,"* Baltimore: Johns Hopkins UP, 1980), McHugh deciphers "Tolv two elf" as 3211, a number which recurs throughout the text (usually as 1132) as an index of some kind, even though its precise significance eludes definition. It thus might stand as an alternative to the midnight hour: "Femelles will be preadaminant as from twentyeight to twelve" (FW: 617.23–4). However, McHugh derived this number from "Tolv two elf" through an inconsistent application of a numerological metamorphosis: 12, 2, 11 = (1+2), 2, 11 = 3211. A consistent application of this additive sequence would yield 322 ([1+2), 2, [1+1]). Although 1132 recurs variously throughout the *Wake*, it appears to be absent here. This gloss is understandably absent from the second edition of the *Annotations*.

[33] James Atherton notes that the line "And low stole o'er the stillness the heartbeats of sleep" is a classical hexameter (James S. Atherton, "Shaun A," *A Conceptual Guide to "Finnegans Wake,"* eds. Michael H. Begnal and Fritz Senn, University Park: The Pennsylvania State UP, 1974. 149–72. 150). An arithmetic persists to organize the words that fall after the numerical sequence.

[34] The allusion Aubert identifies is to Coleridge's *Kubla Kahn*: "'Where Alph, the sacred river, ran.' Mais il serait trop facile d'en appeler ici à l'espace culturel: ce serait ne voir en cette réminiscence qu'un effet décoratif, sinon un clin d'œil entendu. ... L'écho à la fouis signale un *texte* précis et son *absence*" (Jacques Aubert, "Riverrun," *Change* 11 [1972]: 120–30. 128).

[35] An example of misguided syncategoremata occurs in the following passage: "For be all rules of sport 'tis right That youth bedower'd to charm the night Whilst age is dumped to mind the day When wather parted from the say" (FW: 371.18–20). The capitalization of the syntactic particles here orients them *away* from their delimiting role, thereby undermining a coherent reading of the passage at least as much as the estrangement proffered by the various portmanteaux here (there are

other instances of eccentric capitalization in the pages that follow this excerpt). The capitalization brings about additional differentiating contexts through which the passage could be read.

[36] Fritz Senn, "Mean Cosy Turns," *Myriadminded Man,* eds. Rosa Maria Bosinelli, Paola Pugliatti and Romana Zacchi, Bologna: CLUEB, 1986. 263–67. 266.

[37] Laurent Milesi, "Metaphors of the Quest in *Finnegans Wake,*" *"Finnegans Wake": Fifty Years,* ed. Geert Lernout, Amsterdam: Rodopi, 1990. 79–107. 90.

[38] Joyce's feminization of Allah into Annah is perhaps anticipated in the Koran: while the word Allah is masculine in grammatical gender, the words *al-Rahman* (compassionate) and *al-Rahim* (merciful) are both etymologically related to the word for "womb."

[39] For example, although items are ostensibly separated by commas, two of the entries are separated by semi-colons (FW: 104.36 and 105.32) and the final entry is somewhat ambiguous: "*First and Last True Account all about the Honorary Mirsu Earwicker, L.S.D., and the Snake (Nuggets!) by a Woman of the World who only can Tell Naked Truths about a Dear Man and all his Conspirators how they all Tried to Fall him Putting it all around Lucalizod about Privates Earwicker and a Pair of Sloppy Sluts plainly Showing all the Unmentionability falsely Accusing about the Raincoats*" (107.01–7). See also note 30.

[40] "The time is out of joint" (William Shakespeare, *Hamlet, The Oxford Shakespeare: Complete Works,* ed. W.J. Craig, Oxford: Oxford UP, 1905. 870–907. I.v.189).

[41] Accountings of the fate of the letter precede this chapter: "The letter! The litter! And the soother the bitther! Of eyebrow pencilled, by lipstipple penned. ... Wind broke it. Wave bore it. Reed wrote of it. Syce ran with it. Hand tore it and wild went war. Hen trieved it and plight pledged peace. It was folded with cunning, sealed with crime, uptied by a harlot, undone by a child. It was life but was it fair? It was free but was it art?" (FW: 093.24–94.10). This process is later recapitulated: "Letter, carried of Shaun, son of Hek, written of Shem, brother of Shaun, uttered for Alp, mother of Shem, for Hek, father of Shaun. Initialled. Gee. Gone" (420.17–19). The letter is thus associated with litterish dispersal, a dispersal that is at least partially isomorphic with disparition: "in deesperation of deisperation at the diasporation of his diesparition" (257.25–26).

[42] We take the term "paratext" from Gérard Genette who defines it as the convergence of effects around a text that in diverse ways help to constitute the materiality (and thus the survival or maintenance) of that text. The paratext consists of the peritext (the form and format of the text-as-book: typography, binding, dedications, &c.) and the epitext (matter not bound into the book that either leads to it, such as excerpts published in advance, or comes from it, such as interviews, letters, &c.): "le paratexte est lui-même un texte: s'il n'est pas encore *le* texte, il est déjà *du* texte" (Gérard Genette, *Seuils*, Paris: Seuil, 1987. 12; cf. 7–14).

[43] Rita Copeland, *Rhetoric, Hermeneutics, and Translation in the Middle Ages*, Cambridge: Cambridge UP, 1991. 3. Copeland argues that the norms of the commentary tradition emphasize that texts survive only through the rhetorical norms of exegesis: the text is performed *through the* commentary, and thus through the concomitant transformations that such exegetical activity implies (cf. 63–86).

[44] Vladimir Nabokov, *Pale Fire*, New York: Berkley, 1968. 12.

[45] In Hebrew, the word for ox is *aleph* (אָלֶף), the first letter of the alphabet; the word for house is *beth* (בֵּת), the second letter; and the word for the humped camel is *gimmel* (גָמֵל), the third letter. Therefore something that is as simple as an oxhousehumper will *always* (*semper* [Latin]) appeal to the abcedminded. The dis-sense of this portmanteau proffers both pattern and dis-ease.

[46] Hayman has organized such a reading, primarily because a nautical setting is suggested while being nowhere explicit (Hayman 1956, II.47–48). Hayman calls this passage a new version of the following swath from *Un coup de dés*: "né / d'un ébat / la mer par l'aïeul tentant ou l'aïeul contre la mer" (UC: 6a; OC: 464). According to Hayman, the *Wakean* version is configured through tropes from elsewhere in the poem and these could be mapped out thusly:

Mallarméan trope	Joycean modulation
"plume solaire éperdue"	quill
La mer	seer
L'orage	showers
le coup de dés	atosst of a trike
Le Maître	the anonymous author

| La Mère | ALP: the sea-er |

Hayman's reading emphasizes the issue and issuance of disaster, "l'enfant du poète [the text], sa création, un autre aspect de coup: son résultat" (Hayman 1956, II.47). This reading ignores the line that immediately follows and qualifies the passage, "une chance oiseuse" (UC: 6a; OC: 464). The possible birth is a nul issue and the possibility of issue ("PEUT-ÊTRE / UNE CONSTELLATION") is never certain and always annulled in its taking place (see our fourth chapter for a more detailed reading of this passage from *Un coup de dés*).

[47] In his detailed examination of the textual genesis of the letter into the emerging Work in Progress, Laurent Milesi notes that "Detailed genetic analysis, of the 'Letter' motif for instance, has helped to show indirectly how the creation of *Work in Progress* shows a marked tendency to combine paradigmatic selection with syntagmatic combination, thus reshuffling and blurring conceptual demarcations. Similarly, in the narrative, each metaphoric derivation of the quest is in turn a *symbolic* (synecdochic or metonymic) thread of it and the reader-questor going upriver, if he hopes to gain access to the essence of Metaphor and Quest in *Wakean* creation, must trace back every single one of these derivations *and* reconcile them all in order to approach the horizon of the book's production and consumption, when the Metaphor of the Quest cyclically becomes the Metaphor of his endless Quest for the Metaphor in language" (Milesi 1990, 103–4).

[48] Benstock reads this chapter as being alternately voiced by Shaun and Shem in a polemic struggle for authorial control over the discourse concerning the letter, thereby reflecting the antagonism that has been traditionally ascribed to this odd pair ever since Campbell and Robinson's *Skeleton-Key* (Bernard Benstock, "Concerning Lost Historeve," *A Conceptual Guide to "Finnegans Wake,"* eds. Michael H. Begnal and Fritz Senn, University Park: The Pennsylvania State UP, 1974. 33–55. cf. esp. 48–49). In this chapter, there is indeed such a polemic between the writing or creation of the letter (evinced through the scrim of discourse in the tenor of manuscript study) and the delivery of the letter (the postal study). In other words there is a polemic between a "Shem discourse" and a "Shaun discourse," but neither mode is pure and each irreparably contaminates the other. Perhaps Shem and Shaun (as such) are only asymptotic, hypothetical poles around which the discourse concerning the letter is produced and circulates.

[49] The not-entirely-suppressed lasciviousness in this description is not inappropriate to other figurations of *The Book of Kells* in the *Wake*. Atherton's comment on the following line is helpful, "all the French leaves unveilable out of Calomnequiller's Pravities [the manuscript for *The Book of Kells* was discovered in a monastery founded by Colum Cille; also *calumniator*]" (FW: 050.09-10); "'French leaves' means missing leaves—there are at least sixty pages missing from the extant manuscript, but it also means 'obscene pages'—the depravity of which cannot be veiled or concealed" (Atherton 1959, 63). The descriptions of the multiple aspects of the polyhedron are linked (via, among others, *The Book of Kells*) by this notion of the *ob-scene*, it may be smutty, but it has also vanished.

[50] Augustine is illustrative of this tradition. In *On Christian Doctrine* he calls make-up a distortion of natural appearance since it supplements the face that God had created. It adds a layer of human grit and artifice to God's creation, thereby masking God's truth (Augustine, *On Christian Doctrine,* trans. D.W. Robertson, jr, New York: Macmillan, 1958. IV.21). But he also admits that verbal *ornamentation* is necessary for clear discourse if it stands grounded in *caritas*. Through the simile of cosmetics, Augustine illustrates the danger of superfice, the danger of ungrounded supplementarity. But his argument is itself grounded in and by the cosmetic illustration he has proffered. As Leonardi Bruni wrote, in another example of the trope of superfice, the outward garment remains essential to the health of body and mind (quoted in Renato Barilli, *Rhetoric,* trans. Giuliana Menozzi, Minneapolis: U of Minnesota P, 1989. 56). Truth, such as it might have been, is uneasily dissociable from the tropes it wears.

[51] "It is perhaps because Mallarmé does not set out to propose, in *La dernière mode,* an autonomous realm of language, that he very nearly succeeds in doing so" (Judy Kravis, *The Prose of Mallarmé,* Cambridge: Cambridge UP, 1976. 105. cf. 87–107).

[52] Lucia Boldrini, "Let Dante Be Silent... Wakean Transformations of Dante's Theory of Polysemy," unpublished paper.

[53] Alexander Pope, "Dunciad," *Selected Poetry and Prose,* second edition, ed. William K. Wimsatt, New York: Holt, Rinehart and Winston, 1972. 443–514. I.64.

[54] According to one Kabbalistic tradition, all evil and human suffering in this world originally through the gash of a mistranscribed letter when God dictated the

Torah (Ira Nadel, *Joyce and the Jews,* London: Macmillan, 1989. 5). Nadel also identifies other typological affinities between Talmudic Judaism and *Finnegans Wake*, such as the notion of a text intercalated with its own commentary in progress (most notably in the hierarchized marginal commentary in II.2; cf. Nadel, 108–18).

Another resonance to the burial of the letter was discovered by Adaline Glasheen who noted that the dual aspect of Issy derives in part from the account by a Boston psychiatrist of a female patient who suffered multiple personalities. One of these personalities, the vivacious Sally, wrote an autobiography which she then buried secretly near Boston. This would be one reason behind the consistent topographical association of the letter and Boston (Adaline Glasheen, "*Finnegans Wake* and the Girls from Boston, Mass.," *Critical Essays on James Joyce's "Finnegans Wake,"* ed. Patrick A. McCarthy, New York: Macmillan, 1992. 169–75. cf. esp. 173–74; cf. Milesi 1990, 98). The vector of reference in *Finnegans Wake* suffers from multiple personalities.

[55] In this way, the fate of the letter could be taken as an example (albeit extreme) of Jerome McGann's notion of the textual condition (which follows closely from Genette's notion of the paratext): the text is understood as a phenomenal and material event and it is constituted or bound in multiple ways which effect it variously. The text is never self-identical or autotelic due to the variability and inevitable fallibility of its material textualizations (Jerome J. McGann, *The Textual Condition,* Princeton: Princeton UP, 1991. cf. esp. 3–16).

McGann emphasizes the materialism and physicality which is necessary for the transmission and communication, even as this materiality could be said to disturb communication by inscribing it into a sphere of contiguity and circumstantiality. Surprisingly, McGann's work is not entirely without affinity to Blanchot. Blanchot admits of the material and empirical aspect of the book (the book as cultural commodity, cf. *L'entretien infini,* Paris: Gallimard, 1969. 621–22), but for Blanchot there is also something else, neither more nor less, which is intimately consociated with the always flawed publication of the book. We will return to this point at the close of this book.

[56] This of course echoes Stephen's stab at Platonism in *Ulysses*: "Horseness is the whatness of allhorse" (U: 9.84–85). The implication is that the Platonic form is some hypothesized metonymic perfection that subsumes and *in-forms* any and all imperfect equine iterations into a genre of horse (cf. Vincent Cheng, "White Horse, Dark Horse: Joyce's Allhorse of Another Color," *Joyce Studies Annual* 2 [1991]: 101–28.

101–4, 111–12). The possibility of such generic proclamations are *inverted* by the photoist's discovery of his melted negative. There is thus no *horse text*.

[57] The artifact has been discovered by the hen at the fated hour of midnight (FW: 111.08), an hour which is also associated with the crime (see note 25), which would explain the problematic insistence of the twelve o'clock scholars in their efforts of reconstitution and redefinition (see our argument on page 248 and following).

[58] This refers to the incident of Buckley shooting the Russian General because he had been disgusted after seeing the latter absterge his podex with a sod of prime Irish turf (cf. esp. FW: 344.21–345.03). This miniature anecdote is highly woven into the *Wake* as a differently repeated nodal pattern. It appears as one of the names of the untitled mamafesta, "*How Buckling Shut at Rush in January*" (105.21–22). Through the "sod of turb," the artifact is thus a metonym of this story which is itself a metonym of the letter.

[59] The major recurrent epistolary tropes are: "A beautiful present of wedding cakes"; "transhipt from Boston (Mass.)"; "born gentleman"; "poor Father Michael"; "Maggy... Muggy... Maggy"; "dear thankyou"; and "four crosskisses." Benstock lists all of these except for the crosskisses (Benstock 1974, 36–39).

[60] Margaret Solomon has convincingly demonstrated a persistence of a network of consociation in the *Wake* between tea, urine, semen and effluvia. For example, in the letter-version above the post-script, "pee-ess" is a stain supplemented by a teastain (Margaret C. Solomon, *Eternal Geomater,* Carbondale: Southern Illinois UP, 1969. 77–80). Some genre of sexual corruption is always proximate to the textual corruption suffered by the letter.

[61] The crime is more strongly suggested later in this chapter where its tropes are further convolved with the tropes of the letter: "Let a prostitute be whoso stands before a door and winks or parks herself in the fornix near a makeussin wall (sinsin! sinsin!) and the curate one who brings strong waters (gingin! gingin!), but also, and dinna forget, that there is many asleeps between someathome's first and moreinausland's last and that the beautiful presence of waiting kates will until life's (!) be more than enough to make any milkmike in the language of sweet tarts punch hell's hate into his twin nicky and that Maggy's tea, or your majesty, if heard as a boost from a born gentleman is (?)" (FW: 116.16–25).

[62] This also recalls the Museyroom episode by two distinct yet interconnecting paths of refiguration. Shortly after the Museyroom there is a brief and condensed

iteration of the letter out of the heap (recurrent tropes are emphasized and their referent from page 111 is interpolated): "*bostoan nightgarters and masses of shoesets* [transhipt from Boston (Mass.)] and nickelly nacks and *foder allmicheal* [poor Father Michael] and *a lugly parson of cates* [beautiful present of wedding cakes] and howitzer *muchears and midgers and maggets* [Maggy... Muggy... Maggy], ills and ells with loffs of toffs and pleures of bells and the last sigh that come fro the hart (bucklied!) and the fairest sin that sunsaw (that's cearc!). With *Kiss. Kiss Criss. Cross Cris. Kiss Cross* [four crosskisses]. Undo lives 'end. Slain" (FW: 011.22–28). This passage contains all the recurrent tropes except for the "born gentleman (indeed in his list of the recurrent tropes, Benstock omits this one from this passage [Benstock 1974, 37]). The gentleman does unmistakably appear a page earlier in the Museyroom passage when Willingdone is called a "bornstable ghentleman" (FW: 010.17–18) (when asked if he were Irish, Wellington fatuously responded: "If a gentleman happens to be born in a stable, it does not follow that he should be called a horse"). At one point in the Museyroom battle of "loowater carnage" (VI.B. 15:74; JJA 32: 287), Willingdone arms his "Grand *Mons* Injun" (FW: 008.30; emphasis added). And so the born gentleman and his Mons (not to mention the other epistolary tropes) recur with and by the hen, having been retooled into a different engine.

[63] This would be why in III.1 Shaun cannot describe the letter without periphrastic persiflage, his delivery is always highly circuitous. The account of this interrogation is also, appropriately, prevaricated (cf. esp. FW: 412.13–414.21). He is also asked to "vouchsafe to say" (424.15) why he hates Shem and the only answer he can find in the heap of his mind is "For his root language" (424.17), a root language that he shares.

[64] A description of Shem also reinforces the intervallic notion of *hanno o non hanno*: "[Shem] used to stipple endlessly inartistic portraits of himself in the act of reciting old Nichiabelli's monolook interyear *Hanno, o Nonanno, acce'l brubblemm'*as, ser Autore, q.e.d." (FW:182.18–21).

[65] This is a reference to Oliver Wendell Holmes's *The Professor at the Breakfast-Table*. The contextualization or scene-setting is thus accomplished within the same broken or "bruised brogue" (FW: 429.04–5) as the letter and is thus seemingly as liable to misreading.

[66] Only some of these marks are phonetic, bîn is approximate to the phonetic rendering of "been," *bi:n*; there is no consistency underlying this typographic profusion.

[67] This passage thus also refers to the *Book of Kells,* which was dated by a noble analysis of its punctuation marks (Atherton 1959, 66).

Bibliography

Agamben, Giorgio. "Il sogno della lingua: per una lettura di Polifilo." *Lettere italiane* 34.4 (1982): 466–81.

Alighieri, Dante. *Rime*. Ed. Gianfranco Contini. Turin: Einaudi, 1939, 1995.
——. *La divina commedia*. Ed. Fredi Chiappelli. Milan: Mursia, 1965.
——. *Convivio*. Ed. Piero Cudini. Milan: Garzanti, 1980.
——. *La vita nuova*. Ed. Marcello Ciccuto. Milan: Rizzoli, 1984.
——. *Monarchia*. Ed. and trans. Frederico Sanguineti. Milan: Garzanti, 1985.
——. *De vulgari eloquentia*. Ed. Vittorio Coletti. Milan: Garzanti, 1991.
——. *Epistolam ad Canem Grandem della Scalla*. Opere Minori, volume III, tomo II. Eds. Arsenio Frugoni, Giorgio Brugnoli, Enzo Cecchini, and Francesco Mazzoni. Milan: Riccardo Riccardi, 1996. 599–643.

Almansi, Guido. *The Writer as Liar*. London: Routledge and Kegan Paul, 1975.

Aquinas, Thomas. *An Aquinas Reader*. Ed. and trans. Mary T. Clark. New York: Image Books, 1972.

Arnold, Bruce. *The Scandal of "Ulysses."* London: Sinclair-Stevenson, 1991.

Asenjo, F.G. "The General Problem of Sentence Structure: An Analysis Prompted by the Loss of Subject in *Finnegans Wake*." *Centennial Review of Arts and Sciences* VIII (1964): 398–408.

Atherton, James S. *The Books at the Wake*. Carbondale: Southern Illinois UP, 1959.
——. "Shaun A." *A Conceptual Guide to "Finnegans Wake."* Eds. Michael H. Begnal and Fritz Senn. University Park: The Pennsylvania State UP, 1974. 149–72.

Attridge, Derek. "Unpacking the Portmanteau, or Who's Afraid of *Finnegans Wake*?" *On Puns*. Ed. Jonathan Culler. London: Blackwell, 1988. 140–55.
——. *Peculiar Language*. Ithaca: Cornell UP, 1988.
——. "Finnegans Awake: The Dream of Interpretation." *JJQ* 27.1 (Fall 1989): 11–29.

Aubert, Jacques. "Riverrun." *Change* 11 (1972): 120–30.

Augustine. *On Christian Doctrine*. Trans. D.W. Robertson, jr. New York: Macmillan, 1958.

——. *The Confessions*. Trans. John K. Ryan. Garden City: Image, 1960.

——. *De Civitate Dei*. Ed. and trans. Eva Matthews Sanford and William MacAllen Green. Cambridge: Harvard UP, 1965.

Baldelli, Ignazio. "Realtà personale e corporale di Beatrice." *Beatrice nell'opera di Dante e nella memoria europea 1290–1990*. Ed. Maria Picchio Simonelli. Naples: Cadmo, 1994. 137–155.

Barbier, Carl. *Documents Mallarmé I*. Paris: Nizet, 1968.

Barilli, Renato. *Rhetoric*. Trans. Giuliana Menozzi. Minneapolis: U of Minnesota P, 1989.

Barolini, Teodolinda. *The Undivine Comedy: Detheologizing Dante*. Princeton: Princeton UP, 1993.

Baron, Naomi S., and Nikhil Bhattacharya. "Vico and Joyce: The Limits of Language." *Vico and Joyce*. Ed. Donald Phillip Verene. Albany: SUNY P, 1987. 175–95.

Bataille, Georges. *L'expérience intérieure*. Paris: Gallimard, 1954.

——. *La littérature et le mal*. Paris: Gallimard, 1957.

——. *Œuvres complètes, I*. Paris: Gallimard, 1970.

——. *Œuvres complètes, VIII*. Paris: Gallimard, 1976.

——. *Œuvres complètes, X*. Paris: Gallimard, 1987.

——. "Le silence de *Molloy*." *Œuvres complètes, XII*. Paris: Gallimard, 1988. 85–94.

Baudelaire, Charles. *Œuvres complètes, I*. Ed. Claude Pichois. Paris: Gallimard, 1975.

Bauerle, Ruth. *The James Joyce Songbook*. New York: Garland, 1982.

Beckett, Samuel. "Dante... Bruno. Vico.. Joyce" *Our Exagmination Round His Factification For Incamination Of Work In Progress*. Samuel Beckett, *et al*. New York: New Directions, 1939. 1–22.

——. *More Pricks Than Kicks*. London: Calder & Boyars, 1934.

——. *Trilogy: Molloy, Malone Dies, The Unnamable*. London: John Calder, 1959.

——. *Proust*. London: John Calder, 1965.

——. *Worstward Ho*. New York: Grove, 1983.

Begnal, Michael H. *Dreamscheme: Narrative and Voice in Finnegans Wake*. Syracuse: Syracuse UP, 1988.

Bénichou, Paul. *Selon Mallarmé*. Paris: Gallimard, 1995.

Benstock, Bernard. *Joyce-Again's Wake*. Seattle: U of Washington P, 1965.
——. "Every Telling Has a Taling: A Reading of the Narrative of *Finnegans Wake*." *MFS* XV.1 (Spring 1969): 3–25.
——. "Concerning Lost Historeve." *A Conceptual Guide to "Finnegans Wake."* Eds. Michael H. Begnal and Fritz Senn. University Park: Pennsylvania State UP, 1974. 33–55.
——. *James Joyce*. New York: Frederick Ungar, 1985.
——. *Narrative Con/Texts in "Ulysses."* U of Illinois P, 1991.
——. "Cataloguing in *Finnegans Wake*: counting counties." *Joyce in Context*. Eds. Vincent J. Cheng and Timothy Martin. Cambridge: Cambridge UP, 1992. 259–69.

Benstock, Shari. "Is He a Jew or a Gentile or A Holy Roman?" *JJQ* 16.4 (Summer 1979): 493–97.
——. "In Excess of 'And': David Hayman's *Joyce et Mallarmé*." *Re-Viewing Classics of Joyce Scholarship*. Ed. Janet Egleson Dunleavy. Urbana: U of Illinois P, 1991. 186–99.

Benstock, Shari and Bernard Benstock. *Who's He When He's at Home: A James Joyce Directory*. Urbana: U of Illinois P, 1980.
——. "The Benstock Principle." *The Seventh of Joyce*. Ed. Bernard Benstock. Bloomington: Indiana UP, 1982. 10–21.

Bernard, Suzanne. *Mallarmé et la musique*. Paris: Nizet, 1959.

Bersani, Leo. *The Death of Stéphane Mallarmé*. Cambridge: Cambridge UP, 1982.

Bishop, John. *Joyce's Book of the Dark*. Madison: U of Wisconsin P, 1986.

Blanchot, Maurice. *Faux pas*. Paris: Gallimard, 1943.
——. *La part du feu*. Paris: Gallimard, 1949.
——. *L'espace littéraire*. Paris: Gallimard, 1955, 1988.
——. *Le livre à venir*. Paris: Gallimard, 1959, 1986.
——. *Lautréamont et Sade*. Paris: Minuit, 1963.
——. *L'entretien infini*. Paris: Gallimard, 1969.
——. *L'amitié*. Paris: Gallimard, 1971.
——. "Le dernier à parler." *Revue de belles lettres* 2–3 (1972): 171–83.
——. *La folie du jour*. Montpellier: Fata Morgana, 1973.
——. *Le pas au-delà*. Paris: Gallimard, 1973.

——. *L'écriture du désastre.* Paris: Gallimard, 1980.

Blume, Friedrich. *Two Centuries of Bach.* Trans. Stanley Goodman. Oxford: Oxford UP, 1950.

Boccaccio, Giovanni. *Esposizioni sopra la Commedia di Dante.* Ed. Giorgio Padoan. *Tutte le opere di Giovanni Boccaccio, volume 6.* Ed. V. Branca. Milan: Mondadori, 1965.

Boldrini, Lucia. "Let Dante Be Silent... Wakean Transformations of Dante's Theory of Polysemy." Unpublished paper.

Bonheim, Helmut. *A Lexicon of the German in "Finnegans Wake."* Berkeley: U of California P, 1967.

Bonnefoy, Yves. "The Poetics of Mallarmé." Trans. Elaine Ancekewicz. *Yale French Studies* 54 (1977): 9–21.

Booth, Wayne. *The Rhetoric of Fiction.* Second edition. Chicago: U of Chicago P, 1961, 1983.

Borges, Jorge Luis. *Labyrinths.* Trans. John M. Fein *et al.* New York: Penguin, 1964.
——. *A Universal History of Infamy.* Trans. Norman Thomas di Giovanni. Harmondsworth: Penguin, 1975.
——. "The Book of Sand." Trans. Norman Thomas di Giovanni. *The Book of Sand.* Harmondsworth: Penguin, 1975. 87–91.
——. "Beatrice's Last Smile." Trans. Virginia Múzquiz. *Dispositio* XVIII.45 (1993): 23–25.

Boscolo, U. ed. *Enciclopedia Dantesca.* Rome: Instituto dell'Enciclopedia Italiana, 1970–78.

Bougnoux, Daniel. "L'éclat du signe." *Littérature* 14 (May 1974): 83–93.

Bowie, Malcom. *Mallarmé and the Art of Being Difficult.* Cambridge: Cambridge UP, 1978.
——. "The Question of *Un coup de dés.*" *Baudelaire, Mallarmé, Valéry: New Essays in Honour of Lloyd Austin.* Eds. Malcom Bowie, Alison Fairlie, and Alison Finch. Cambridge: Cambridge UP, 1982. 142–50.

Budgen, Frank. *James Joyce and the Making of "Ulysses."* Oxford: Oxford UP, 1968.

Buttigieg, Joseph A. *"A Portrait of the Artist" in Different Perspective*. Athens: Ohio UP, 1987.

Cachey, Theodore J., Jr. *Introduction. Renaissance Dante in Print (1472–1629)*. Online. Internet. January 3, 1996.

Cadbury, Bill. "The Development of the 'Eye, Ear, Nose and Throat Witness' Testimony in I.4." *Probes: Genetic Studies in Joyce*. Eds. David Hayman and Sam Slote. Amsterdam: Rodopi, 1995. 203–54.

Campbell, Joseph, and Henry Morton Robinson. *A Skeleton Key to "Finnegans Wake."* Harmondsworth: Penguin, 1961.

Carpenter, William. *Death and Marriage: Structural Metaphors for the Work of Art in Joyce and Mallarmé*. New York: Garland, 1988.

Celan, Paul. *Collected Prose*. Trans. Rosmarie Waldrop. New York: Sheep Meadow Press, 1986.

Cheng, Vincent. *Shakespeare and Joyce*. Gerrards Cross: Colin Smythe, 1984.
———. "White Horse, Dark Horse: Joyce's Allhorse of Another Color." *Joyce Studies Annual* 2 (1991): 101–28.

Chiarenza, Marguerite Mills. "The Imageless Vision and Dante's *Paradiso*." *Dante Studies* XC (1972): 77–91.

Christiani, Dounia. *Scandinavian Elements of "Finnegans Wake."* Evanston: Northwestern UP, 1965.

Cohn, R.G. *L'œuvre de Mallarmé: "Un coup de dés."* Paris: Les Lettres, 1951.
———. *Mallarmé's Masterwork: New Findings*. The Hague: Mouton, 1966.
———. *Towards the Poems of Mallarmé*. Revised edition. Berkeley: U of California P, 1980.
———. *Mallarmé's "Divagations."* New York: Peter Lang, 1990.
———. *Vues sur Mallarmé*. Paris: Nizet, 1991.

Collin, Françoise. *Maurice Blanchot et la question de l'écriture*. Paris: Gallimard, 1971, 1986.

Colum, Mary and Padraic Colum. *Our Friend James Joyce*. New York: Doubleday, 1958.

Costa, Paolo. Commentary, 1819. *Dartmouth Dante Project.* Online, Internet. October 27, 1995.

Copeland, Rita. *Rhetoric, Hermeneutics, and Translation in the Middle Ages.* Cambridge: Cambridge UP, 1991.

Curtius, Ernst Robert. *European Literature and the Latin Middle Ages.* Trans. Willard R. Trask. Princeton: Princeton UP, 1953.

Dalton, Jack. "The Text of *Ulysses.*" *New Light on Joyce.* Ed. Fritz Senn. Bloomington: Indiana UP, 1972. 99–119.

D'Andria, Michele. *Beatrice simbolo della poesia con Dante dalla terra a dio.* Rome: Ateneo and Bizzarri, 1979.

Davies, Gardner. *Mallarmé et la « couche suffisante d'intelligibilité ».* Paris: José Corti, 1988.

———. *Vers une explication rationnelle du « coup de dés ».* Nouvelle edition. Paris: José Corti, 1992.

de Campos, Augusto. "Le coup de dés de *Finnegans Wake.*" Trans. Isabelle Meyreles. *Revue Littéraire Mensuelle.* 657–58 (January–February 1984): 112–15.

de Lungo, Isidoro. Commentary, 1926. *Dartmouth Dante Project.* Online, Internet. October 26, 1995.

de Man, Paul. *Allegories of Reading.* New Haven: Yale UP, 1979.

———. *Blindness and Insight.* Revised edition. Minneapolis: U of Minnesota P, 1983.

———. *The Rhetoric of Romanticism.* New York: Columbia UP, 1984.

———. "Lyrical Voice in Contemporary Theory: Riffaterre and Jauss." *Lyric Poetry: Beyond New Criticism.* Ed. Chaviva Hošek and Patricia Parker. Ithaca: Cornell UP, 1985. 55–72.

———. *The Resistance to Theory.* Minneapolis: U of Minnesota P, 1986.

———. *Critical Writings, 1953–1978.* Ed. Lindsay Waters. Minneapolis: U of Minnesota P, 1989.

della Lana, Jacopo. Commentary, 1324. *Dartmouth Dante Project.* Online, Internet. October 24, 1995.

De Robertis, Domenico. *Il libro della "Vita Nuova."* Second edition. Florence: Sansoni, 1970.

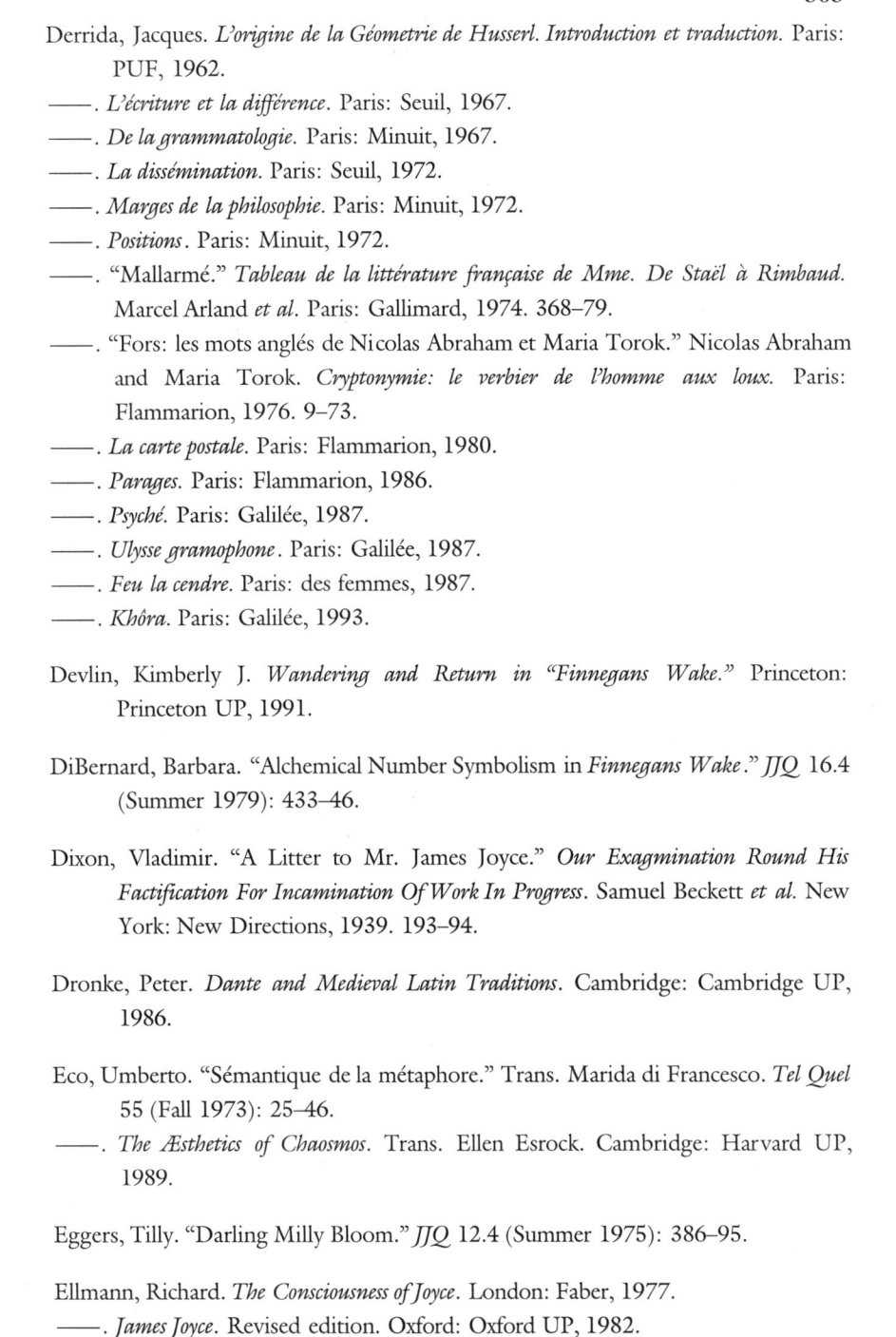

Derrida, Jacques. *L'origine de la Géometrie de Husserl. Introduction et traduction.* Paris: PUF, 1962.
———. *L'écriture et la différence.* Paris: Seuil, 1967.
———. *De la grammatologie.* Paris: Minuit, 1967.
———. *La dissémination.* Paris: Seuil, 1972.
———. *Marges de la philosophie.* Paris: Minuit, 1972.
———. *Positions.* Paris: Minuit, 1972.
———. "Mallarmé." *Tableau de la littérature française de Mme. De Staël à Rimbaud.* Marcel Arland *et al.* Paris: Gallimard, 1974. 368–79.
———. "Fors: les mots anglés de Nicolas Abraham et Maria Torok." Nicolas Abraham and Maria Torok. *Cryptonymie: le verbier de l'homme aux loux.* Paris: Flammarion, 1976. 9–73.
———. *La carte postale.* Paris: Flammarion, 1980.
———. *Parages.* Paris: Flammarion, 1986.
———. *Psyché.* Paris: Galilée, 1987.
———. *Ulysse gramophone.* Paris: Galilée, 1987.
———. *Feu la cendre.* Paris: des femmes, 1987.
———. *Khôra.* Paris: Galilée, 1993.

Devlin, Kimberly J. *Wandering and Return in "Finnegans Wake."* Princeton: Princeton UP, 1991.

DiBernard, Barbara. "Alchemical Number Symbolism in *Finnegans Wake*." *JJQ* 16.4 (Summer 1979): 433–46.

Dixon, Vladimir. "A Litter to Mr. James Joyce." *Our Exagmination Round His Factification For Incamination Of Work In Progress.* Samuel Beckett *et al.* New York: New Directions, 1939. 193–94.

Dronke, Peter. *Dante and Medieval Latin Traditions.* Cambridge: Cambridge UP, 1986.

Eco, Umberto. "Sémantique de la métaphore." Trans. Marida di Francesco. *Tel Quel* 55 (Fall 1973): 25–46.
———. *The Æsthetics of Chaosmos.* Trans. Ellen Esrock. Cambridge: Harvard UP, 1989.

Eggers, Tilly. "Darling Milly Bloom." *JJQ* 12.4 (Summer 1975): 386–95.

Ellmann, Richard. *The Consciousness of Joyce.* London: Faber, 1977.
———. *James Joyce.* Revised edition. Oxford: Oxford UP, 1982.

Ferris, Kathleen. *James Joyce and the Burden of Disease*. Lexington: UP of Kentucky, 1995.

Flaubert, Gustave. *Bouvard et Pécuchet*. Paris: Flammarion, 1966.
———. *Correspondance, Volume II*. Ed. Jean Bruneau. Paris: Gallimard, 1980.

Fontanier, Pierre. *Les figures du discours*. Paris: Flammarion, 1968.

Franke, William. *Dante's Interpretive Journey*. Chicago: The U of Chicago P, 1996.

Freccero, John. *Dante: The Poetics of Conversion*. Ed. Rachel Jacoff. Cambridge: Harvard UP, 1986.

Freud, Sigmund. *Jokes and their Relationship to the Unconscious. Standard Edition of the Complete Psychological Works of Sigmund Freud*, volume 8. Ed. and trans. James Strachey. London: Hogarth, 1960.

Frey, Hans-Jost. *Studies in Poetic Discourse*. Trans. William Whobry. Stanford: Stanford UP, 1996.

Froment-Meurice, Marc. *Solitudes*. Paris: Galilée, 1989.

Gasché, Rodolphe. *Inventions of Difference*. Cambridge: Harvard UP, 1994.

Gaskell, Philip and Clive Hart. *"Ulysses": A Review of Three Texts*. Gerrards Cross: Colin Smythe, 1989.

Genette, Gérard. "Bonheur de Mallarmé?" *Figures I*. Paris: Seuil, 1966. 91–100.
———. *Figures III*. Paris: Seuil, 1972.
———. *Seuils*. Paris: Seuil, 1987.

Gifford, Don. *Joyce Annotated*. Second edition. Berkeley: U of California P, 1982.

Gifford, Don, and Robert J. Seidman. *"Ulysses" Annotated*. Second edition. Berkeley: U of California P, 1988.

Gilbert, Stuart. "Prolegomena to Work in Progress." *Our Exagmination Round His Factification For Incamination Of Work In Progress*. Samuel Beckett *et al*. New York: New Directions, 1939. 47–75.
———. *James Joyce's "Ulysses."* Revised edition. New York: Vintage, 1952.
———. *Reflections on James Joyce, Stuart Gilbert's Paris Journal*. Ed. T. Staley and R. Lewis. Austin: U of Texas P, 1993.

Gillespie, Michael Patrick. *Reading the Book of Himself.* Columbus: Ohio State UP, 1989.

Gillet, Louis. *Claybook for James Joyce.* Trans. George Markow-Totevy. London: Abelard-Schuman, 1958.

Gilson, Étienne. *Dante et Béatrice.* Paris: Vrin, 1974.

Glasheen, Adaline. *Third Census of "Finnegans Wake."* Berkeley: U of California P, 1977.

———. *"Finnegans Wake* and the Girls from Boston, Mass." *Critical Essays on James Joyce's "Finnegans Wake."* Ed. Patrick A. McCarthy. New York: Macmillan, 1992. 169–75.

Goldwasser, Thomas A. "Who Was Vladimir Dixon? Was He Vladimir Dixon?" *JJQ* 16.3 (Spring 1979): 219–22.

Goodkin, Richard E. *The Symbolist Home and the Tragic Home: Mallarmé and Œdipus.* Amsterdam: John Benjamins Publishing, 1984.

Gordon, John. *"Finnegans Wake": A Plot Summary.* Syracuse: Syracuse UP, 1986.

Green, Richard Hamilton. "Dante's 'Allegory of the Poets' and Medieval Theory of Poetic Fiction." *Comparative Literature* 9.2 (Spring 1957): 118–28.

Harrison, Robert Pogue. *The Body of Beatrice.* Baltimore: Johns Hopkins UP, 1988.

Hart, Clive. *Structure and Motif in "Finnegans Wake."* London: Faber, 1962.

———. *A Concordance to "Finnegans Wake."* Corrected edition. Mamaroneck: Paul P. Appel, 1974.

———. *"Finnegans Wake* in Adjusted Perspective." *Critical Essays on James Joyce's "Finnegans Wake."* Ed. Patrick A. McCarthy. New York: Macmillan, 1992. 15–33.

———. "Fritz in the Early Awning." *A Collideorscape of Joyce.* Eds. Ruth Frehner and Ursula Zeller. Dublin: Lilliput, 1998. 4–10.

Hart, Clive, and G.C. Sandulescu. Eds. *Assessing the 1984 "Ulysses."* Gerrards Cross: Colin Smythe, 1986.

Hawkins, Peter S. "Dante's *Paradiso* and the Dialectic of Ineffability." *Ineffability.* Eds. Peter S. Hawkins and Anne Howland Schotter. New York: AMS, 1984. 5–21.

Hayman, David. *Joyce et Mallarmé*. 2 volumes. Paris: Lettres Modernes, 1956.

———. "Dramatic Motion in *Finnegans Wake*." *The University of Texas Studies in English* XXXVII (1958): 155–76.

———. "From *Finnegans Wake*: A Sentence in Progress." *PMLA* 63 (March 1958): 136–54.

———. "Dædalian Imagery in *A Portrait of the Artist as a Young Man*." *Hereditas: Seven Essays on the Modern Experience of the Classical*. Ed. Frederick Will. Austin: U of Texas P, 1964. 33–54.

———. "The Empirical Molly." *Approaches to "Ulysses": Ten Essays*. Eds. Thomas Staley and Bernard Benstock. Pittsburgh: U of Pittsburgh P, 1970. 103–35.

———. "Language Of/As Gesture in Joyce." *Ulysse: Cinquante ans après*. Ed. Louis Bonnerot. Paris: Didier, 1974. 209–21.

———. "Cyclops." *James Joyce's "Ulysses."* Eds. Clive Hart and David Hayman. Berkeley: U of California P, 1974. 243–75.

———. "Two Eyes at Two Levels: A Response to Herbert Schneidau on Joyce's 'Cyclops.'" *JJQ* 16.1–2 (Fall 1978–Winter 1979): 105–9.

———. *"Ulysses": The Mechanics of Meaning*. Revised edition. Madison: U of Wisconsin P, 1982.

———. "James Joyce, Paratactitian." *Contemporary Literature* XXVI.2 (1985): 155–78.

———. "Reading the End of a Wake." *Myriadminded Man*. Eds. Rosa Maria Bosinelli, Paola Pugliatti, and Romana Zacchi. Bologna: CLUEB, 1986. 269–76.

———. *Re-Forming the Narrative*. Ithaca: Cornell UP, 1987.

———. *The "Wake" in Transit*. Ithaca: Cornell UP, 1990.

———. "The Manystorytold of the *Wake*: How Narrative Was Made to Inform the Non-Narrativity of the Night." *Joyce Studies Annual* 8 (1997): 81–114.

———. "Beckett." Unpublished.

Heath, Stephen. "'Ambiviolences': Notes pour la lecture de Joyce." *Tel Quel* 50 (Summer 1972): 22–43.

———. "'Ambiviolences' 2." *Tel Quel* 51 (Autumn 1972): 64–76.

Heidegger, Martin. *An Introduction to Metaphysics*. Trans. Ralph Manheim. New Haven: Yale UP, 1959.

———. *Being and Time*. Trans. John Macquarrie and Edward Robinson. New York: Harper and Row, 1962.

———. *On the Way to Language*. Trans. Peter D. Hertz. San Francisco: Harper and Row, 1971.

———. *Poetry, Language, Thought*. Trans. Albert Hofstadter. New York: Harper and Row, 1971.

———. *The Question Concerning Technology*. Trans. William Lovitt. New York: Harper and Row, 1977.

———. "Letter on Humanism." Trans. Frank Capuzzi, J. Glenn Gray, and David Krell. *Basic Writings*. Ed. David Krell. New York: Harper and Row, 1977. 189–242.

———. *Early Greek Thinking*. Trans. David Farrell Krell and Frank A. Capuzzi. New York: Harper and Row, 1984.

Heraclitus. *Fragments*. Ed. and trans. T. M. Robinson. Toronto: U of Toronto P, 1987.

Hill, Archibald A. "A Philologist Looks at *Finnegans Wake*." *Virginia Quarterly Review* XV (1939): 650–56.

Hill, Leslie. "Blanchot and Mallarmé." *MLN* 105 (1990): 889–913.

Hodgart, Matthew and Mabel Worthington. *Songs in the Work of James Joyce*. New York: Columbia UP, 1959.

Hollander, Robert. *Allegory in Dante's "Commedia."* Princeton: Princeton UP, 1969.
———. "Dante *Theologus-Poeta*." *Studies in Dante*. Ravenna: Longo, 1980. 39–89.
———. *Dante's Epistle to Cangrande*. Ann Arbor: U of Michigan P, 1993.

Hollier, Denis. "La littérature ne repose sur rien." *Critique* 431 (April 1983): 271–86.

Homer. *The Odyssey*. Trans. Richmond Lattimore. New York: Harper Collins, 1965.

Horace. *Ars Poetica. Épitres*. Ed. François Villeneuve. Paris: Belles Lettres, 1967. 181–227.

Huysmans, Joris-Karl. *À rebours*. Paris: Flammarion, 1978.

Irving, Washington. *Rip Van Winkle and The Legend of Sleepy Hollow*. San Diego: Harper Brace Jovanovich, 1984.

Johnson, Barbara. "*Les fleurs du mal armé*." *Lyric Poetry*. Eds. Chaviva Hošek and Patricia Parker. Ithaca: Cornell UP, 1985. 264–80.

Jolas, Eugene. "The Revolution of Language and James Joyce." *Our Exagmination Round His Factification For Incamination Of Work In Progress*. Samuel Beckett, et al. New York: New Directions, 1939. 77–92.

Josipovici, Gabriel. *The World and the Book*. London: Stanford UP, 1971.

Joyce, James. *Finnegans Wake*. New York: Viking, 1939.
———. *Letters; Volume I*. Ed. Stuart Gilbert. New York: Viking Press, 1957.
———. *Stephen Hero*. Eds. Theodore Spencer, John J. Slocum, and Herbert Cahoon. New York: New Directions, 1963.
———. *Letters; Volume II and III*. Ed. Richard Ellmann. New York: Viking Press, 1966.
———. *A Portrait of the Artist as a Young Man*. Ed. Chester G. Anderson. New York: Viking, 1968.
———. *Dubliners*. Eds. Robert Scholes and A. Walton Litz. New York: Viking, 1969.
———. *Selected Letters*. Ed. Richard Ellmann. London: Faber and Faber, 1975.
———. *The James Joyce Archive*. Eds. Michael Groden, Hans Walter Gabler, David Hayman, A. Walton Litz, and Danis Rose. New York: Garland, 1978.
———. *Ulysses: A Critical and Synoptic Edition*. Eds. Hans Walter Gabler, Wolfhard Steppe, and Claus Melchior. New York: Garland, 1984, 1986.
———. *Ulysses*. Eds. Hans Walter Gabler *et al*. New York: Vintage, 1986.
———. *Critical Writings*. Eds. Ellsworth Mason and Richard Ellmann. Ithaca: Cornell UP, 1989.
———. *Exiles*. London: Paladin, 1991.
———. *Poems and Shorter Writings*. Eds. Richard Ellmann, A. Walton Litz, and John Whittier-Ferguson. London: Faber and Faber, 1991.

Kaufmann, Vincent. *Le livre et ses adresses*. Paris: Méridiens Klincksieck, 1986.

Kenner, Hugh. *The Stoic Comedians*. Berkeley: U of California P, 1974.
———. *Joyce's Voices*. Berkeley: U of California P, 1978.
———. *Ulysses*. London: George Allen and Unwin, 1980.
———. *Dublin's Joyce*. New York: Columbia UP, 1987.

Kravis, Judy. *The Prose of Mallarmé*. Cambridge: Cambridge UP, 1976.

Kristeva, Julia. *La révolution du langage poétique*. Paris: Seuil 1974.
———. *Polylogue*. Paris: Seuil, 1977.

Kromer, Gretchen. "The Redoubtable PTYX." *MLN* 86.4 (May 1971): 563–72.

Kumar, Udaya. *The Joycean Labyrinth*. Oxford: Oxford UP, 1991.

Lacan, Jacques. "Joyce le symptôme I." *Joyce avec Lacan*. Ed. Jacques Aubert. Paris: Navarin, 1987. 21–29.

La Charité, Virginia A. *The Dynamics of Space*. Lexington: French Forum, 1987.

Lacoue-Labarthe, Philippe. *Musica ficta (figures de Wagner)*. Paris: Christian Bourgois, 1991.

Lansing, Richard H. *From Image to Idea*. Ravenna: Longo, 1977.

Laporte, Roger. *À l'extrême pointe: Bataille et Blanchot*. Montpellier: Fata Morgana, 1994.

Lawrence, Karen. *The Odyssey of Style in "Ulysses."* Princeton: Princeton UP, 1981.

Lebenstejn, Jean-Claude. "Note relative au *Coup de dés*." *Critique* 397–98 (June–July 1980): 633–59.

Lernout, Geert. "Dutch in *Finnegans Wake*." *JJQ* 23.1 (Fall 1985): 45–66.
———. *The French Joyce*. Ann Arbor: U of Michigan P, 1990.
———. "La critique textuelle anglo-américaine et le cas de *Ulysses* édité par Hans Walter Gabler." *Genesis* 9 (1996): 45–65.

Levin, Harry. *James Joyce*. Revised edition. Norfolk: New Directions, 1959.

Libertson, Joseph. *Proximity*. The Hague: Martinus Nijhoff, 1982.

Liddell, Henry George, and Robert Scott. Revised by Henry Stuart Jones, Roderick McKenzie, *et al*. *A Greek-English Lexicon*. 9th edition. Oxford: Oxford UP, 1940.

Littré, Emile. *Dictionnaire de la langue française*. Paris: Gallimard, 1965–68.

Lowe, Catherine. "Le mirage de ptyx: implications à la rime." *Poétqiue* 59 (September 1984): 325–45.

MacCabe, Colin. *James Joyce and the Revolution of the Word*. London: Macmillan, 1978.

Mallarmé, Stéphane. *Un coup de dés jamais n'abolira le hasard*. Paris: Gallimard, 1914, 1993.
———. *Œuvres complètes*. Eds. Henri Mondor and G. Jean-Aubry. Paris: Gallimard, 1945.
———. *Correspondances*. Volume I. Eds. Henri Mondor and Jean-Pierre Richard. Paris: Gallimard, 1956.
———. *Pour un tombeau d'Anatole*. Ed. Jean-Pierre Richard. Paris: Seuil, 1961.

———. *Correspondances*. Volumes II–XI. Eds. Henri Mondor and Lloyd James Austin. Paris: Gallimard, 1965–84.

———. *Un coup de dés jamais n'abolira le hasard*. Eds. Mitsou Ronat et al. Paris: Change/d'Atelier, 1980.

———. *Œuvres complètes. I. Poésies*. Eds. Carl Paul Barbier and Charles Gordon Millan. Paris: Flammarion, 1983.

Marchal, Bertrand. *Lecture de Mallarmé*. Paris: José Corti, 1985.

———. *La religion de Mallarmé*. Paris: José Corti, 1988.

———. "Éditer Mallarmé." *Genesis* 6 (1994): 167–77.

Marasso, Arturo. *El pensamiento secreto de Mallarmé*. Buenos Ares: Ollantay, 1948.

Martin, Jean-Paul. "La condensation." *Poétique* 26 (1976): 180–206.

Mauron, Charles. *Mallarmé l'obscur*. Paris: Champion-Slatkine, 1941.

Mazzotta, Guiseppe. *Dante, Poet of the Desert*. Princeton: Princeton UP, 1979.

———. "The Language of Poetry in the *Vita Nuova*." *Rivista di studi italiani*, 1.1 (June 1983): 3–15.

McCarthy, Patrick A. "The Last Epistle of *Finnegans Wake*." *Critical Essays on James Joyce's "Finnegans Wake."* Ed. Patrick A. McCarthy. New York: Macmillan, 1992. 96–103.

McGann, Jerome J. *The Textual Condition*. Princeton: Princeton UP, 1991.

McHugh, Roland. *The Sigla of "Finnegans Wake."* London: Edward Arnold, 1976.

———. *Annotations to "Finnegans Wake."* Baltimore: Johns Hopkins UP, 1980.

———. *The "Finnegans Wake" Experience*. Berkeley: U of California P, 1981.

———. *Annotations to "Finnegans Wake."* Revised edition. Baltimore: Johns Hopkins UP, 1991.

McLuhan, Eric. "The Rhetorical Structure of *Finnegans Wake*." *JJQ* 11.4 (Summer 1974): 394–403.

McLuhan, Marshall. "Joyce, Mallarmé and the Press." *Sewanee Review* 62 (1954): 38–55.

Mengaldo, Pier Vincenzo. *Linguistica e retorica di Dante*. Pisa: Nistri-Lischi, 1978.

Milesi, Laurent. "L'idiome babélien de *Finnegans Wake*." *Genèse de Babel, Joyce et la création*. Ed. Claude Jacquet. Paris: CNRS, 1986. 155–215.

——. "Vico... Jousse. Joyce.. Langue." *James Joyce: "Scribble" 1, genèse des textes*. Ed. Claude Jacquet. Paris: Lettres Modernes, 1988.

——. "Toward a Female Grammar of Sexuality: The De/Recomposition of 'Storiella as she is syung.'" *MFS* 35.3 (1989): 569–86.

——. "Metaphors of the Quest in *Finnegans Wake*." *"Finnegans Wake": Fifty Years*. Ed. Geert Lernout. Amsterdam: Rodopi, 1990. 79–107.

——. "The Perversions of 'Aerse' and the Anglo-Irish Middle Voice in *Finnegans Wake*." *Joyce Studies Annual* 4 (1993): 98–118.

Miller, Paul Allen. "Black and White Myths: Etymology and Dialectics in Mallarmé's 'Sonnet en yx.'" *Texas Studies in Literature and Language* 36.2 (Summer 1994): 184–211.

Mink, Louis O. *A "Finnegans Wake" Gazetteer*. Bloomington: Indiana UP, 1978.

Mirham, Danielle. "The Abortive Didot/Vollard Edition of *Un coup de dés*." *French Studies* XXXIII.1 (January 1979): 39–56.

Mondor, Henri. *Vie de Mallarmé*. Paris: Gallimard, 1941.

Montbertrand, Gérard. "'À la nue...' ou le déshabillage d'un poème de Mallarmé." *Nineteenth Century French Studies* 15.3 (Spring 1987): 285–301.

Morris, D. Hampton. *Stéphane Mallarmé, 20th Century Criticism 1901–71*. Valencia: Romance Monographs, 1977.

Murray, James, *et al*. Eds. *The Complete Oxford English Dictionary*. Oxford: Oxford UP, 1933.

Myers, Peter. *The Sound of "Finnegans Wake."* London: Macmillan, 1992.

Nabokov, Vladimir. *Pale Fire*. New York: Berkley, 1968.

Nadel, Ira. *Joyce and the Jews*. London: Macmillan, 1989.

Nagy, Gregory. *The Best of the Achæans*. Baltimore: Johns Hopkins UP, 1979.

Nancy, Jean-Luc. "Exscription." Trans. Katherine Lydon. *The Birth to Presence*. Stanford: Stanford UP, 1993. 319–40.

Nardi, Bruno. *Dante e la cultura medievale*. New edition. Ed. Paolo Mazzantini. Bari: Laterza, 1983.

Newman, Francis X. "St. Augustine's Three Visions and the Structure of the *Comedy*." *MLN* LXXXII (1967): 58–76.

Niebylski, Dianna C. *The Poem on the Edge of the Word*. New York: Peter Lang, 1993.

Nietzsche, Friedrich. "Description of Ancient Rhetoric." *Friedrich Nietzsche on Rhetoric and Language*. Eds. and trans. Sander L. Gilman, Carole Blair, and David J. Parent. Oxford: Oxford UP, 1989.

Norris, Margot. *The Decentered Universe of "Finnegans Wake."* Baltimore: Johns Hopkins UP, 1976.

———. *Joyce's Web*. Austin: U of Texas P, 1992.

O'Hehir, Brendan. *A Gaelic Lexicon for "Finnegans Wake."* Berkeley: U of California P, 1967.

O'Hehir, Brendan, and John Dillon. *A Classical Lexicon for "Finnegans Wake."* Berkeley: U of California P, 1977.

Page, D.L. *The Homeric Odyssey*. Oxford: Oxford UP, 1955.

Pagliaro, Antonino. *Ulisse: ricerche semantiche sulla "Divina Commedia."* Florence: Messina, 1967.

Paris, Jean. "Finnegan, Wake!" *Tel Quel* 30 (Summer 1967): 58–66.

Pépin, Jean. *La tradition de l'allégorie: de Philon d'Alexandrie à Dante*. Paris: Études Augustiniennes, 1987.

Petrocchi, Giorgio. *L'ultima Dea*. Rome: Bonacci, 1977.

Piette, Adam. *Remembering and the Sound of Words*. Oxford: Oxford UP, 1996.

Pindar. *The Odes*. Ed. and trans. John Sandys. Cambridge: Harvard UP, 1915.

Poe, Edgar Allan. *The Complete Tales and Poems*. Eds. Arthur Hobson Quinn and Edward H. O'Neill. New York: Barnes and Noble, 1992.

Pope, Alexander. "Dunciad." *Selected Poetry and Prose*. Second edition. Ed. William K. Wimsatt. New York: Holt, Rinehart and Winston, 1972. 443–514.

Porter, Laurence M. "The Disappearing Muse: Erasure of Inspiration in Mallarmé." *Romanic Review* 76.4 (1985): 389–404.

Psaki, Regina. "La critica dantesca ortodossa e gli allegoristi." *L'idea deforme*. Ed. Maria Pia Pozzato. Milan: Bompiani, 1989. 263–79.

Pugliatti, Paola. "The New *Ulysses* Between Philology, Semiotics and Textual Genetics." *Dispositio* 12 (1987): 113–40.

Purdy, Strother B. "Mind Your Genderous: Toward a *Wake* Grammar." *New Light on Joyce*. Ed. Fritz Senn. Bloomington: Indiana UP, 1972. 46–78.

Quintillian. *Institutio Oratoria*. Ed. and trans. H.E. Butler. Cambridge: Harvard UP, 1921.

Rabaté, Jean-Michel. *Joyce: Portrait de l'auteur en autre lecteur*. Paris: Cistre-Essais, 1984.
——. "Narratology and the Subject of *Finnegans Wake*." *James Joyce: The Centennial Symposium*. Eds. Morris Beja, Phillip Herring, Maurice Harmon, and David Norris. Urbana: U of Illinois P, 1986. 137–46.
——. "'Alphybettyformed verbage': the shape of sounds and letters in *Finnegans Wake*." *Word and Image* 2.3 (July–September 1986): 237–43.
——. "'Rien n'aura eu lieu que le lieu': Mallarmé and Postmodernism." *Writing the Future*. Ed. David Wood. London: Routledge, 1990. 37–54.
——. *Joyce upon the Void*. New York: St. Martin's, 1991.
——. "Back to Beria! Genetic Joyce and Eco's 'Ideal Readers.'" *Probes: Genetic Studies in Joyce*. Eds. David Hayman and Sam Slote. Amsterdam: Rodopi, 1995. 65–83.

de Rambaldis (de Imola), Benvenuti. *Comentum super Dantis Aldigherij Comoediam*. Ed. J.P. Lacaita. Florence: Barbera, 1887.

Reynolds, Mary T. *Joyce and Dante*. Princeton: Princeton UP, 1981.

Rice, Thomas Jackson. "The Complexity of *Finnegans Wake*." *Joyce Studies Annual* 6 (1995): 78–98.
——. *Joyce, Chaos, and Complexity*. Urbana: U of Illinois P, 1997.

Richard, Jean-Pierre. *L'univers imaginaire de Mallarmé*. Paris: Seuil, 1961.

Riquelme, John Paul. *Teller and Tale in Joyce's Fiction*. Baltimore: Johns Hopkins UP, 1983.

Robb, Graham. "Mallarmé's False Friends." *French Studies Bulletin* 49 (Winter 1993): 13–15.

———. *Unlocking Mallarmé*. New Haven: Yale UP, 1996.

Ronat, Mitsou. "*Un coup de dés*, mystère hurlé?" *Cahiers cistre* 5 (1978): 59–92.

———. "Réponse à Robert Greer Cohn." *Critique* 418 (March 1982): 276–77.

Rose, Danis, and John O'Hanlon. *Understanding "Finnegans Wake."* New York: Garland, 1982.

de Sade, Donatien Alphonse François. *Histoire de Juliette, ou les prospérités du vice*. Eds. Annie le Brun and Jean-Jacques Pauvert. Paris: Pauvert, 1987.

Sailer, Susan Shaw. *On the Void of To Be*. Ann Arbor: U of Michigan P, 1993.

Sarolli, Gian Roberto. *Prolegomena alla "Divina Commedia."* Florence: Olschki, 1971.

Saunders, Rebecca. "The Syntactic Panopticon and Mallarméan Resistance." *The Romanic Review* 87.3 (May 1996): 363–75.

———. "Shaking Down the Pillars: Lamentation, Purity, and Mallarmé's 'Hommage' to Wagner." *PMLA* 111.5 (October 1996): 1106–20.

Scherer, Jacques. *L'expression littéraire dans l'œuvre de Mallarmé*. Paris: Nizet, 1947.

———. *Le "livre" de Mallarmé*. nouvelle édition. Paris: Gallimard, 1957, 1977.

———. *Grammaire de Mallarmé*. Paris: Nizet, 1977.

Schneidau, Herbert. "One Eye at Two Levels: On Joyce's 'Cyclops.'" *JJQ* 16.1–2 (Fall 1978–Winter 1979): 95–103.

Schoenbaum, Samuel. *Shakespeare's Lives*. Oxford: Oxford UP, 1970.

Schute, William M. *Index of Recurrent Elements in James Joyce's "Ulysses."* Carbondale: Southern Illinois UP, 1982.

Scott, David H.T. "Mallarmé and the Octosyllabic Sonnet." *French Studies* XXXI.2 (April 1977): 149–63.

———. *Pictorialist Poetics*. Cambridge: Cambridge UP, 1988.

Scott, John A. "Dante's Allegory." *Romance Philology* 26.3 (February 1973): 558–91.

Seidel, Michael. *Epic Geography: James Joyce's "Ulysses."* Princeton: Princeton UP, 1976.

Senn, Fritz. *Joyce's Dislocutions*. Baltimore: Johns Hopkins UP, 1984.

———. "Mean Cosy Turns." *Myriadminded Man*. Eds. Rosa Maria Bosinelli, Paola Pugliatti and Romana Zacchi. Bologna: CLUEB, 1986. 263–67.

———. *Inductive Scrutinies*. Ed. Christine O'Neill. Dublin: Lilliput, 1995.

Shakespeare, William. *The Oxford Shakespeare: Complete Works*. Ed. W.J. Craig. Oxford: Oxford UP, 1905.

Sharpless, F. Parvin. "Irony in Joyce's *Portrait:* The Stasis of Pity." *Twentieth Century Interpretations of "A Portrait of the Artist as a Young Man."* Ed. William M. Schute. Englewood Cliffs: Prentice-Hall, 1968. 96–106.

Shaw, Mary Lewis. *Performance in the Texts of Mallarmé*. University Park: Pennsylvania State UP, 1993.

Shklovsky, Victor. "Sterne's *Tristram Shandy*: Stylistic Commentary." *Russian Formalist Criticism: Four Essays*. Eds. and trans. Lee T. Lemon and Marion J. Reis. Lincoln: U of Nebraska P, 1965. 25–57.

Singleton, Charles S. *An Essay on the "Vita Nuova."* Baltimore: Johns Hopkins UP, 1949.

———. *"Commedia": Elements of Structure. (Dante Studies 1)*. Cambridge: Harvard UP, 1954.

———. "The Irreducible Dove." *Comparative Literature* 9.2 (Spring 1957): 129–35.

———. *Journey to Beatrice. (Dante Studies* 2). Baltimore: Johns Hopkins UP, 1958.

———. *Commentary on "The Divine Comedy."* Princeton: Princeton UP, 1970–75.

Sollers, Philippe. *Logiques*. Paris: Seuil, 1968.

———. *H*. Paris: Seuil, 1973.

———. "Joyce et c^{ie}." *Tel Quel* 64 (Winter 1975): 15–24.

Solomon, Margaret C. *Eternal Geomater*. Carbondale: Southern Illinois UP, 1969.

Sophocles. *Philoctetes*. Trans. David Grene. *Sophocles*. Eds. David Grene and Richmond Lattimore. Chicago: U of Chicago P, 1959. 401–60.

Spoo, Robert. *James Joyce and the Language of History*. Oxford: Oxford UP, 1994.

Staley, Thomas F. *An Annotated Critical Bibliography of James Joyce*. New York: Harvester Wheatsheaf, 1989.

Staudt, Kathleen Henderson. "The Poetics of 'Black on White': Stéphane Mallarmé's *Un coup de dés*." *Ineffability*. Eds. Peter S. Hawkins and Anne Howland Schotter. New York: AMS, 1984. 147–61.

Steiner, Carlo. Commentary, 1921. *Dartmouth Dante Project*. Online, Internet. October 27, 1995.

Steiner, George. *Language and Silence*. Harmondsworth: Penguin, 1969.

Stewart, Garrett. *Reading Voices: Literature and the Phonotext*. Berkeley: U of California P, 1990.

Sugano, Marion Zwerling. *The Poetics of the Occasion*. Stanford: Stanford UP, 1992.

Tambling, Jeremy. *Dante and Difference*. Cambridge: Cambridge UP, 1988.
——. "Dante and Benjamin: Melancholy and Allegory." *Exemplaria* 4.2 (Fall 1992): 341–63.
——. "'Nostro peccato fu ermafrodito': Dante and the Moderns." *Exemplaria* 6.2 (Fall 1994): 405–27.

Thibaudet, Albert. *La poésie de Stéphane Mallarmé*. Ninth edition. Paris: Gallimard, 1926.

Tindall, William York. *A Reader's Guide to James Joyce*. New York: Farrar, Strauss and Giroux, 1969.

Tommaseo, Niccolò. Commentary, 1837. *Dartmouth Dante Project*. Online, Internet. October 24, 1995.

Ulmer, Gregory. "The Puncept in Grammatology." *On Puns*. Ed. Jonathan Culler. London: Blackwell, 1988. 164–89.

Valente, Joseph. "Beyond Truth and Freedom: The New Faith of Joyce and Nietzsche." *JJQ* 25.1 (Fall 1987): 87–103.

Valéry, Paul. *Écrits divers sur Stéphane Mallarmé*. Paris: Gallimard, 1951.

van Boheemen-Saaf, Christine. "Deconstruction after Joyce." *New Alliances in Joyce Studies*. Ed. Bonnie Kime Scott. Newark: U of Delaware P, 1988. 29–36.

Verdin, Simonne. "Mallarmé et Joyce, somptuosités vitales et magnifique veille de la pensée." *Courrier de Centre International d'Études Poétiques* 84 (1971): 17–28.

———. *Le presque contradictoire, précédé d'une Étude de variantes*. Paris: Nizet, 1975.

Virgil. *Æneid*. Trans. Allen Mandelbaum. Berkeley: U of California P, 1971.

Wall, Richard. *An Anglo-Irish Dialect Glossary for Joyce's Works*. Syracuse: Syracuse UP, 1986.

Whitman, Jon. *Allegory*. Oxford: Oxford UP, 1987.

Whittier-Ferguson, John. "The Voice Behind the Echo: Vladimir Dixon's Letters to James Joyce and Sylvia Beach." *JJQ* 29.3 (Spring 1992): 511–31.

Index

A

Adam, 41–45, 48, 67
"À la nue accablante tu," 11, 102–5, 143, 150, 158, 177
Alexandrine, the, 82–83, 95, 171
allegory, 24–28, 30, 35, 60–61, 74, 75, 251, 266
apophasis, 37–40, 48, 65
Aquinas, Thomas, 1
Asenjo, F.G., 230
Atherton, James S., 280, 287, 291
Attridge, Derek, 236, 240
Aubert, Jacques, 208, 252–53, 287
Auerbach, Erich, 26
Augustine, 19, 40–41, 62, 66, 70, 291

B

Babel, 28, 40–44, 66, 67, 87, 208–16, 252
Bach, J.S., 241, 252, 254, 283
Balzac, Honoré de, 1
Barolini, Teodolinda, 61
Bataille, Georges, 3, 5
Baudelaire, Charles, 1, 121
Beatrice, 8, 18–19, 21, 30, 32, 57, 59, 63, 66, 69, 70, 81, 167, 286–87
Beckett, Samuel, 15, 20, 105, 125, 198, 209–10, 226, 232, 245
Bénichou, Paul, 92–93, 103, 113, 118, 121–23
Benjamin, Walter, 86, 117, 230
Benstock, Bernard and Shari, 187, 192, 202, 220, 222
Benstock, Bernard, 235–36, 286, 290
Bérard, Victor, 222
Bernard, Jean-Marc, 114
Bernard, Suzanne, 20, 76, 109, 113, 125, 171
Bersani, Leo, 74, 85, 107–9, 112
Bishop, John, 207, 230
Blake, William, 1
Blanchot, Maurice, 2–6, 10–13, 16, 18, 73, 75–77, 83–87, 89, 90, 99, 102, 108–10, 114–20, 127–34, 136–39, 159–60, 164, 168, 172–73, 175, 178, 181, 183–84, 185–86, 202, 204, 217, 219, 275–76, 278–79, 292–93

Boccaccio, Giovanni, 70
Boldrini, Lucia, 26, 62, 265–66
Bonnefoy, Yves, 78
Book, the, 4, 6, 10, 13, 33, 54, 57, 90, 117, 168–69

Book of Kells, The, 268, 278, 291, 295
Borges, Jorge Luis, 69, 283
Bougnoux, Daniel, 124
Bowie, Malcom, 100, 123, 139–40, 161, 167, 175, 177, 179, 247
Brahe, Tycho, 197
Brise marine, 11, 94–98, 155

C

Califf, David, 287
Campbell, Joseph, 208, 228
Carpenter, William, 15
Cazalis, Henri, 10, 74, 88, 95, 120, 122, 173
Celan, Paul, 6
Cervantes, Miguel de, 1
Cheng, Vincent, 293
Chiarenza, Marguerite, 36, 54, 55
Cohn, R.G., 1, 15, 20, 92–93, 95, 98–100, 103, 109, 111, 116, 121–23, 127–28, 132, 142, 149, 151, 157, 165, 170–72, 174, 176, 178, 181, 284
Coleridge, Samuel Taylor, 287
Colum, Padraic, 222
Convivio, 24–25, 27, 31, 68, 70, 224–25, 265–66
Copeland, Rita, 289
Costa, Paolo, 67

Coup de dés, Un, 12, 14, 81, 104, 105, 110, 124, 127–29, 131–34, 138–69, 173, 247, 249, 251, 260–61
Crise de vers, 74, 76–77, 81–87
Curtius, Ernst Robert, 8, 59

D

Dante, 1, 6–12, 16, 17, 19, 20, 72, 75, 81, 87, 90, 105, 169, 198, 209–210, 217, 232, 279, *et passim*
Davies, Gardner, 20, 104, 125, 127, 134, 142, 151–52, 157, 172, 174, 176–78, 180
della Lana, Jacopo, 70
de Lungo, Isidoro, 65
de Man, Paul, 27, 62, 63, 78, 109, 115–17
de Rambaldis, Benvenuti, 60
dernière mode, La, 265, 291
Derrida, Jacques, 5, 16, 37–39, 55–57, 65, 67, 68, 73, 78–79, 86–89, 107–8, 110–11, 114, 117–18, 145–46, 172–73, 178–79, 183–84, 201–5, 211–15, 227–28, 244, 249, 251–52, 281
de Robertis, Domenico, 8
désœuvrement, 3–5, 10, 89
De Vulgari Eloquentia, 40–41, 43–44, 61, 67, 81, 211

différance, 201, 203, 227, 233
dissemination, 80, 145–46, 251–52
Divagations, 73
Dixon, Vladimir, 238–39, 281–82
Du Bellay, Joachim, 231

E

Eco, Umberto, 206, 229
Ellmann, Richard, 281
Epistle to Can Grande, 24–26, 30, 61, 62, 265–66
exscription, 5, 6, 14, 22, 23, 52, 55, 57, 73, 77, 83, 145, 162, 185

F

ference, 201–4, 240, 257, 266, 278
Finnegans Wake, 12–14, 87, 147, 164, 185, 205–18, 219, 235–79
Flaubert, Gustave, 5, 18, 219
Franke, William, 27–28
Freccero, John, 30, 32–33, 175, 177
Freud, Sigmund, 55–57, 78, 280–81
Frey, Hans-Jost, 108, 125–26
Froment-Meurice, Marc, 173

G

Garryowen, 200, 219–220
Gasché, Rodolphe, 227–28
Genette, Gérard, 108, 206–7, 289

Gide, André, 127, 171
Gifford, Don, 195, 226
Gilbert, Stuart, 221
Gillespie, Michael Patrick, 186–87, 200
Gillet, Louis, 15
Glasheen, Adaline, 292
Goldwasser, Thomas, 282
Green, Richard Hamilton, 61

H

Hamlet, 157, 181, 190–92, 197, 200, 288
Hart, Clive, 205–8, 228–29, 242
Hawkins, Peter, 33–34, 37–38, 49, 64
Hayman, David, 15, 20, 187, 206, 220, 221, 229, 230, 234, 246, 260, 284, 289–90
HCE, 168, 215–17, 230–31, 233–34, 271–72
Heath, Stephen, 243
Hegel, G.W.F., 260
Heidegger, Martin, 4, 16, 27–28, 63, 75, 87, 116, 130, 211–12, 227, 232–33
Hérodiade, 74, 114, 123–24
Hill, Archibald, 282
Hölderlin, Friedrich, 83
Hollander, Robert, 26, 60, 62, 63

Hollier, Denis, 109, 119
Homer, 193, 198
Horace, 44, 68, 77
Hugo, Victor, 1
Husserl, Edmund, 202

I

Igitur, 74, 110, 128–31, 140, 152, 156, 160, 173, 174, 246
Inferno, 11, 21, 53–54, 58–59, 63, 66, 69–70, 135–36
ingegno, 23, 30, 34, 37–38, 40, 45, 49, 60, 255, 274

J

Johnson, Barbara, 110
Josipovici, Gabriel, 28, 61
Joubert, Joseph, 119
Joyce, James, 1, 7, 12–13, 16, 19, 20, 59, 67, 169, 185–86, 231, 280, *et passim*

K

Kafka, Franz, 175
Kaufmann, Vincent, 103, 113, 119–21
Kenner, Hugh, 188–89, 205, 220–21
Koran, The, 255
Kravis, Judy, 291
Kristeva, Julia, 177, 284

Kromer, Gretchen, 119
Kumar, Udaya, 188–89, 200, 205, 222–25

L

Lacan, Jacques, 281
La Charité, Virginia A., 171, 176
Lacoue-Labarthe, Philippe, 77, 107
Lansing, Richard, 35, 64, 68
Laporte, Roger, 117
Lawrence, Karen, 187–88, 200
Lebenstejn, Jean-Claude, 128, 170, 181
Le livre, instrument spirituel, 1, 90, 149–150, 274
Le nénuphar blanc, 124
Lernout, Geert, 16, 285
Lethe, 21–23
"Le vierge, le vivace et le bel aujourd'hui," 11, 98–103, 146, 148
Levin, Harry, 240
Lewis, Wyndam, 16
Libertson, Joseph, 175
Lowe, Catherine, 118

M

MacCabe, Colin, 232

Mallarmé, Stéphane, 1, 7, 10–13, 19, 20, 51, 54, 56–58, 73–74, 83, 127, 185–86, 204, 209, 210, 231, 236, 240, 247, 254, 260, 265–66, 274–76, 279, *et passim*
Marchal, Bertrand, 91–93, 98–99, 101, 103, 104, 112, 123–25, 133, 135, 141–43, 157, 167, 174, 176–78
Mauclair, Camille, 147
Mauron, Charles, 4
Mazzotta, Guiseppe, 19, 22, 24, 27, 30, 32, 36, 48, 49, 53–55, 57, 70, 135
McGann, Jerome, 292
McHugh, Roland, 233, 285, 287
McLuhan, Marshall, 15
Mendès, Catulle, 76
Milesi, Laurent, 208–10, 215–16, 230, 255, 290
Miller, Paul Allen, 119
Mimique, 78
Mirham, Danielle, 170
Monarchia, 67
Mondor, Henri, 7, 111–12
Montbertrand, Gérard, 103, 104, 124, 125
mots anglais, Les, 209, 240
music, 76–77, 144–45, 242

Myers, Peter, 282

N
Nabokov, Vladimir, 258–59
Nadel, Ira, 223, 292
Nagy, Gregory, 222–23
Nancy, Jean-Luc, 5–6
Nardi, Bruno, 60
negative theology, 37–39, 64
Nieblyski, Dianna, 173
Nordau, Max, 16

O
Odysseus, 11, 51, 135–38, 142, 152, 159, 168, 175, 189, 193–94, 198–200, 202, 204, 206, 221–23
Ovid, 1, 31, 175

P
Page, D.L., 222
Pagliaro, Antonio, 64
Paradiso, 9–10, 23, 29–37, 41–55, 58, 64, 67–71, 81, 132, 143, 168, 201, 279
parapolylogic, 246, 252, 254, 257, 279, 284
Pépin, Jean, 61
Piette, Adam, 15
Pindar, 119

Plato, 39, 56, 121, 268, 293
Poe, Edgar Allan, 75, 118, 181–83
Pope, Alexander, 267
Porter, Laurence, 108, 118
Portrait of the Artist as a Young Man, A, 66, 123, 186, 225
Poulet, Georges, 130
Pound, Ezra, 16
Purdy, Strother, 208
Purgatorio, 21–23, 64, 67, 71

Q

Quant au livre, 148–49, 275
Queneau, Raymond, 1
Quintillian, 61
quoits, 198–200

R

Rabaté, Jean-Michel, 15, 176, 206, 224, 225, 233, 284
récit, 137–38, 175
Reynolds, Mary, 15
Rice, Thomas, 237–38, 286
Richard, Jean-Pierre, 108, 123, 127–28, 172, 178
Rip Van Winkle, 193–97, 200, 225
Riquelme, John Paul, 206, 229
Robb, Graham, 87, 110, 118
Ronat, Mitsou, 167, 170–71, 177

rhythm, 78, 145–46

S

Sade, Donatien Alphonse François, 3, 10
Sailer, Susan Shaw, 206, 229
Salut, 11, 91–94, 102, 127, 132, 165, 178
Saunders, Rebecca, 107
Scherer, Jacques, 10–11, 109, 111–12, 119, 122–23, 132, 178
Scott, David, 82, 103, 135, 141, 174, 176, 179
Scott, John A., 61
Schutte, William, 222
"Ses purs ongles," 87–89, 144
Seidel, Michael, 221
Senn, Fritz, 253
Shakespeare, William, 190–92, 197, 204, 224
Shaw, Mary Lewis, 141
Shklovsky, Vladimir, 234
silence, 2–5, 57, 76–77, 144, 185
Singleton, Charles, 18, 23, 59, 60–61, 64, 69
Sollers, Philippe, 7, 15–16, 18, 32, 40–41, 53, 54, 57, 66, 87, 118, 211, 244, 284
Solomon, Margaret, 293

Sophocles, 175
Spoo, Robert, 222
Steiner, Carlo, 67
Steiner, George, 19
Stephen Hero, 237
Sterne, Laurence, 234
Stewart, Garrett, 283
Sugano, Marion, 112–13, 173–74, 179
symbolism, 75–77, 108
syntax, 79–81, 141, 144, 179, 208, 247, 252–53, 258, 288

T

Tambling, Jeremy, 26–27, 63, 67, 68, 70
Thibaudet, Albert, 17, 20, 170
translation, 86–87
Tombeau d'Edgar Poe, Le, 181–83
Tommaseo, Niccolò, 71

U

Ulysses, 12, 185–205, 217–18, 219, 242, 272, 277

V

Valéry, Paul, 20, 114
Verdin, Simone, 15, 284
Vico, Giambattista, 207

Virgil, 7, 51, 59, 66, 135, 175
Vita Nuova, 8–9, 19, 21–22, 49, 53, 58, 286–87

W

Wagner, Richard, 109
wandering Jew, the, 189–91, 193, 200, 222
Weaver, Harriet Shaw, 237
Whitman, Jon, 25, 61

Currents in Comparative
Romance Languages and Literatures

This series was founded in 1987, and actively solicits book-length manuscripts (approximately 200–400 pages) which treat aspects of Romance Languages and Literatures. Originally established for works dealing with two or more Romance literatures, the series has broadened its horizons and now includes studies on themes within a single literature or between different literatures, civilizations, art, music, film and social movements, as well as comparative linguistics. Studies on individual writers with an influence on other literatures/civilizations are also welcome. We entertain a variety of approaches and formats, provided the scholarship and methodology are appropriate.

For additional information about the series or for the submission of manuscripts, please contact:

Tamara Alvarez-Detrell and Michael G. Paulson
c/o Dr. Heidi Burns
Peter Lang Publishing, Inc.
516 N. Charles St., 2nd Floor
Baltimore, MD 21201